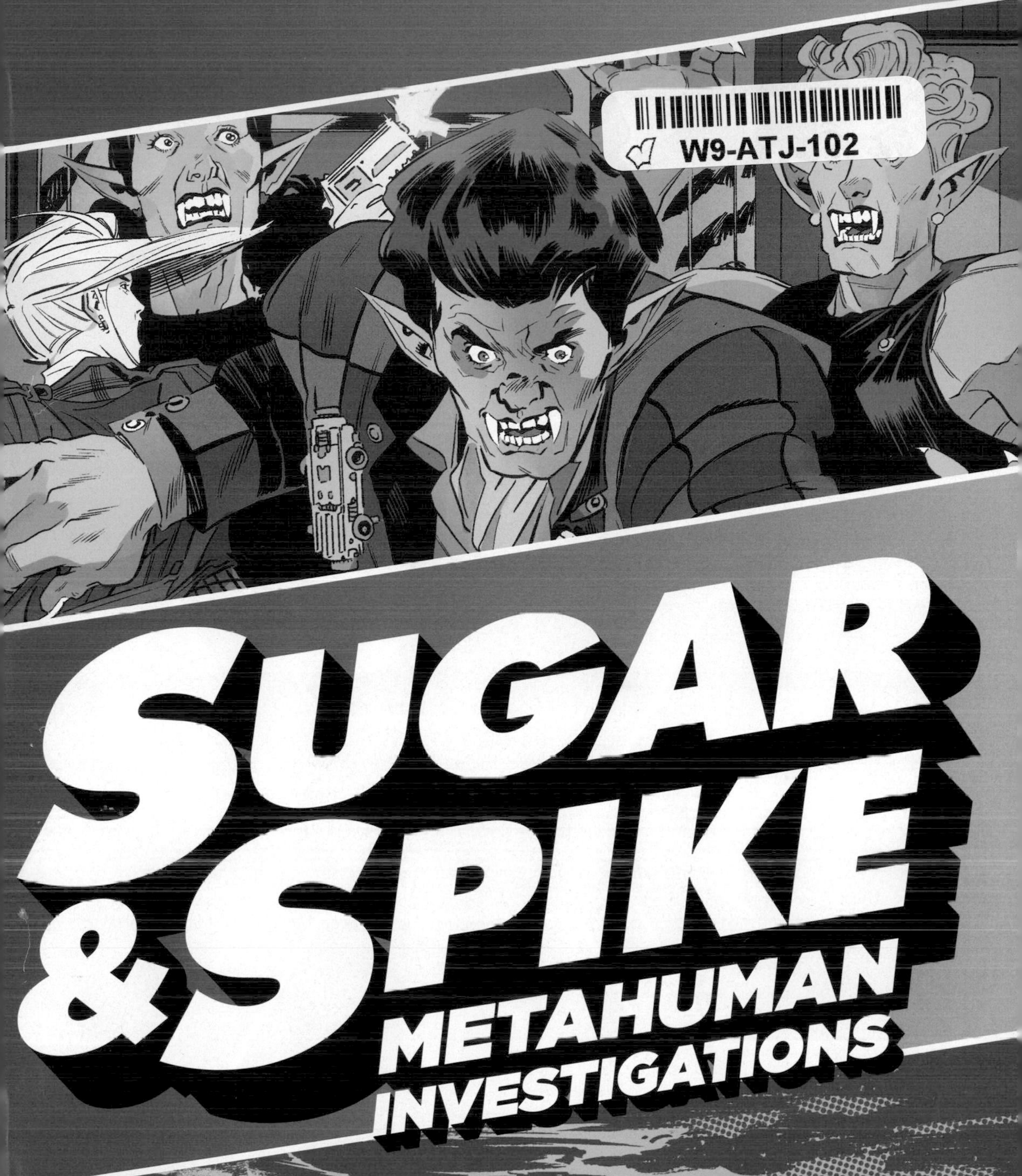

SUGAR & SPIKE
METAHUMAN INVESTIGATIONS

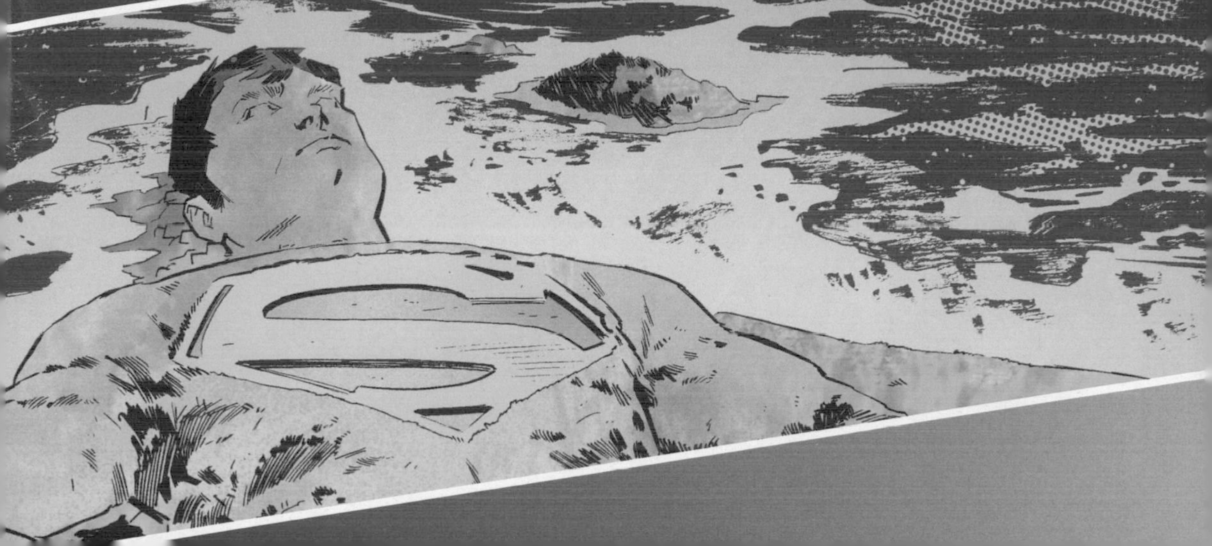

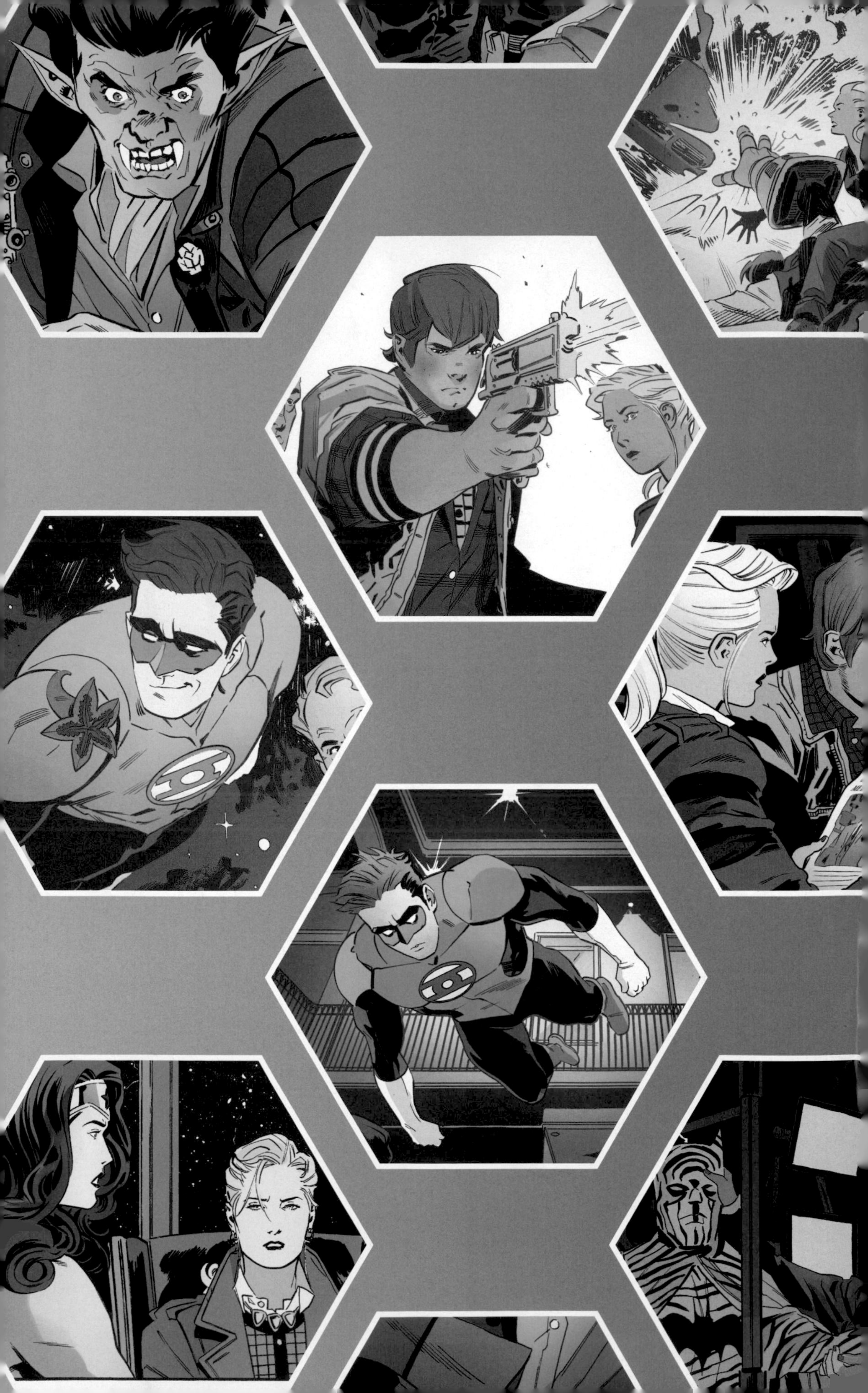

SUGAR & SPIKE
METAHUMAN INVESTIGATIONS

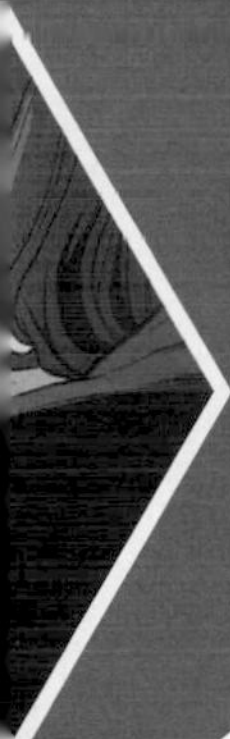

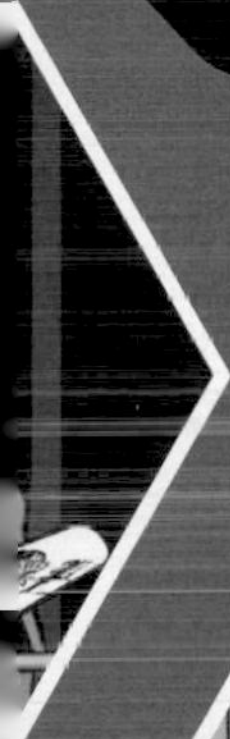

KEITH GIFFEN
writer

BILQUIS EVELY
artist

IVAN PLASCENCIA
colorist

TOM NAPOLITANO
letterer

BILQUIS EVELY
collection cover artist

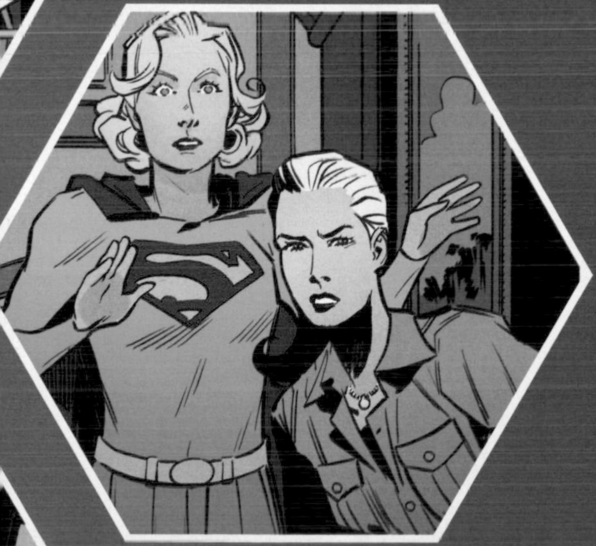

SUPERMAN created by
JERRY SIEGEL
and **JOE SHUSTER.**

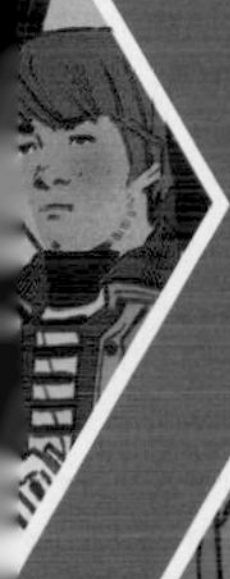

SUPERGIRL based on
characters created by
JERRY SIEGEL
and **JOE SHUSTER.**

By special arrangement
with the JERRY SIEGEL family.

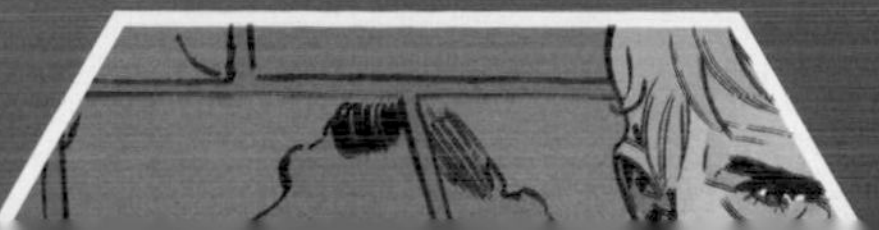

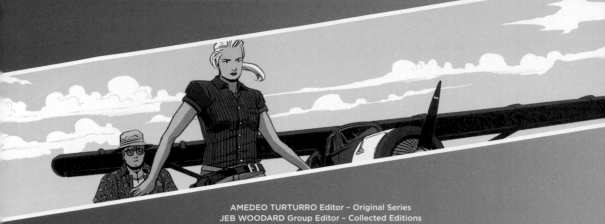

AMEDEO TURTURRO Editor – Original Series
JEB WOODARD Group Editor – Collected Editions
SUZANNAH ROWNTREE Editor – Collected Edition
STEVE COOK Design Director – Books
SARABETH KETT Publication Design

BOB HARRAS Senior VP – Editor-in-Chief, DC Comics

DIANE NELSON President
DAN DiDIO Publisher
JIM LEE Publisher
GEOFF JOHNS President & Chief Creative Officer
AMIT DESAI Executive VP – Business & Marketing Strategy, Direct to Consumer & Global Franchise Management
SAM ADES Senior VP – Direct to Consumer
BOBBIE CHASE VP – Talent Development
MARK CHIARELLO Senior VP – Art, Design & Collected Editions
JOHN CUNNINGHAM Senior VP – Sales & Trade Marketing
ANNE DePIES Senior VP – Business Strategy, Finance & Administration
DON FALLETTI VP – Manufacturing Operations
LAWRENCE GANEM VP – Editorial Administration & Talent Relations
ALISON GILL Senior VP – Manufacturing & Operations
HANK KANALZ Senior VP – Editorial Strategy & Administration
JAY KOGAN VP – Legal Affairs
THOMAS LOFTUS VP – Business Affairs
JACK MAHAN VP – Business Affairs
NICK J. NAPOLITANO VP – Manufacturing Administration
EDDIE SCANNELL VP – Consumer Marketing
COURTNEY SIMMONS Senior VP – Publicity & Communications
JIM (SKI) SOKOLOWSKI VP – Comic Book Specialty Sales & Trade Marketing
NANCY SPEARS VP – Mass, Book, Digital Sales & Trade Marketing

SUGAR & SPIKE: METAHUMAN INVESTIGATIONS

DC Comics, 2900 West Alameda Ave., Burbank, CA 91505
Printed by RR Donnelley, Salem, VA, USA. 10/7/16. First Printing.
ISBN: 978-1-4012-6482-6

Library of Congress Cataloging-in-Publication Data is available.

PEFC Certified
Printed on paper from sustainably managed forests and controlled sources
PEFC/29-31-75
www.pefc.org

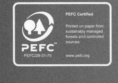

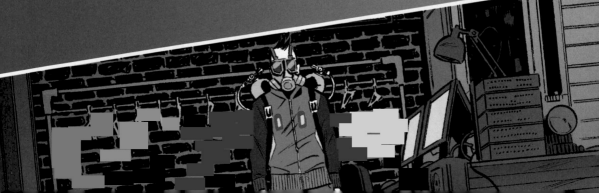

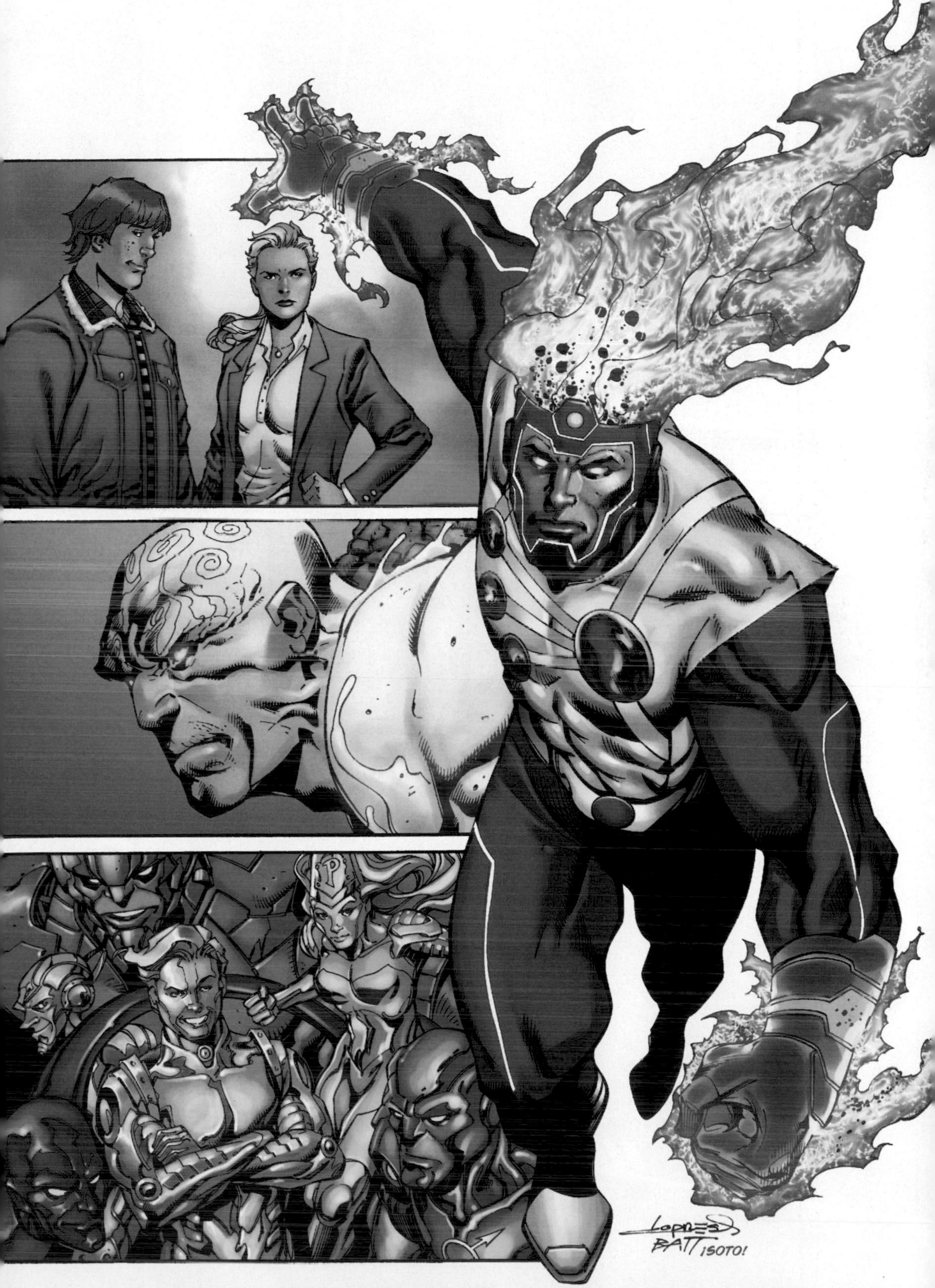
BATT ¡SOTO!

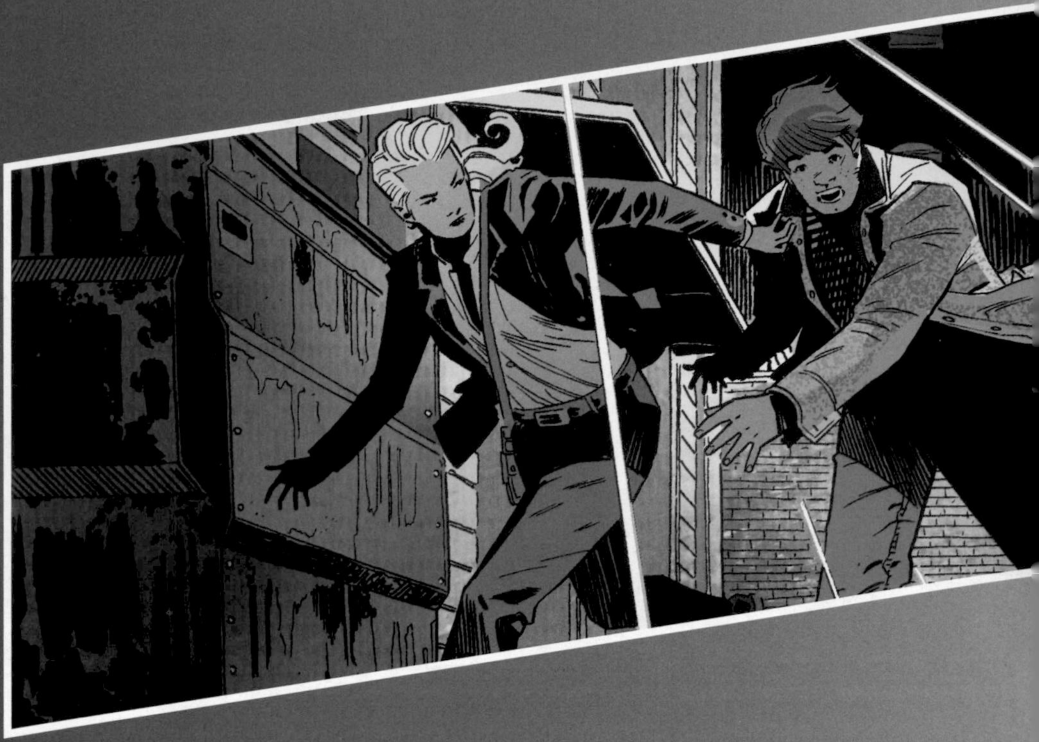

AARON LOPRESTI
with **CHRIS SOTOMAYOR**
cover

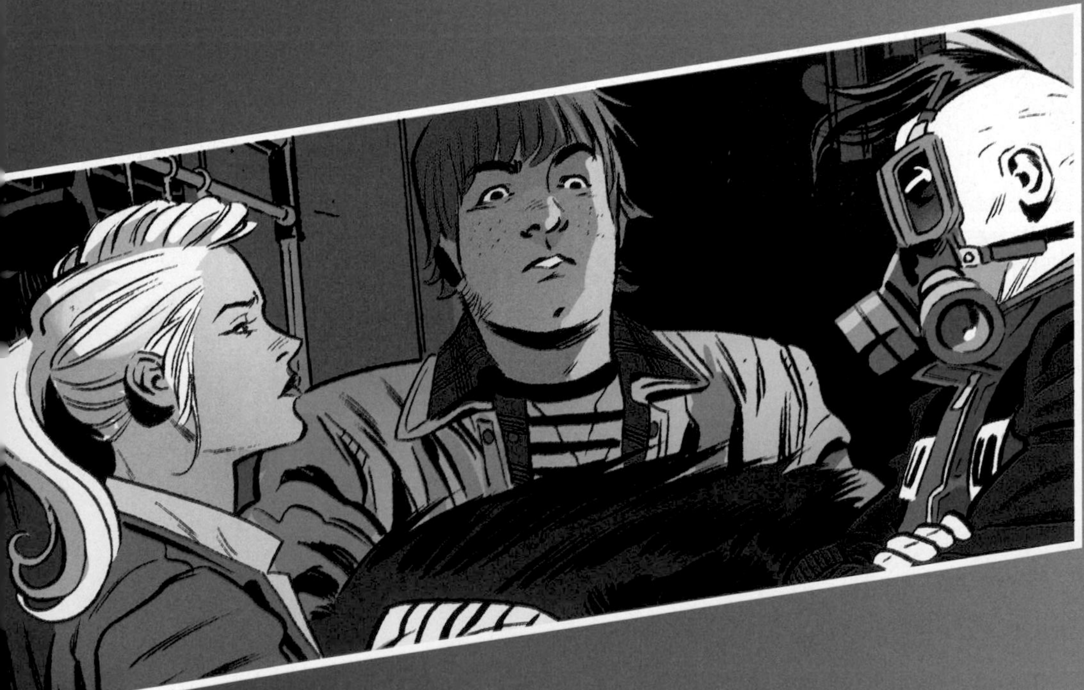

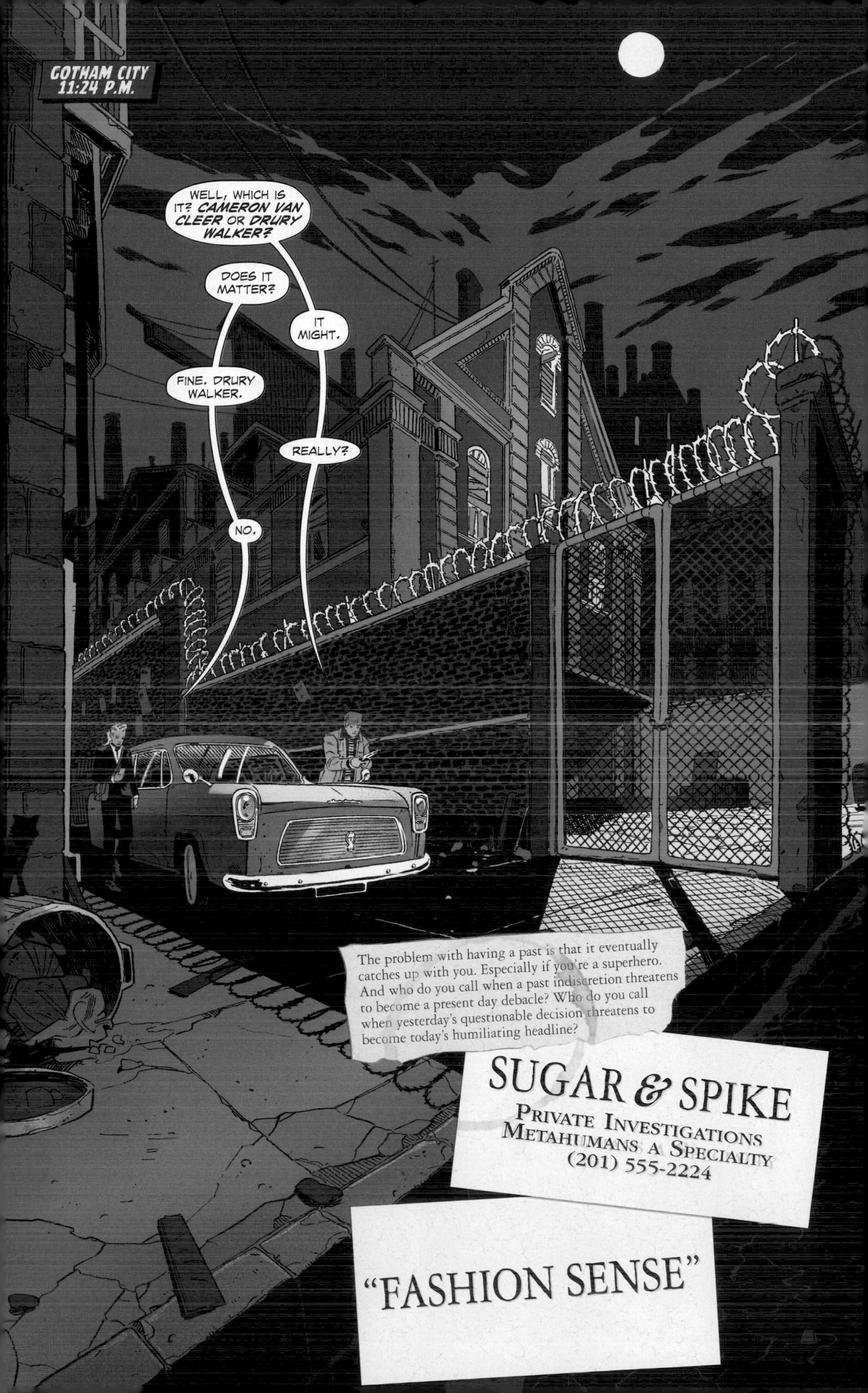
GOTHAM CITY
11:24 P.M.
WELL, WHICH IS IT? CAMERON VAN CLEER OR DRURY WALKER?
DOES IT MATTER?
IT MIGHT.
FINE. DRURY WALKER.
REALLY?
NO.
The problem with having a past is that it eventually catches up with you. Especially if you're a superhero. And who do you call when a past indiscretion threatens to become a present day debacle? Who do you call when yesterday's questionable decision threatens to become today's humiliating headline?
SUGAR & SPIKE
PRIVATE INVESTIGATIONS
METAHUMANS A SPECIALTY
(201) 555-2224
"FASHION SENSE"

SPIKE, IT DOESN'T SAY.

HOW CAN IT NOT SAY, SUGAR? THE GUY'S A FELON.

YOU'VE GOT TO START HACKING INTO BETTER SITES.

DULY NOTED.

ANYTHING ELSE WE SHOULD KNOW?

Umm...A.K.A. KILLER MOTH... PROPORTIONATE ABILITIES OF A MOTH; FLIGHT, GOOEY COCOON MUCUS...

...NOPE.

GOOEY COCOON MUCUS?

NOT GOING THERE. WE ARE NOT GOING THERE.

FINE. FINE.

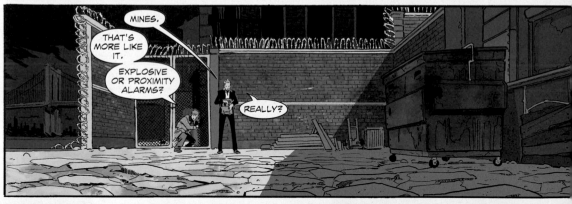

MINES.

THAT'S MORE LIKE IT.

EXPLOSIVE OR PROXIMITY ALARMS?

REALLY?

IT DOESN'T CONCERN YOU?

IT SHOULD?

DEAD OR DISCOVERED.

HELL YEAH IT SHOULD CONCERN--

PROXIMITY.

BREEE

BREEE B

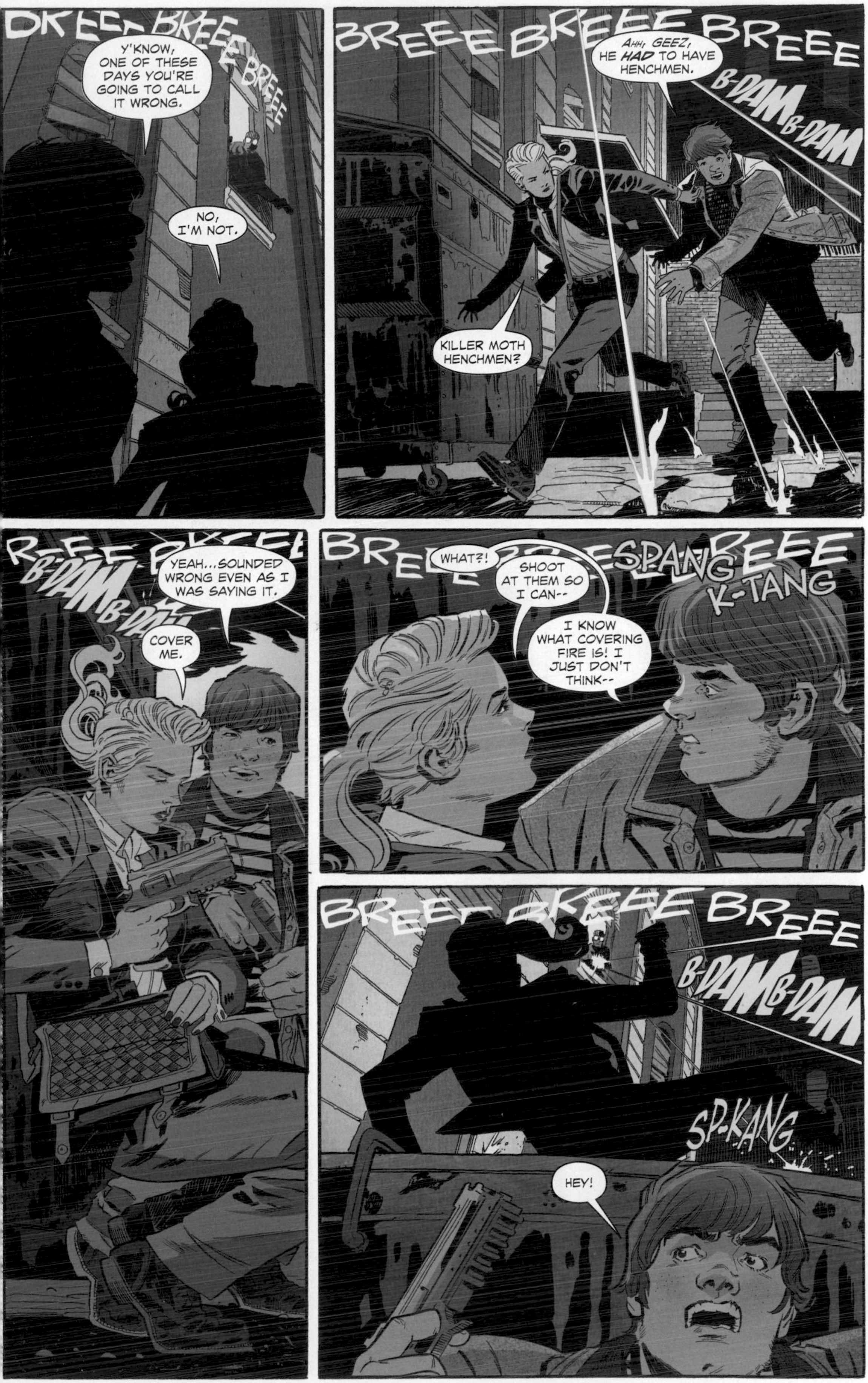

BREEE BREEE BREEE
Y'KNOW, ONE OF THESE DAYS YOU'RE GOING TO CALL IT WRONG.
NO, I'M NOT.
BREEE BREEE BREEE
AHH, GEEZ, HE HAD TO HAVE HENCHMEN.
B-DAM B-DAM
KILLER MOTH HENCHMEN?
B-DAM B-DAM
YEAH...SOUNDED WRONG EVEN AS I WAS SAYING IT.
COVER ME.
BREEE
WHAT?!
SHOOT AT THEM SO I CAN--
SPANG
BREEE
K-TANG
I KNOW WHAT COVERING FIRE IS! I JUST DON'T THINK--
BREEE BREEE BREEE
B-DAM B-DAM
SP-KANG
HEY!

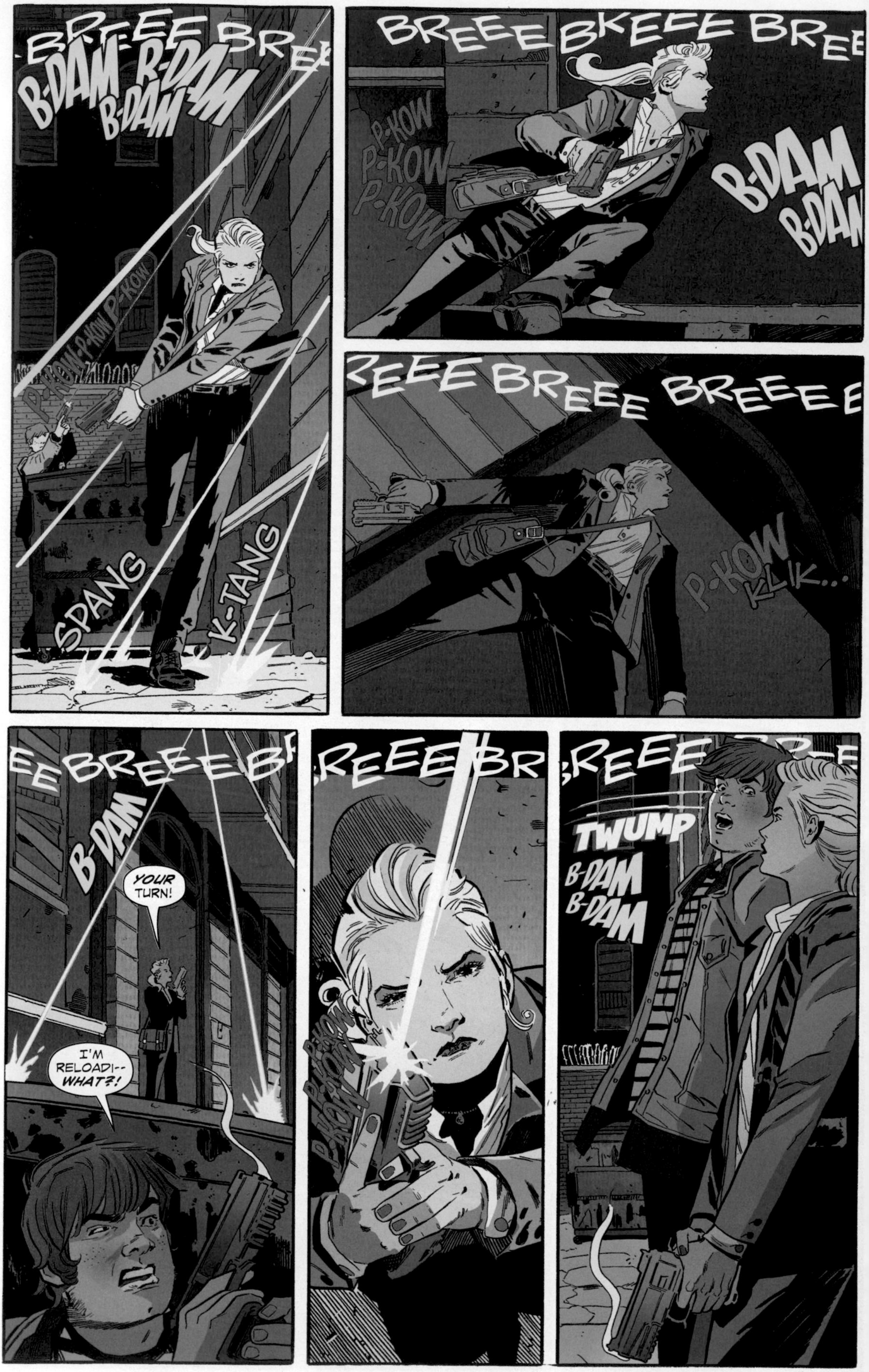
BRRREEE BREE
B-DAM R-DAM
B-DAM
P-KOW P-KOW P-KOW
SPANG
K-TANG
BREEE BREEE BREE
P-KOW
P-KOW
P-KOW
B-DAM
B-DAM
BREEE BREEE BREEEEE
P-KOW
KLIK...
BREEEEE BR
B-DAM
YOUR TURN!
I'M RELOADI-- WHAT?!
BREEEE BR
BREEE
TWUMP
B-DAM
B-DAM

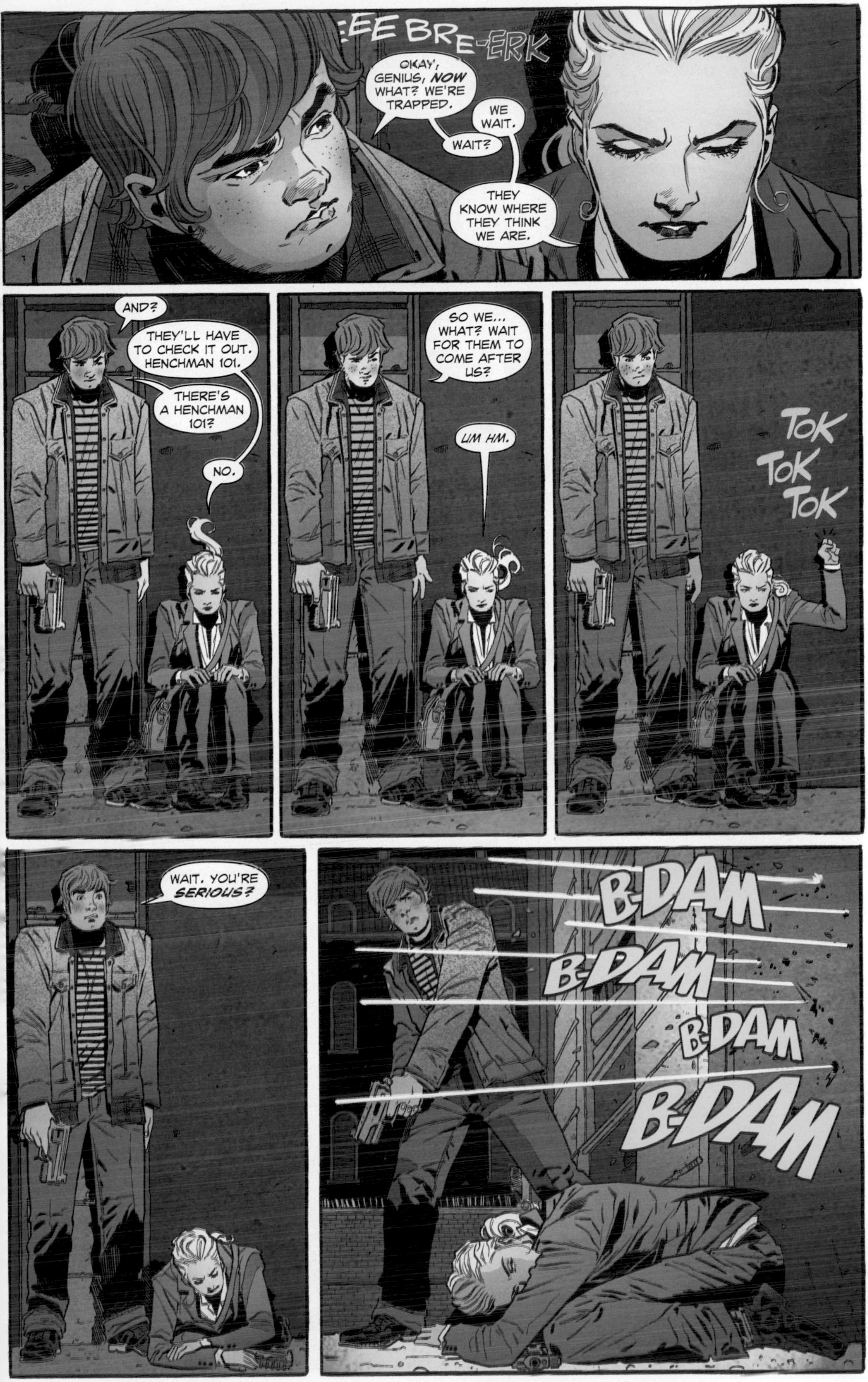
EEE BRE-ERK
OKAY, GENIUS, NOW WHAT? WE'RE TRAPPED.
WE WAIT.
WAIT?
THEY KNOW WHERE THEY THINK WE ARE.
AND?
THEY'LL HAVE TO CHECK IT OUT. HENCHMAN 101.
THERE'S A HENCHMAN 101?
NO.
SO WE... WHAT? WAIT FOR THEM TO COME AFTER US?
UM HM.
TOK
TOK
TOK
WAIT. YOU'RE SERIOUS?
B-DAM
B-DAM
B-DAM
B-DAM

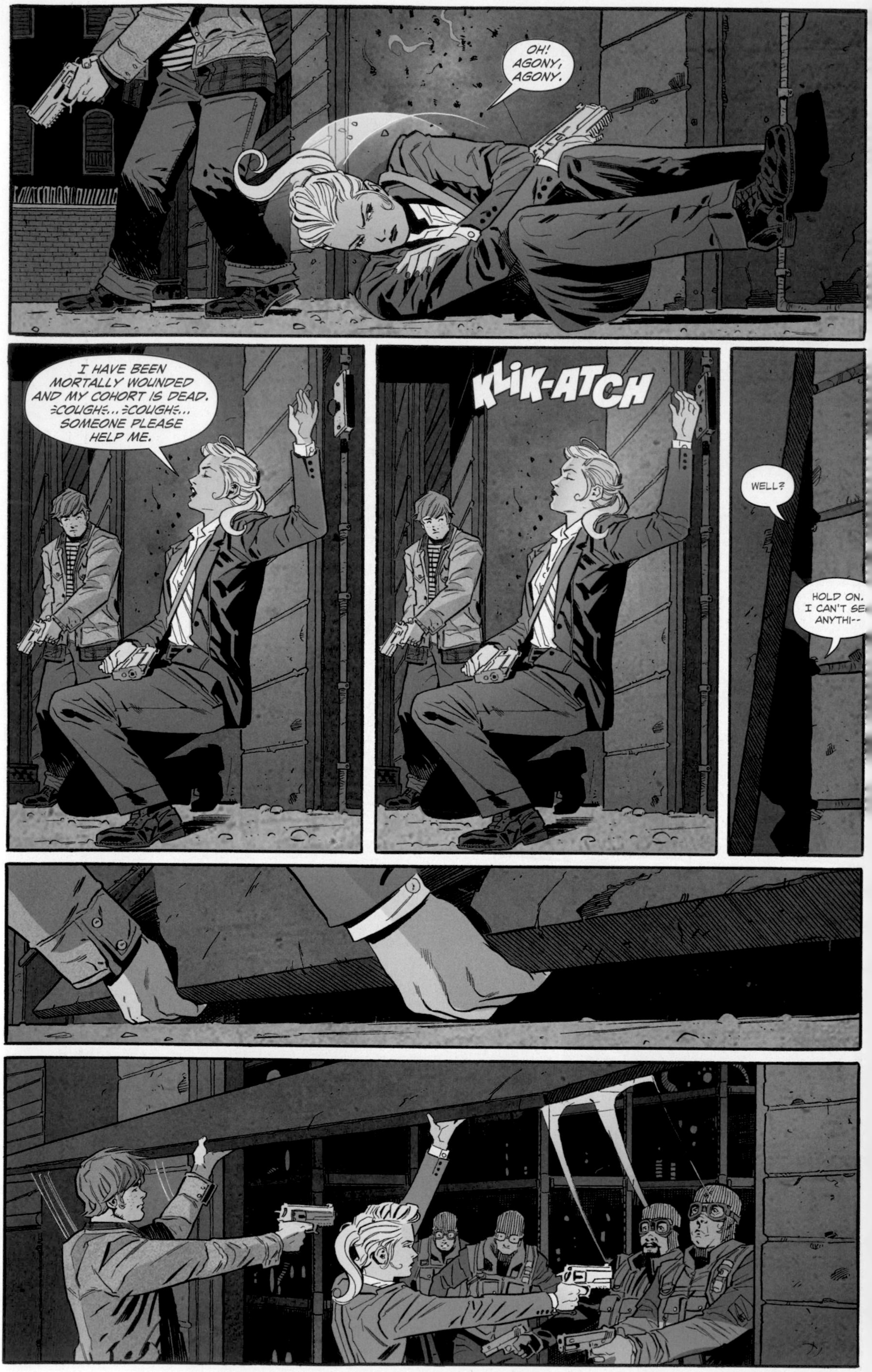
OH! AGONY, AGONY.
I HAVE BEEN MORTALLY WOUNDED AND MY COHORT IS DEAD. *COUGH*... *COUGH*... SOMEONE PLEASE HELP ME.
KLIK-ATCH
WELL?
HOLD ON. I CAN'T SE ANYTHI--

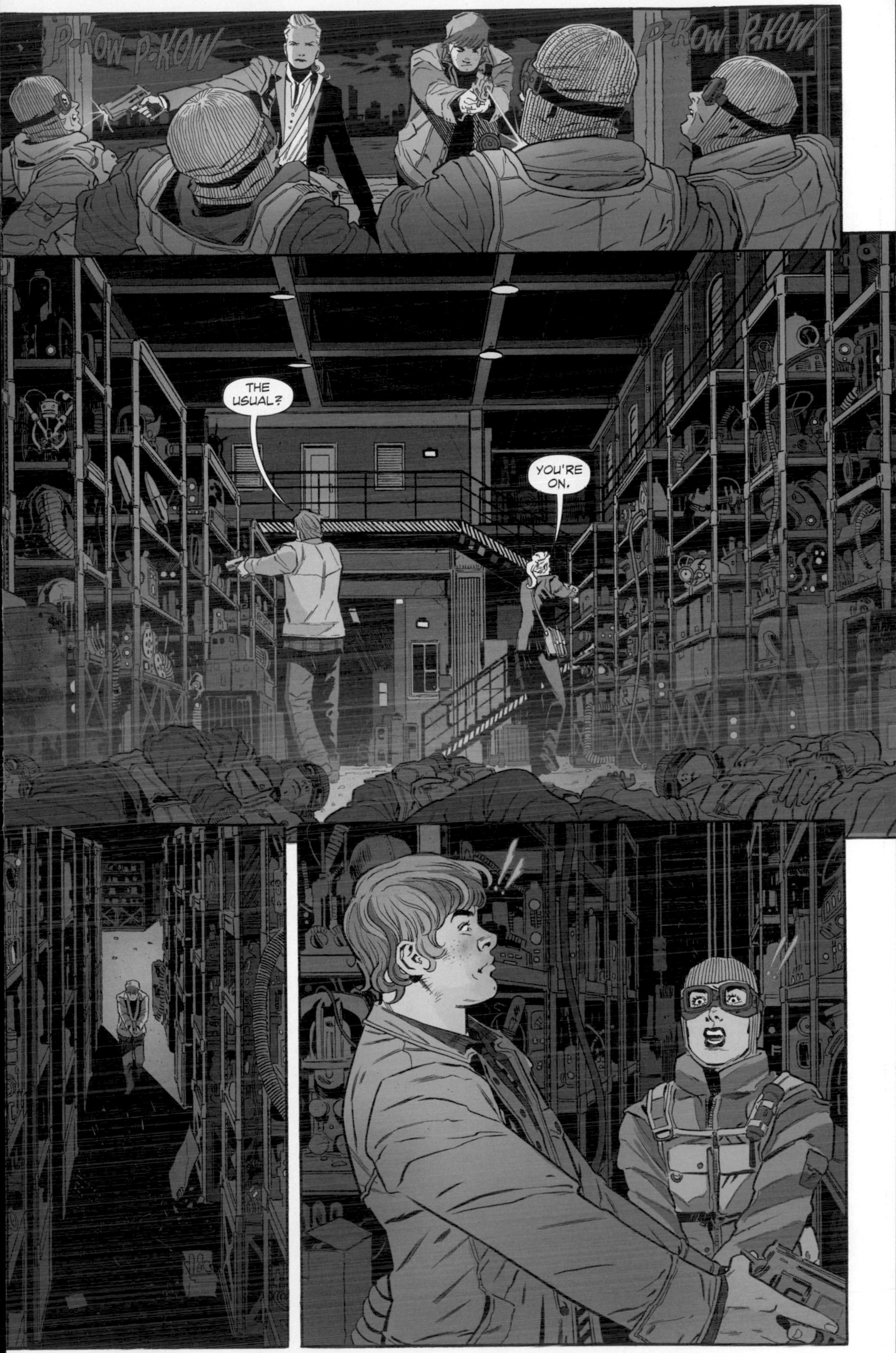
P-KOW P-KOW
P-KOW P-KOW
THE USUAL?
YOU'RE ON.
!!

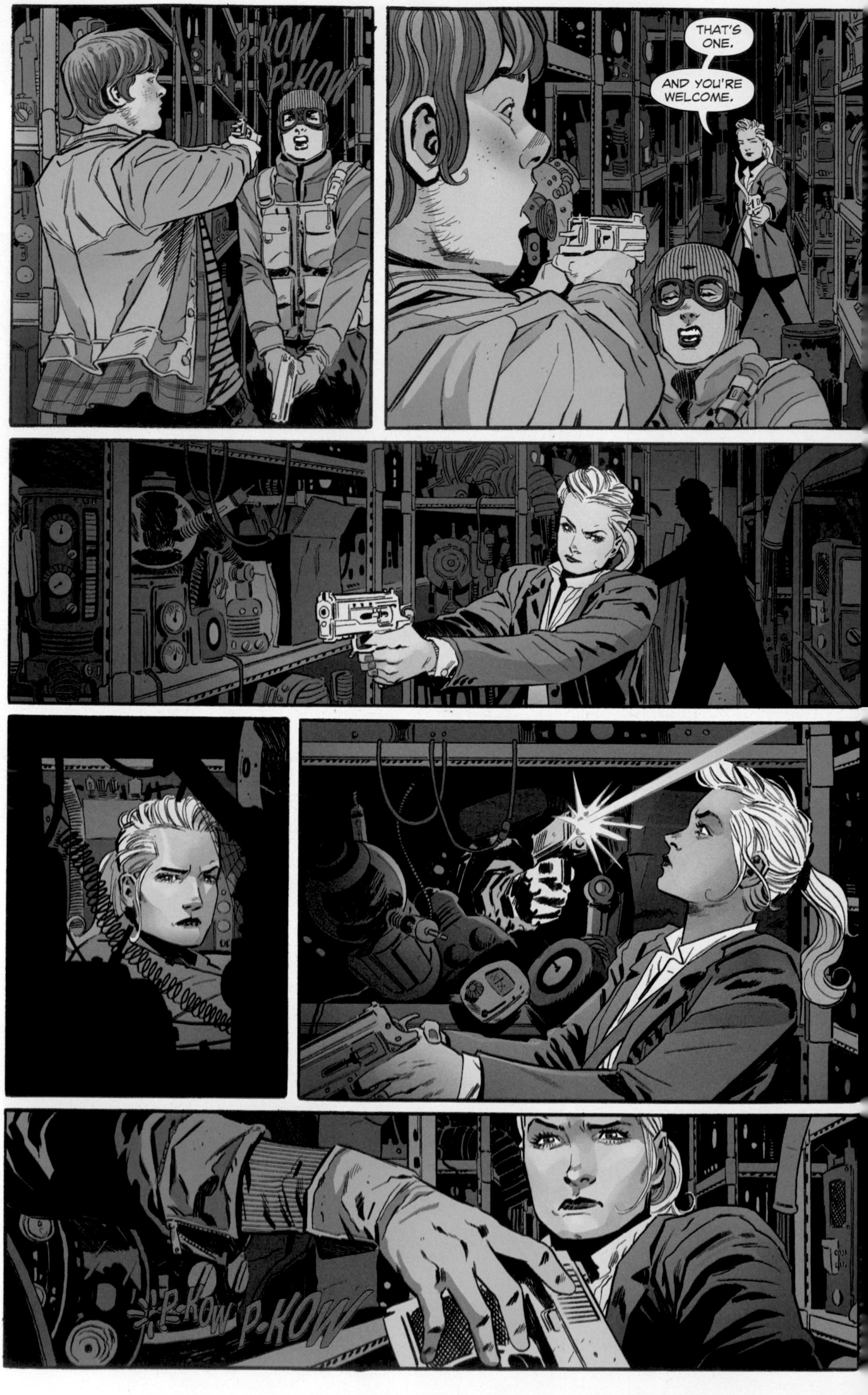
P-KOW P-KOW
THAT'S ONE.
AND YOU'RE WELCOME.
P-KOW P-KOW

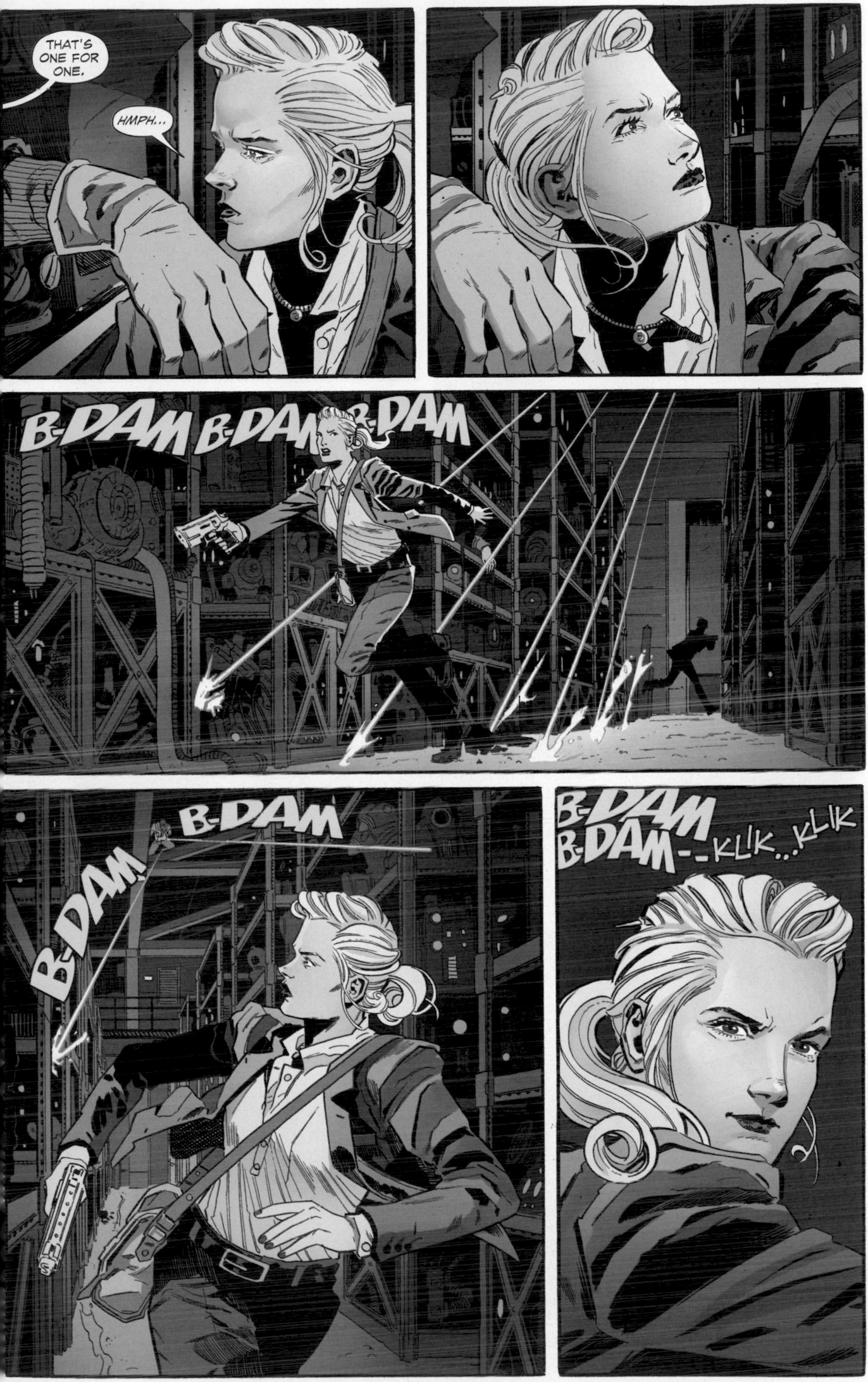
THAT'S ONE FOR ONE.
HMPH...
B-DAM B-DAM B-DAM
B-DAM
B-DAM
B-DAM
B-DAM--KLIK..KLIK

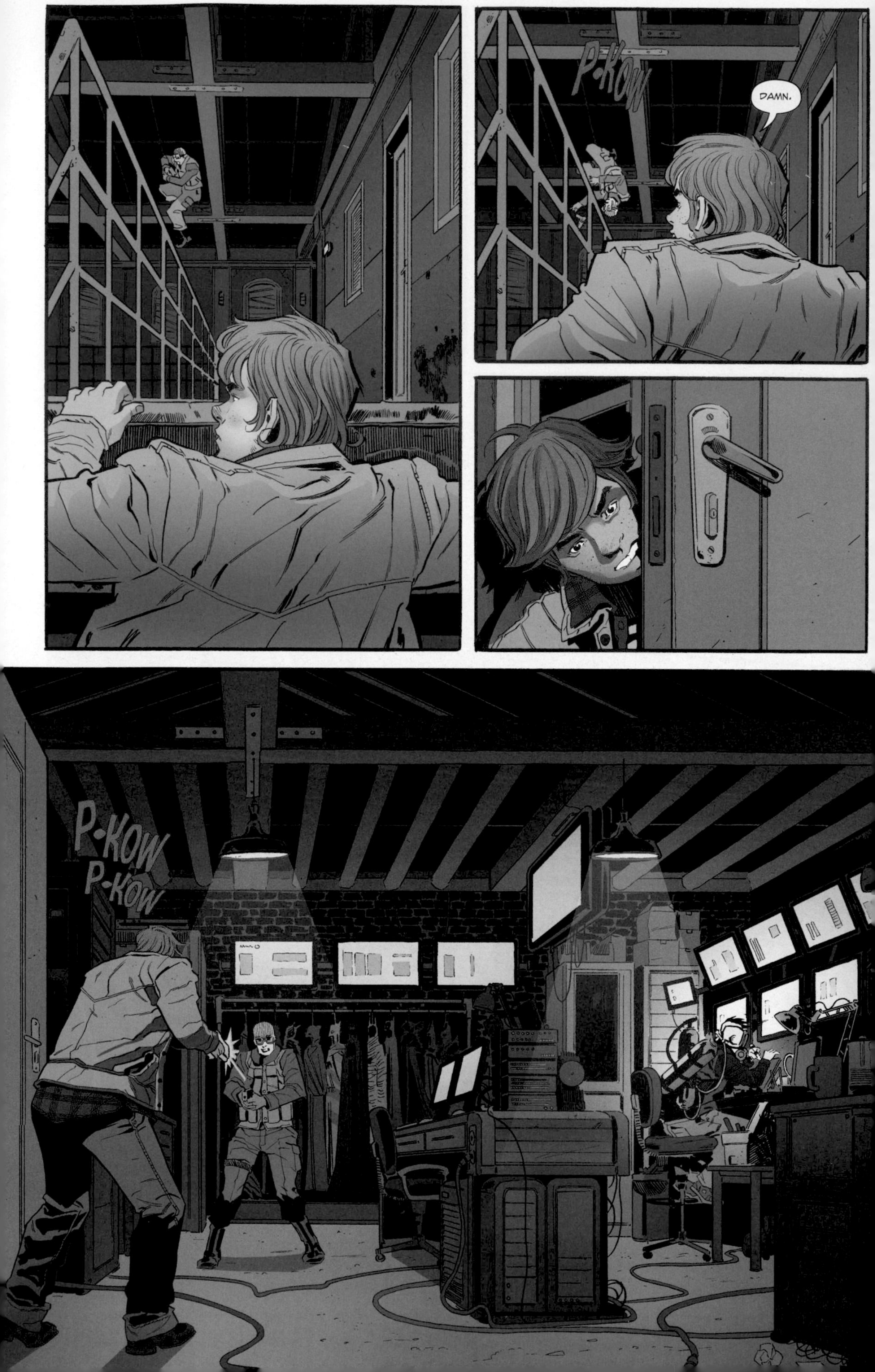
P-KOW
DAMN.
P-KOW
P-KOW

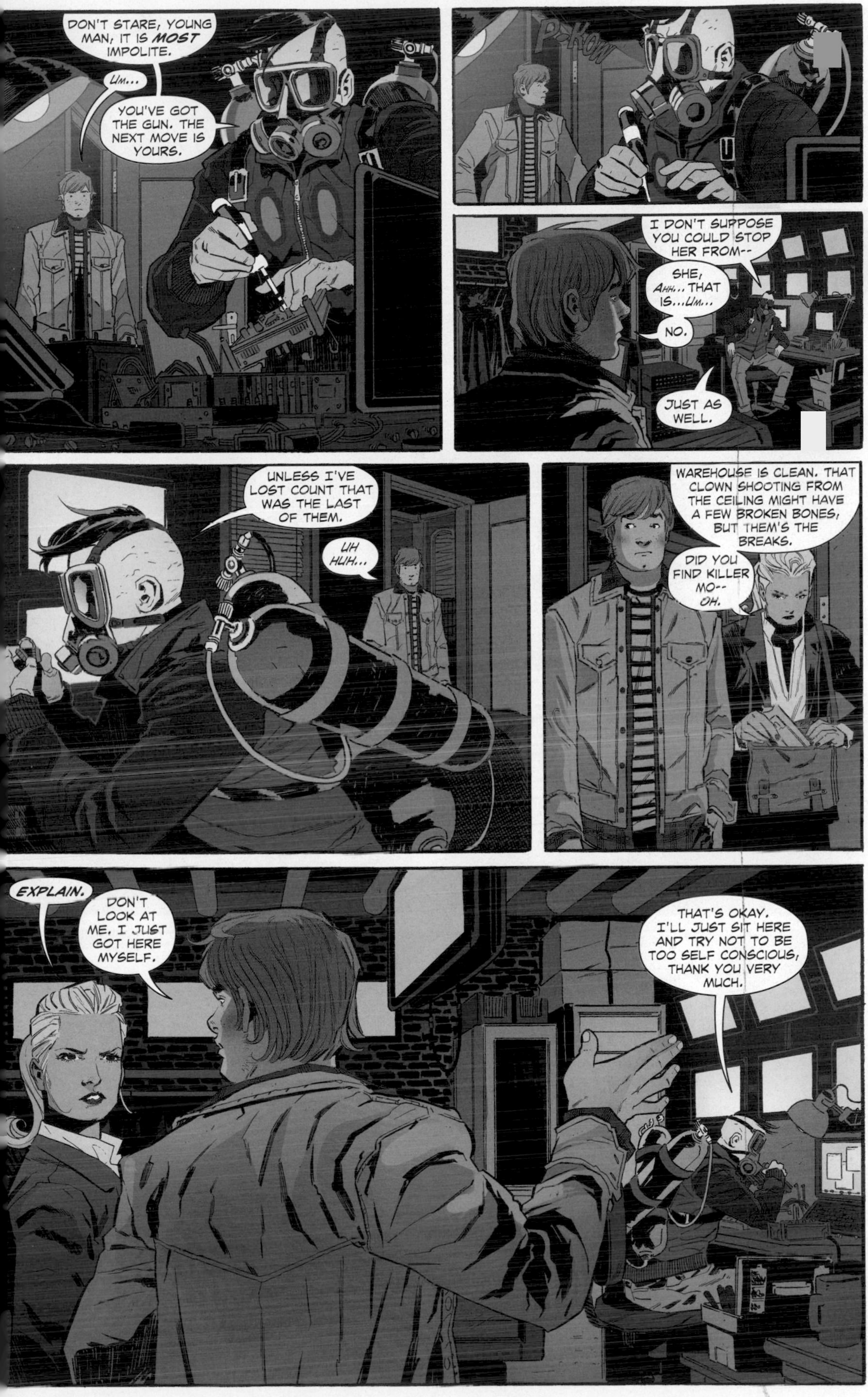
DON'T STARE, YOUNG MAN, IT IS MOST IMPOLITE.
UM...
YOU'VE GOT THE GUN. THE NEXT MOVE IS YOURS.
P-KOW
I DON'T SUPPOSE YOU COULD STOP HER FROM--
SHE, AHH... THAT IS... UM...
NO.
JUST AS WELL.
UNLESS I'VE LOST COUNT THAT WAS THE LAST OF THEM.
UH HUH...
WAREHOUSE IS CLEAN. THAT CLOWN SHOOTING FROM THE CEILING MIGHT HAVE A FEW BROKEN BONES, BUT THEM'S THE BREAKS.
DID YOU FIND KILLER MO-- OH.
EXPLAIN.
DON'T LOOK AT ME. I JUST GOT HERE MYSELF.
THAT'S OKAY. I'LL JUST SIT HERE AND TRY NOT TO BE TOO SELF CONSCIOUS, THANK YOU VERY MUCH.

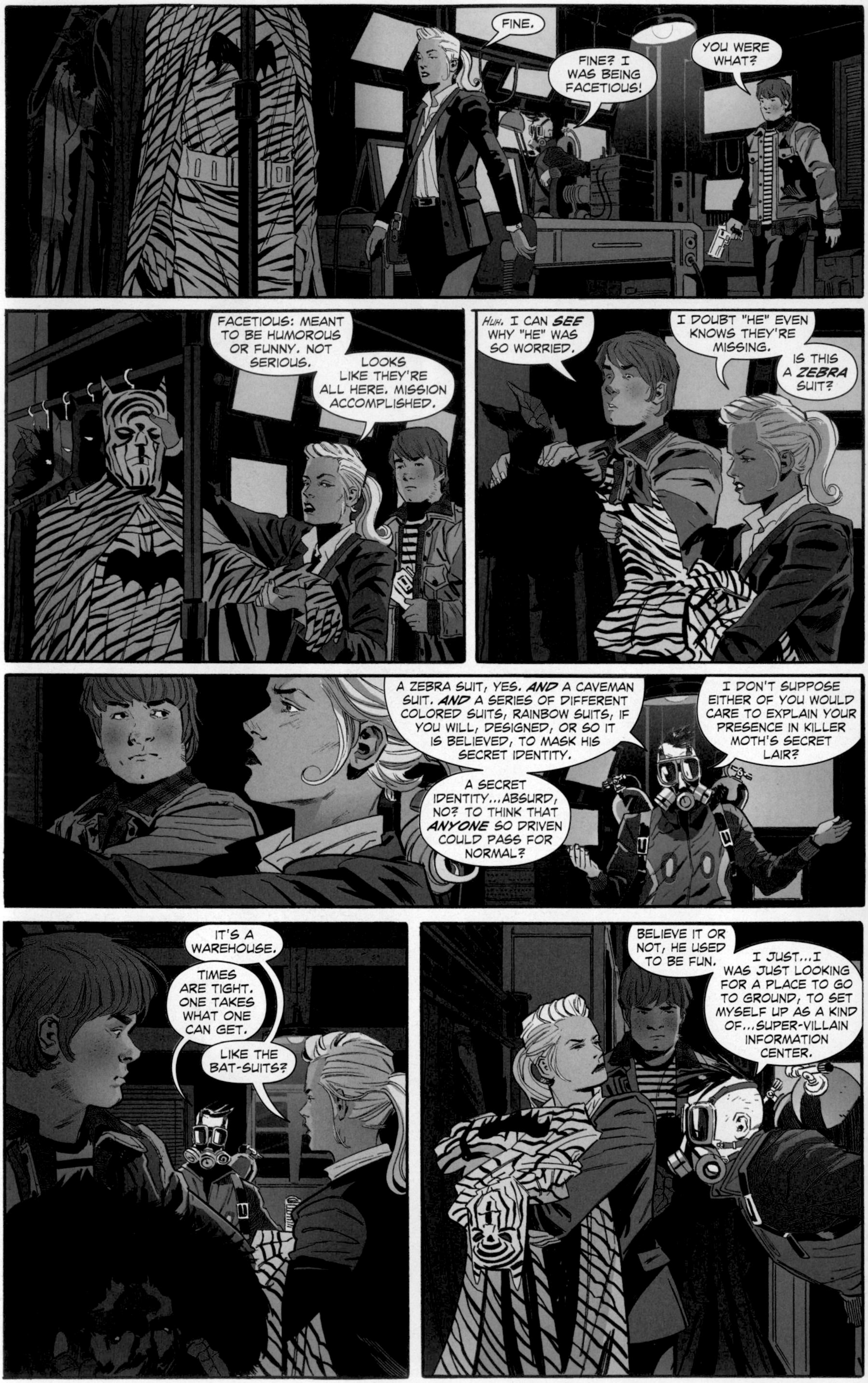
FINE.
FINE? I WAS BEING FACETIOUS!
YOU WERE WHAT?
FACETIOUS: MEANT TO BE HUMOROUS OR FUNNY. NOT SERIOUS.
LOOKS LIKE THEY'RE ALL HERE. MISSION ACCOMPLISHED.
HUH. I CAN SEE WHY "HE" WAS SO WORRIED.
I DOUBT "HE" EVEN KNOWS THEY'RE MISSING.
IS THIS A ZEBRA SUIT?
A ZEBRA SUIT, YES. AND A CAVEMAN SUIT. AND A SERIES OF DIFFERENT COLORED SUITS, RAINBOW SUITS, IF YOU WILL, DESIGNED, OR SO IT IS BELIEVED, TO MASK HIS SECRET IDENTITY.
A SECRET IDENTITY...ABSURD, NO? TO THINK THAT ANYONE SO DRIVEN COULD PASS FOR NORMAL?
I DON'T SUPPOSE EITHER OF YOU WOULD CARE TO EXPLAIN YOUR PRESENCE IN KILLER MOTH'S SECRET LAIR?
IT'S A WAREHOUSE.
TIMES ARE TIGHT. ONE TAKES WHAT ONE CAN GET.
LIKE THE BAT-SUITS?
BELIEVE IT OR NOT, HE USED TO BE FUN.
I JUST...I WAS JUST LOOKING FOR A PLACE TO GO TO GROUND, TO SET MYSELF UP AS A KIND OF...SUPER-VILLAIN INFORMATION CENTER.

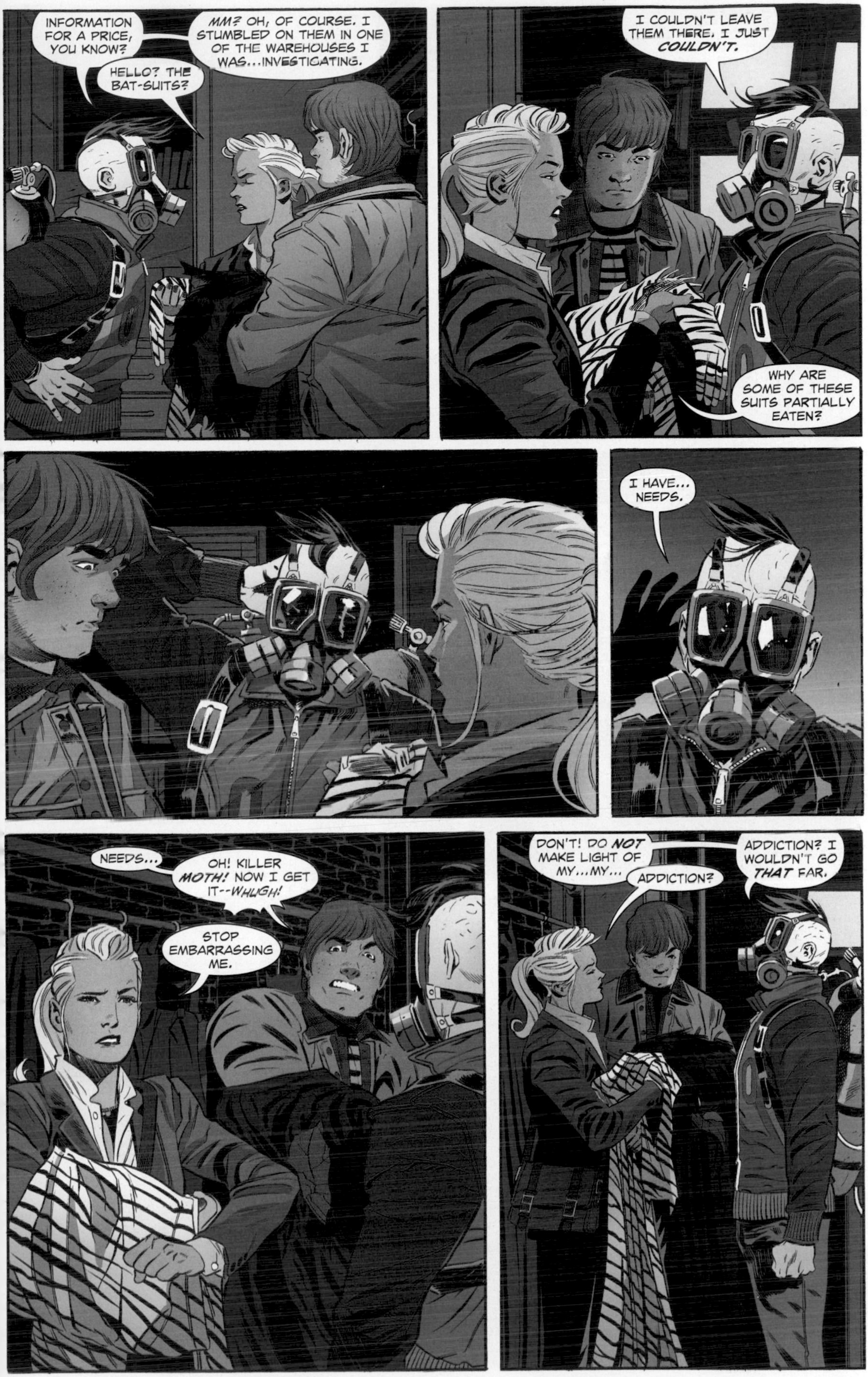
INFORMATION FOR A PRICE, YOU KNOW?
HELLO? THE BAT-SUITS?
MM? OH, OF COURSE. I STUMBLED ON THEM IN ONE OF THE WAREHOUSES I WAS...INVESTIGATING.
I COULDN'T LEAVE THEM THERE. I JUST *COULDN'T.*
WHY ARE SOME OF THESE SUITS PARTIALLY EATEN?
I HAVE... NEEDS.
NEEDS...
OH! KILLER *MOTH!* NOW I GET IT--*WHUGH!*
STOP EMBARRASSING ME.
DON'T! DO *NOT* MAKE LIGHT OF MY...MY...
ADDICTION?
ADDICTION? I WOULDN'T GO *THAT* FAR.

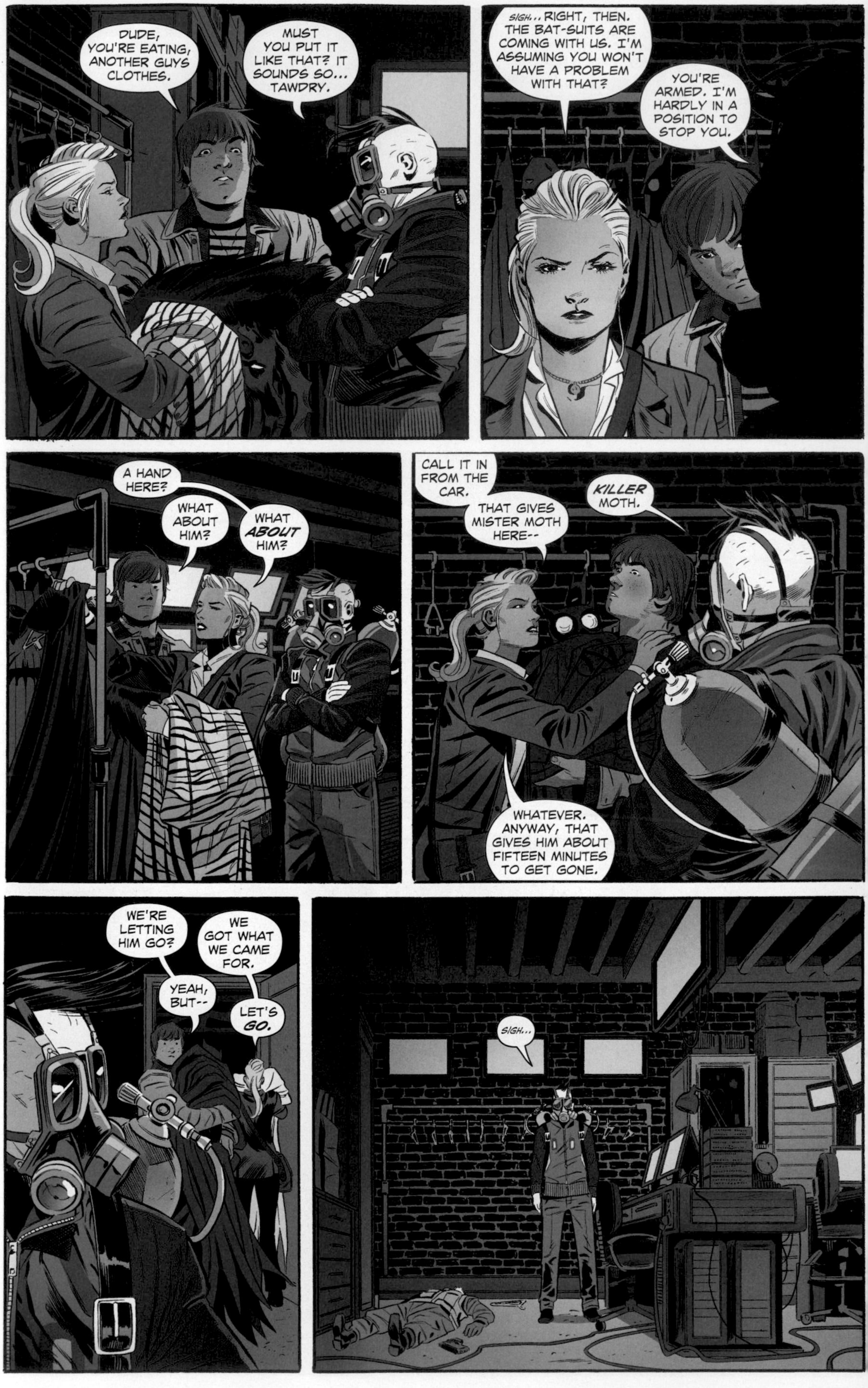
DUDE, YOU'RE EATING, ANOTHER GUYS CLOTHES.
MUST YOU PUT IT LIKE THAT? IT SOUNDS SO... TAWDRY.
SIGH... RIGHT, THEN. THE BAT-SUITS ARE COMING WITH US. I'M ASSUMING YOU WON'T HAVE A PROBLEM WITH THAT?
YOU'RE ARMED. I'M HARDLY IN A POSITION TO STOP YOU.
A HAND HERE?
WHAT ABOUT HIM?
WHAT ABOUT HIM?
CALL IT IN FROM THE CAR.
THAT GIVES MISTER MOTH HERE--
KILLER MOTH.
WHATEVER. ANYWAY, THAT GIVES HIM ABOUT FIFTEEN MINUTES TO GET GONE.
WE'RE LETTING HIM GO?
WE GOT WHAT WE CAME FOR.
YEAH, BUT--
LET'S GO.
SIGH...

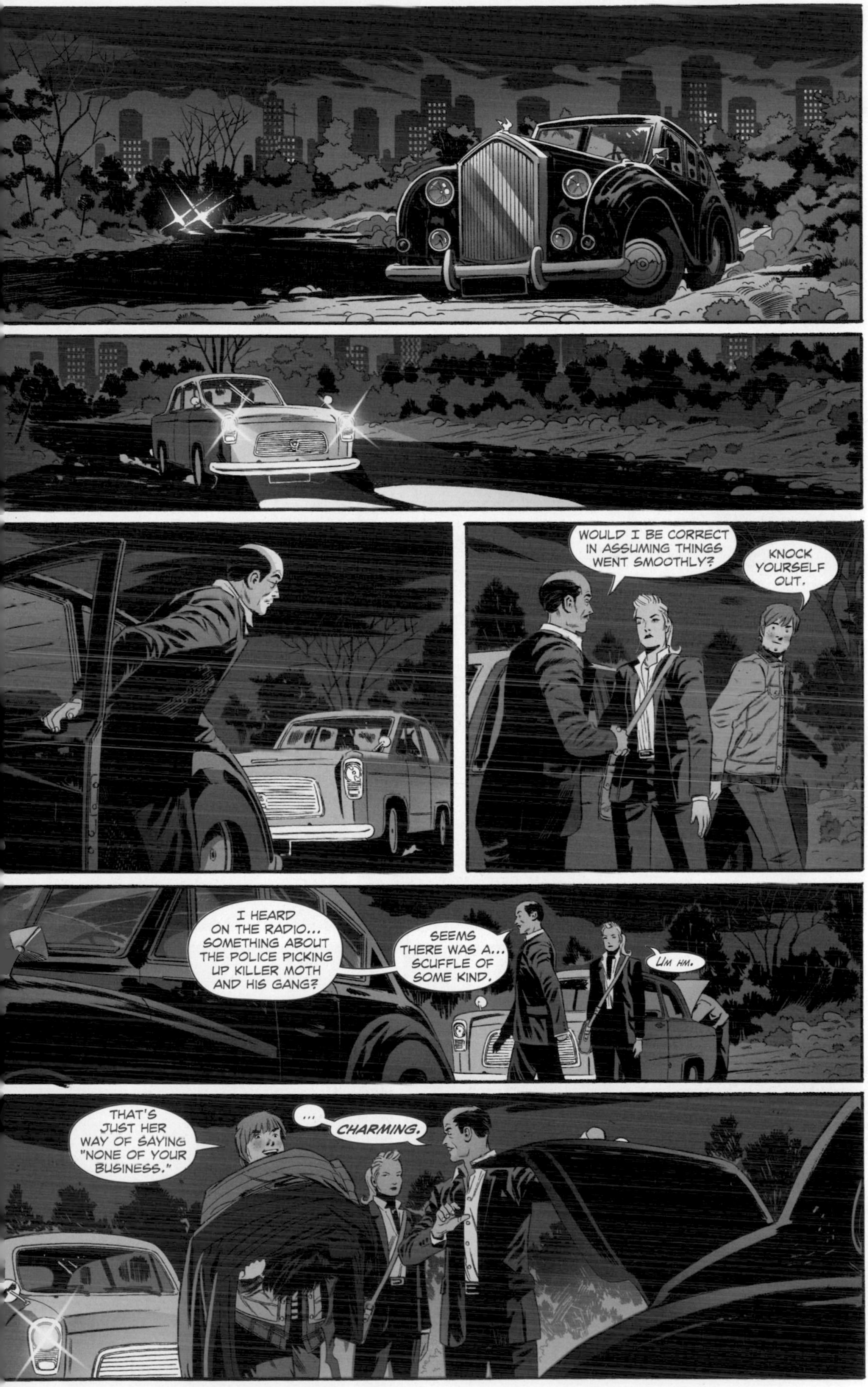
WOULD I BE CORRECT IN ASSUMING THINGS WENT SMOOTHLY?
KNOCK YOURSELF OUT.
I HEARD ON THE RADIO... SOMETHING ABOUT THE POLICE PICKING UP KILLER MOTH AND HIS GANG?
SEEMS THERE WAS A... SCUFFLE OF SOME KIND.
UM HM.
THAT'S JUST HER WAY OF SAYING "NONE OF YOUR BUSINESS."
... CHARMING.

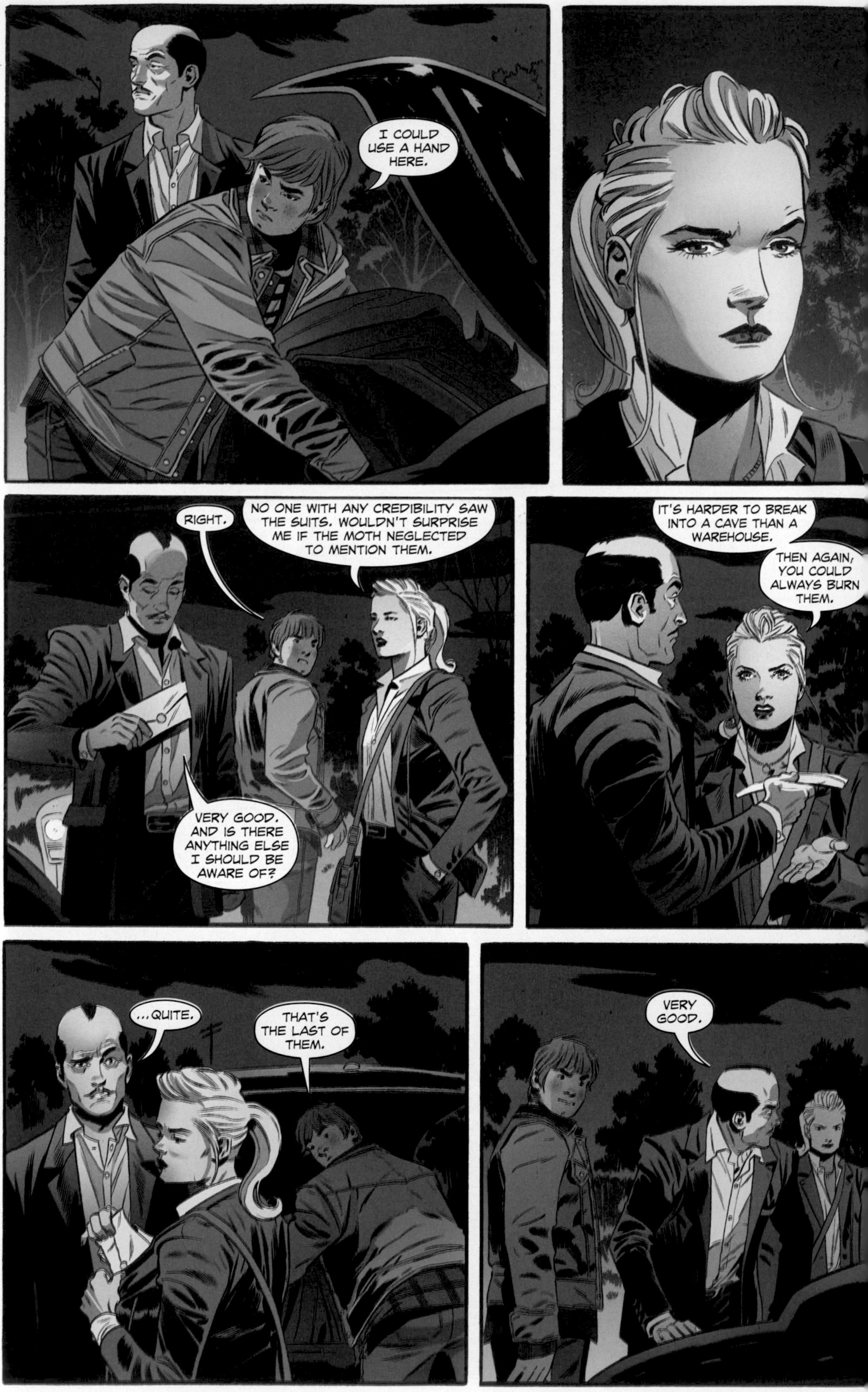
I COULD USE A HAND HERE.
RIGHT.
NO ONE WITH ANY CREDIBILITY SAW THE SUITS. WOULDN'T SURPRISE ME IF THE MOTH NEGLECTED TO MENTION THEM.
VERY GOOD. AND IS THERE ANYTHING ELSE I SHOULD BE AWARE OF?
IT'S HARDER TO BREAK INTO A CAVE THAN A WAREHOUSE.
THEN AGAIN, YOU COULD ALWAYS BURN THEM.
...QUITE.
THAT'S THE LAST OF THEM.
VERY GOOD.

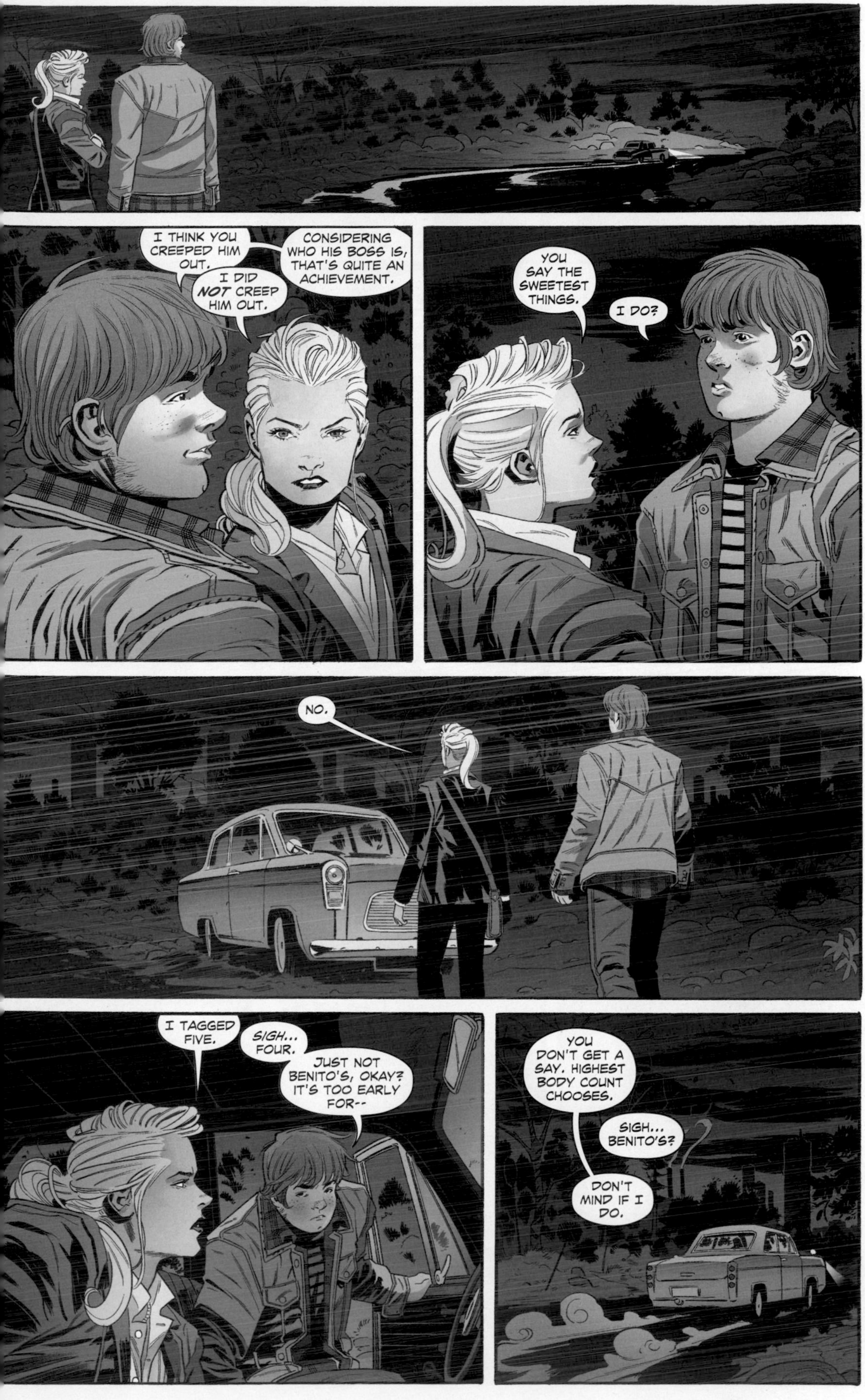
I THINK YOU CREEPED HIM OUT.
CONSIDERING WHO HIS BOSS IS, THAT'S QUITE AN ACHIEVEMENT.
I DID *NOT* CREEP HIM OUT.
YOU SAY THE SWEETEST THINGS.
I DO?
NO.
I TAGGED FIVE.
SIGH... FOUR.
JUST NOT BENITO'S, OKAY? IT'S TOO EARLY FOR--
YOU DON'T GET A SAY. HIGHEST BODY COUNT CHOOSES.
SIGH... BENITO'S?
DON'T MIND IF I DO.

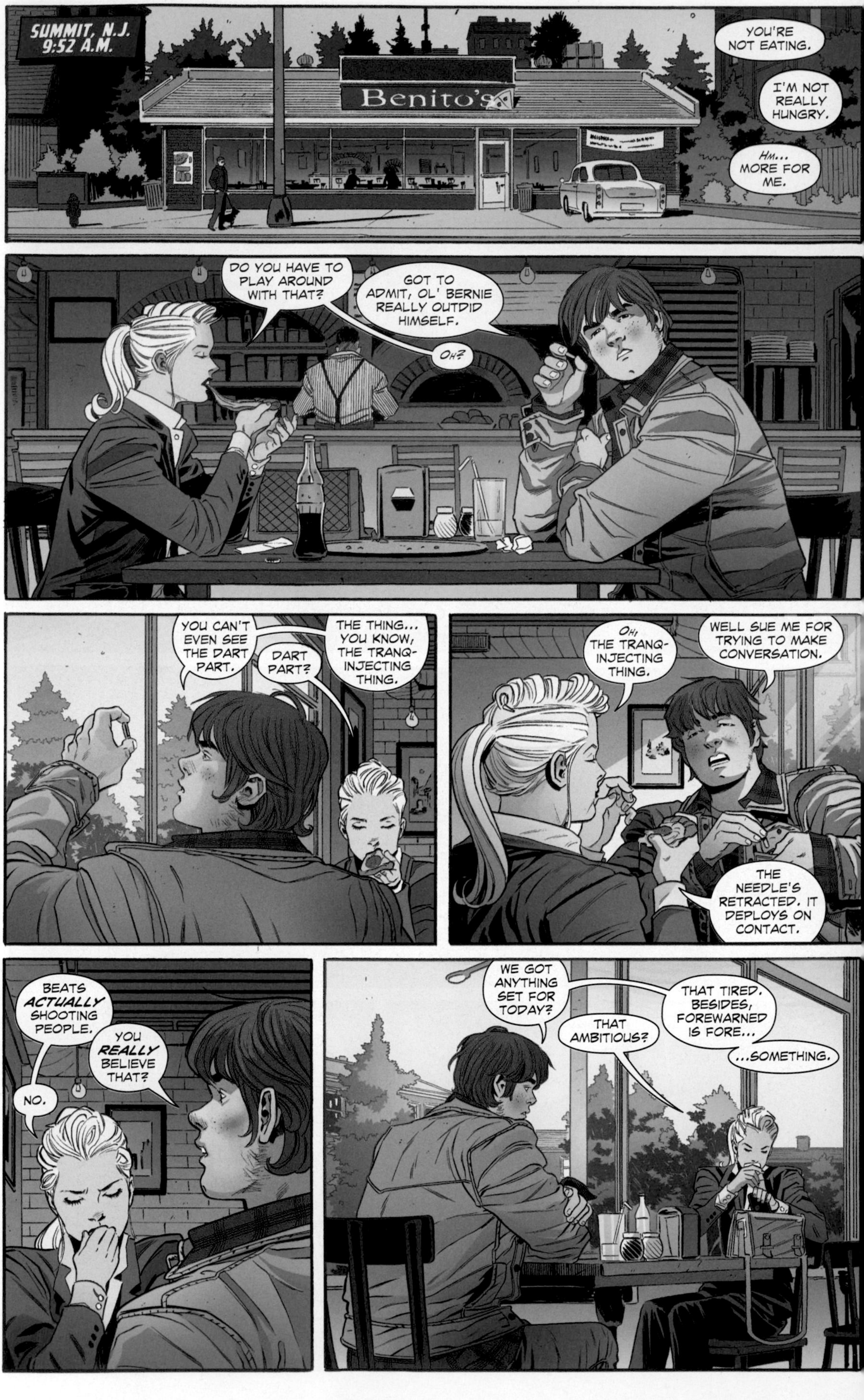
SUMMIT, N.J. 9:52 A.M.
Benito's
YOU'RE NOT EATING.
I'M NOT REALLY HUNGRY.
HM... MORE FOR ME.
DO YOU HAVE TO PLAY AROUND WITH THAT?
GOT TO ADMIT, OL' BERNIE REALLY OUTDID HIMSELF.
OH?
YOU CAN'T EVEN SEE THE DART PART.
DART PART?
THE THING... YOU KNOW, THE TRANQ-INJECTING THING.
OH, THE TRANQ-INJECTING THING.
WELL SUE ME FOR TRYING TO MAKE CONVERSATION.
THE NEEDLE'S RETRACTED. IT DEPLOYS ON CONTACT.
BEATS ACTUALLY SHOOTING PEOPLE.
YOU REALLY BELIEVE THAT?
NO.
WE GOT ANYTHING SET FOR TODAY?
THAT AMBITIOUS?
THAT TIRED. BESIDES, FOREWARNED IS FORE...
...SOMETHING.

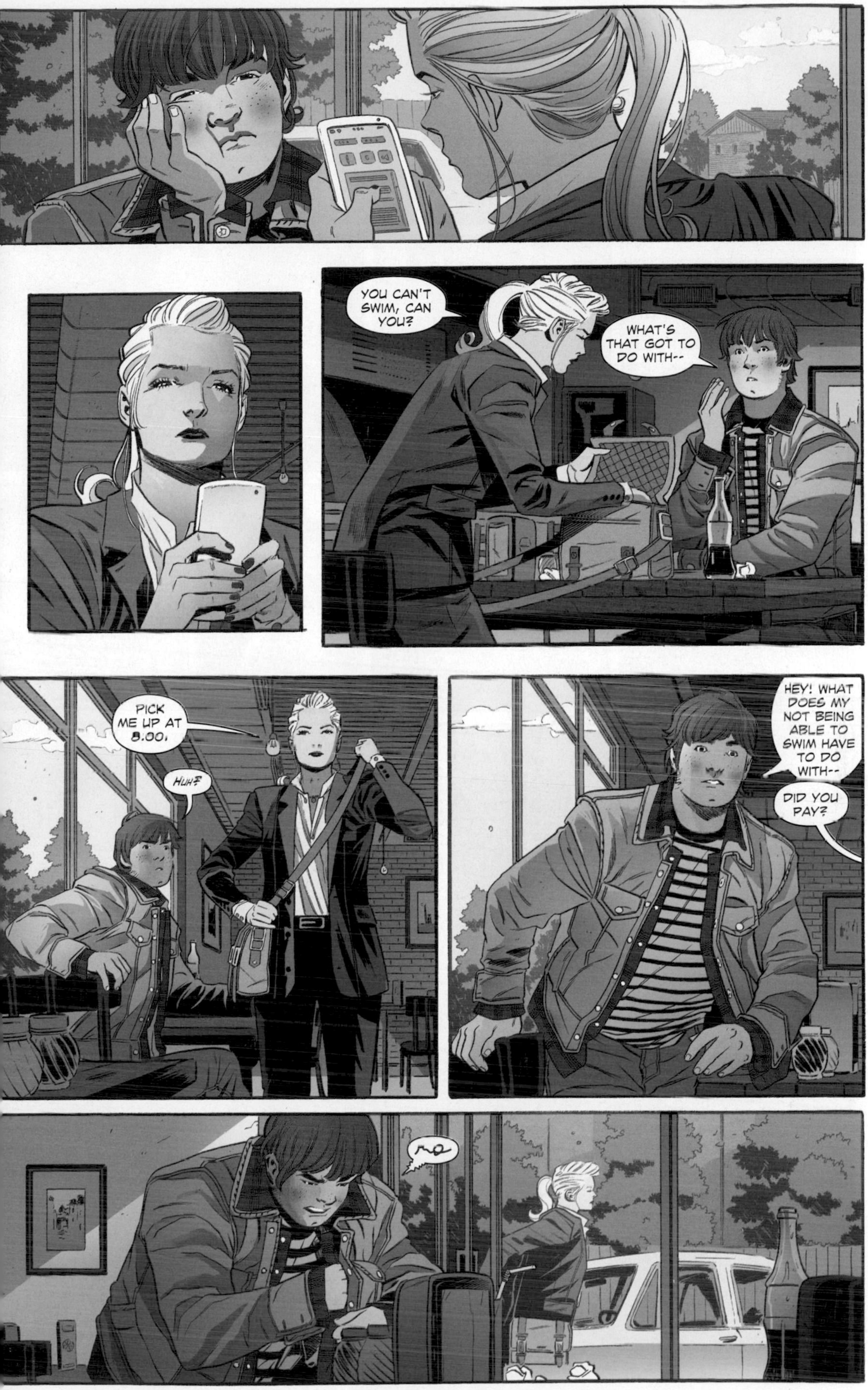
YOU CAN'T SWIM, CAN YOU?
WHAT'S THAT GOT TO DO WITH--
PICK ME UP AT 8.00.
HUH?
HEY! WHAT DOES MY NOT BEING ABLE TO SWIM HAVE TO DO WITH--
DID YOU PAY?

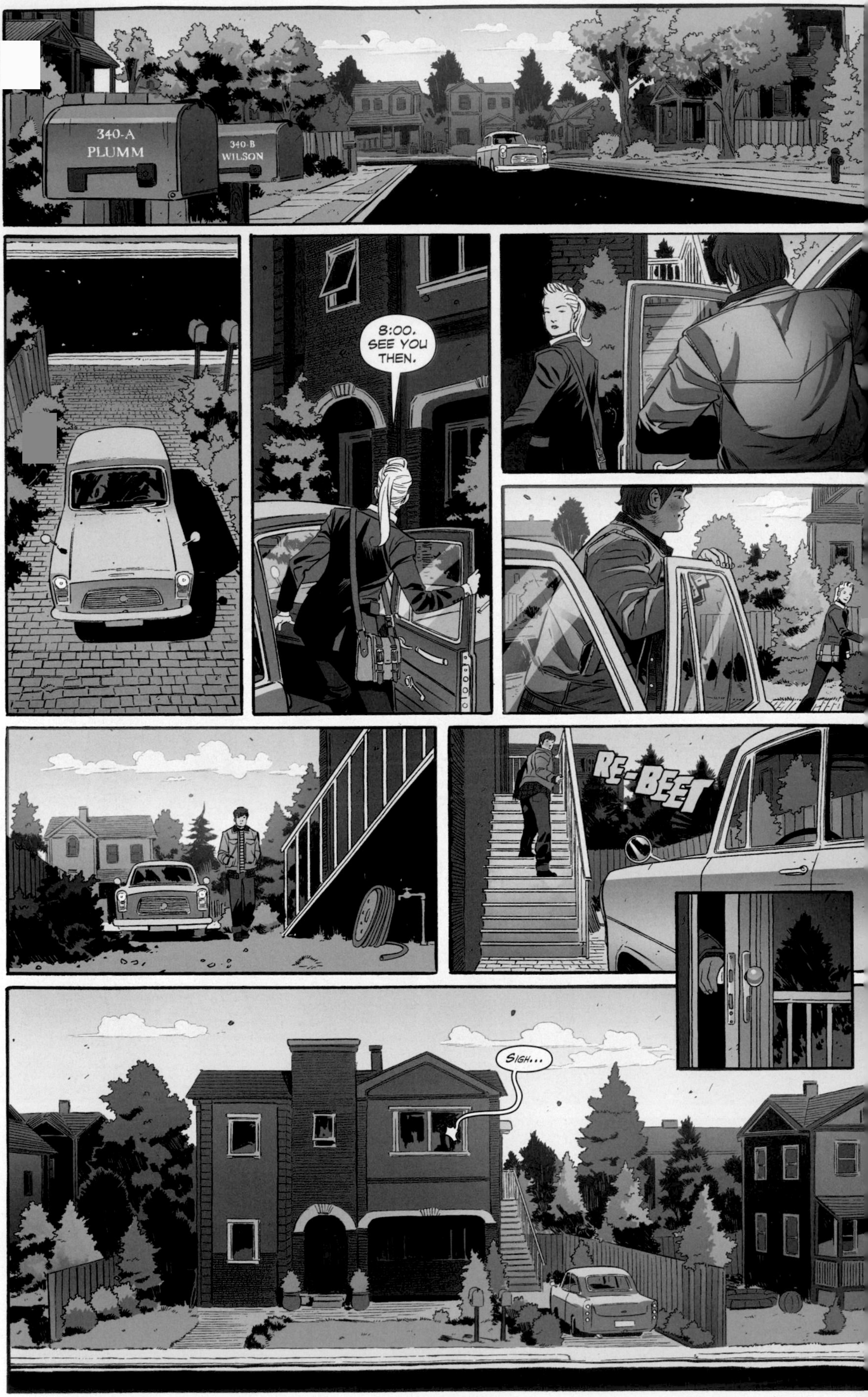
340-A
PLUMM
340-B
WILSON
8:00. SEE YOU THEN.
RE-BEET
SIGH...

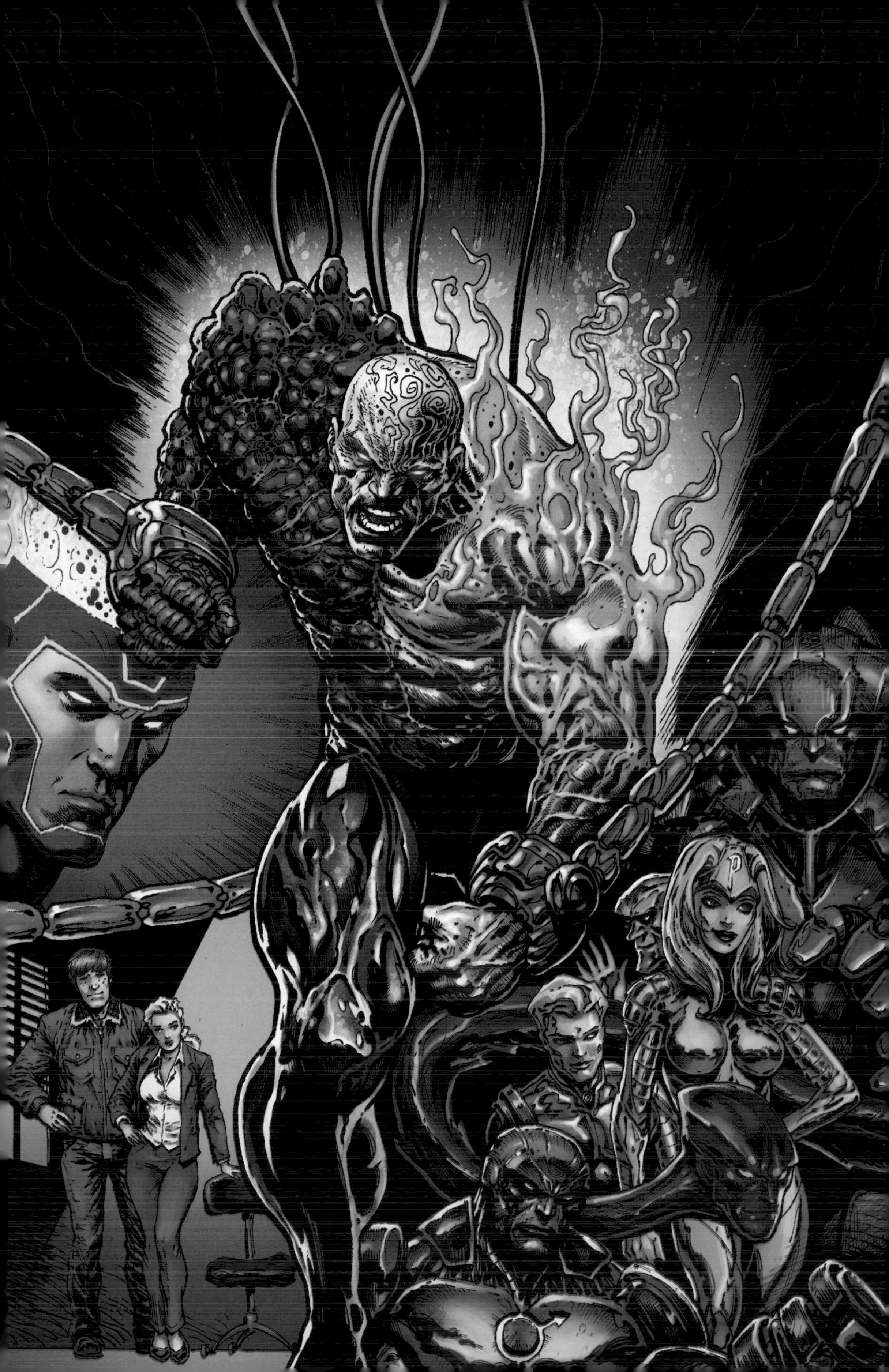

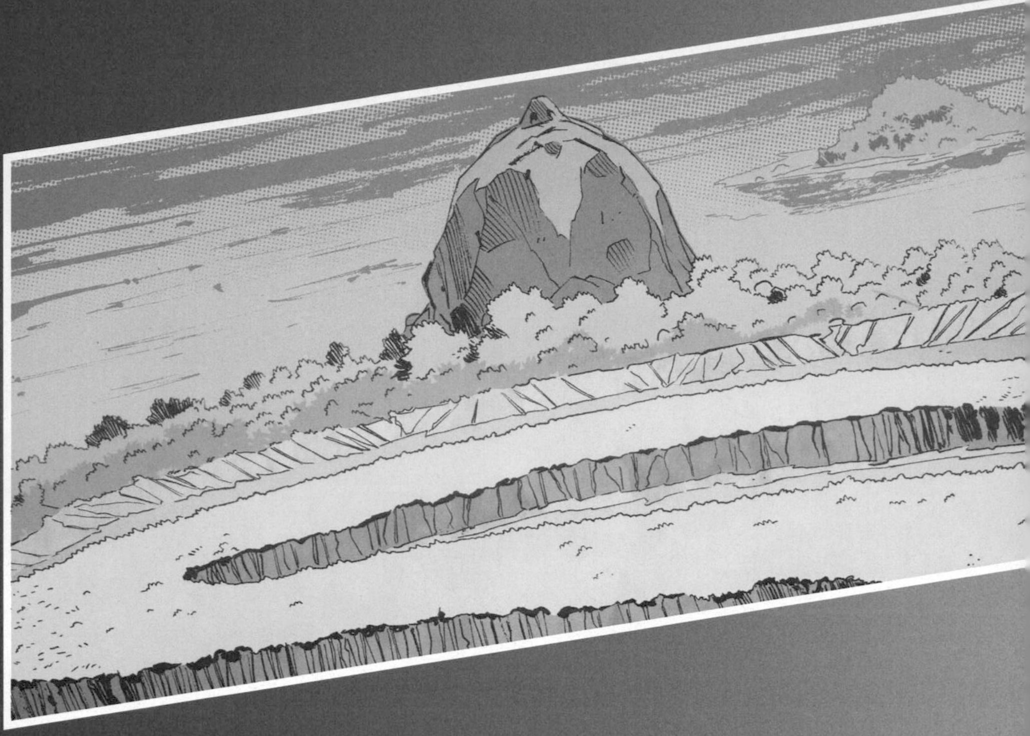

LIAM SHARP
with **CHRIS SOTOMAYOR**
cover

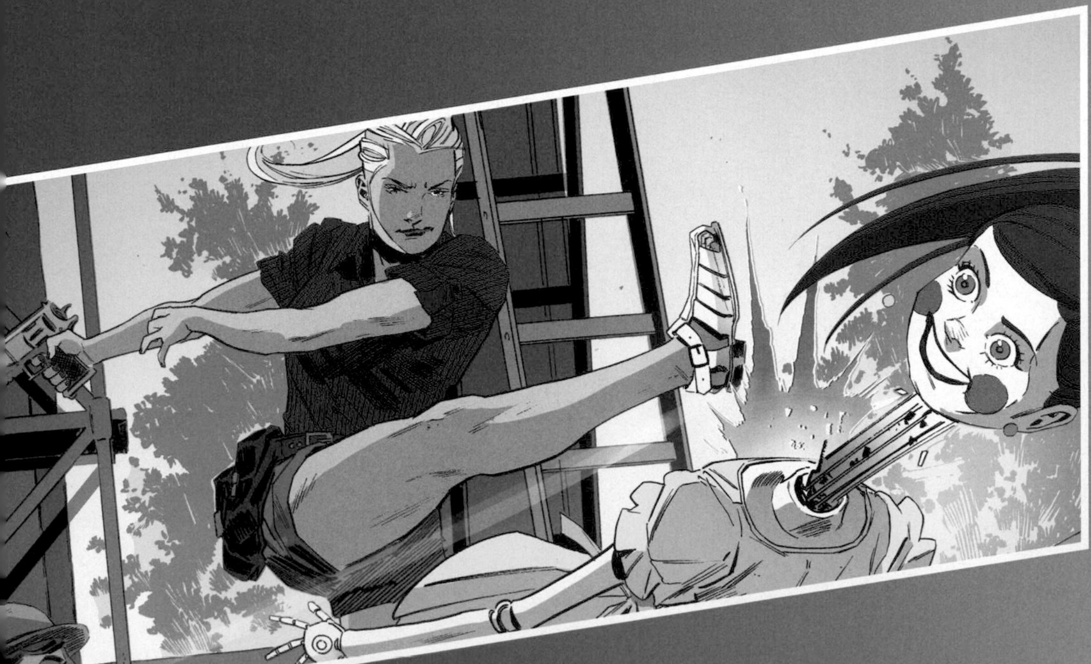

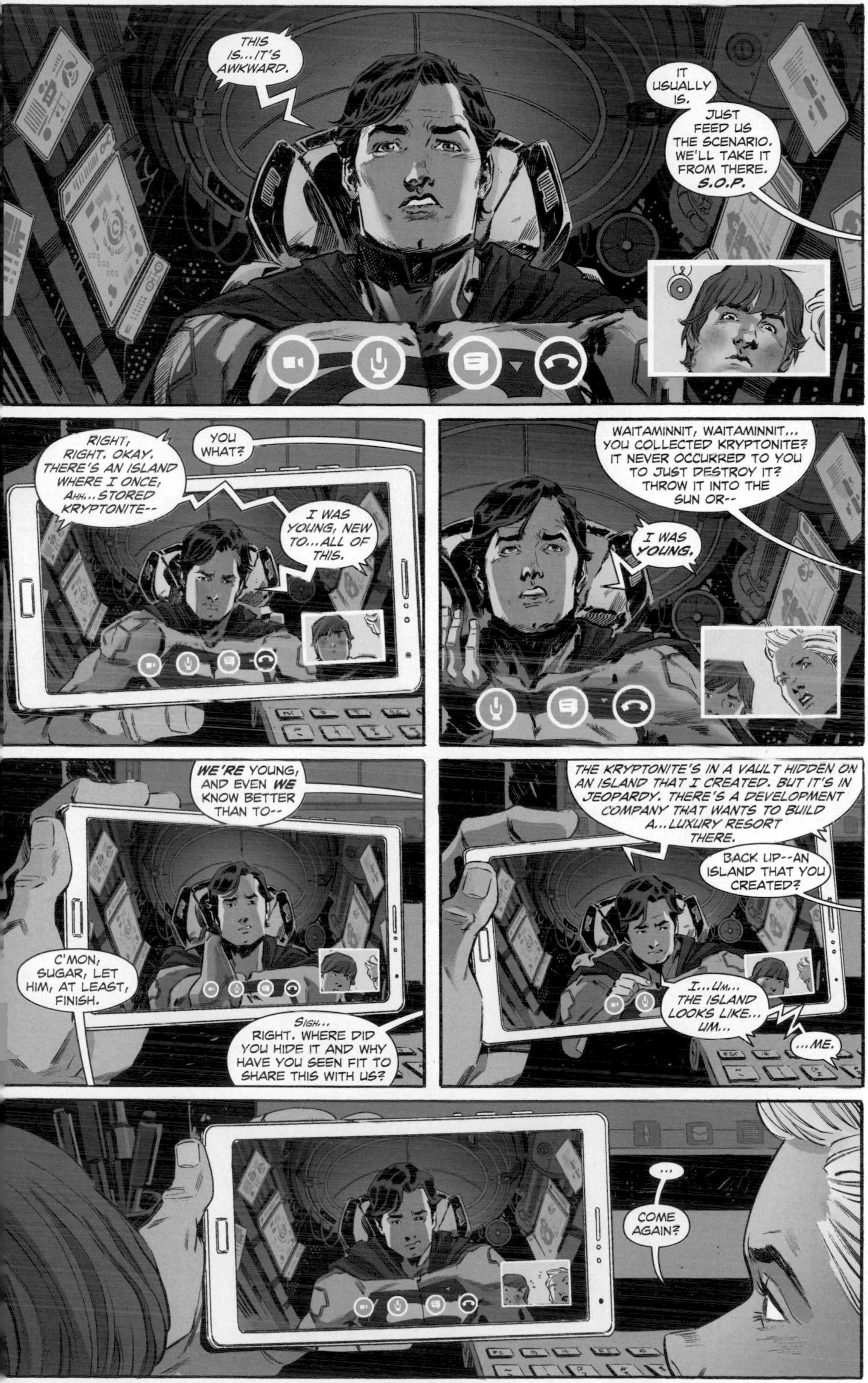

THIS IS...IT'S AWKWARD.
IT USUALLY IS.
JUST FEED US THE SCENARIO. WE'LL TAKE IT FROM THERE. S.O.P.
RIGHT, RIGHT. OKAY. THERE'S AN ISLAND WHERE I ONCE, AHH...STORED KRYPTONITE--
YOU WHAT?
I WAS YOUNG, NEW TO...ALL OF THIS.
WAITAMINNIT, WAITAMINNIT... YOU COLLECTED KRYPTONITE? IT NEVER OCCURRED TO YOU TO JUST DESTROY IT? THROW IT INTO THE SUN OR--
I WAS YOUNG.
WE'RE YOUNG, AND EVEN WE KNOW BETTER THAN TO--
C'MON, SUGAR, LET HIM, AT LEAST, FINISH.
SIGH...
RIGHT. WHERE DID YOU HIDE IT AND WHY HAVE YOU SEEN FIT TO SHARE THIS WITH US?
THE KRYPTONITE'S IN A VAULT HIDDEN ON AN ISLAND THAT I CREATED. BUT IT'S IN JEOPARDY. THERE'S A DEVELOPMENT COMPANY THAT WANTS TO BUILD A...LUXURY RESORT THERE.
BACK UP--AN ISLAND THAT YOU CREATED?
I...UM... THE ISLAND LOOKS LIKE... UM...
...ME.
...
COME AGAIN?

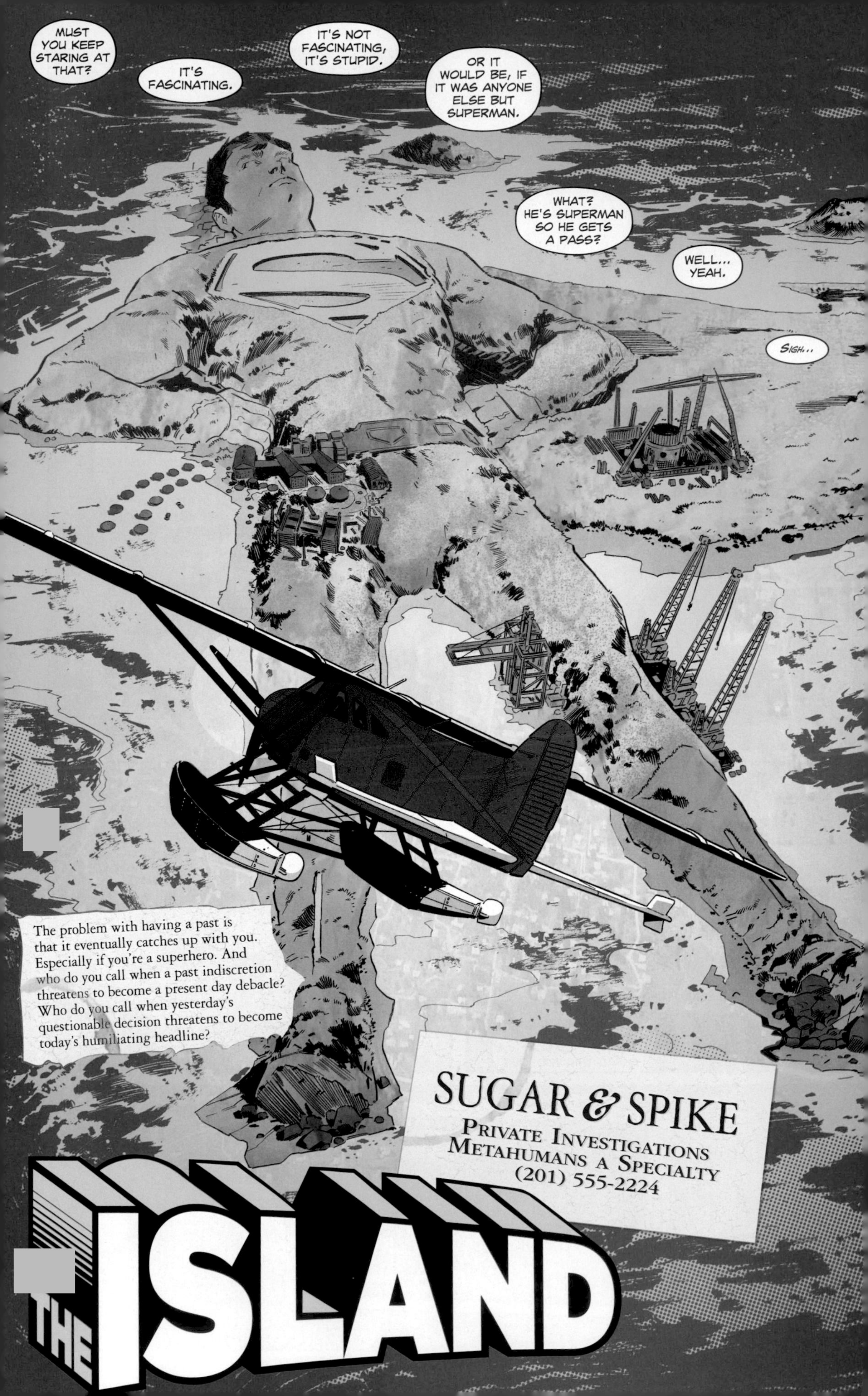
MUST YOU KEEP STARING AT THAT?
IT'S FASCINATING.
IT'S NOT FASCINATING, IT'S STUPID.
OR IT WOULD BE, IF IT WAS ANYONE ELSE BUT SUPERMAN.
WHAT? HE'S SUPERMAN SO HE GETS A PASS?
WELL... YEAH.
SIGH...
The problem with having a past is that it eventually catches up with you. Especially if you're a superhero. And who do you call when a past indiscretion threatens to become a present day debacle? Who do you call when yesterday's questionable decision threatens to become today's humiliating headline?
SUGAR & SPIKE
PRIVATE INVESTIGATIONS
METAHUMANS A SPECIALTY
(201) 555-2224
THE ISLAND

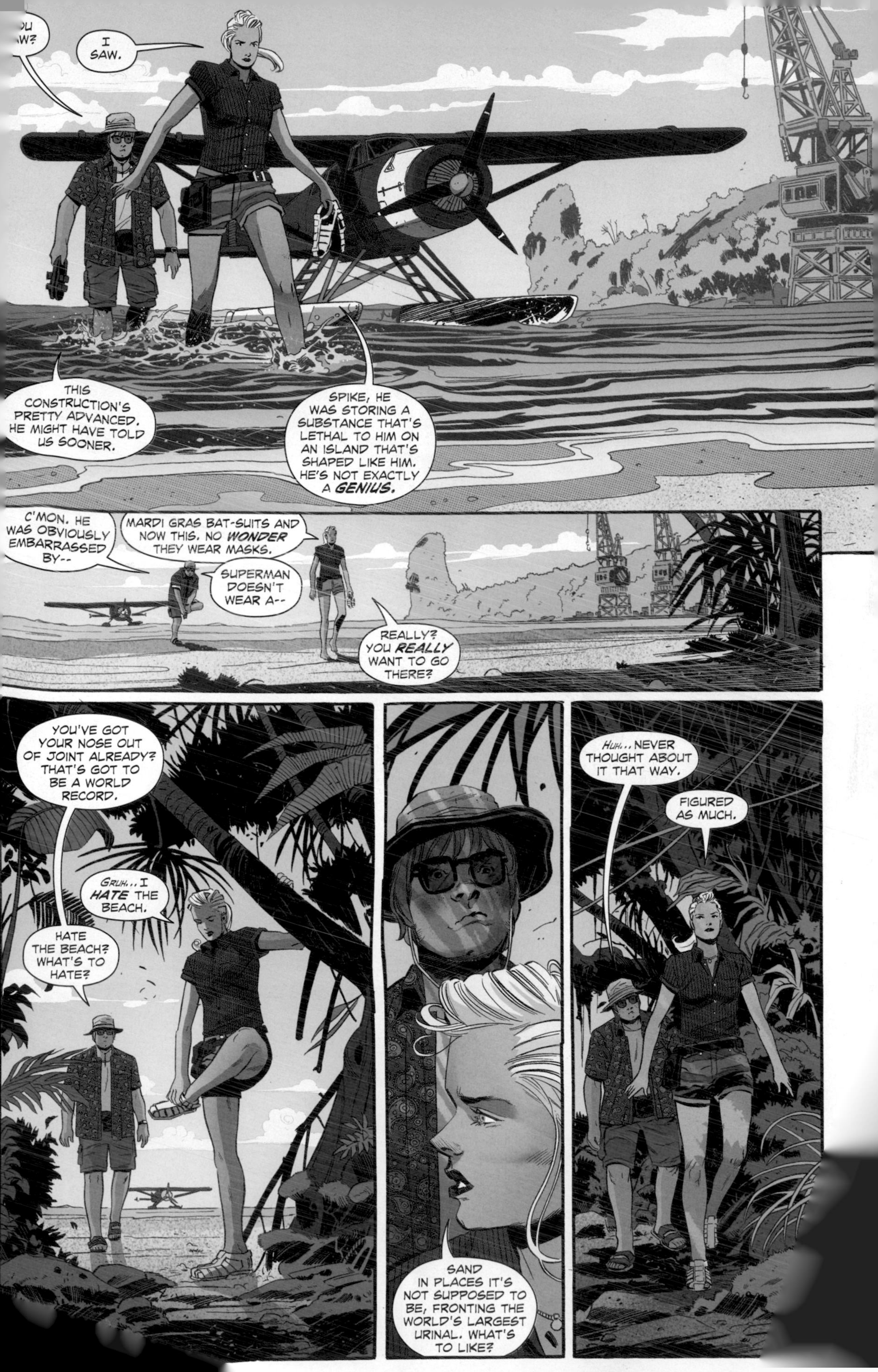
I SAW.
THIS CONSTRUCTION'S PRETTY ADVANCED. HE MIGHT HAVE TOLD US SOONER.
SPIKE, HE WAS STORING A SUBSTANCE THAT'S LETHAL TO HIM ON AN ISLAND THAT'S SHAPED LIKE HIM. HE'S NOT EXACTLY A GENIUS.
C'MON. HE WAS OBVIOUSLY EMBARRASSED BY--
MARDI GRAS BAT-SUITS AND NOW THIS. NO WONDER THEY WEAR MASKS.
SUPERMAN DOESN'T WEAR A--
REALLY? YOU REALLY WANT TO GO THERE?
YOU'VE GOT YOUR NOSE OUT OF JOINT ALREADY? THAT'S GOT TO BE A WORLD RECORD.
GRUH... I HATE THE BEACH.
HATE THE BEACH? WHAT'S TO HATE?
SAND IN PLACES IT'S NOT SUPPOSED TO BE, FRONTING THE WORLD'S LARGEST URINAL. WHAT'S TO LIKE?
HUH... NEVER THOUGHT ABOUT IT THAT WAY.
FIGURED AS MUCH.

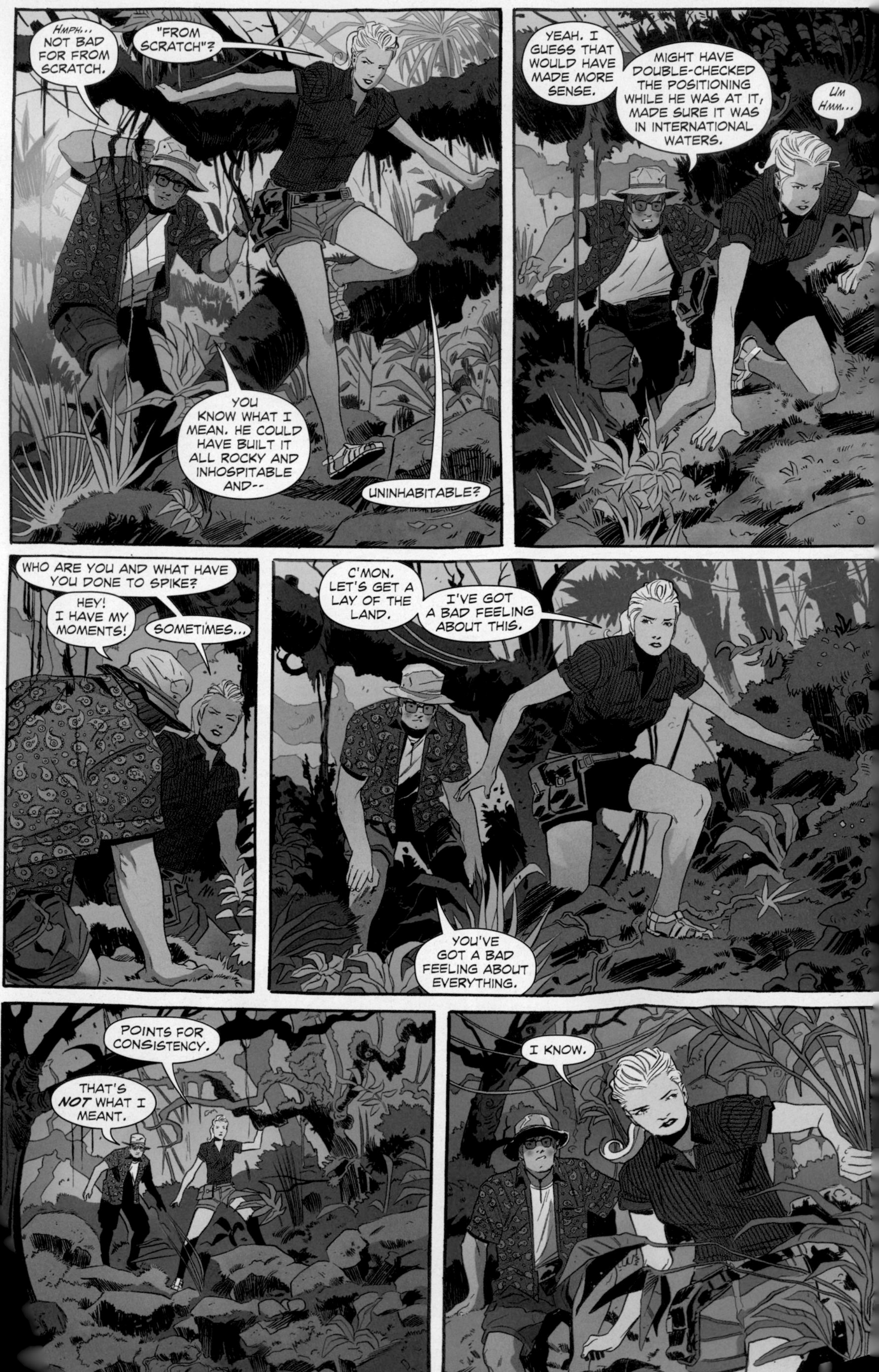
HMPH... NOT BAD FOR FROM SCRATCH.
"FROM SCRATCH"?
YOU KNOW WHAT I MEAN. HE COULD HAVE BUILT IT ALL ROCKY AND INHOSPITABLE AND--
UNINHABITABLE?
YEAH. I GUESS THAT WOULD HAVE MADE MORE SENSE.
MIGHT HAVE DOUBLE-CHECKED THE POSITIONING WHILE HE WAS AT IT, MADE SURE IT WAS IN INTERNATIONAL WATERS.
UM HMM...
WHO ARE YOU AND WHAT HAVE YOU DONE TO SPIKE?
HEY! I HAVE MY MOMENTS!
SOMETIMES...
C'MON. LET'S GET A LAY OF THE LAND.
I'VE GOT A BAD FEELING ABOUT THIS.
YOU'VE GOT A BAD FEELING ABOUT EVERYTHING.
POINTS FOR CONSISTENCY.
THAT'S NOT WHAT I MEANT.
I KNOW.

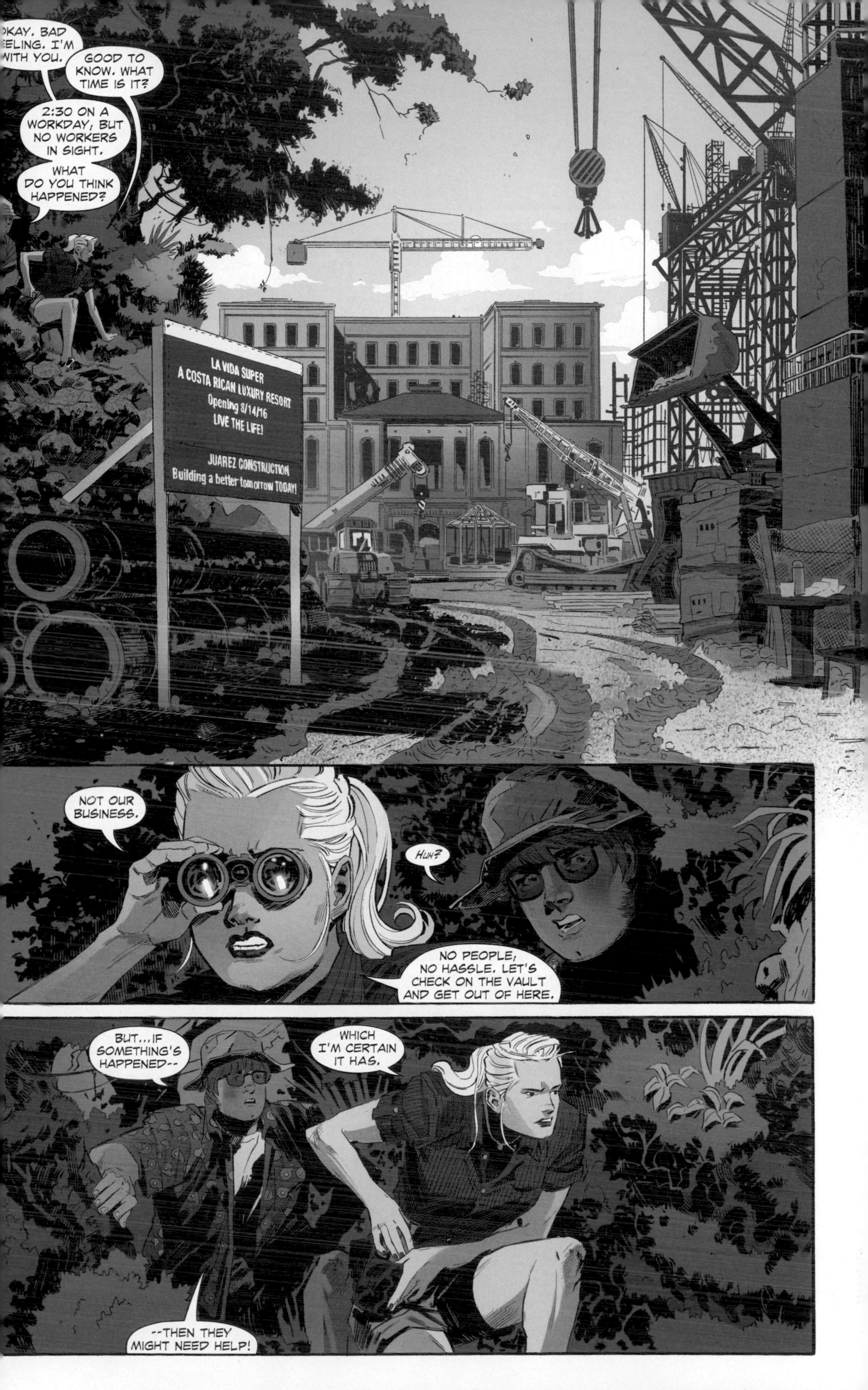
OKAY. BAD FEELING. I'M WITH YOU.
GOOD TO KNOW. WHAT TIME IS IT?
2:30 ON A WORKDAY, BUT NO WORKERS IN SIGHT.
WHAT DO YOU THINK HAPPENED?
LA VIDA SUPER
A COSTA RICAN LUXURY RESORT
Opening 8/14/16
LIVE THE LIFE!
JUAREZ CONSTRUCTION
Building a better tomorrow TODAY!
NOT OUR BUSINESS.
HUH?
NO PEOPLE, NO HASSLE. LET'S CHECK ON THE VAULT AND GET OUT OF HERE.
BUT...IF SOMETHING'S HAPPENED--
WHICH I'M CERTAIN IT HAS.
--THEN THEY MIGHT NEED HELP!

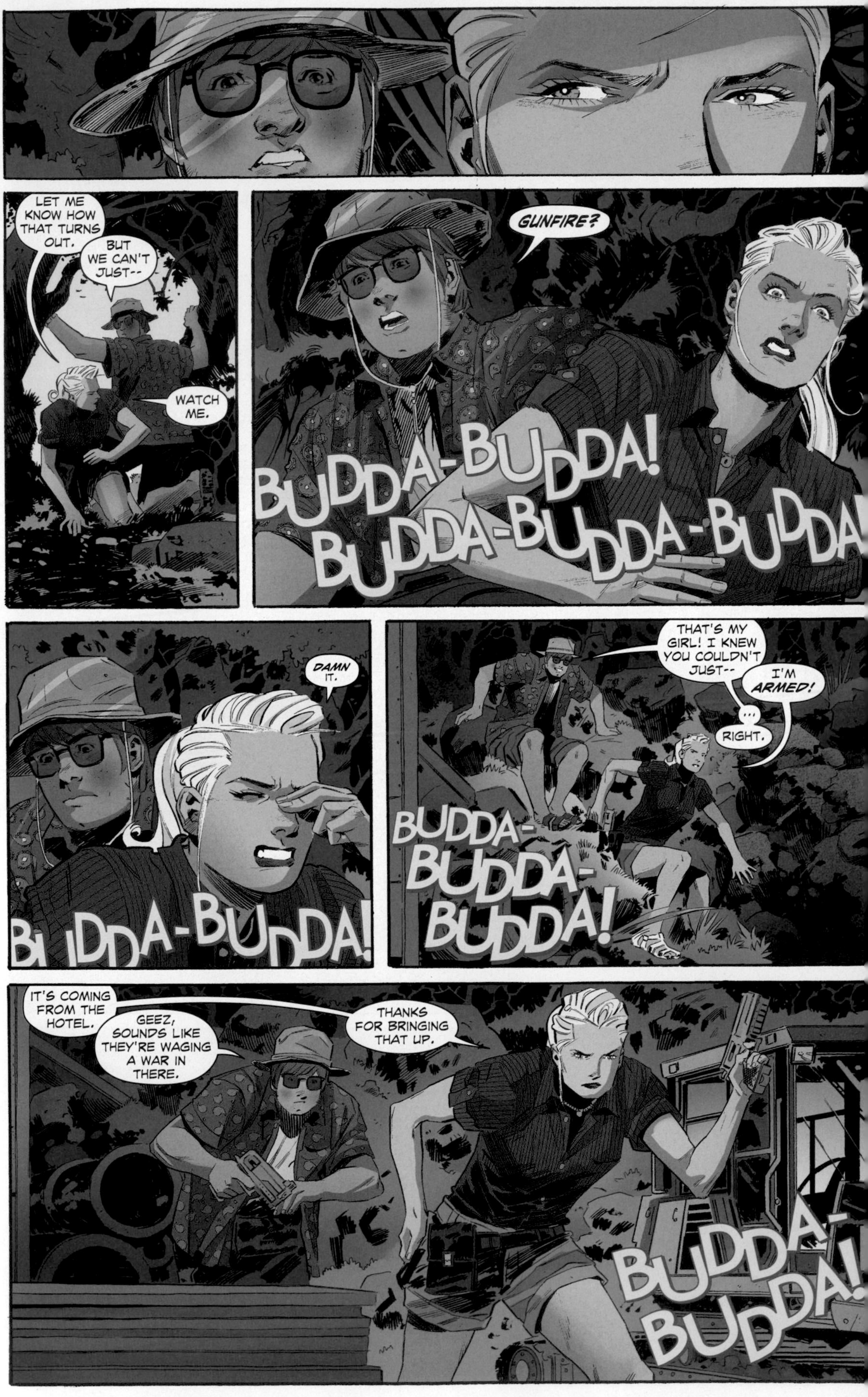
LET ME KNOW HOW THAT TURNS OUT.
BUT WE CAN'T JUST--
WATCH ME.
GUNFIRE?
BUDDA-BUDDA!
BUDDA-BUDDA-BUDDA
DAMN IT.
BUDDA-BUDDA!
THAT'S MY GIRL! I KNEW YOU COULDN'T JUST--
I'M ARMED!
...
RIGHT.
BUDDA-BUDDA-BUDDA!
IT'S COMING FROM THE HOTEL.
GEEZ, SOUNDS LIKE THEY'RE WAGING A WAR IN THERE.
THANKS FOR BRINGING THAT UP.
BUDDA-BUDDA!

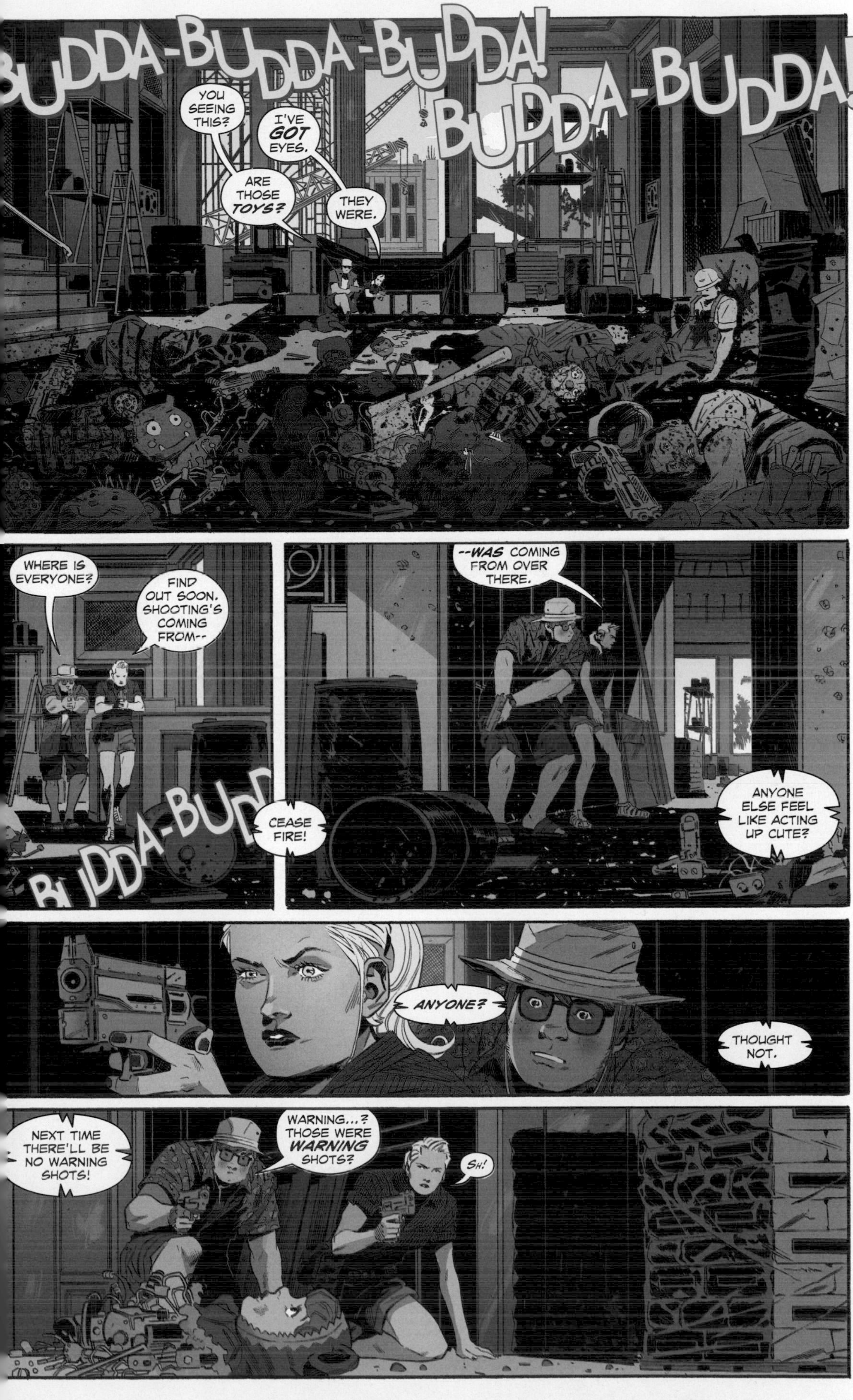
BUDDA-BUDDA-BUDDA!
BUDDA-BUDDA!
YOU SEEING THIS?
I'VE GOT EYES.
ARE THOSE TOYS?
THEY WERE.
WHERE IS EVERYONE?
FIND OUT SOON. SHOOTING'S COMING FROM--
BUDDA-BUD
CEASE FIRE!
--WAS COMING FROM OVER THERE.
ANYONE ELSE FEEL LIKE ACTING UP CUTE?
ANYONE?
THOUGHT NOT.
NEXT TIME THERE'LL BE NO WARNING SHOTS!
WARNING...? THOSE WERE WARNING SHOTS?
SH!

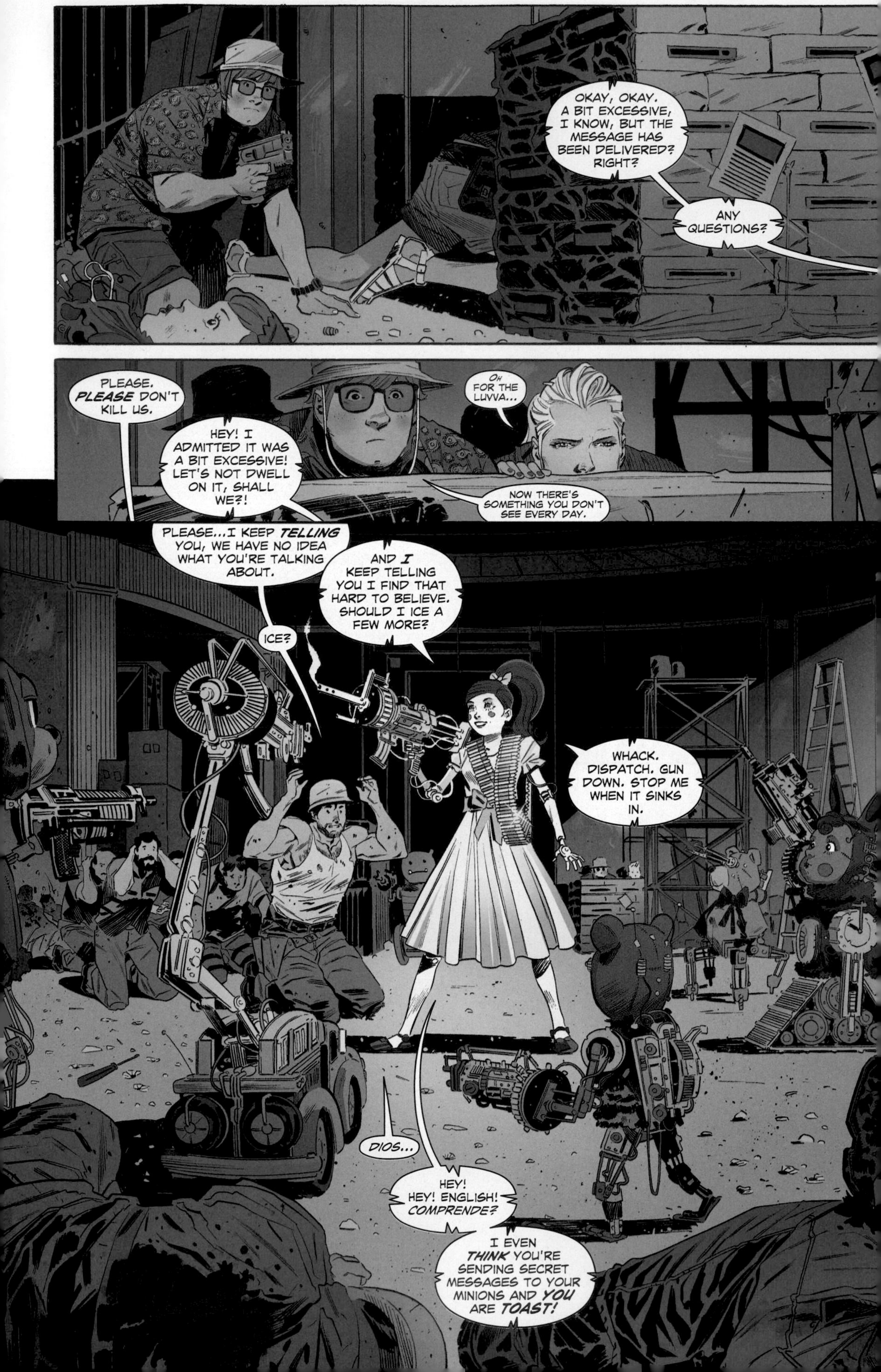
OKAY, OKAY. A BIT EXCESSIVE, I KNOW, BUT THE MESSAGE HAS BEEN DELIVERED? RIGHT?
ANY QUESTIONS?
PLEASE. *PLEASE* DON'T KILL US.
HEY! I ADMITTED IT WAS A BIT EXCESSIVE! LET'S NOT DWELL ON IT, SHALL WE?!
OH FOR THE LUVVA...
NOW THERE'S SOMETHING YOU DON'T SEE EVERY DAY.
PLEASE...I KEEP *TELLING* YOU, WE HAVE NO IDEA WHAT YOU'RE TALKING ABOUT.
AND *I* KEEP TELLING YOU I FIND THAT HARD TO BELIEVE. SHOULD I ICE A FEW MORE?
ICE?
WHACK. DISPATCH. GUN DOWN. STOP ME WHEN IT SINKS IN.
DIOS...
HEY! HEY! ENGLISH! *COMPRENDE?*
I EVEN *THINK* YOU'RE SENDING SECRET MESSAGES TO YOUR MINIONS AND *YOU* ARE *TOAST!*

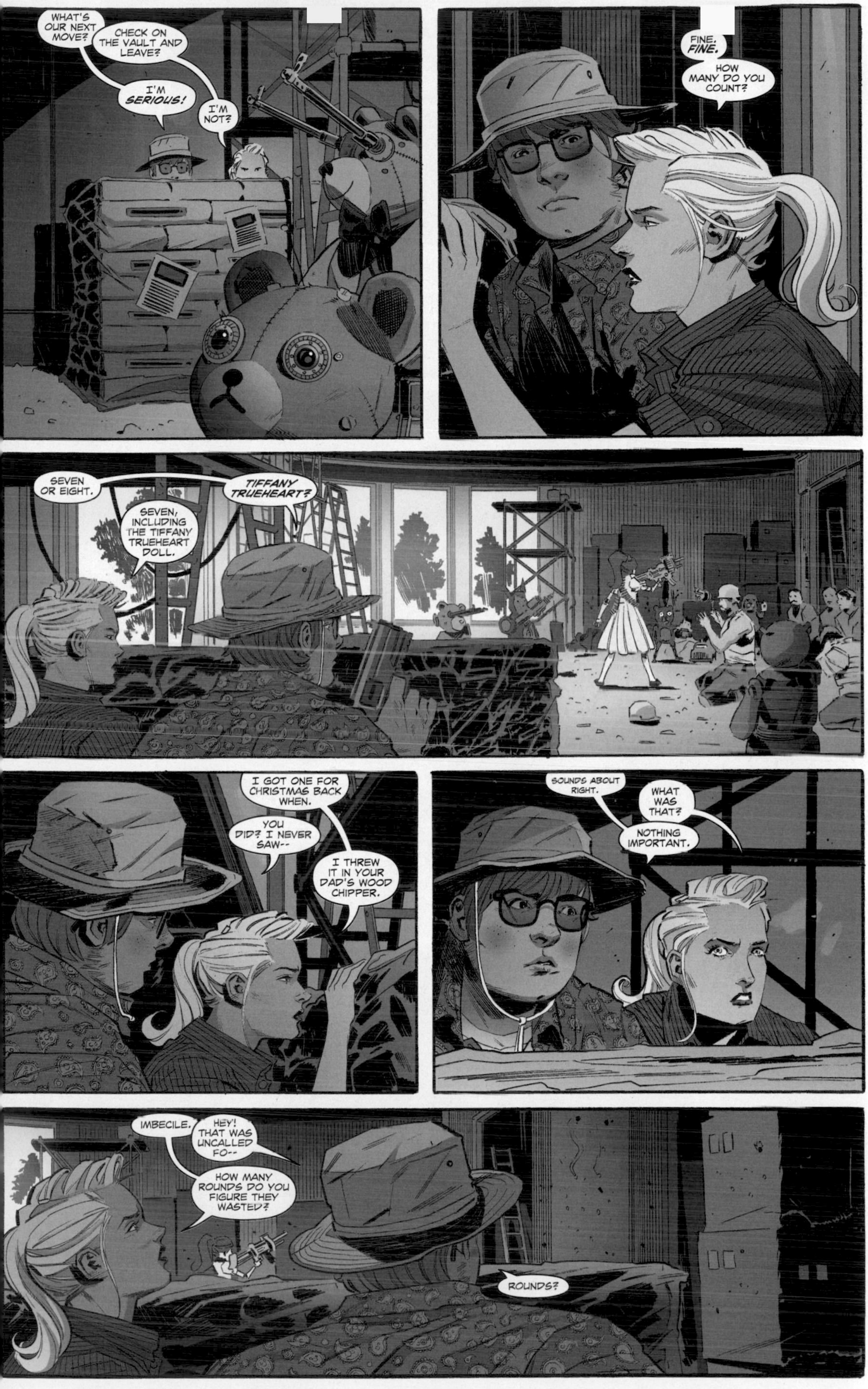

WHAT'S OUR NEXT MOVE?
CHECK ON THE VAULT AND LEAVE?
I'M *SERIOUS!*
I'M NOT?
FINE. *FINE.*
HOW MANY DO YOU COUNT?
SEVEN OR EIGHT.
TIFFANY TRUEHEART?
SEVEN, INCLUDING THE TIFFANY TRUEHEART DOLL.
I GOT ONE FOR CHRISTMAS BACK WHEN.
YOU DID? I NEVER SAW--
I THREW IT IN YOUR DAD'S WOOD CHIPPER.
SOUNDS ABOUT RIGHT.
WHAT WAS THAT?
NOTHING IMPORTANT.
IMBECILE.
HEY! THAT WAS UNCALLED FO--
HOW MANY ROUNDS DO YOU FIGURE THEY WASTED?
ROUNDS?

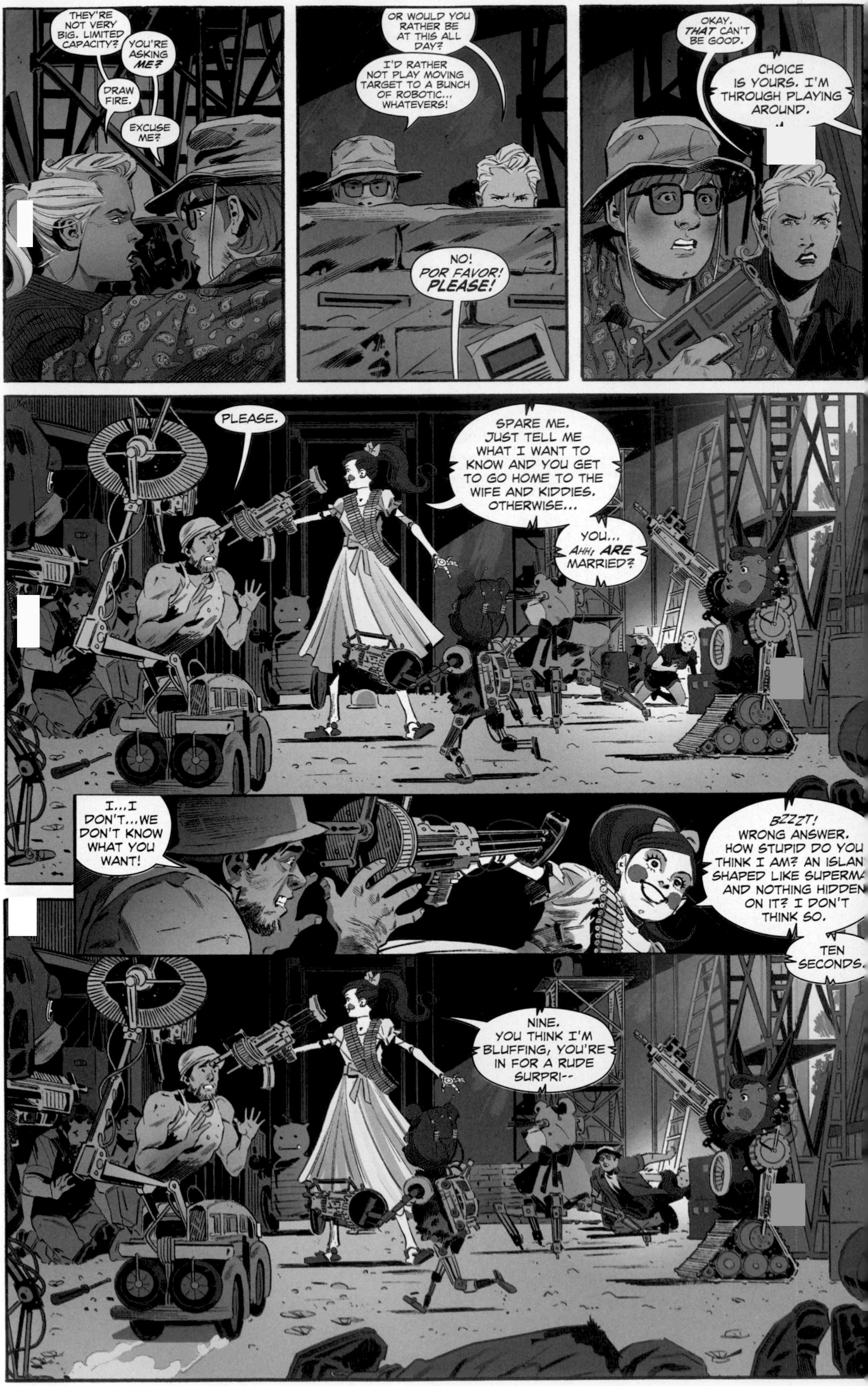
THEY'RE NOT VERY BIG. LIMITED CAPACITY?
YOU'RE ASKING *ME?*
DRAW FIRE.
EXCUSE ME?
OR WOULD YOU RATHER BE AT THIS ALL DAY?
I'D RATHER NOT PLAY MOVING TARGET TO A BUNCH OF ROBOTIC... WHATEVERS!
NO! *POR FAVOR!* ***PLEASE!***
OKAY. *THAT* CAN'T BE GOOD.
CHOICE IS YOURS. I'M THROUGH PLAYING AROUND.
PLEASE.
SPARE ME. JUST TELL ME WHAT I WANT TO KNOW AND YOU GET TO GO HOME TO THE WIFE AND KIDDIES. OTHERWISE...
YOU... *AHH,* ***ARE*** MARRIED?
I...I DON'T...WE DON'T KNOW WHAT YOU WANT!
BZZZT! WRONG ANSWER. HOW STUPID DO YOU THINK I AM? AN ISLAN SHAPED LIKE SUPERMA AND NOTHING HIDDEN ON IT? I DON'T THINK SO.
TEN SECONDS.
NINE. YOU THINK I'M BLUFFING, YOU'RE IN FOR A RUDE SURPRI--

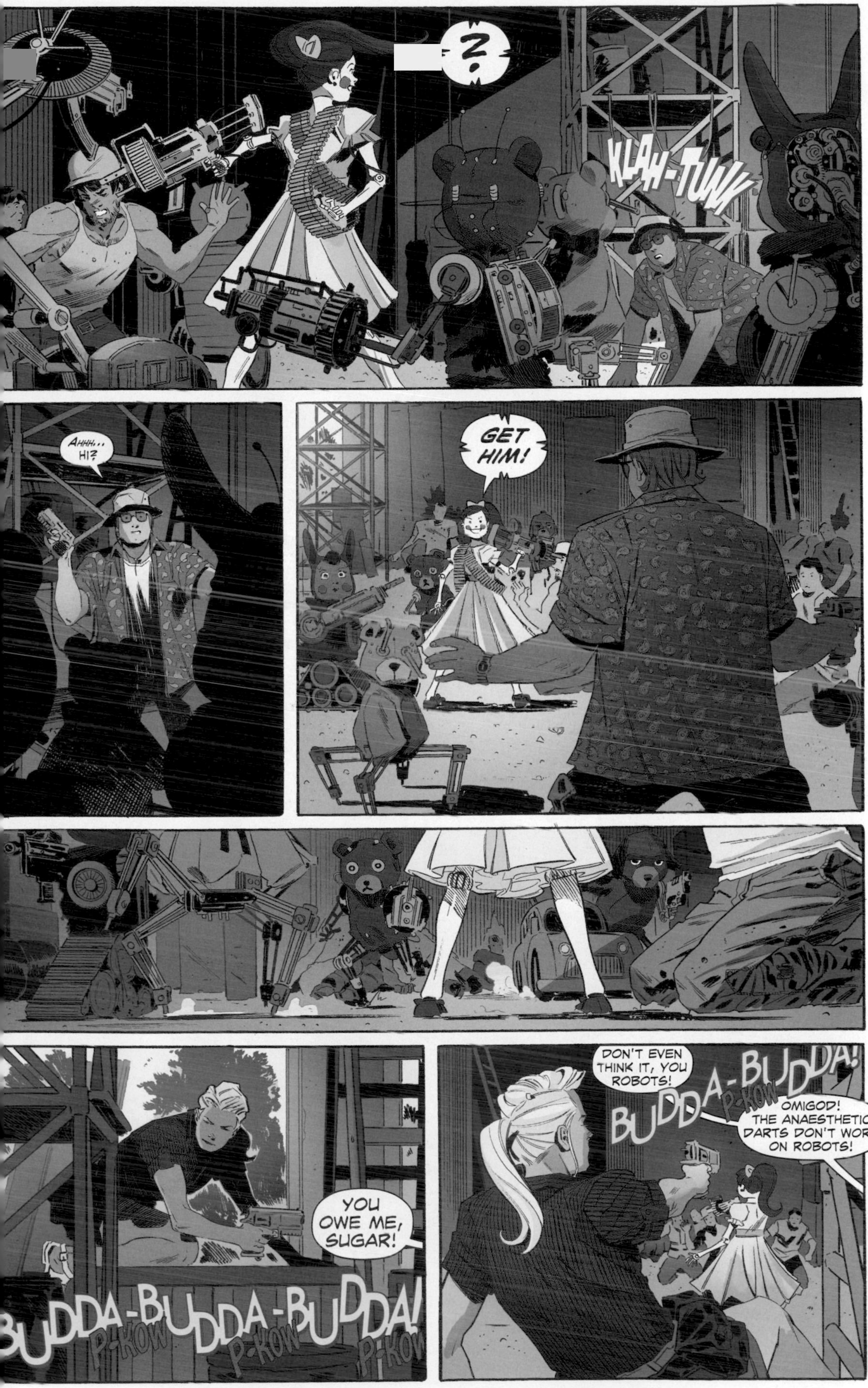
?
KLAH-TUNK
AHHH... HI?
GET HIM!
YOU OWE ME, SUGAR!
BUDDA-BUDDA-BUDDA!
P-KOW
P-KOW
P-KOW
DON'T EVEN THINK IT, YOU ROBOTS!
BUDDA-BUDDA!
P-KOW
OMIGOD! THE ANAESTHETIC DARTS DON'T WORK ON ROBOTS!

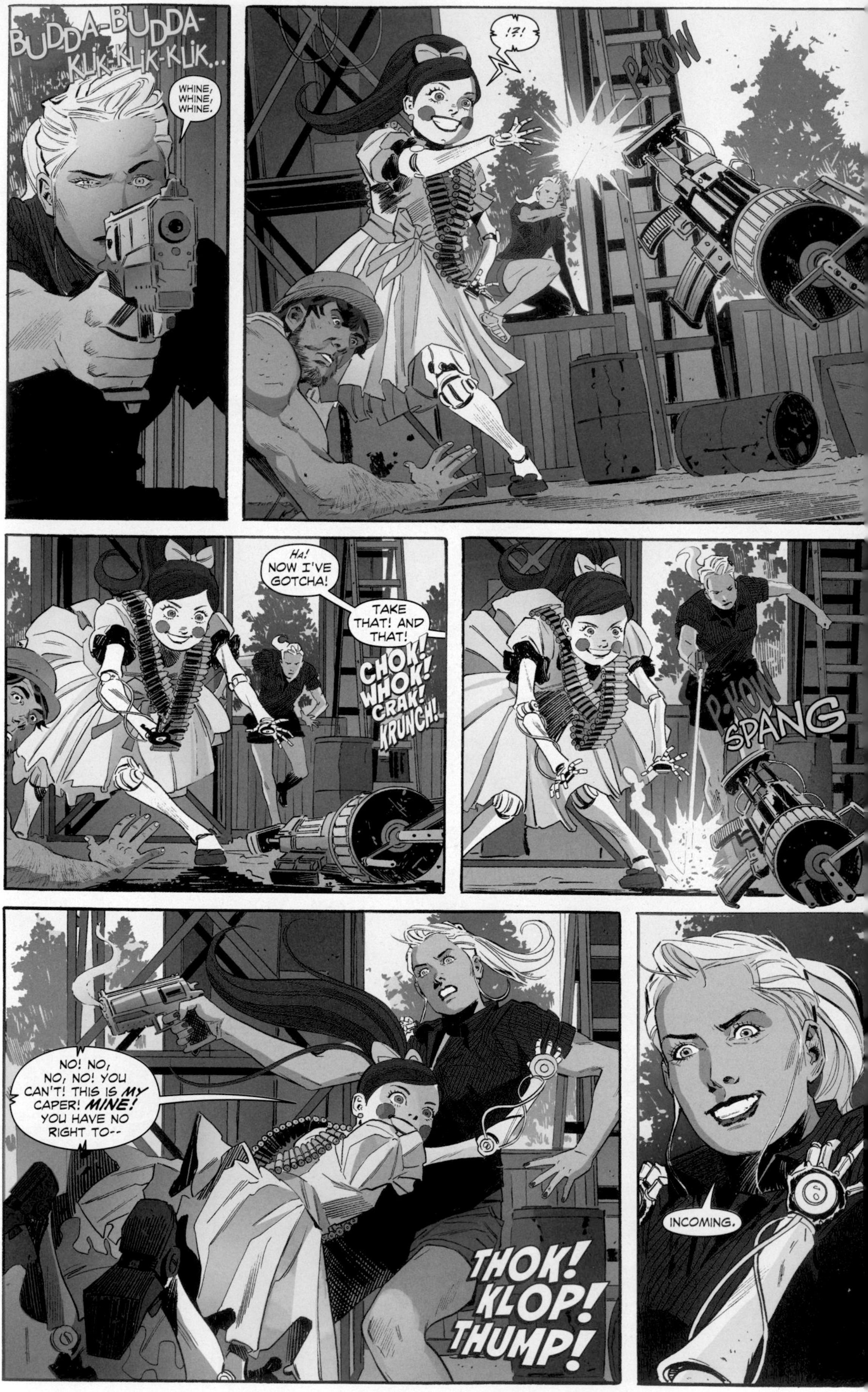
BUDDA-BUDDA-
KLIK-KLIK-KLIK...
WHINE, WHINE, WHINE.
!?!
P-KOW
HA! NOW I'VE GOTCHA!
TAKE THAT! AND THAT!
CHOK! WHOK! CRAK! KRUNCH!
P-KOW
SPANG
NO! NO, NO, NO! YOU CAN'T! THIS IS MY CAPER! MINE! YOU HAVE NO RIGHT TO--
THOK! KLOP! THUMP!
INCOMING.

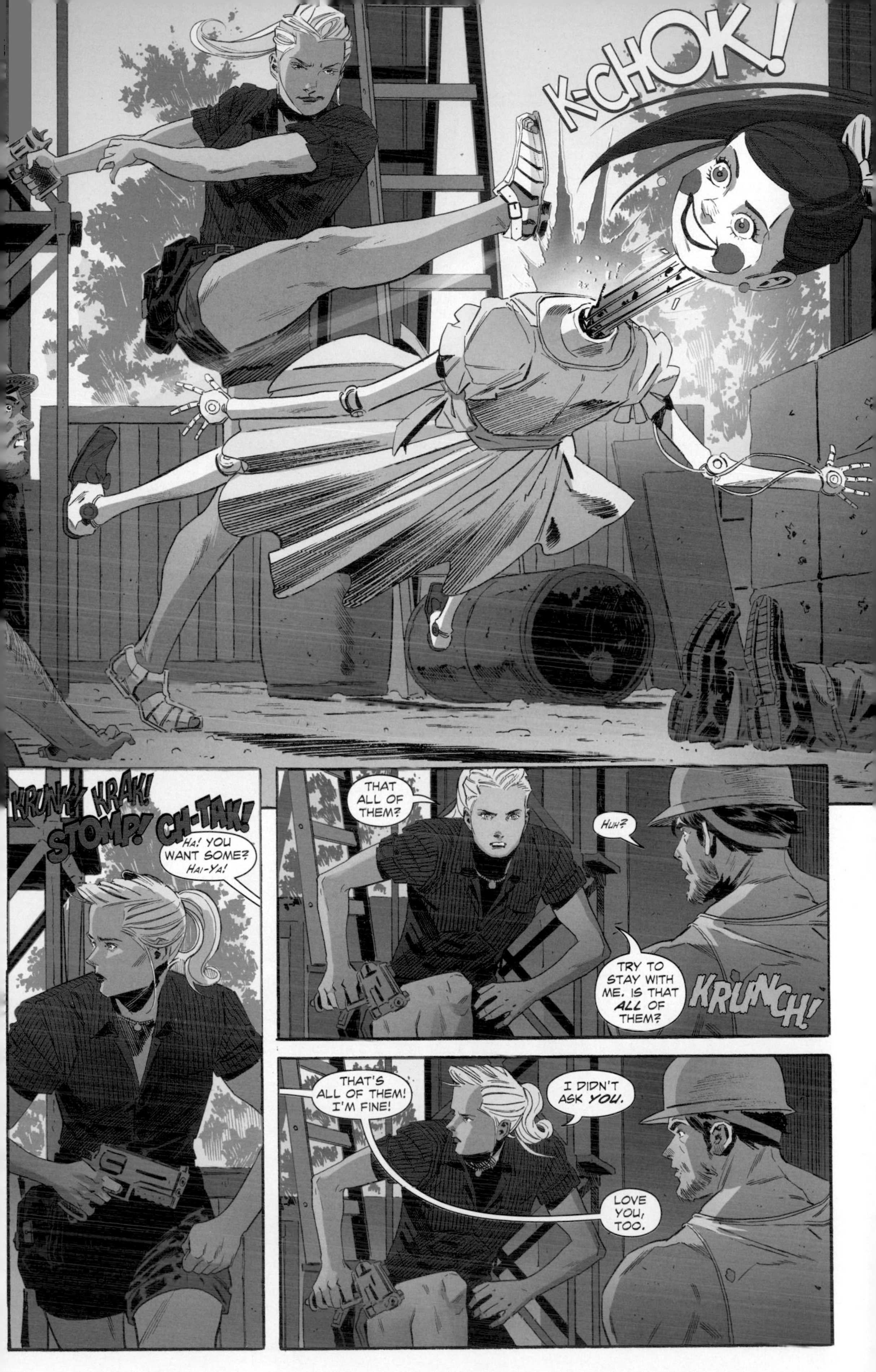
K-CHOK!
KRUNK! KRAK!
STOMP! CH-TAK!
HA! YOU WANT SOME? HAI-YA!
THAT ALL OF THEM?
HUH?
TRY TO STAY WITH ME. IS THAT ALL OF THEM?
KRUNCH!
THAT'S ALL OF THEM! I'M FINE!
I DIDN'T ASK YOU.
LOVE YOU, TOO.

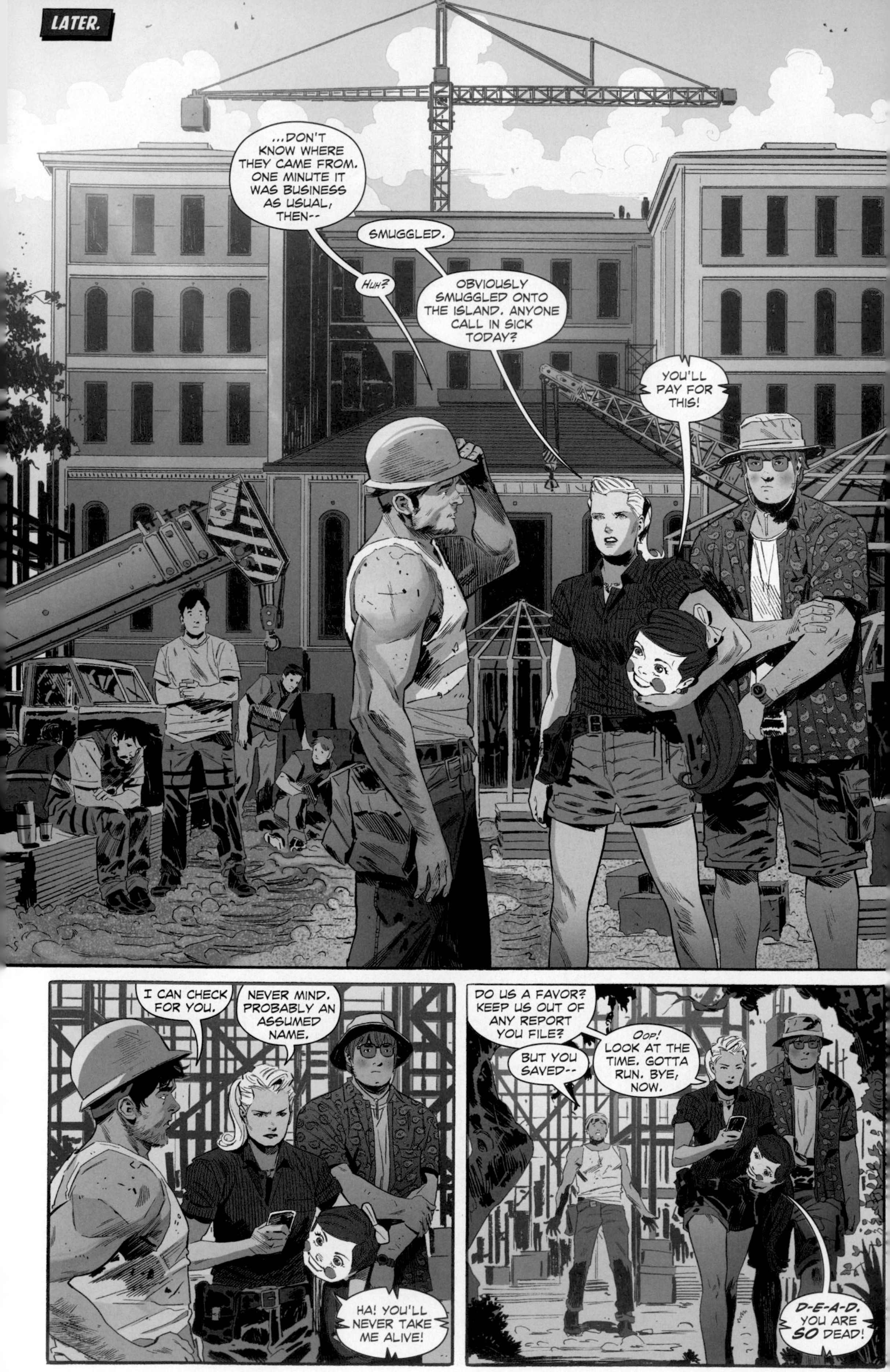
LATER.
...DON'T KNOW WHERE THEY CAME FROM. ONE MINUTE IT WAS BUSINESS AS USUAL, THEN--
SMUGGLED.
HUH?
OBVIOUSLY SMUGGLED ONTO THE ISLAND. ANYONE CALL IN SICK TODAY?
YOU'LL PAY FOR THIS!
I CAN CHECK FOR YOU.
NEVER MIND. PROBABLY AN ASSUMED NAME.
HA! YOU'LL NEVER TAKE ME ALIVE!
DO US A FAVOR? KEEP US OUT OF ANY REPORT YOU FILE?
BUT YOU SAVED--
OOP! LOOK AT THE TIME. GOTTA RUN. BYE, NOW.
D-E-A-D. YOU ARE SO DEAD!

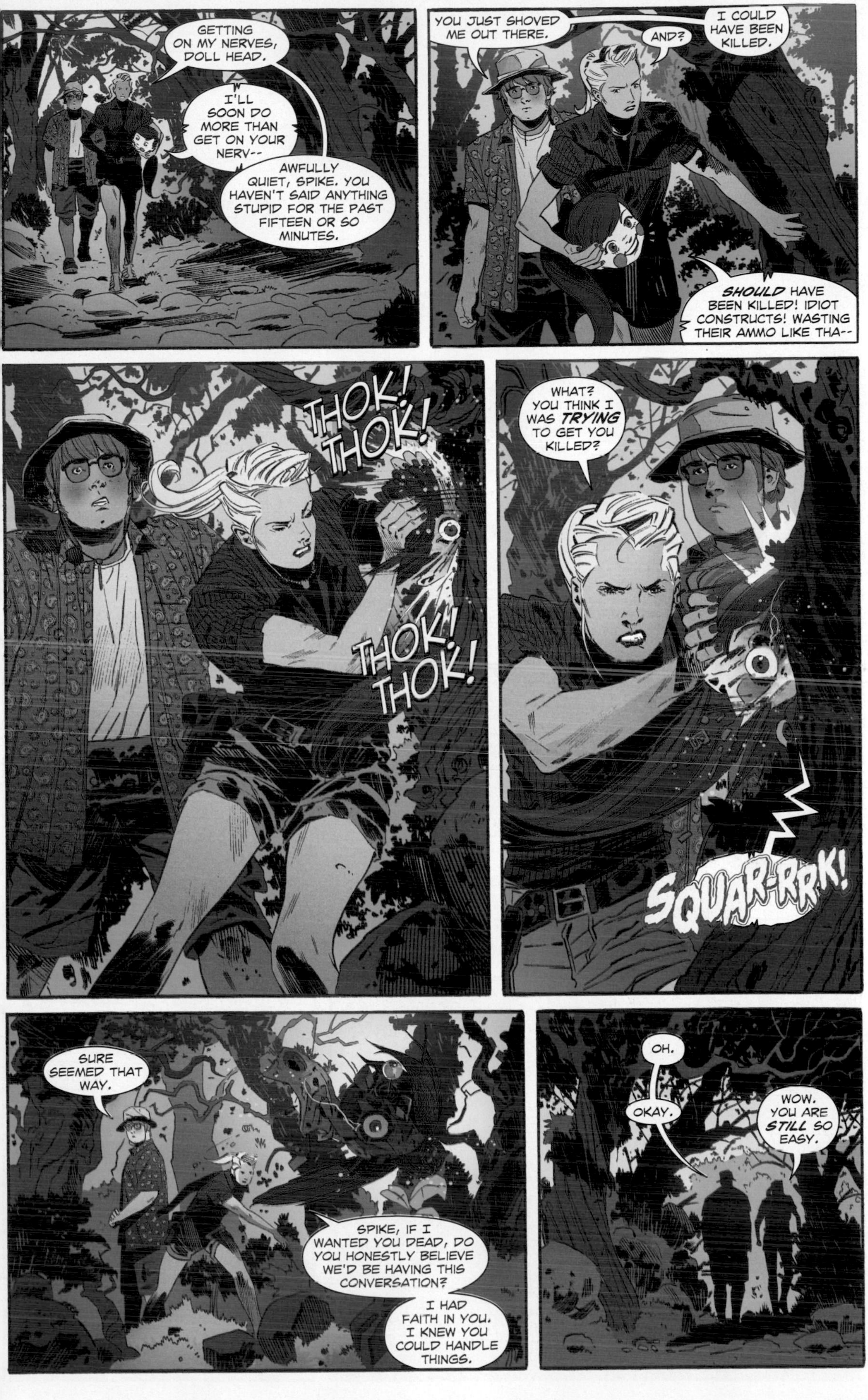
GETTING ON MY NERVES, DOLL HEAD.
I'LL SOON DO MORE THAN GET ON YOUR NERV--
AWFULLY QUIET, SPIKE. YOU HAVEN'T SAID ANYTHING STUPID FOR THE PAST FIFTEEN OR SO MINUTES.
YOU JUST SHOVED ME OUT THERE.
AND?
I COULD HAVE BEEN KILLED.
SHOULD HAVE BEEN KILLED! IDIOT CONSTRUCTS! WASTING THEIR AMMO LIKE THA--
THOK! THOK!
THOK! THOK!
WHAT? YOU THINK I WAS TRYING TO GET YOU KILLED?
SQUAR-RRK!
SURE SEEMED THAT WAY.
SPIKE, IF I WANTED YOU DEAD, DO YOU HONESTLY BELIEVE WE'D BE HAVING THIS CONVERSATION?
I HAD FAITH IN YOU. I KNEW YOU COULD HANDLE THINGS.
OH.
OKAY.
WOW. YOU ARE STILL SO EASY.

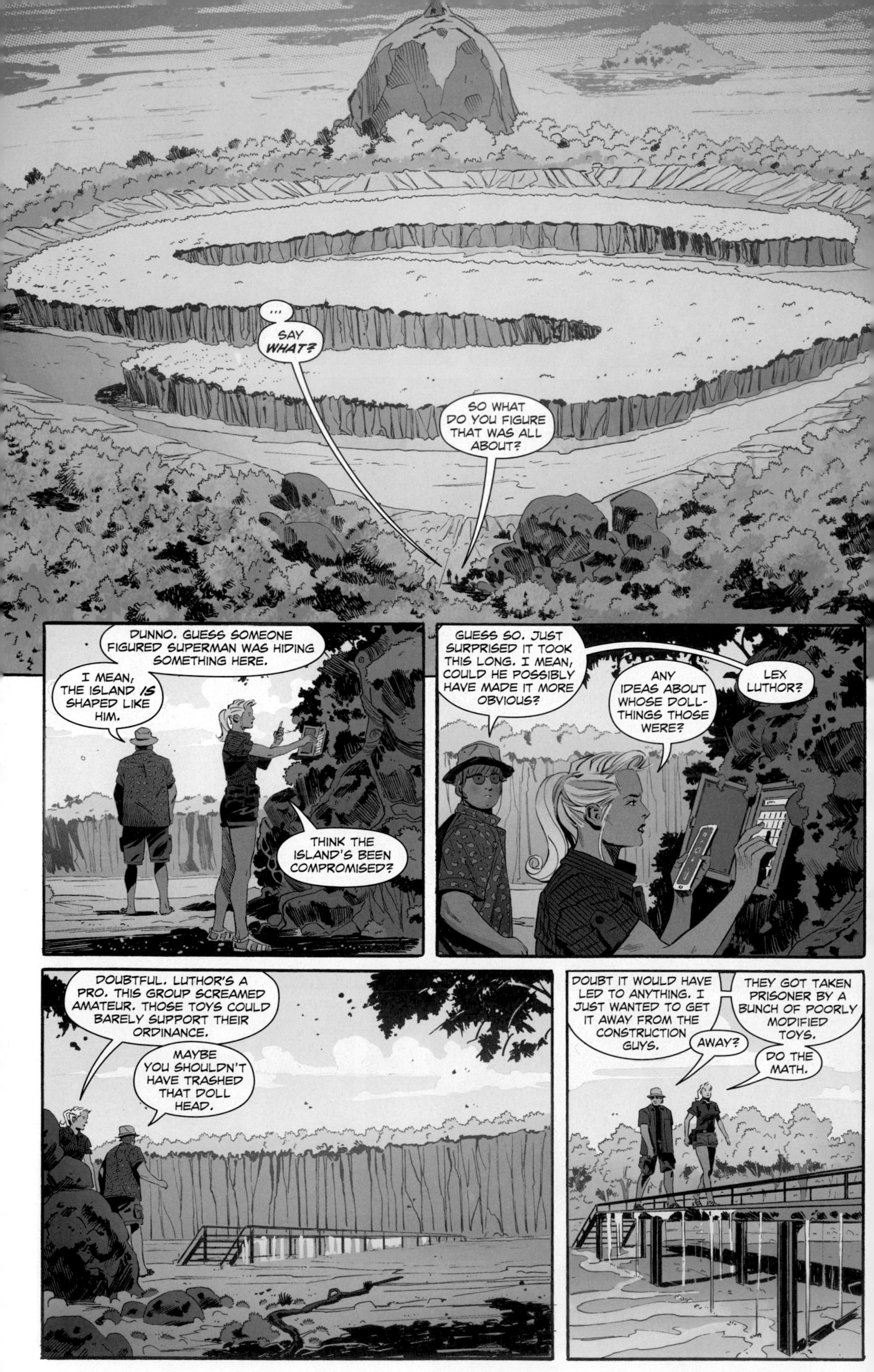
...
SAY *WHAT?*
SO WHAT DO YOU FIGURE THAT WAS ALL ABOUT?
DUNNO. GUESS SOMEONE FIGURED SUPERMAN WAS HIDING SOMETHING HERE.
I MEAN, THE ISLAND *IS* SHAPED LIKE HIM.
THINK THE ISLAND'S BEEN COMPROMISED?
GUESS SO. JUST SURPRISED IT TOOK THIS LONG. I MEAN, COULD HE POSSIBLY HAVE MADE IT MORE OBVIOUS?
ANY IDEAS ABOUT WHOSE DOLL-THINGS THOSE WERE?
LEX LUTHOR?
DOUBTFUL. LUTHOR'S A PRO. THIS GROUP SCREAMED AMATEUR. THOSE TOYS COULD BARELY SUPPORT THEIR ORDINANCE.
MAYBE YOU SHOULDN'T HAVE TRASHED THAT DOLL HEAD.
DOUBT IT WOULD HAVE LED TO ANYTHING. I JUST WANTED TO GET IT AWAY FROM THE CONSTRUCTION GUYS.
AWAY?
THEY GOT TAKEN PRISONER BY A BUNCH OF POORLY MODIFIED TOYS.
DO THE MATH.

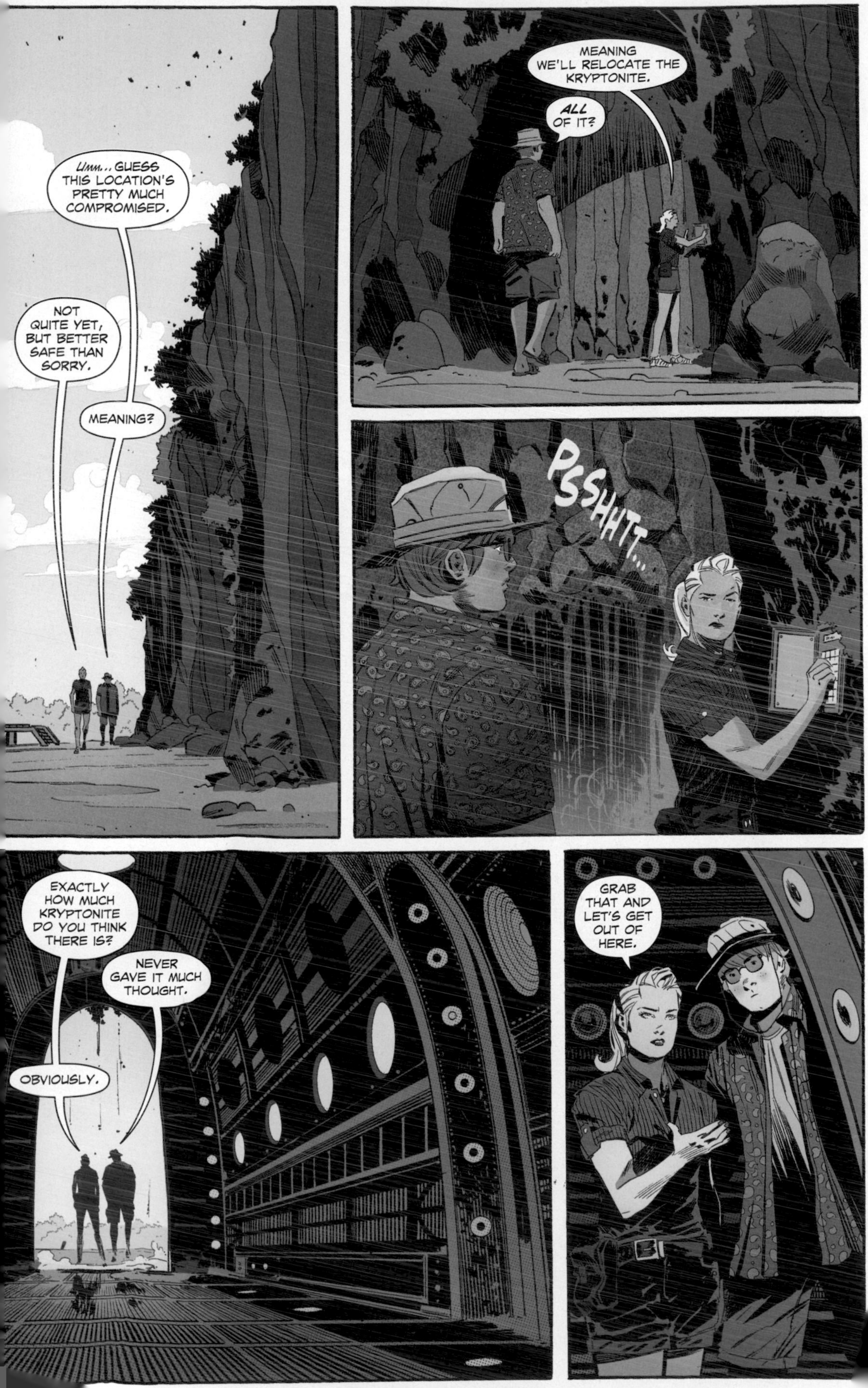
Umm... GUESS THIS LOCATION'S PRETTY MUCH COMPROMISED.
NOT QUITE YET, BUT BETTER SAFE THAN SORRY.
MEANING?
MEANING WE'LL RELOCATE THE KRYPTONITE.
ALL OF IT?
PSSHHTT...
EXACTLY HOW MUCH KRYPTONITE DO YOU THINK THERE IS?
NEVER GAVE IT MUCH THOUGHT.
OBVIOUSLY.
GRAB THAT AND LET'S GET OUT OF HERE.

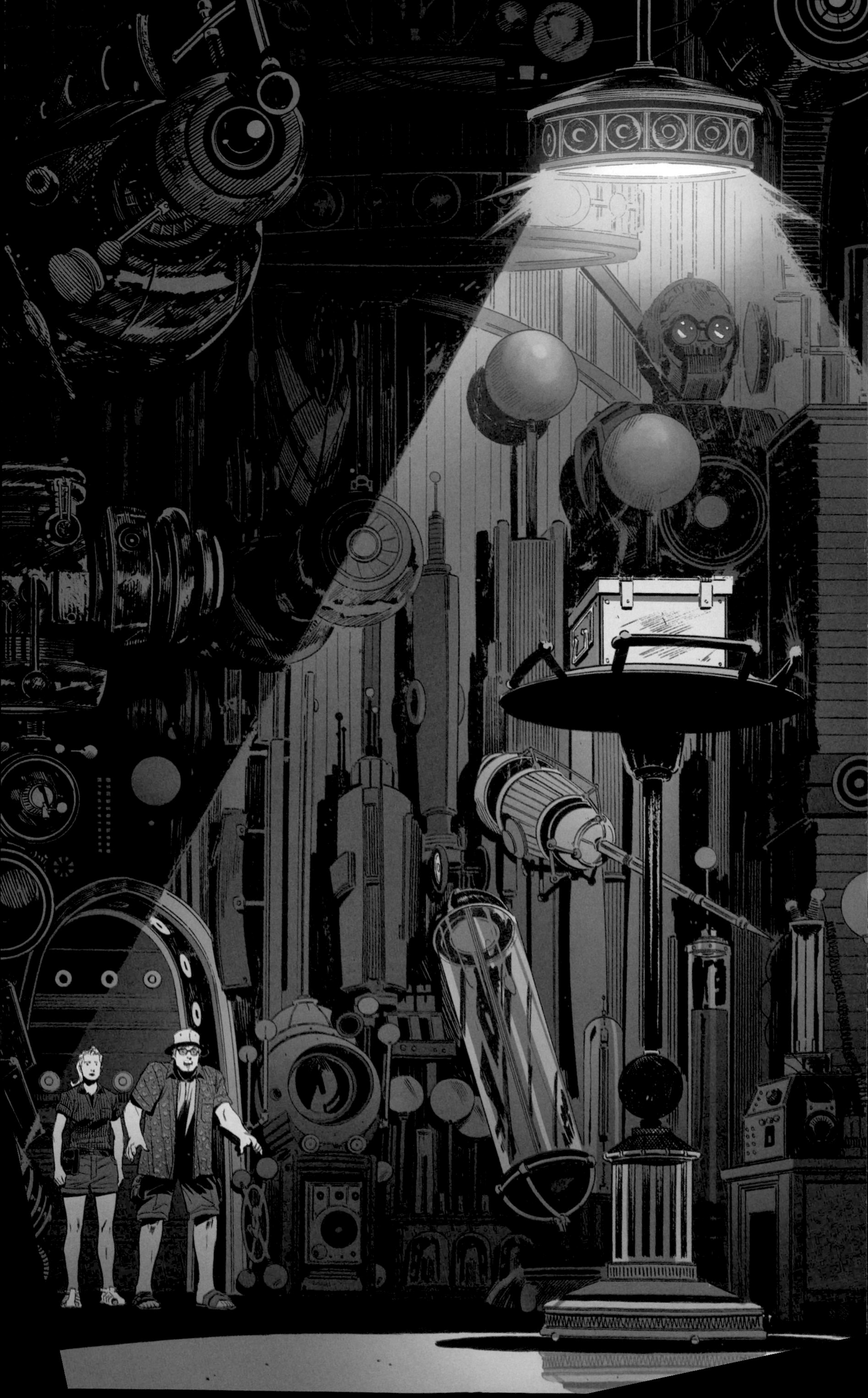

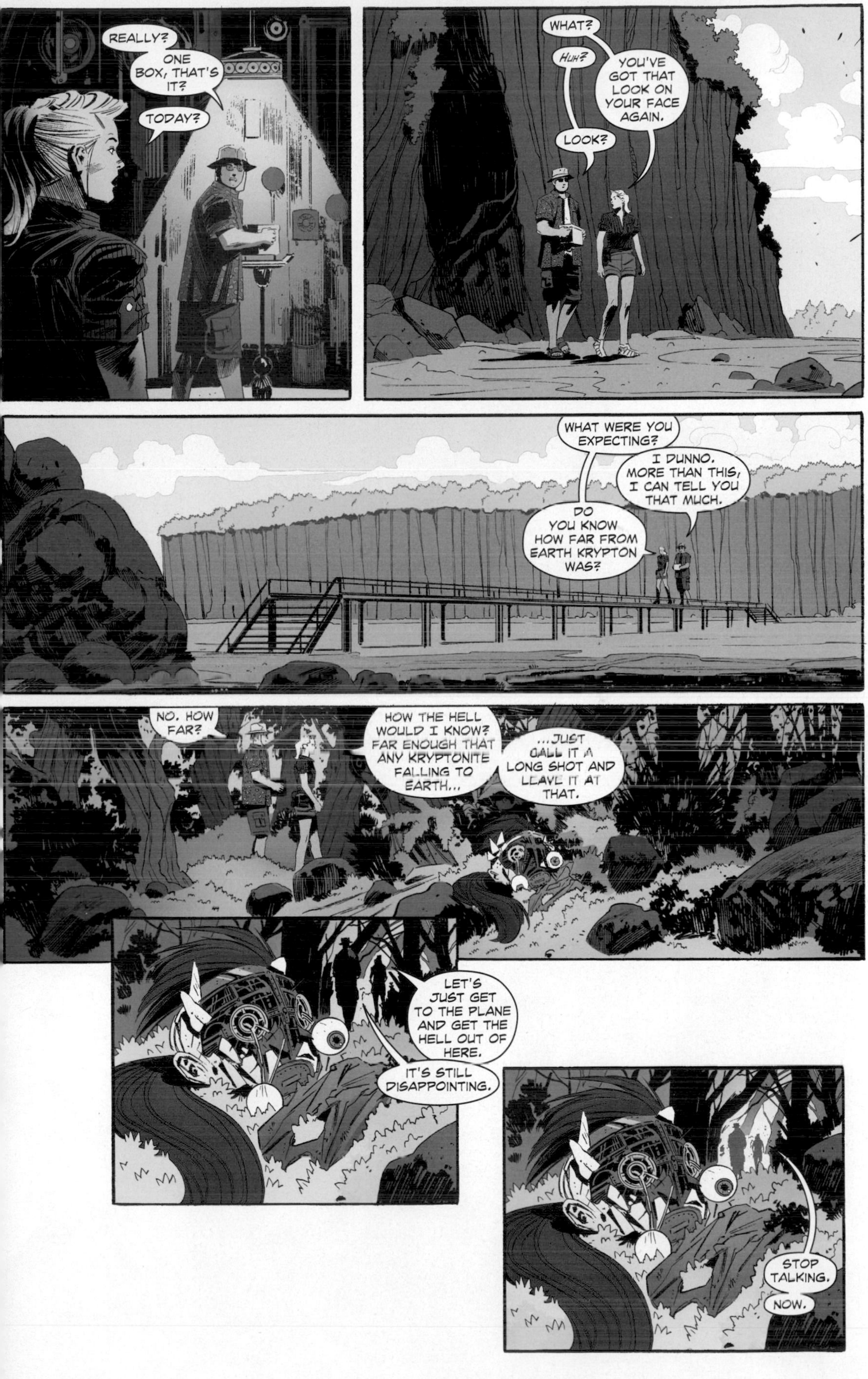
REALLY?
ONE BOX, THAT'S IT?
TODAY?
WHAT?
HUH?
YOU'VE GOT THAT LOOK ON YOUR FACE AGAIN.
LOOK?
WHAT WERE YOU EXPECTING?
I DUNNO. MORE THAN THIS, I CAN TELL YOU THAT MUCH.
DO YOU KNOW HOW FAR FROM EARTH KRYPTON WAS?
NO. HOW FAR?
HOW THE HELL WOULD I KNOW? FAR ENOUGH THAT ANY KRYPTONITE FALLING TO EARTH...
...JUST CALL IT A LONG SHOT AND LEAVE IT AT THAT.
LET'S JUST GET TO THE PLANE AND GET THE HELL OUT OF HERE.
IT'S STILL DISAPPOINTING.
STOP TALKING.
NOW.

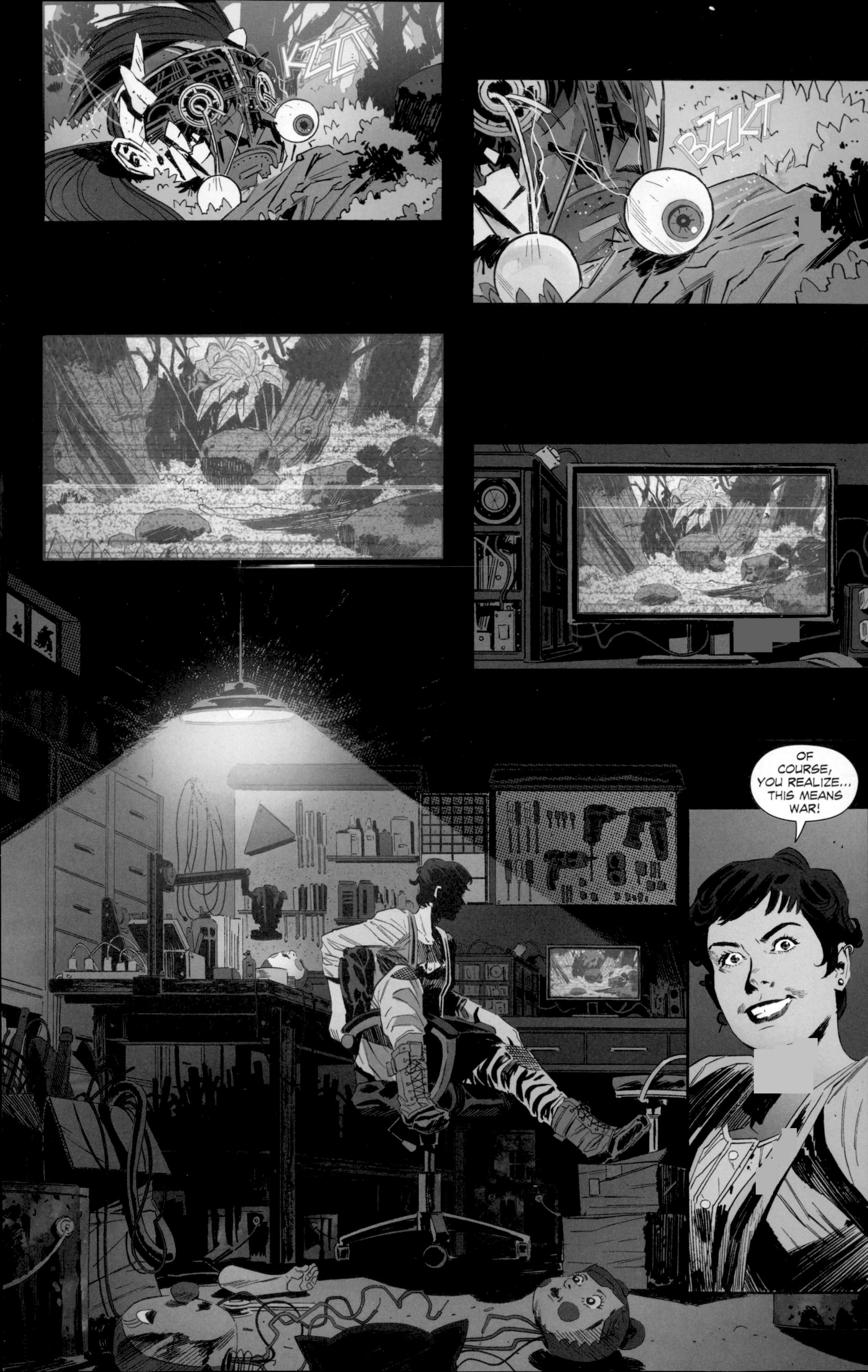
KZZZT
BZZKT
OF COURSE, YOU REALIZE... THIS MEANS WAR!

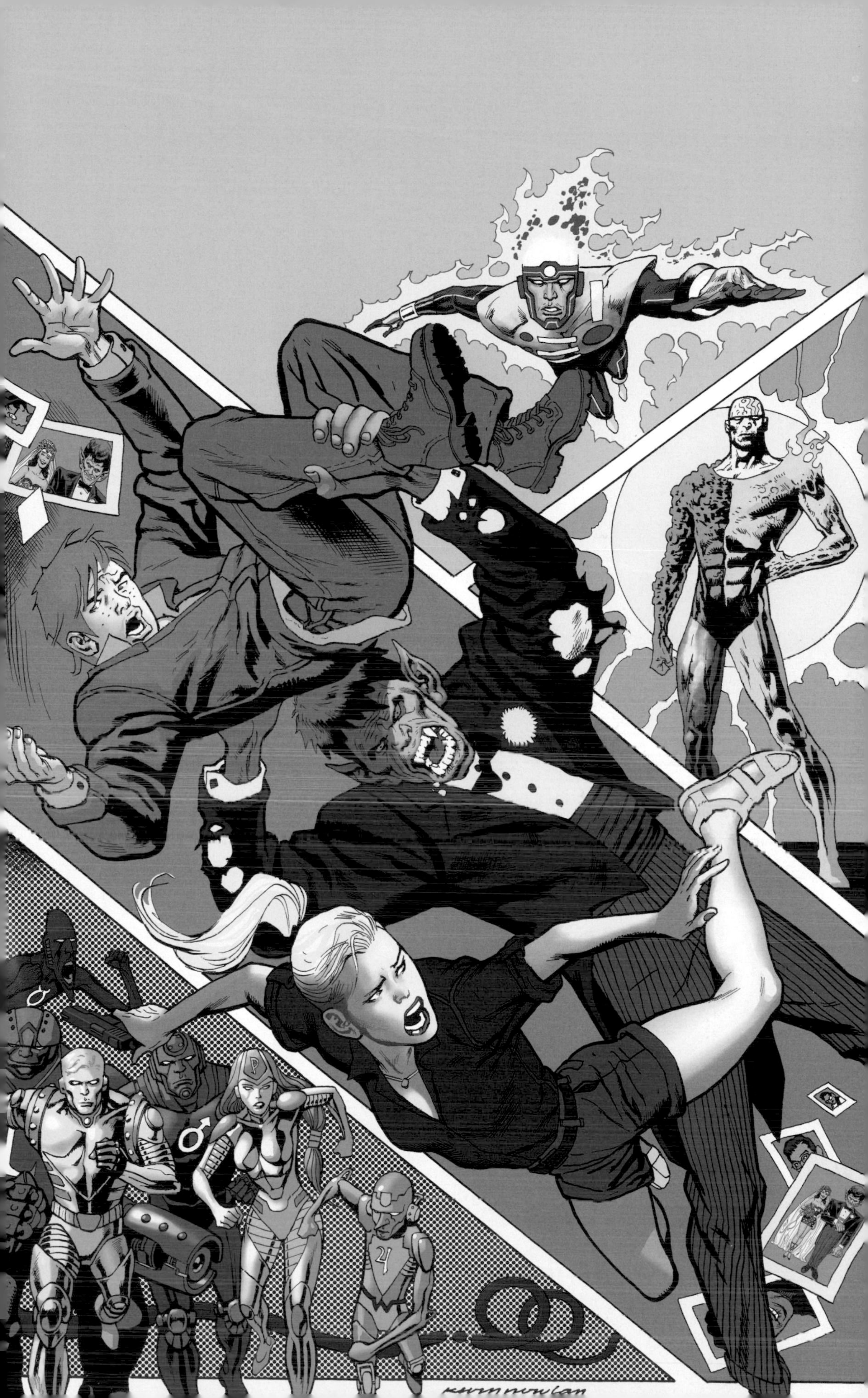
kevin nowlan

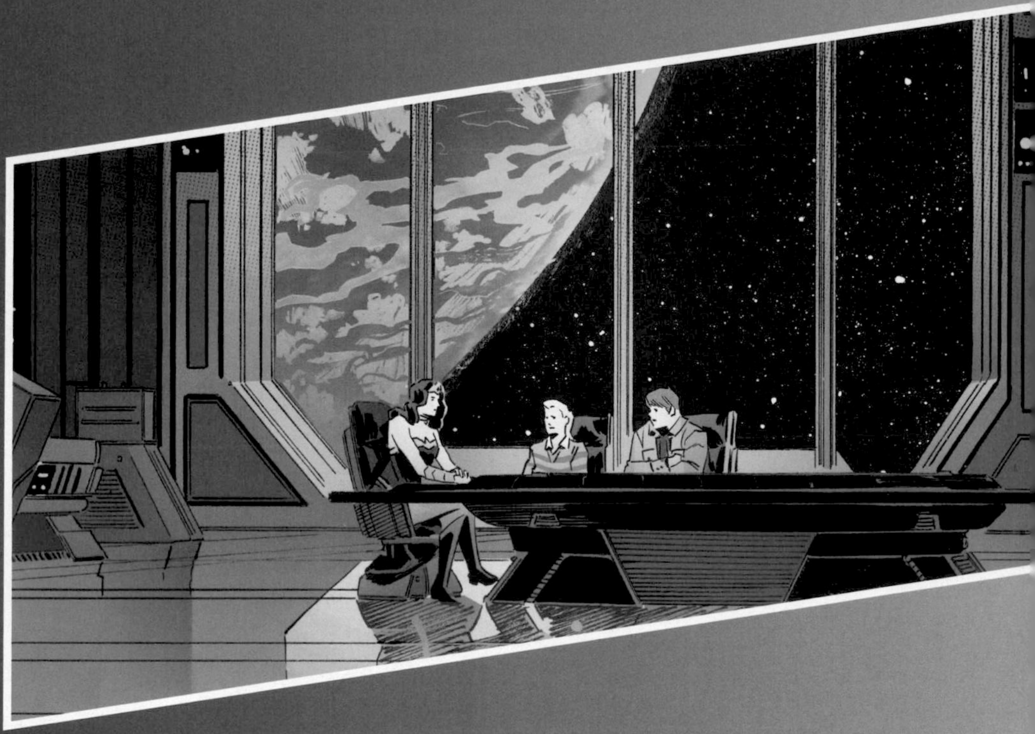

KEVIN NOWLAN
cover

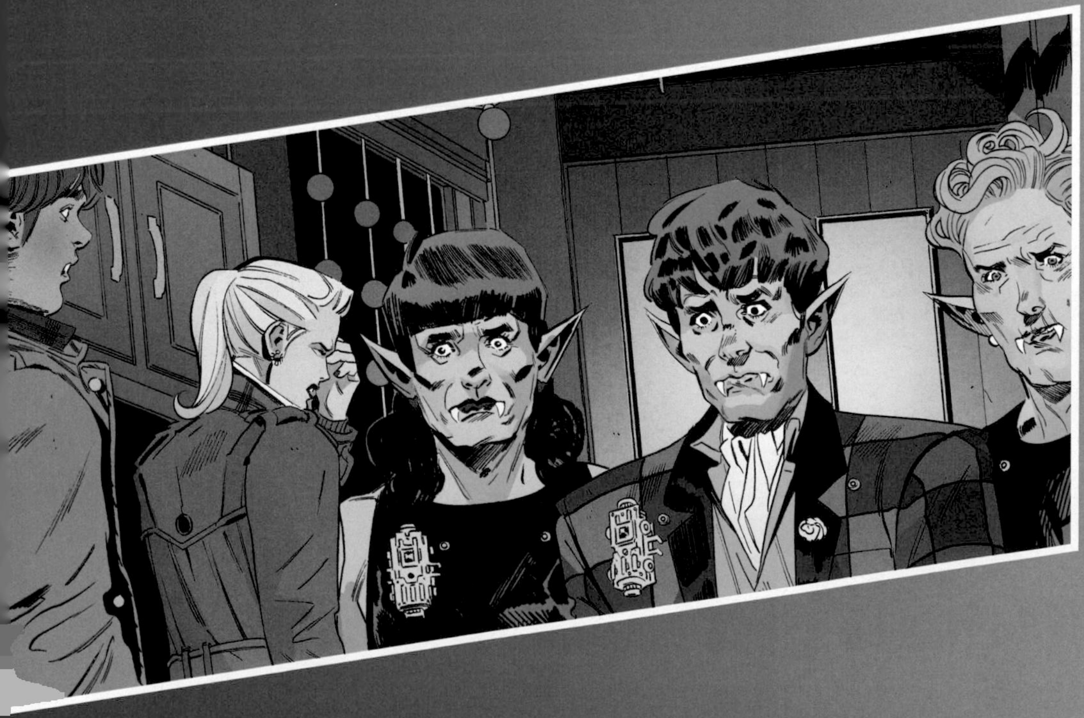

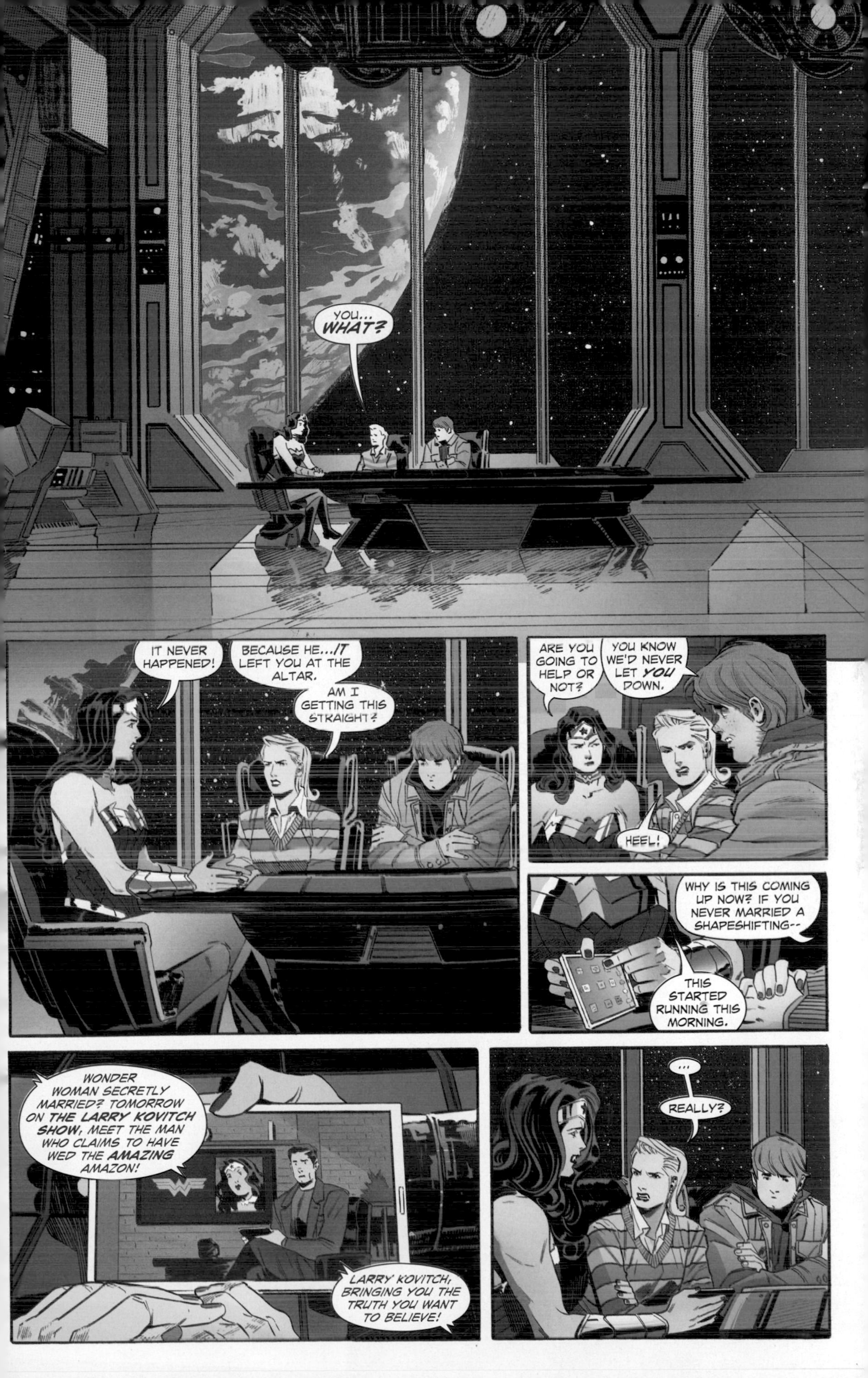
YOU... WHAT?
IT NEVER HAPPENED!
BECAUSE HE...IT LEFT YOU AT THE ALTAR.
AM I GETTING THIS STRAIGHT?
ARE YOU GOING TO HELP OR NOT?
YOU KNOW WE'D NEVER LET YOU DOWN.
HEEL!
WHY IS THIS COMING UP NOW? IF YOU NEVER MARRIED A SHAPESHIFTING--
THIS STARTED RUNNING THIS MORNING.
WONDER WOMAN SECRETLY MARRIED? TOMORROW ON THE LARRY KOVITCH SHOW, MEET THE MAN WHO CLAIMS TO HAVE WED THE AMAZING AMAZON!
LARRY KOVITCH, BRINGING YOU THE TRUTH YOU WANT TO BELIEVE!
...
REALLY?

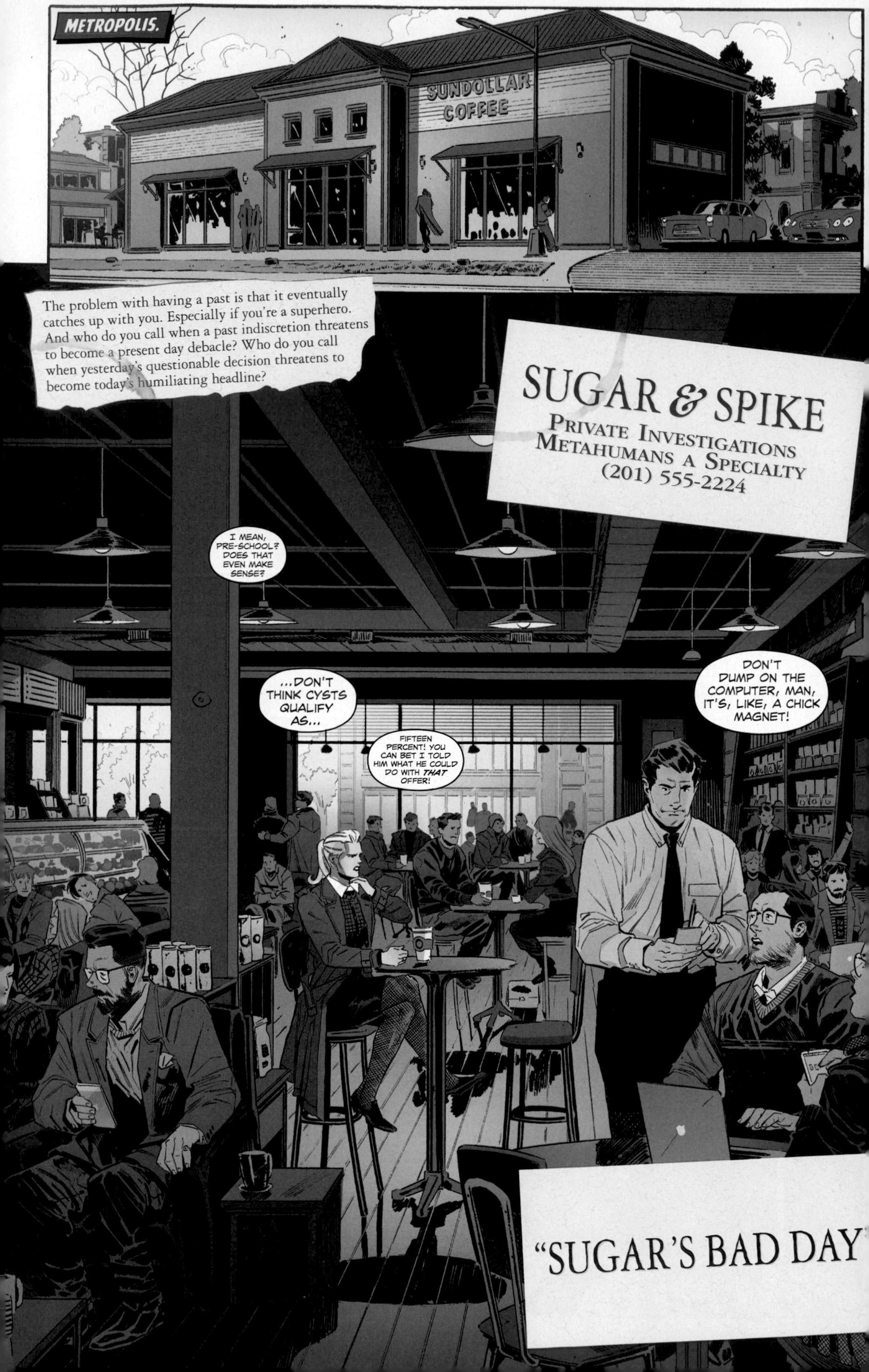
METROPOLIS.
SUNDOLLAR COFFEE
The problem with having a past is that it eventually catches up with you. Especially if you're a superhero. And who do you call when a past indiscretion threatens to become a present day debacle? Who do you call when yesterday's questionable decision threatens to become today's humiliating headline?
SUGAR & SPIKE
PRIVATE INVESTIGATIONS
METAHUMANS A SPECIALTY
(201) 555-2224
I MEAN, PRE-SCHOOL? DOES THAT EVEN MAKE SENSE?
...DON'T THINK CYSTS QUALIFY AS...
FIFTEEN PERCENT! YOU CAN BET I TOLD HIM WHAT HE COULD DO WITH THAT OFFER!
DON'T DUMP ON THE COMPUTER, MAN, IT'S, LIKE, A CHICK MAGNET!
"SUGAR'S BAD DAY"

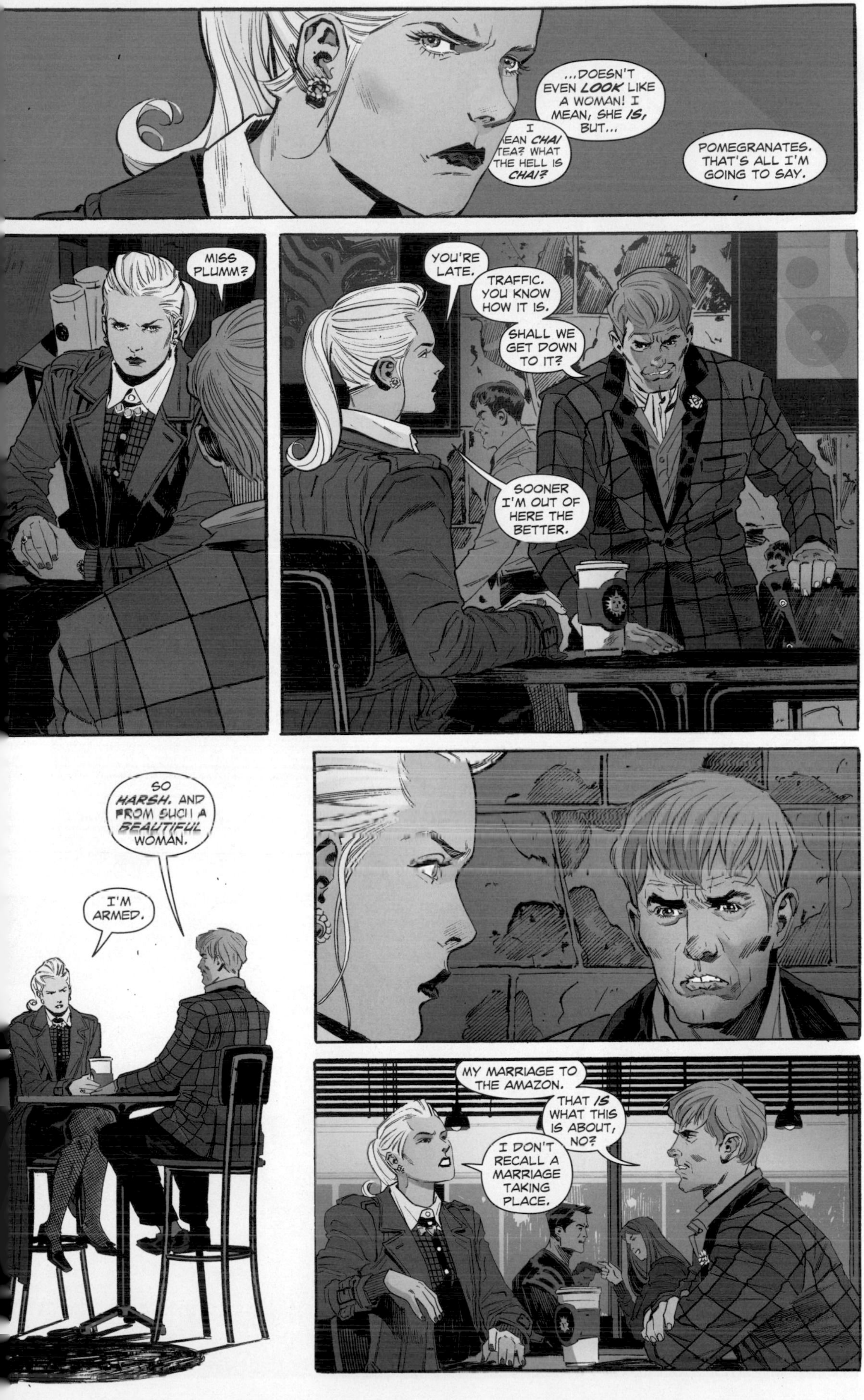
...DOESN'T EVEN LOOK LIKE A WOMAN! I MEAN, SHE IS, BUT...
I MEAN CHAI TEA? WHAT THE HELL IS CHAI?
POMEGRANATES. THAT'S ALL I'M GOING TO SAY.
MISS PLUMM?
YOU'RE LATE.
TRAFFIC. YOU KNOW HOW IT IS.
SHALL WE GET DOWN TO IT?
SOONER I'M OUT OF HERE THE BETTER.
SO HARSH. AND FROM SUCH A BEAUTIFUL WOMAN.
I'M ARMED.
MY MARRIAGE TO THE AMAZON.
THAT IS WHAT THIS IS ABOUT, NO?
I DON'T RECALL A MARRIAGE TAKING PLACE.

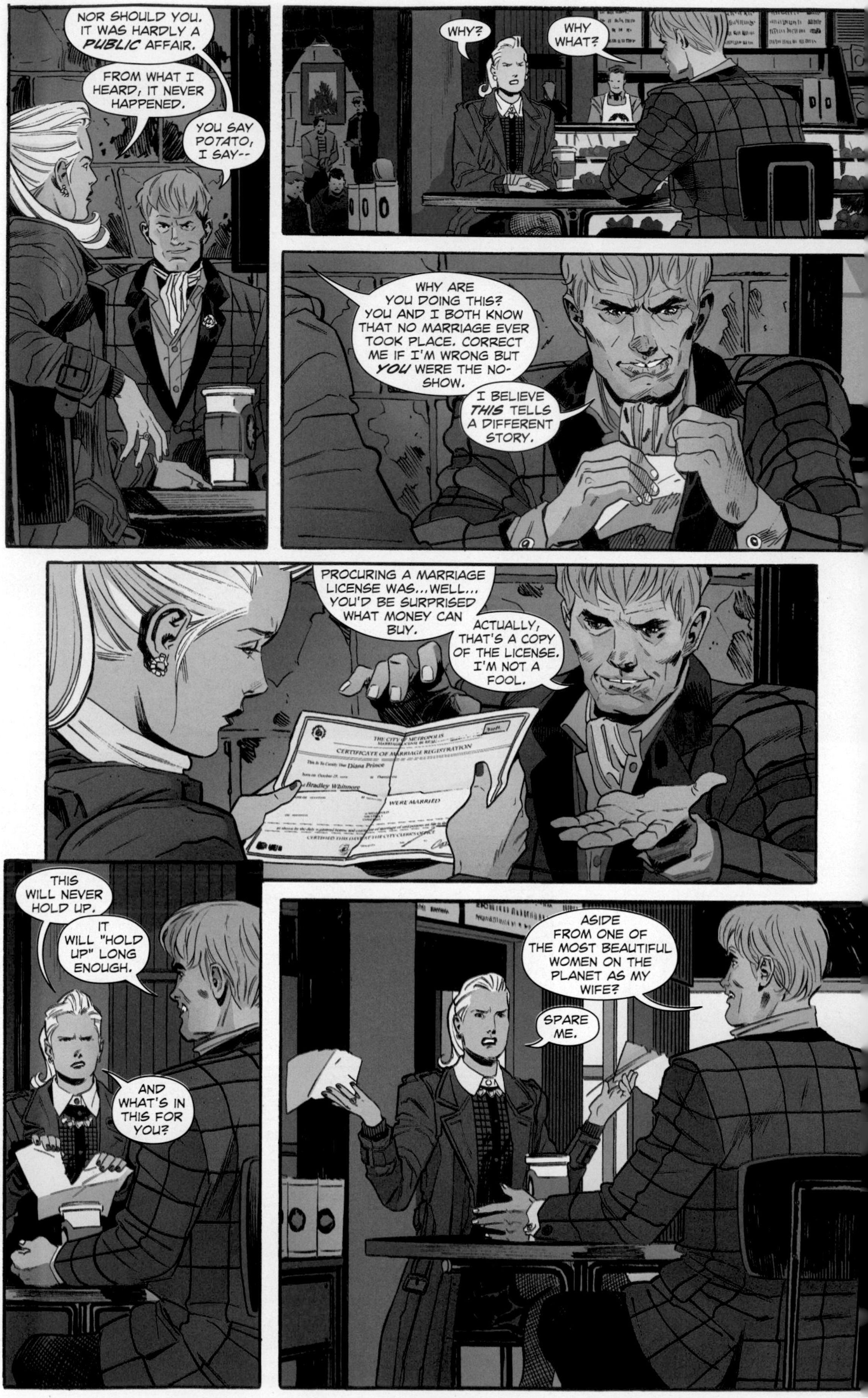
NOR SHOULD YOU. IT WAS HARDLY A *PUBLIC* AFFAIR.
FROM WHAT I HEARD, IT NEVER HAPPENED.
YOU SAY POTATO, I SAY--
WHY?
WHY WHAT?
WHY ARE YOU DOING THIS? YOU AND I BOTH KNOW THAT NO MARRIAGE EVER TOOK PLACE. CORRECT ME IF I'M WRONG BUT *YOU* WERE THE NO-SHOW.
I BELIEVE *THIS* TELLS A DIFFERENT STORY.
PROCURING A MARRIAGE LICENSE WAS...WELL... YOU'D BE SURPRISED WHAT MONEY CAN BUY.
ACTUALLY, THAT'S A COPY OF THE LICENSE. I'M NOT A FOOL.
CERTIFICATE OF MARRIAGE REGISTRATION
Diana Prince
Bradley Whitmore
WERE MARRIED
THIS WILL NEVER HOLD UP.
IT WILL "HOLD UP" LONG ENOUGH.
AND WHAT'S IN THIS FOR YOU?
ASIDE FROM ONE OF THE MOST BEAUTIFUL WOMEN ON THE PLANET AS MY WIFE?
SPARE ME.

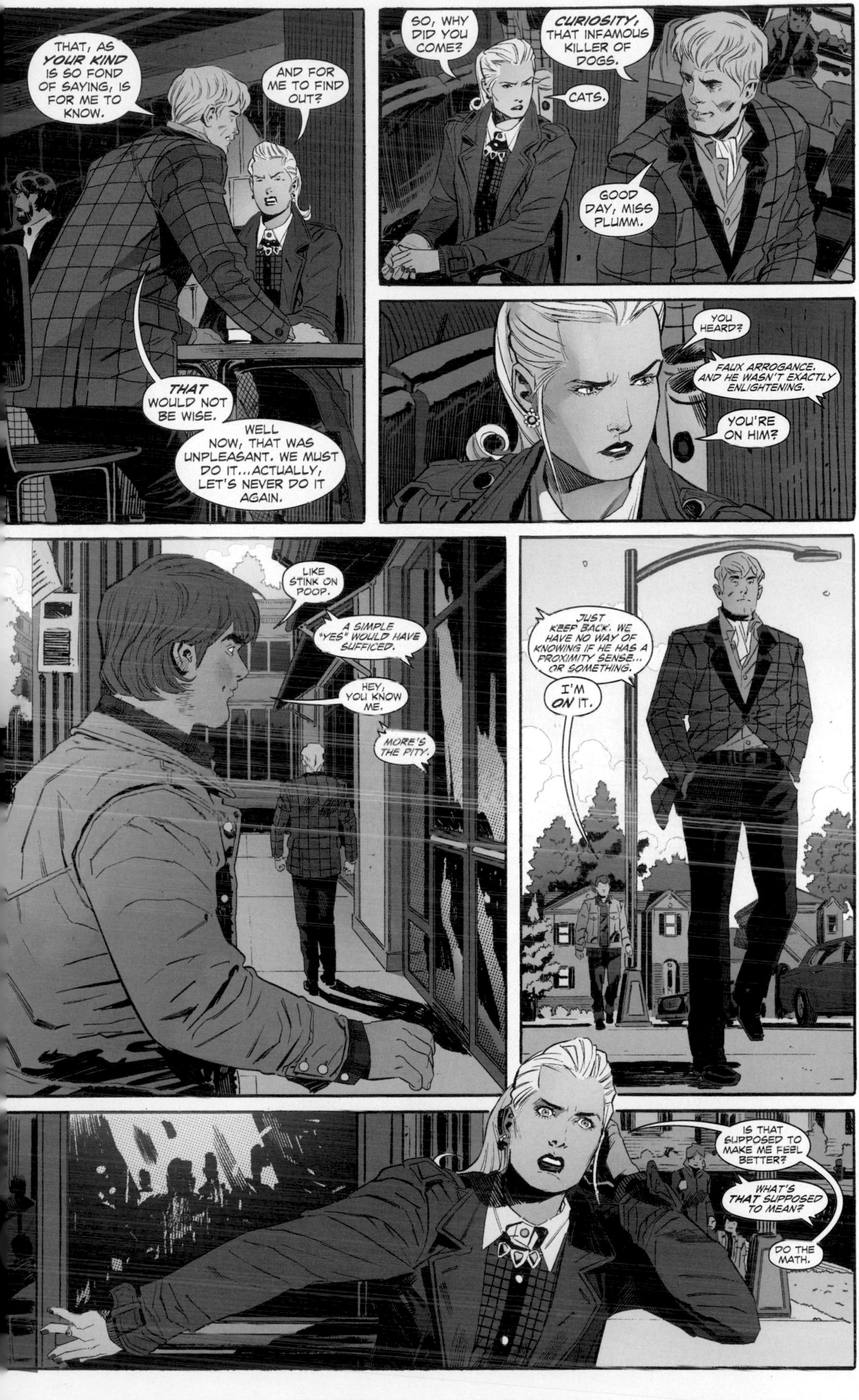
THAT, AS YOUR KIND IS SO FOND OF SAYING, IS FOR ME TO KNOW.
AND FOR ME TO FIND OUT?
THAT WOULD NOT BE WISE.
WELL NOW, THAT WAS UNPLEASANT. WE MUST DO IT...ACTUALLY, LET'S NEVER DO IT AGAIN.
SO, WHY DID YOU COME?
CURIOSITY, THAT INFAMOUS KILLER OF DOGS.
CATS.
GOOD DAY, MISS PLUMM.
YOU HEARD?
FAUX ARROGANCE. AND HE WASN'T EXACTLY ENLIGHTENING.
YOU'RE ON HIM?
LIKE STINK ON POOP.
A SIMPLE "YES" WOULD HAVE SUFFICED.
HEY, YOU KNOW ME.
MORE'S THE PITY.
JUST KEEP BACK. WE HAVE NO WAY OF KNOWING IF HE HAS A PROXIMITY SENSE... OR SOMETHING.
I'M ON IT.
IS THAT SUPPOSED TO MAKE ME FEEL BETTER?
WHAT'S THAT SUPPOSED TO MEAN?
DO THE MATH.

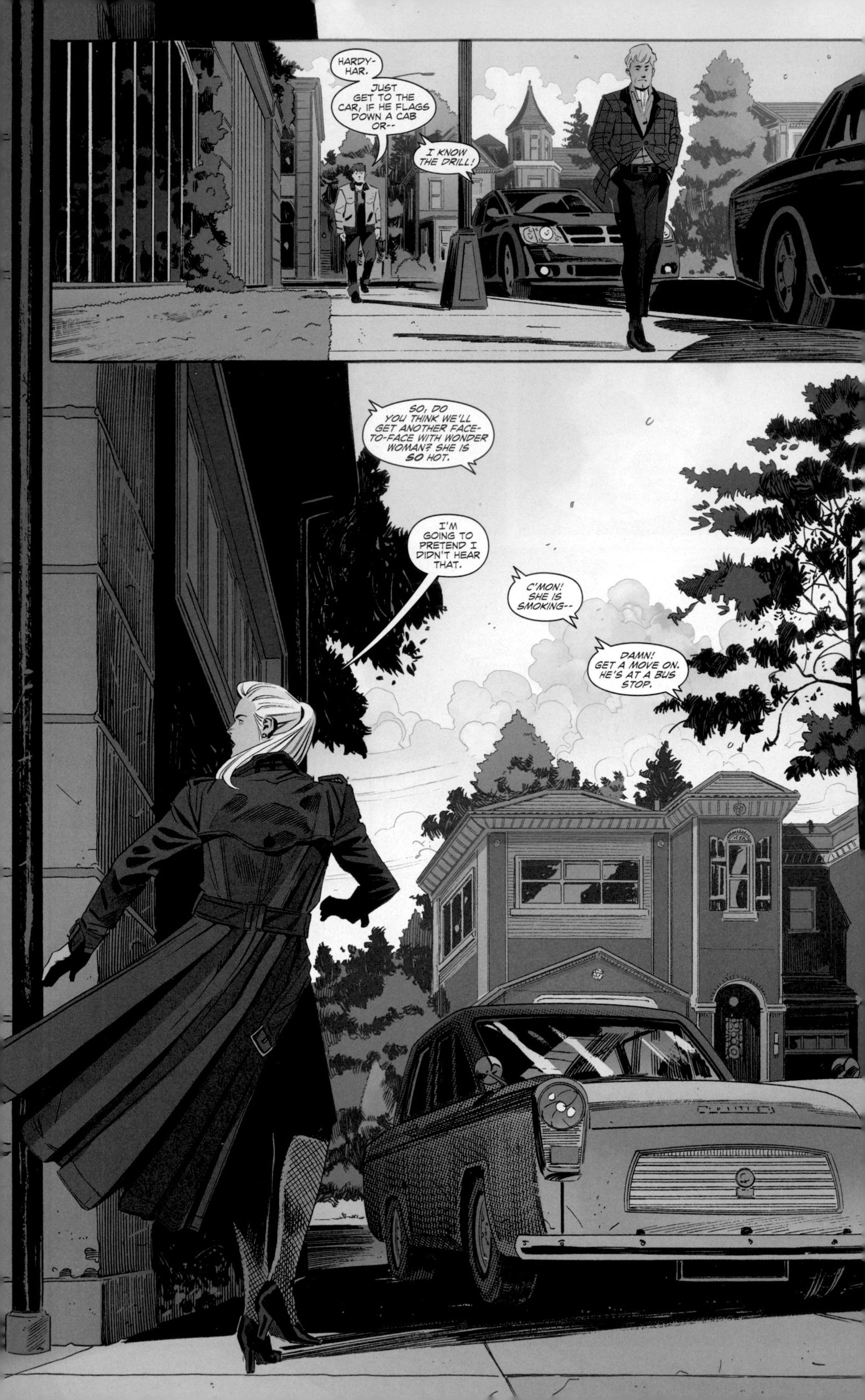
HARDY-HAR.
JUST GET TO THE CAR, IF HE FLAGS DOWN A CAB OR--
I KNOW THE DRILL!
SO, DO YOU THINK WE'LL GET ANOTHER FACE-TO-FACE WITH WONDER WOMAN? SHE IS SO HOT.
I'M GOING TO PRETEND I DIDN'T HEAR THAT.
C'MON! SHE IS SMOKING--
DAMN! GET A MOVE ON. HE'S AT A BUS STOP.

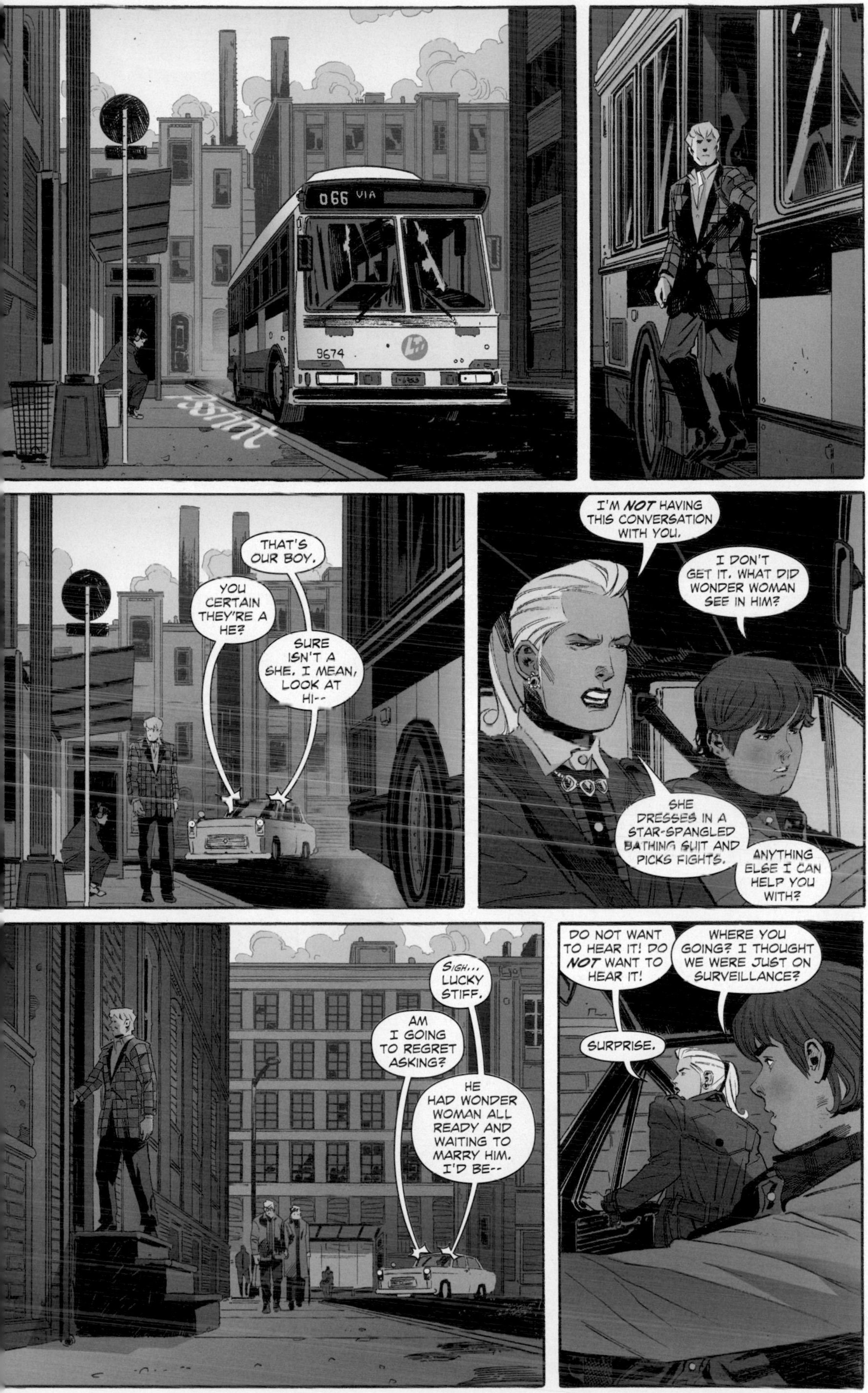
066 VIA
9674
THAT'S OUR BOY.
YOU CERTAIN THEY'RE A HE?
SURE ISN'T A SHE. I MEAN, LOOK AT HI--
I'M NOT HAVING THIS CONVERSATION WITH YOU.
I DON'T GET IT. WHAT DID WONDER WOMAN SEE IN HIM?
SHE DRESSES IN A STAR-SPANGLED BATHING SUIT AND PICKS FIGHTS.
ANYTHING ELSE I CAN HELP YOU WITH?
SIGH... LUCKY STIFF.
AM I GOING TO REGRET ASKING?
HE HAD WONDER WOMAN ALL READY AND WAITING TO MARRY HIM. I'D BE--
DO NOT WANT TO HEAR IT! DO NOT WANT TO HEAR IT!
WHERE YOU GOING? I THOUGHT WE WERE JUST ON SURVEILLANCE?
SURPRISE.

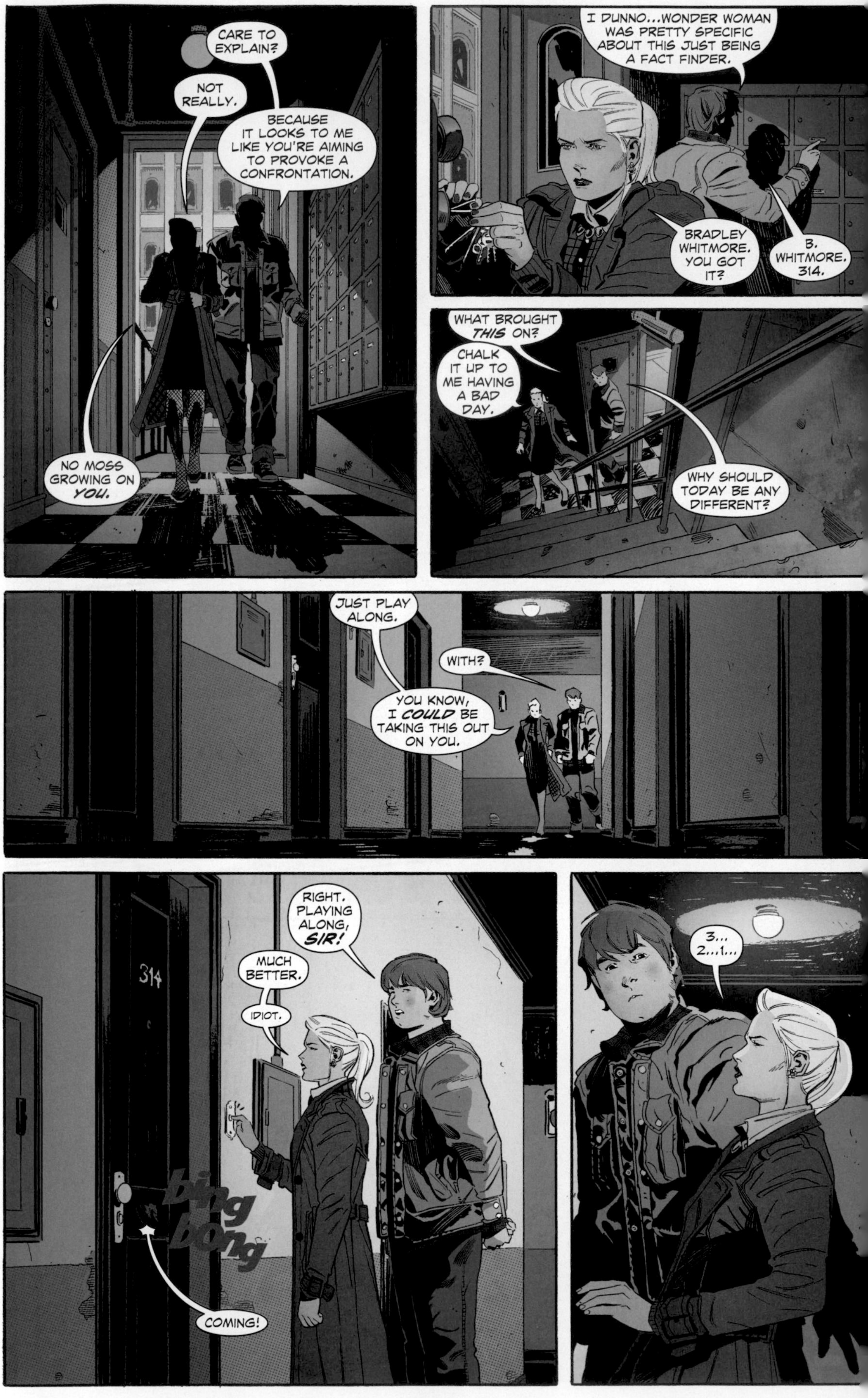
CARE TO EXPLAIN?
NOT REALLY.
BECAUSE IT LOOKS TO ME LIKE YOU'RE AIMING TO PROVOKE A CONFRONTATION.
NO MOSS GROWING ON YOU.
I DUNNO...WONDER WOMAN WAS PRETTY SPECIFIC ABOUT THIS JUST BEING A FACT FINDER.
BRADLEY WHITMORE. YOU GOT IT?
B. WHITMORE. 314.
WHAT BROUGHT THIS ON?
CHALK IT UP TO ME HAVING A BAD DAY.
WHY SHOULD TODAY BE ANY DIFFERENT?
JUST PLAY ALONG.
WITH?
YOU KNOW, I COULD BE TAKING THIS OUT ON YOU.
RIGHT. PLAYING ALONG, SIR!
MUCH BETTER.
IDIOT.
314
bing bong
COMING!
3... 2...1...

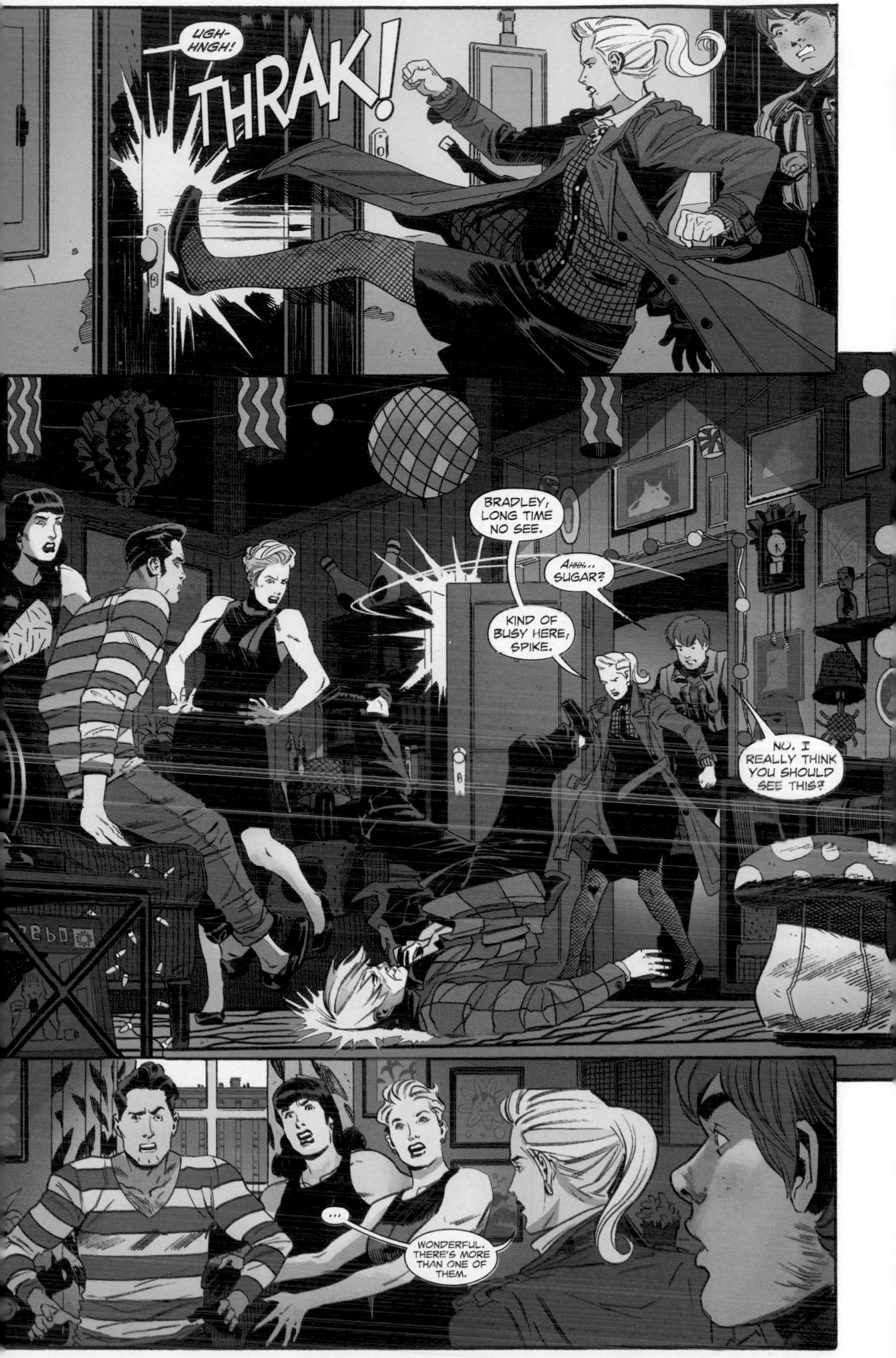
UGH-HNGH!
THRAK!
BRADLEY, LONG TIME NO SEE.
AHHH... SUGAR?
KIND OF BUSY HERE, SPIKE.
NO. I REALLY THINK YOU SHOULD SEE THIS?
...
WONDERFUL. THERE'S MORE THAN ONE OF THEM.

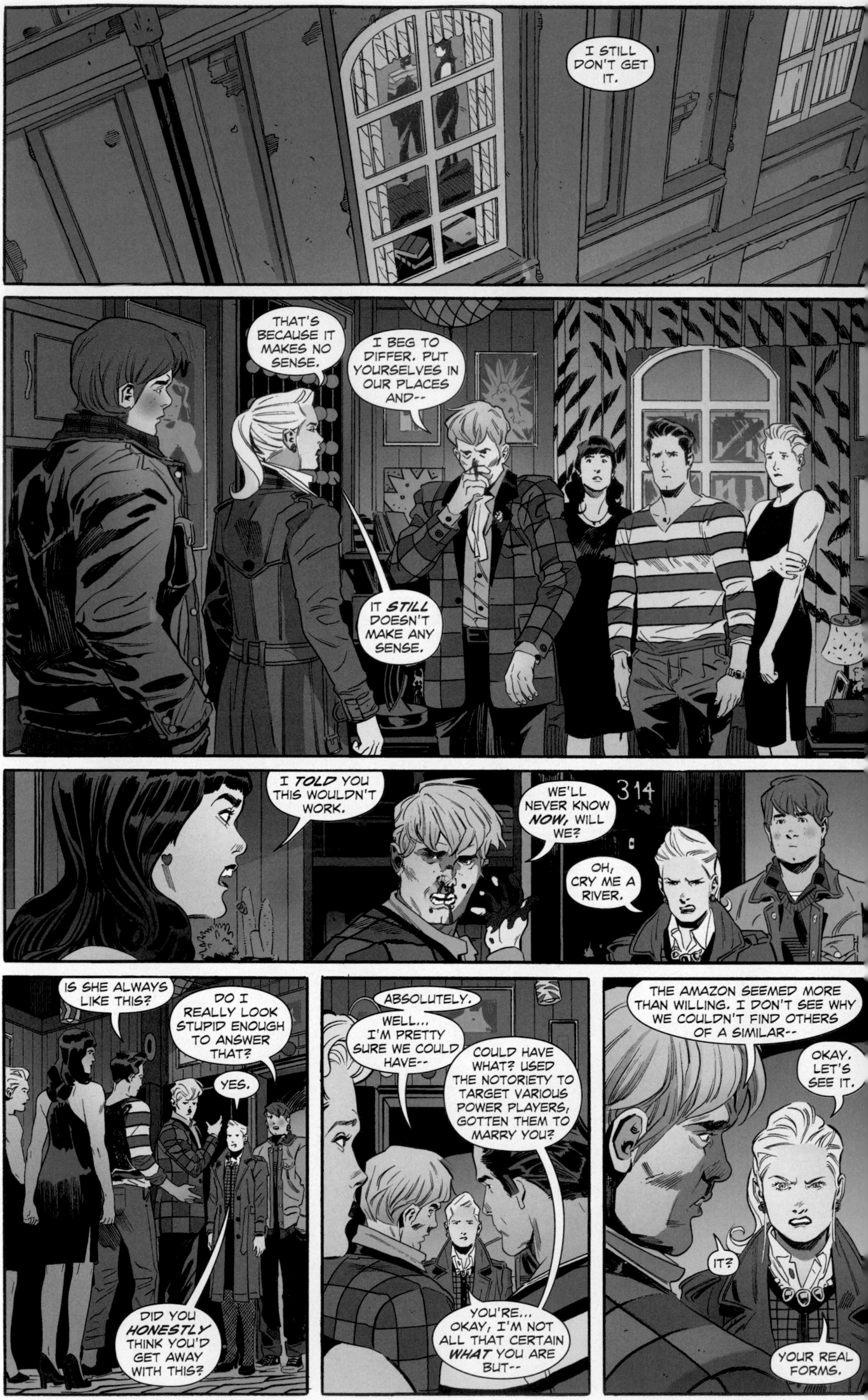
I STILL DON'T GET IT.
THAT'S BECAUSE IT MAKES NO SENSE.
I BEG TO DIFFER. PUT YOURSELVES IN OUR PLACES AND--
IT STILL DOESN'T MAKE ANY SENSE.
I TOLD YOU THIS WOULDN'T WORK.
WE'LL NEVER KNOW NOW, WILL WE?
OH, CRY ME A RIVER.
314
IS SHE ALWAYS LIKE THIS?
DO I REALLY LOOK STUPID ENOUGH TO ANSWER THAT?
YES.
DID YOU HONESTLY THINK YOU'D GET AWAY WITH THIS?
ABSOLUTELY.
WELL... I'M PRETTY SURE WE COULD HAVE--
COULD HAVE WHAT? USED THE NOTORIETY TO TARGET VARIOUS POWER PLAYERS, GOTTEN THEM TO MARRY YOU?
YOU'RE... OKAY, I'M NOT ALL THAT CERTAIN WHAT YOU ARE BUT--
THE AMAZON SEEMED MORE THAN WILLING. I DON'T SEE WHY WE COULDN'T FIND OTHERS OF A SIMILAR--
OKAY. LET'S SEE IT.
IT?
YOUR REAL FORMS.

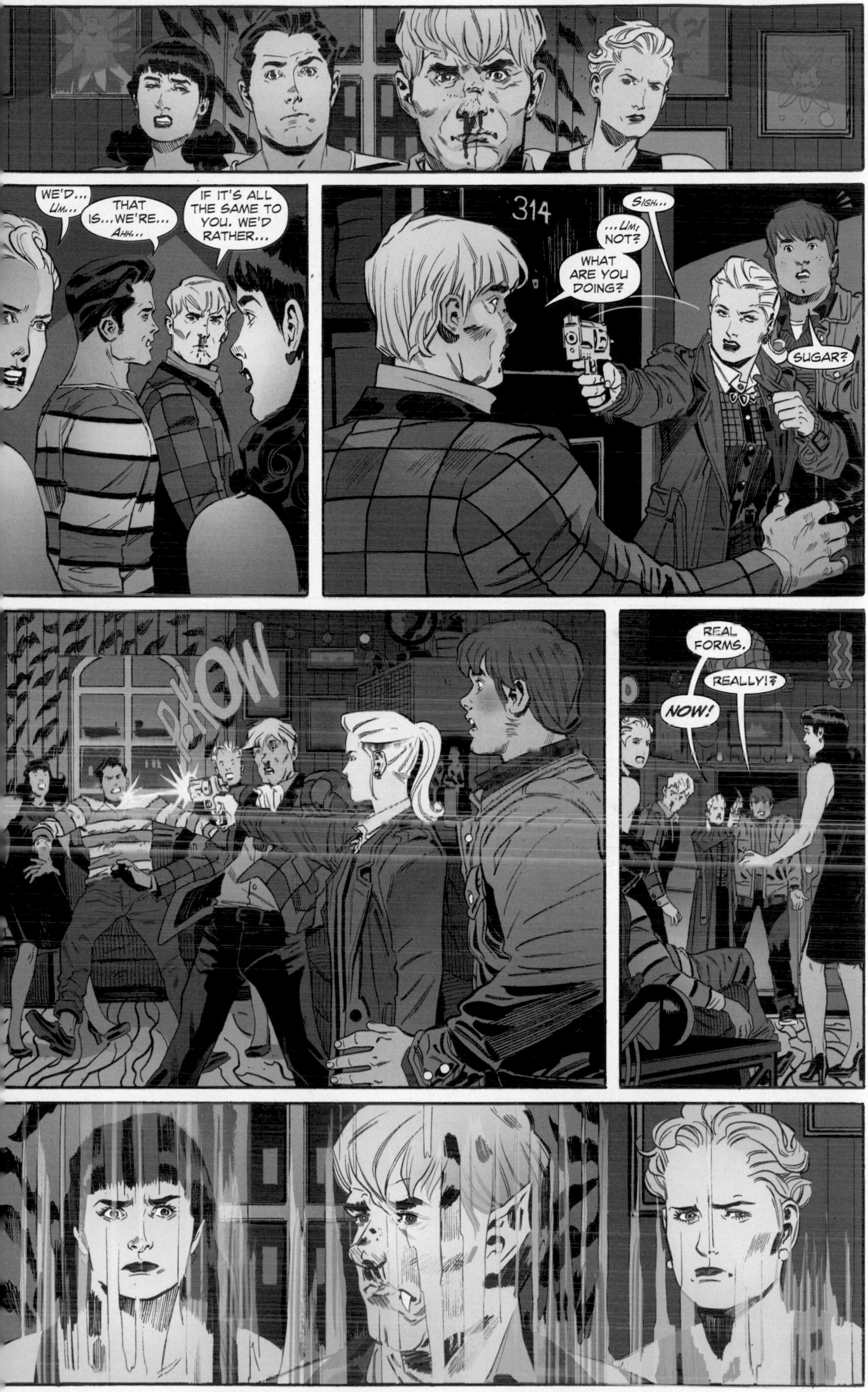
WE'D... UM...
THAT IS...WE'RE... AHH...
IF IT'S ALL THE SAME TO YOU, WE'D RATHER...
314
SIGH...
...UM, NOT?
WHAT ARE YOU DOING?
SUGAR?
BLOW
REAL FORMS.
NOW!
REALLY!?

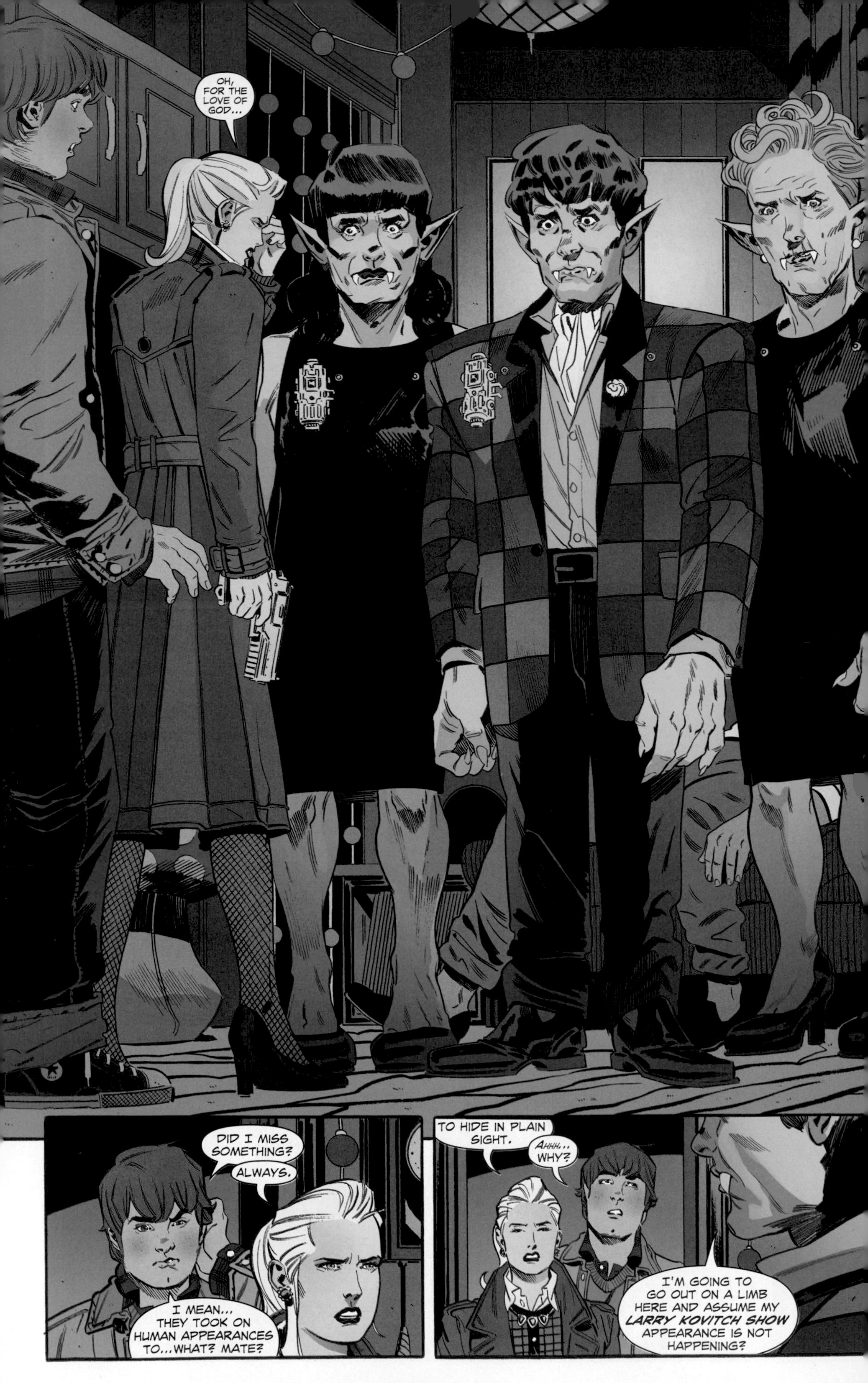
OH, FOR THE LOVE OF GOD...
DID I MISS SOMETHING?
ALWAYS.
I MEAN... THEY TOOK ON HUMAN APPEARANCES TO... WHAT? MATE?
TO HIDE IN PLAIN SIGHT.
AHHH... WHY?
I'M GOING TO GO OUT ON A LIMB HERE AND ASSUME MY *LARRY KOVITCH SHOW* APPEARANCE IS NOT HAPPENING?

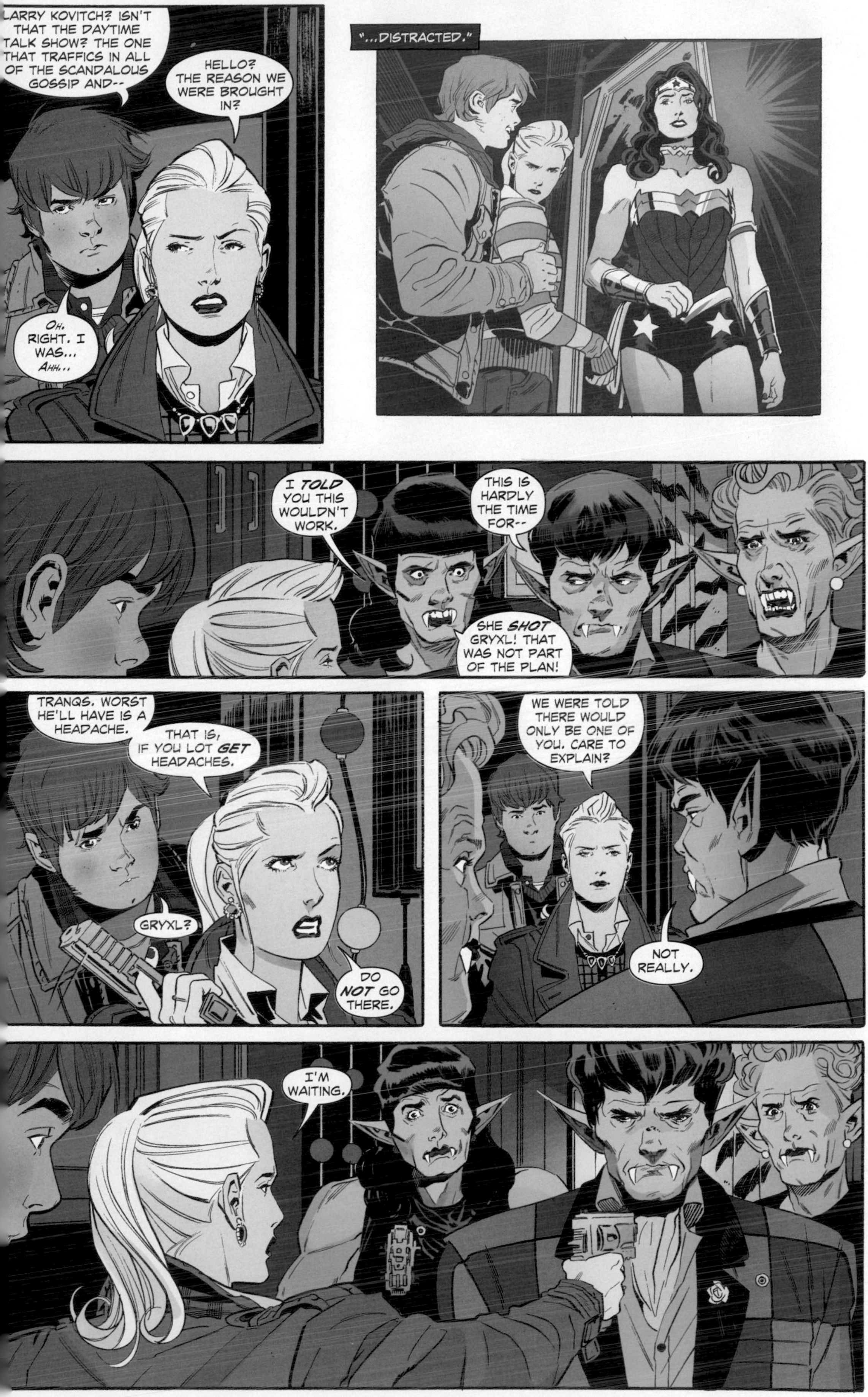
LARRY KOVITCH? ISN'T THAT THE DAYTIME TALK SHOW? THE ONE THAT TRAFFICS IN ALL OF THE SCANDALOUS GOSSIP AND--
HELLO? THE REASON WE WERE BROUGHT IN?
OH. RIGHT. I WAS... AHH...
"...DISTRACTED."
I TOLD YOU THIS WOULDN'T WORK.
THIS IS HARDLY THE TIME FOR--
SHE SHOT GRYXL! THAT WAS NOT PART OF THE PLAN!
TRANQS. WORST HE'LL HAVE IS A HEADACHE.
THAT IS, IF YOU LOT GET HEADACHES.
GRYXL?
DO NOT GO THERE.
WE WERE TOLD THERE WOULD ONLY BE ONE OF YOU. CARE TO EXPLAIN?
NOT REALLY.
I'M WAITING.

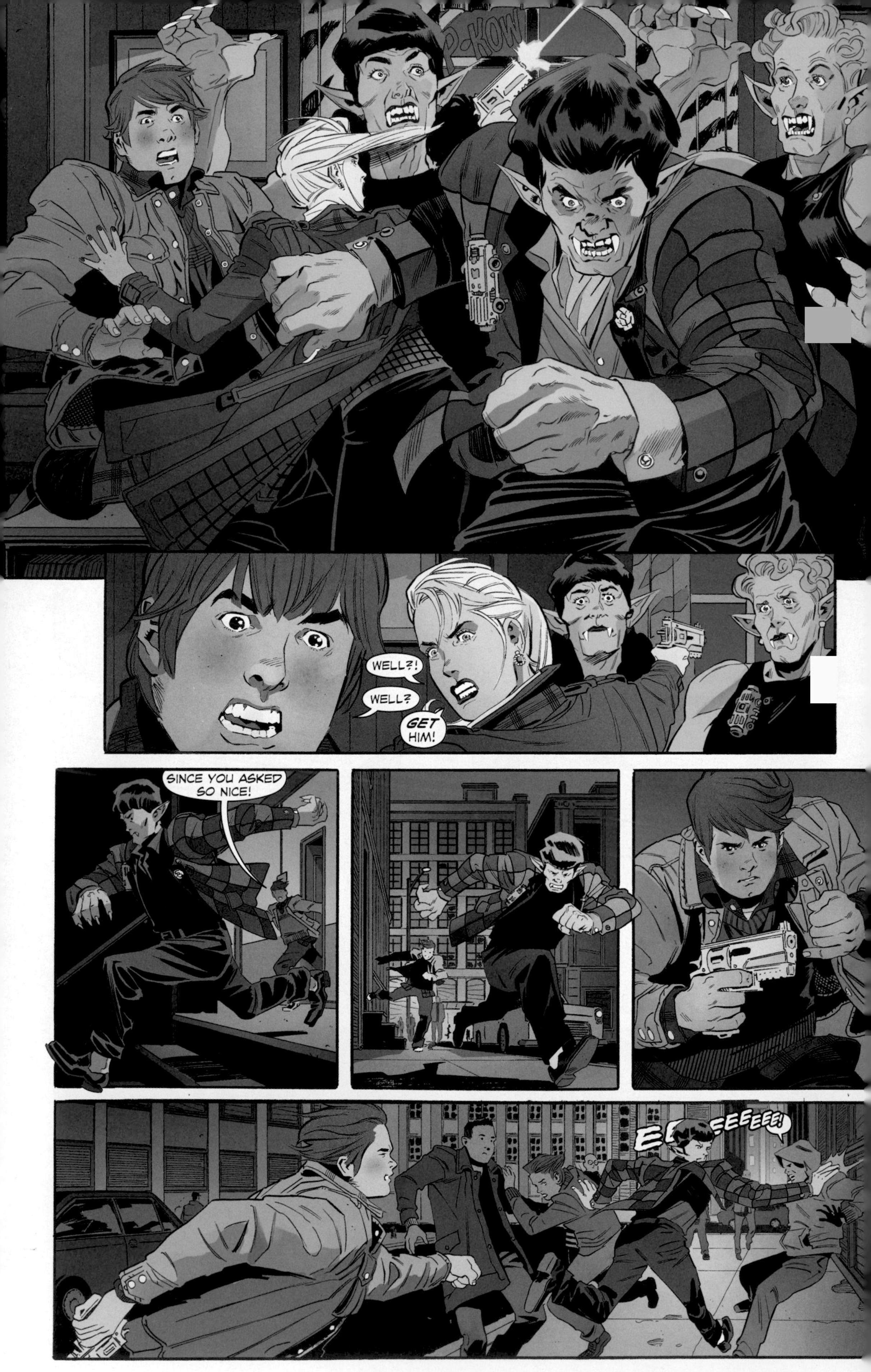
WELL?!
WELL?
GET HIM!
SINCE YOU ASKED SO NICE!

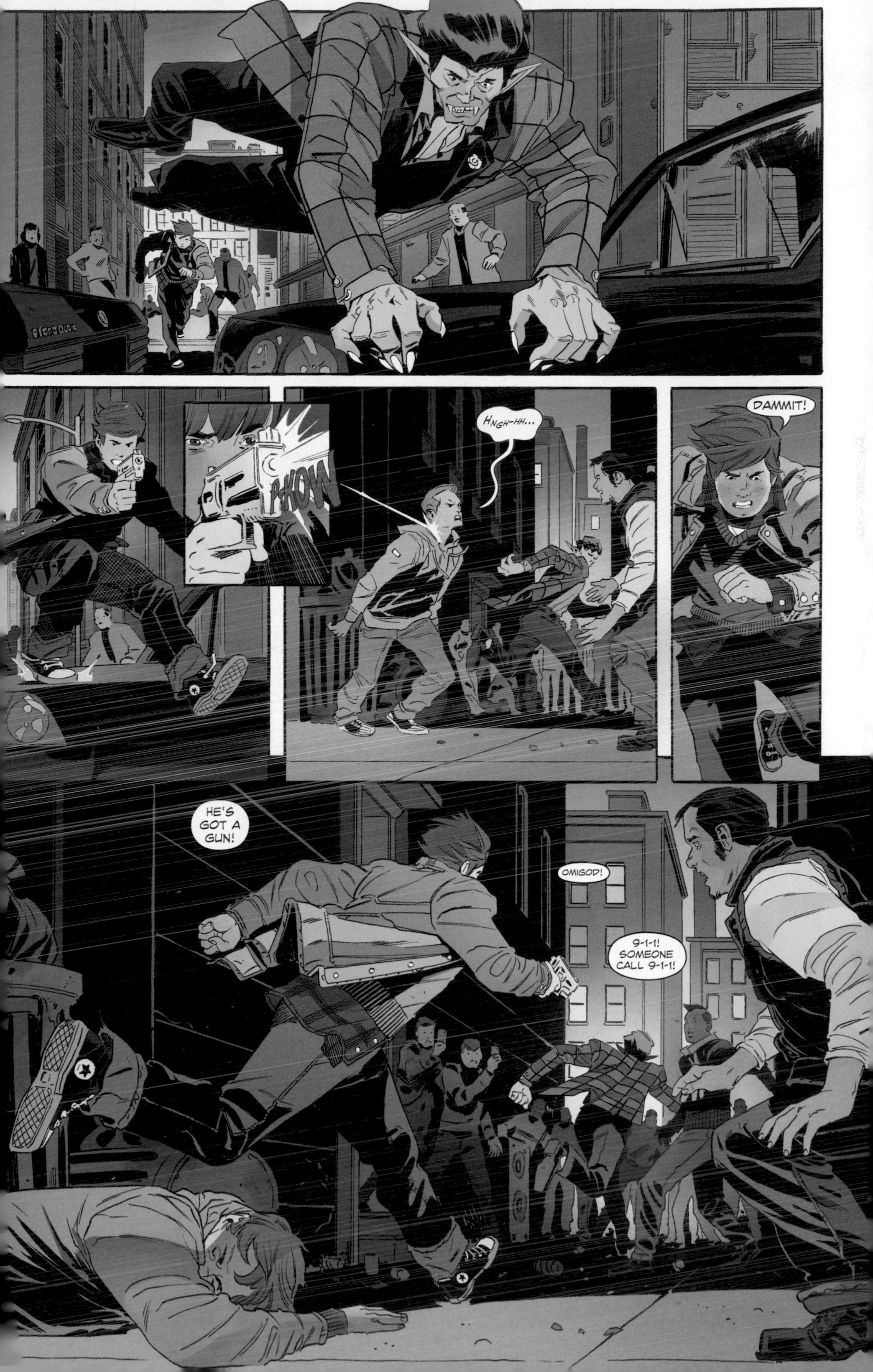
PHOW
HNGH-HH...
DAMMIT!
HE'S GOT A GUN!
OMIGOD!
9-1-1! SOMEONE CALL 9-1-1!

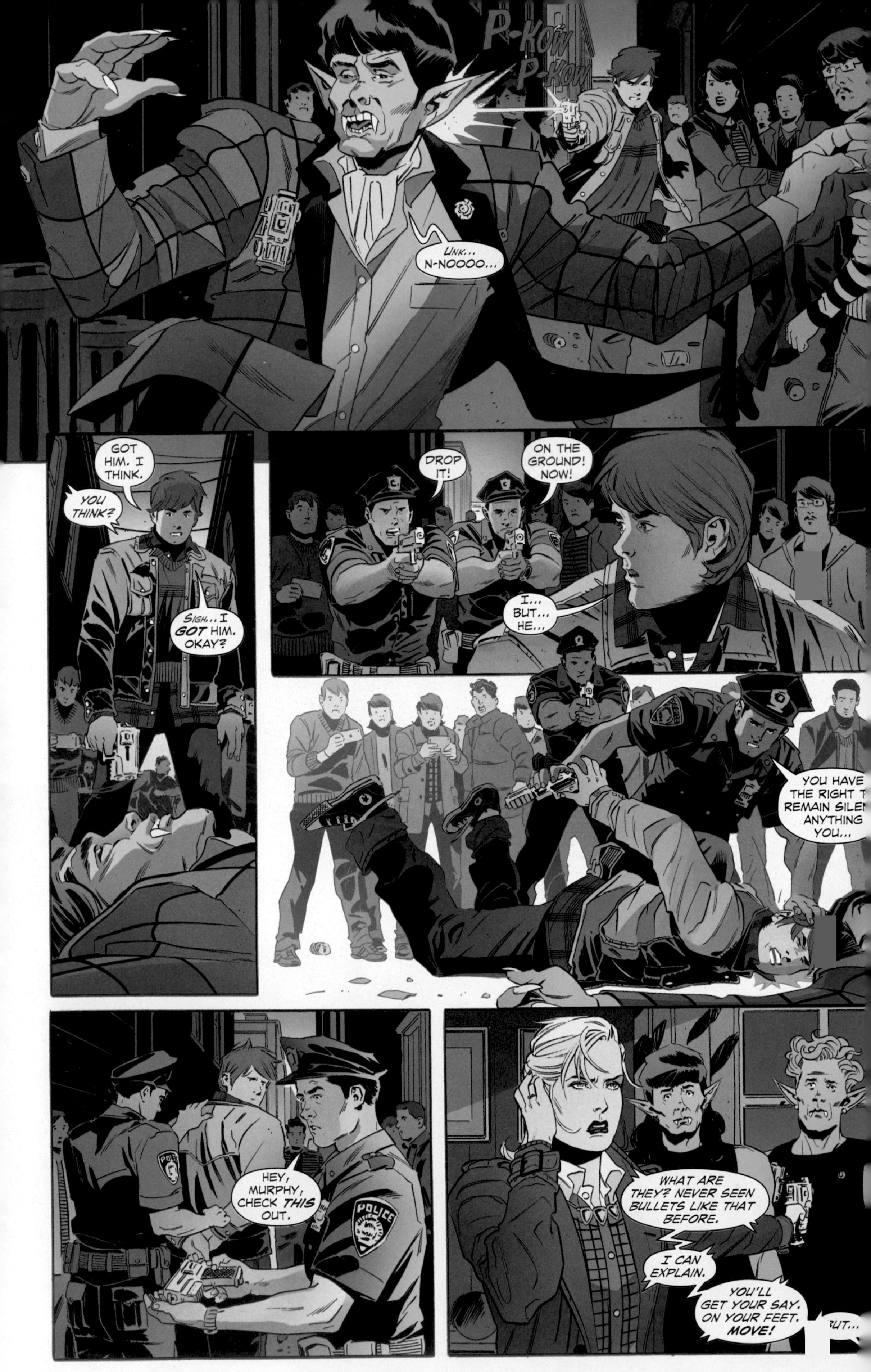
P-KOW
P-KOW
UNK... N-NOOOO...
GOT HIM. I THINK.
YOU THINK?
SIGH... I GOT HIM. OKAY?
DROP IT!
ON THE GROUND! NOW!
I... BUT... HE...
YOU HAVE THE RIGHT T REMAIN SILE ANYTHING YOU...
HEY, MURPHY, CHECK THIS OUT.
WHAT ARE THEY? NEVER SEEN BULLETS LIKE THAT BEFORE.
I CAN EXPLAIN.
YOU'LL GET YOUR SAY. ON YOUR FEET. MOVE!
UT...

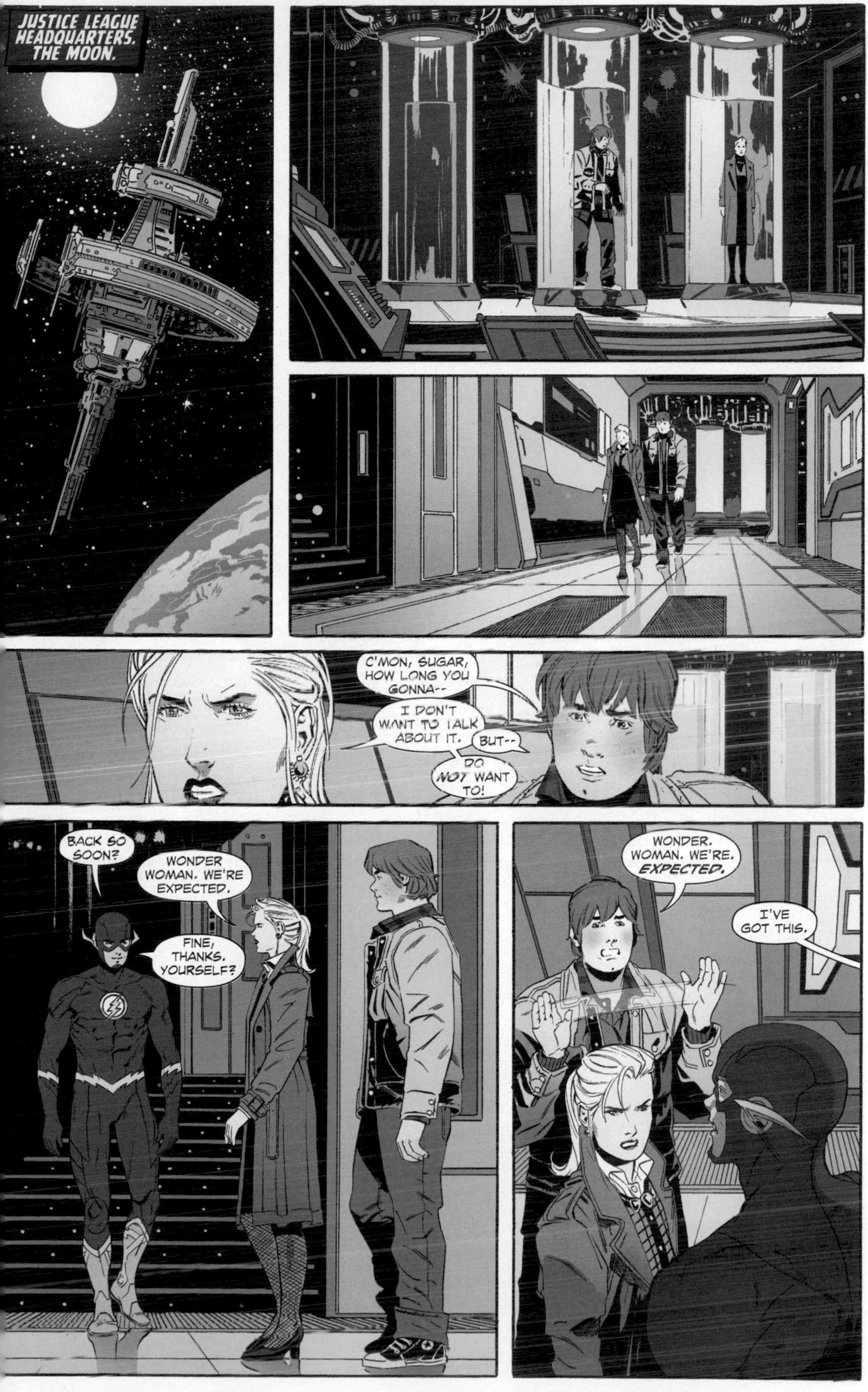
JUSTICE LEAGUE HEADQUARTERS. THE MOON.
C'MON, SUGAR, HOW LONG YOU GONNA--
I DON'T WANT TO TALK ABOUT IT.
BUT--
DO NOT WANT TO!
BACK SO SOON?
WONDER WOMAN. WE'RE EXPECTED.
FINE, THANKS. YOURSELF?
WONDER. WOMAN. WE'RE. EXPECTED.
I'VE GOT THIS.

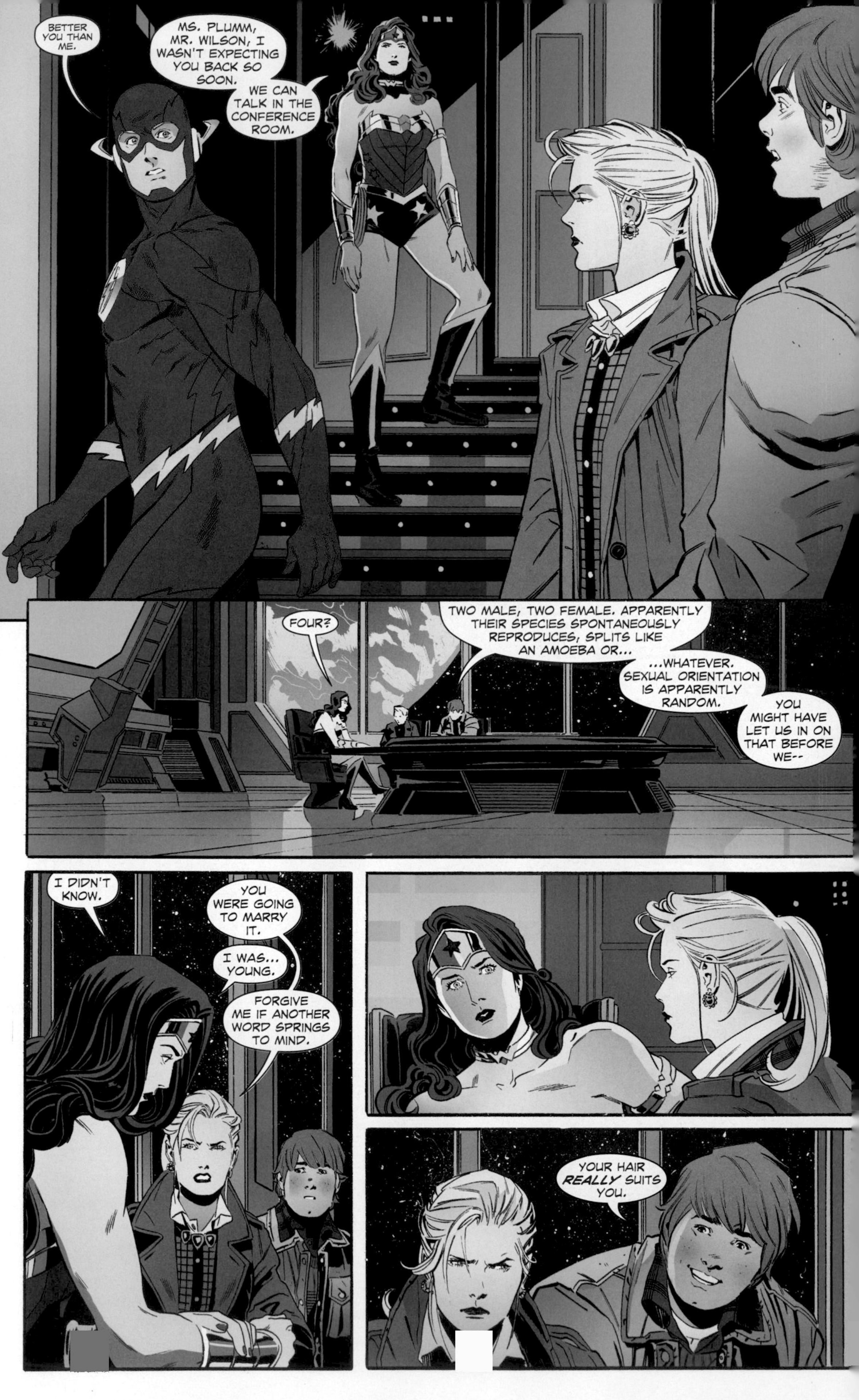
BETTER YOU THAN ME.
MS. PLUMM, MR. WILSON, I WASN'T EXPECTING YOU BACK SO SOON.
WE CAN TALK IN THE CONFERENCE ROOM.
FOUR?
TWO MALE, TWO FEMALE. APPARENTLY THEIR SPECIES SPONTANEOUSLY REPRODUCES, SPLITS LIKE AN AMOEBA OR...
...WHATEVER. SEXUAL ORIENTATION IS APPARENTLY RANDOM.
YOU MIGHT HAVE LET US IN ON THAT BEFORE WE--
I DIDN'T KNOW.
YOU WERE GOING TO MARRY IT.
I WAS... YOUNG.
FORGIVE ME IF ANOTHER WORD SPRINGS TO MIND.
YOUR HAIR REALLY SUITS YOU.

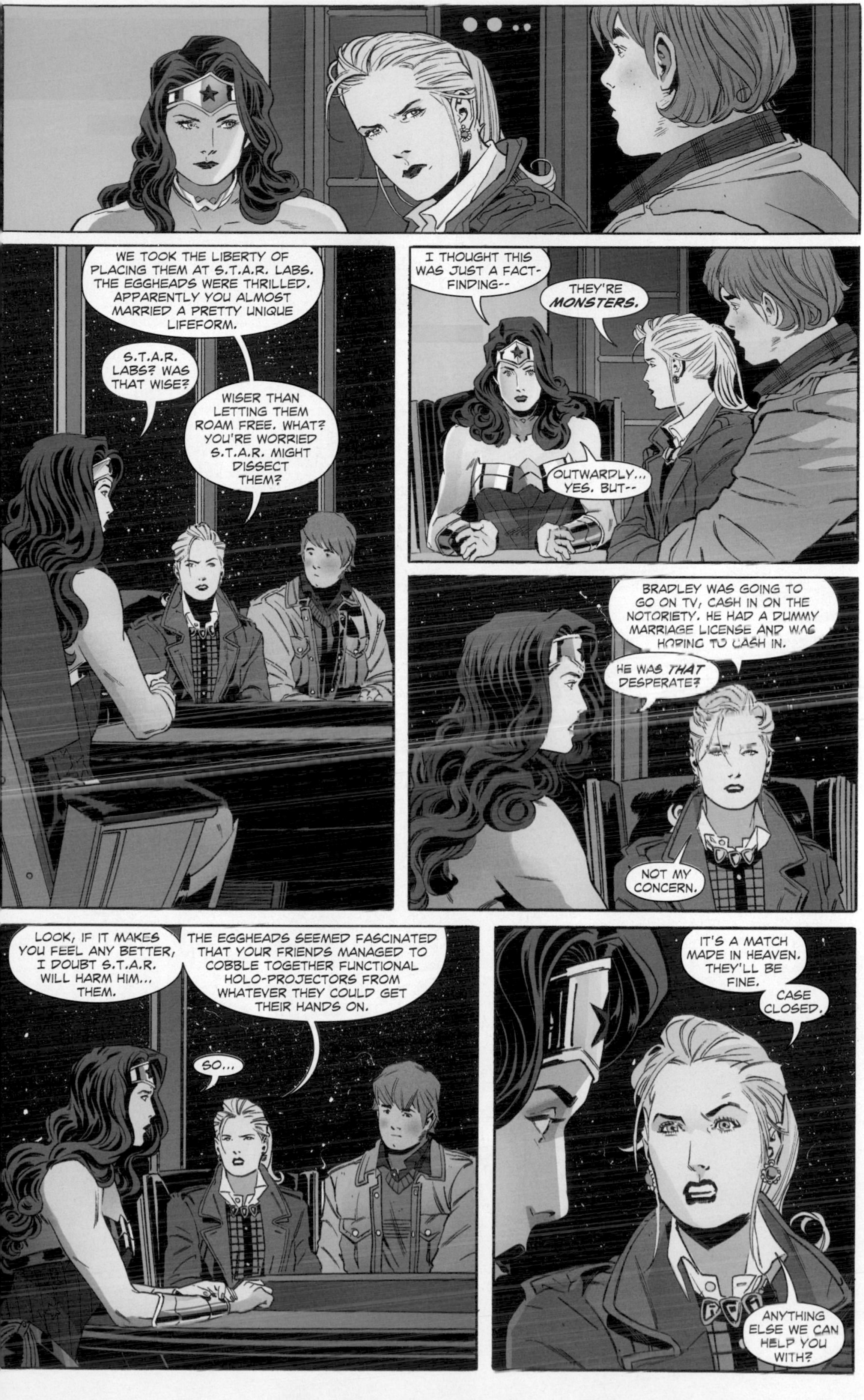
...
WE TOOK THE LIBERTY OF PLACING THEM AT S.T.A.R. LABS. THE EGGHEADS WERE THRILLED. APPARENTLY YOU ALMOST MARRIED A PRETTY UNIQUE LIFEFORM.
S.T.A.R. LABS? WAS THAT WISE?
WISER THAN LETTING THEM ROAM FREE. WHAT? YOU'RE WORRIED S.T.A.R. MIGHT DISSECT THEM?
I THOUGHT THIS WAS JUST A FACT-FINDING--
THEY'RE *MONSTERS.*
OUTWARDLY... YES. BUT--
BRADLEY WAS GOING TO GO ON TV, CASH IN ON THE NOTORIETY. HE HAD A DUMMY MARRIAGE LICENSE AND WAS HOPING TO CASH IN.
HE WAS *THAT* DESPERATE?
NOT MY CONCERN.
LOOK, IF IT MAKES YOU FEEL ANY BETTER, I DOUBT S.T.A.R. WILL HARM HIM... THEM.
THE EGGHEADS SEEMED FASCINATED THAT YOUR FRIENDS MANAGED TO COBBLE TOGETHER FUNCTIONAL HOLO-PROJECTORS FROM WHATEVER THEY COULD GET THEIR HANDS ON.
SO...
IT'S A MATCH MADE IN HEAVEN. THEY'LL BE FINE.
CASE CLOSED.
ANYTHING ELSE WE CAN HELP YOU WITH?

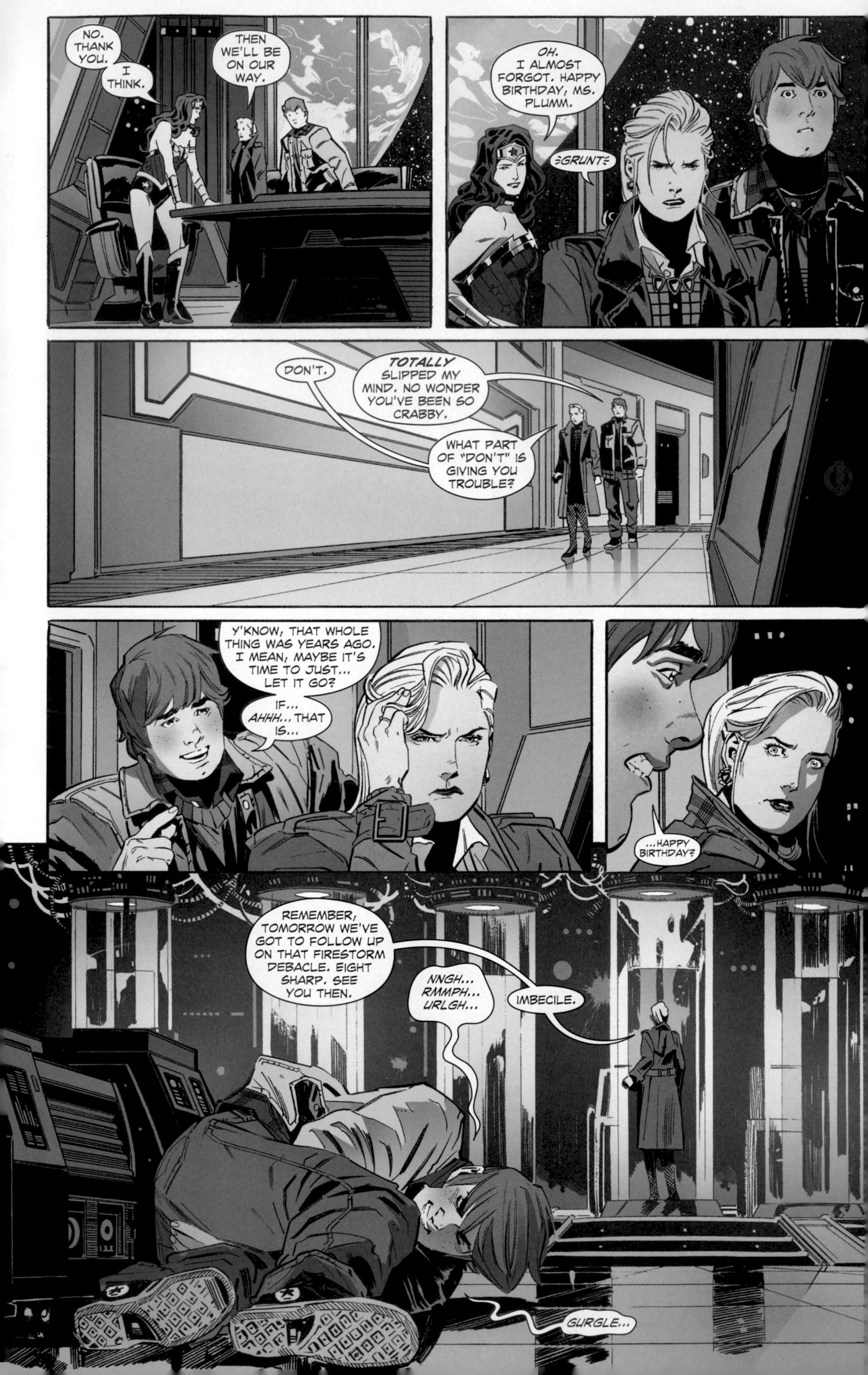
NO. THANK YOU.
I THINK.
THEN WE'LL BE ON OUR WAY.
OH. I ALMOST FORGOT. HAPPY BIRTHDAY, MS. PLUMM.
GRUNT
TOTALLY SLIPPED MY MIND. NO WONDER YOU'VE BEEN SO CRABBY.
DON'T.
WHAT PART OF "DON'T" IS GIVING YOU TROUBLE?
Y'KNOW, THAT WHOLE THING WAS YEARS AGO. I MEAN, MAYBE IT'S TIME TO JUST... LET IT GO?
IF... AHHH... THAT IS...
...HAPPY BIRTHDAY?
REMEMBER, TOMORROW WE'VE GOT TO FOLLOW UP ON THAT FIRESTORM DEBACLE. EIGHT SHARP. SEE YOU THEN.
NNGH... RMMPH... URLGH...
IMBECILE.
GURGLE...

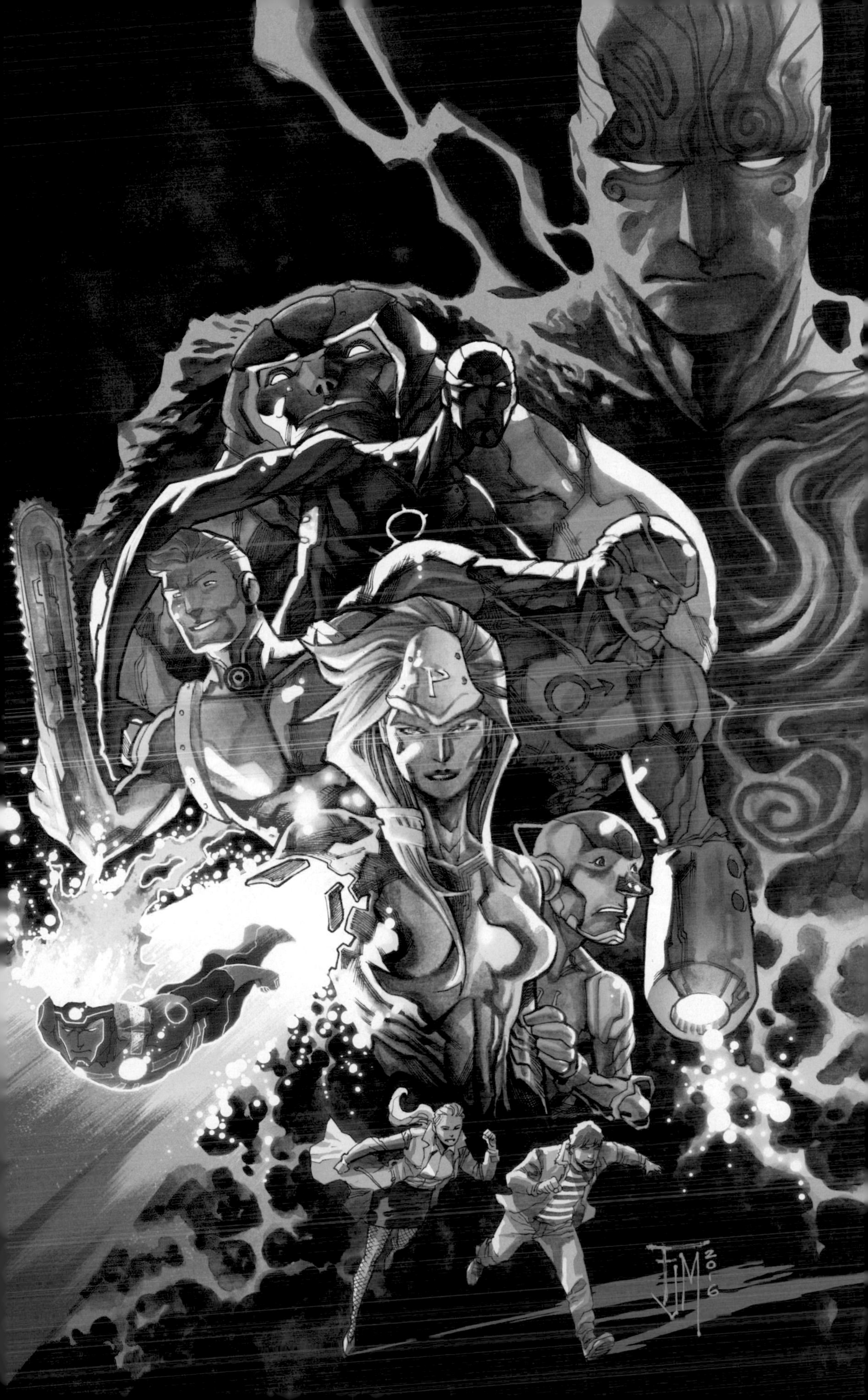

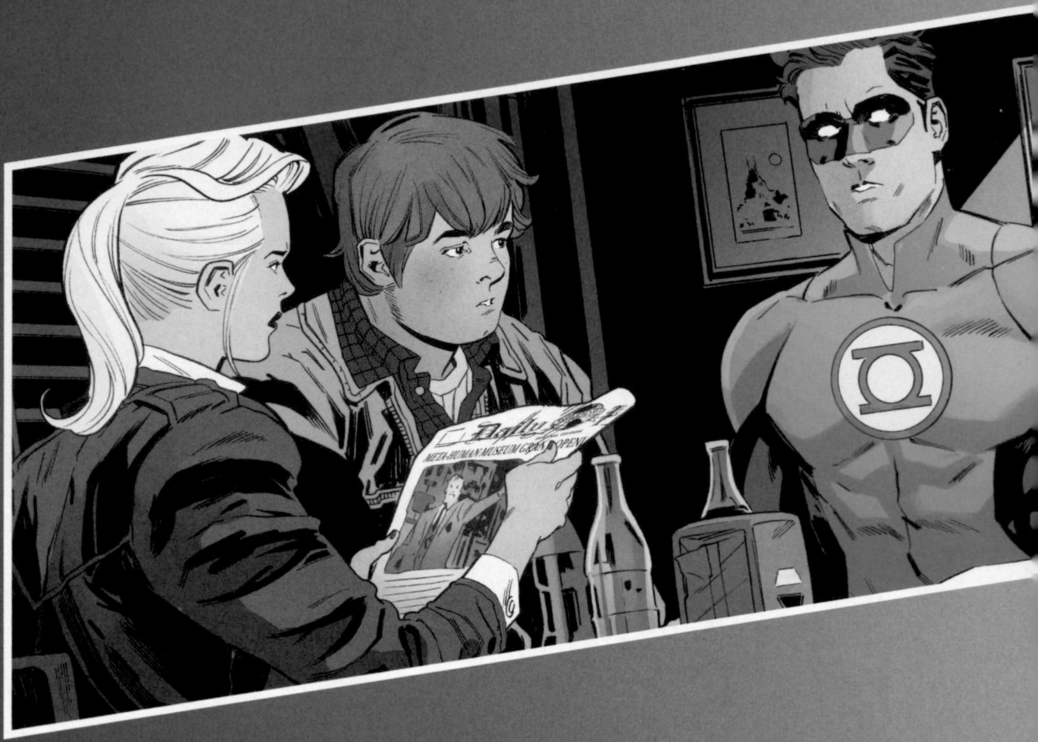

FRANCIS MANAPUL
cover

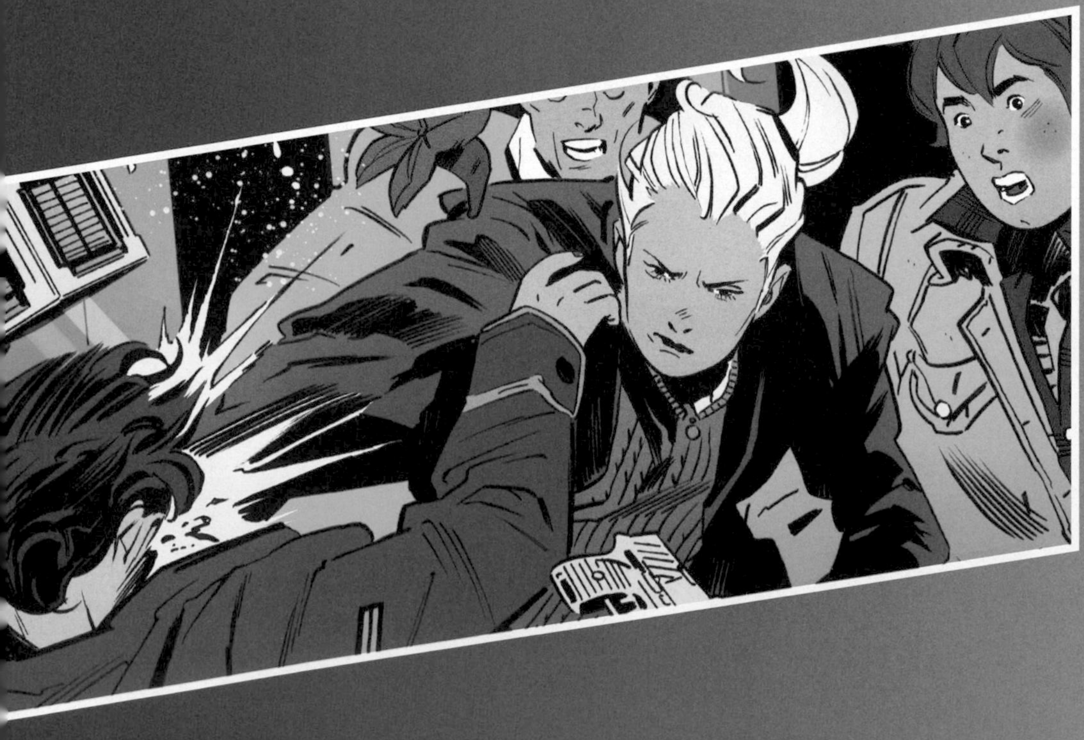

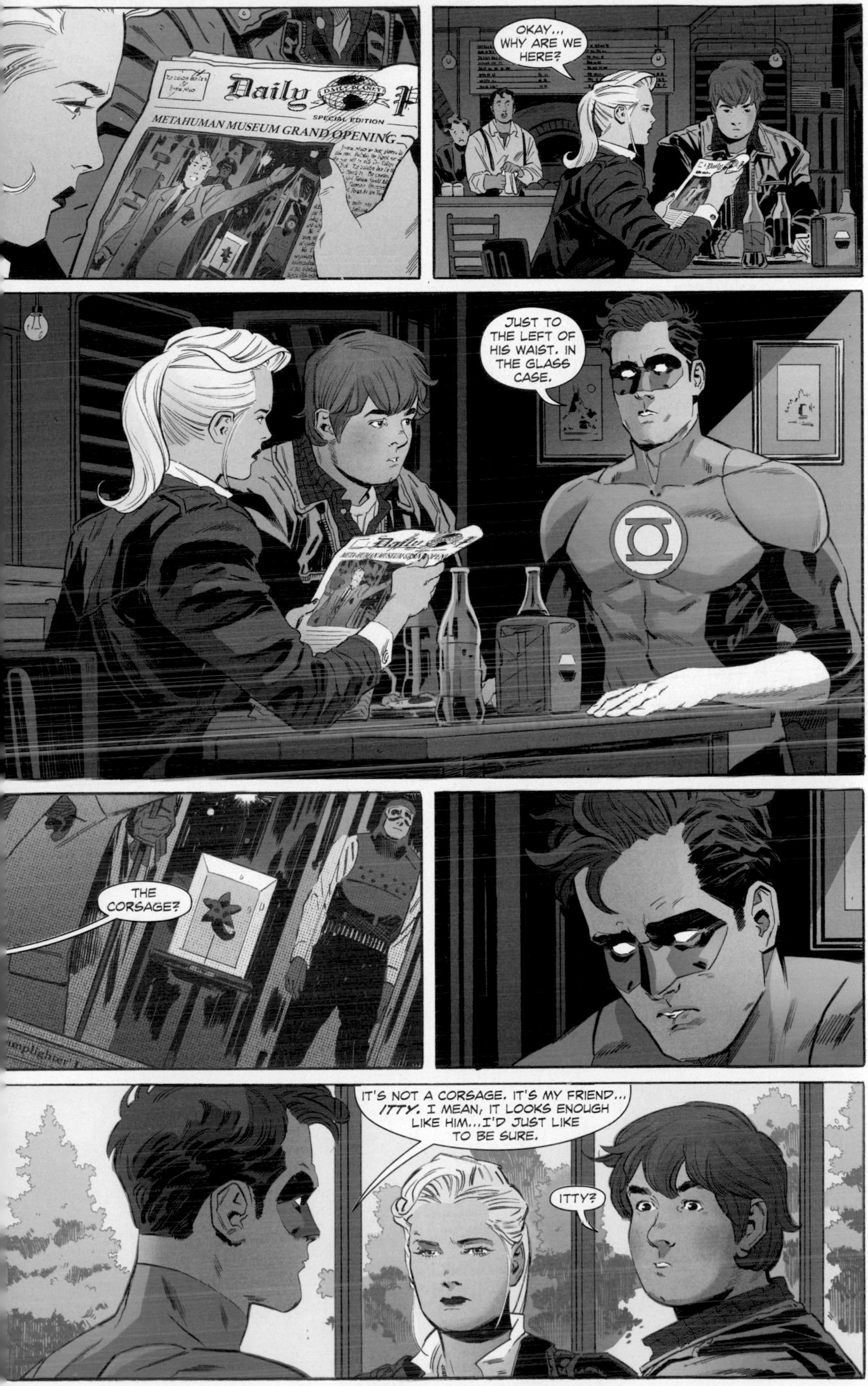
Daily
SPECIAL EDITION
METAHUMAN MUSEUM GRAND OPENING
OKAY... WHY ARE WE HERE?
JUST TO THE LEFT OF HIS WAIST. IN THE GLASS CASE.
THE CORSAGE?
IT'S NOT A CORSAGE. IT'S MY FRIEND... *ITTY.* I MEAN, IT LOOKS ENOUGH LIKE HIM...I'D JUST LIKE TO BE SURE.
ITTY?

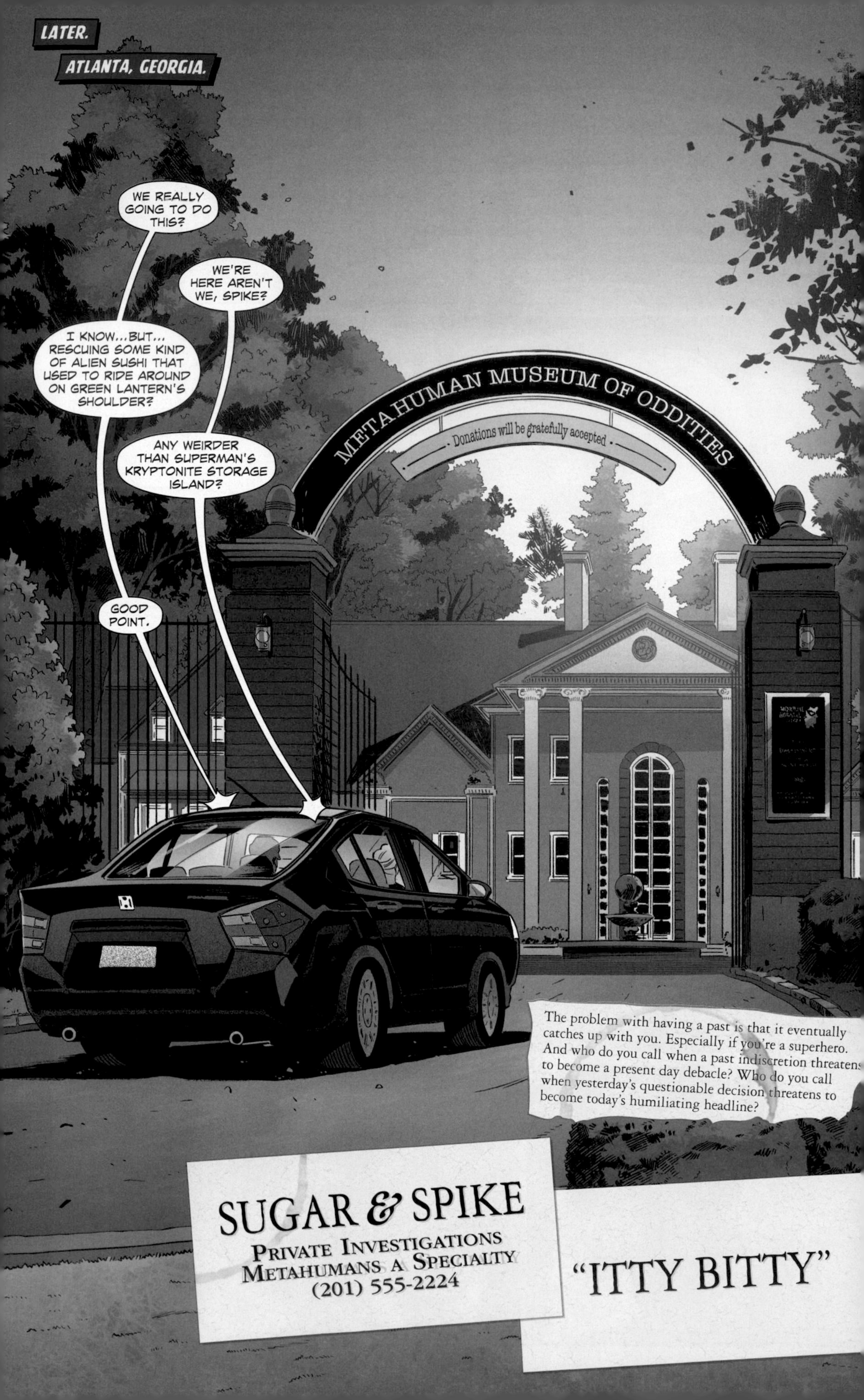
LATER.
ATLANTA, GEORGIA.
WE REALLY GOING TO DO THIS?
WE'RE HERE AREN'T WE, SPIKE?
I KNOW...BUT... RESCUING SOME KIND OF ALIEN SUSHI THAT USED TO RIDE AROUND ON GREEN LANTERN'S SHOULDER?
ANY WEIRDER THAN SUPERMAN'S KRYPTONITE STORAGE ISLAND?
GOOD POINT.
METAHUMAN MUSEUM OF ODDITIES
Donations will be gratefully accepted
The problem with having a past is that it eventually catches up with you. Especially if you're a superhero. And who do you call when a past indiscretion threatens to become a present day debacle? Who do you call when yesterday's questionable decision threatens to become today's humiliating headline?
SUGAR & SPIKE
PRIVATE INVESTIGATIONS
METAHUMANS A SPECIALTY
(201) 555-2224
"ITTY BITTY"

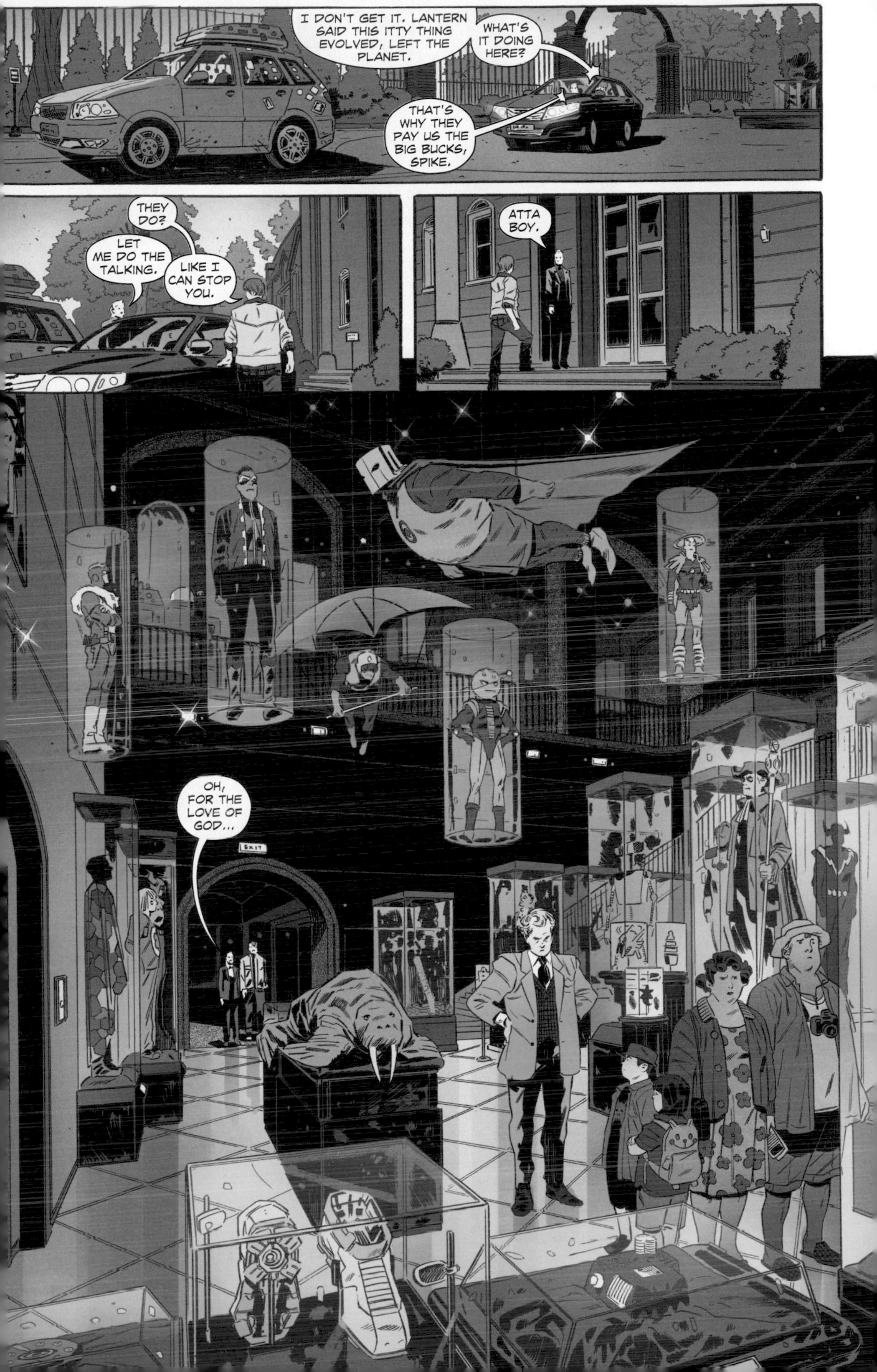
I DON'T GET IT. LANTERN SAID THIS ITTY THING EVOLVED, LEFT THE PLANET.
WHAT'S IT DOING HERE?
THAT'S WHY THEY PAY US THE BIG BUCKS, SPIKE.
THEY DO?
LET ME DO THE TALKING.
LIKE I CAN STOP YOU.
ATTA BOY.
OH, FOR THE LOVE OF GOD...
EXIT

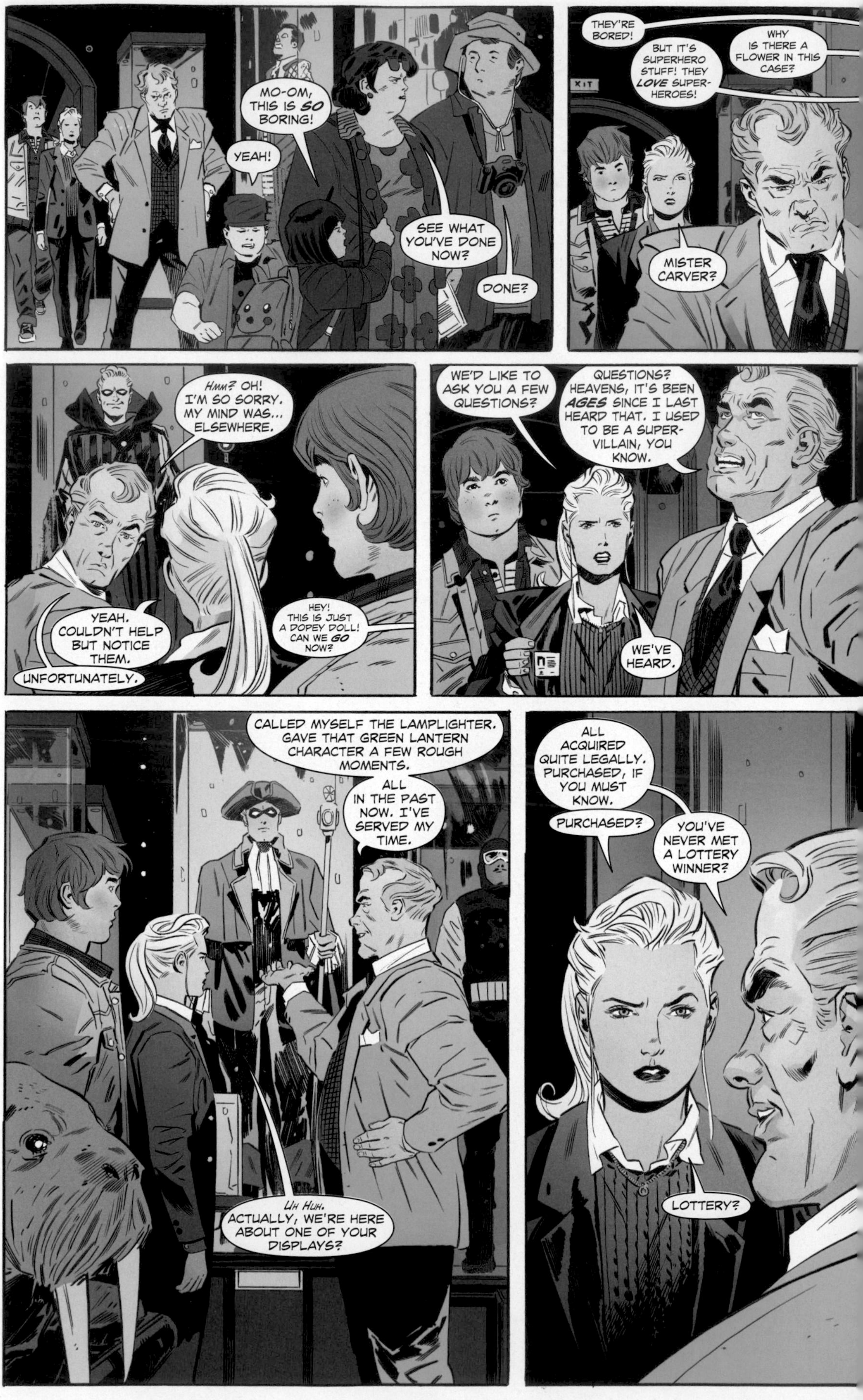
MO-OM, THIS IS SO BORING!
YEAH!
SEE WHAT YOU'VE DONE NOW?
DONE?
THEY'RE BORED!
BUT IT'S SUPERHERO STUFF! THEY LOVE SUPER-HEROES!
WHY IS THERE A FLOWER IN THIS CASE?
MISTER CARVER?
HMM? OH! I'M SO SORRY. MY MIND WAS... ELSEWHERE.
YEAH. COULDN'T HELP BUT NOTICE THEM.
UNFORTUNATELY.
HEY! THIS IS JUST A DOPEY DOLL! CAN WE GO NOW?
WE'D LIKE TO ASK YOU A FEW QUESTIONS?
QUESTIONS? HEAVENS, IT'S BEEN AGES SINCE I LAST HEARD THAT. I USED TO BE A SUPER-VILLAIN, YOU KNOW.
WE'VE HEARD.
CALLED MYSELF THE LAMPLIGHTER. GAVE THAT GREEN LANTERN CHARACTER A FEW ROUGH MOMENTS.
ALL IN THE PAST NOW. I'VE SERVED MY TIME.
UH HUH. ACTUALLY, WE'RE HERE ABOUT ONE OF YOUR DISPLAYS?
ALL ACQUIRED QUITE LEGALLY. PURCHASED, IF YOU MUST KNOW.
PURCHASED?
YOU'VE NEVER MET A LOTTERY WINNER?
LOTTERY?

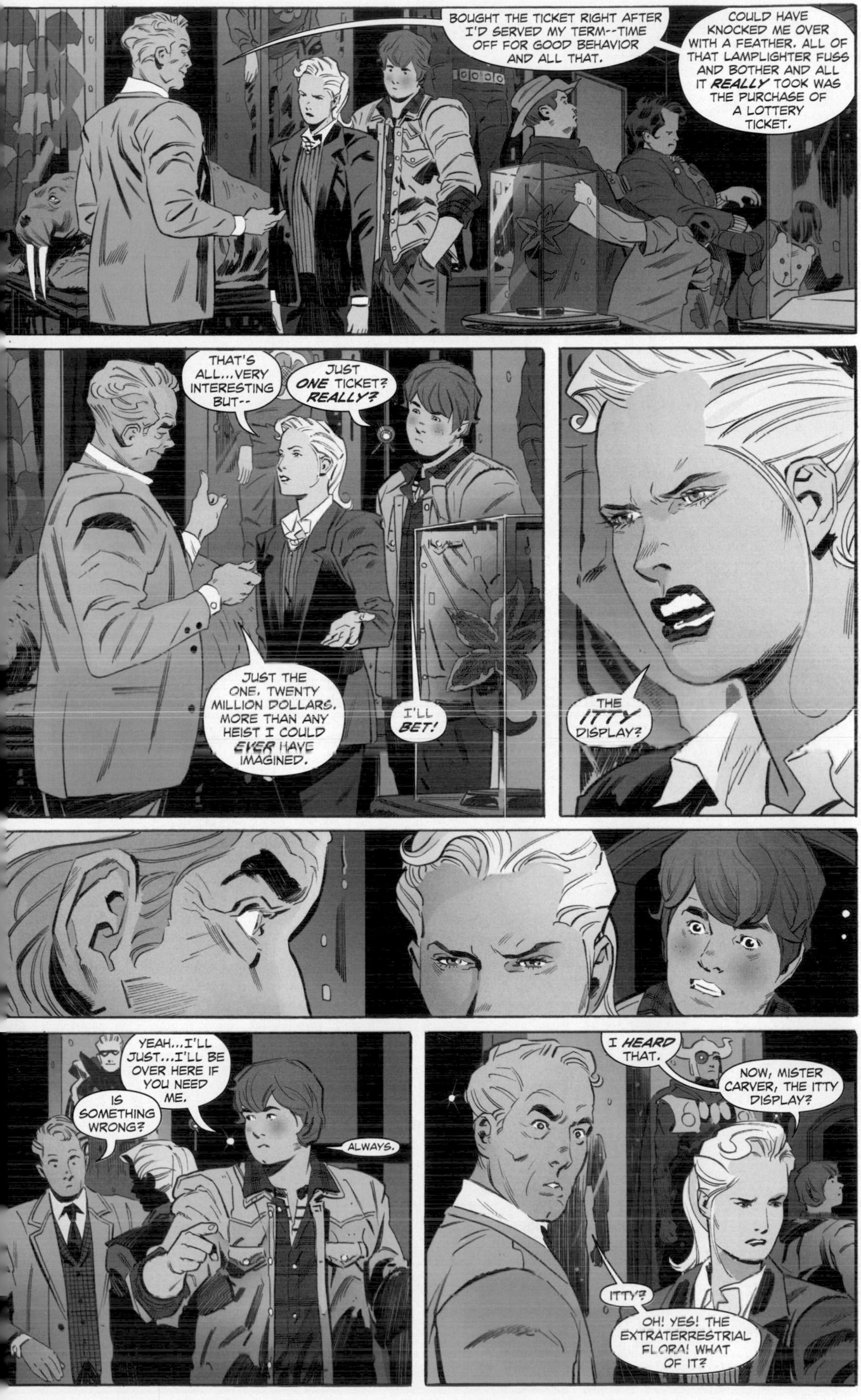
BOUGHT THE TICKET RIGHT AFTER I'D SERVED MY TERM--TIME OFF FOR GOOD BEHAVIOR AND ALL THAT.
COULD HAVE KNOCKED ME OVER WITH A FEATHER. ALL OF THAT LAMPLIGHTER FUSS AND BOTHER AND ALL IT REALLY TOOK WAS THE PURCHASE OF A LOTTERY TICKET.
THAT'S ALL...VERY INTERESTING BUT--
JUST ONE TICKET? REALLY?
JUST THE ONE. TWENTY MILLION DOLLARS. MORE THAN ANY HEIST I COULD EVER HAVE IMAGINED.
I'LL BET!
THE ITTY DISPLAY?
YEAH...I'LL JUST...I'LL BE OVER HERE IF YOU NEED ME.
IS SOMETHING WRONG?
ALWAYS.
I HEARD THAT.
NOW, MISTER CARVER, THE ITTY DISPLAY?
ITTY?
OH! YES! THE EXTRATERRESTRIAL FLORA! WHAT OF IT?

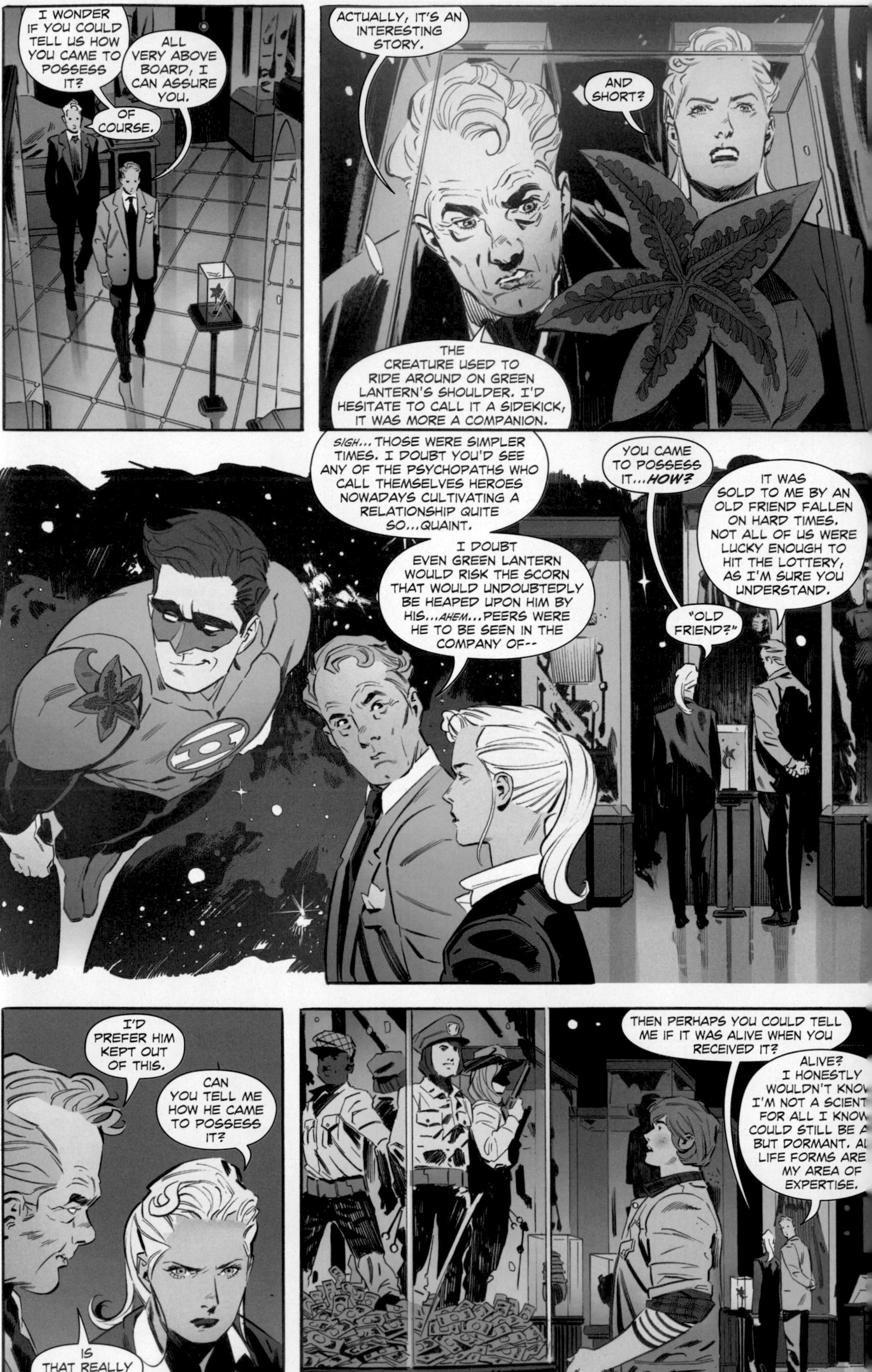
I WONDER IF YOU COULD TELL US HOW YOU CAME TO POSSESS IT?
OF COURSE.
ALL VERY ABOVE BOARD, I CAN ASSURE YOU.
ACTUALLY, IT'S AN INTERESTING STORY.
AND SHORT?
THE CREATURE USED TO RIDE AROUND ON GREEN LANTERN'S SHOULDER. I'D HESITATE TO CALL IT A SIDEKICK, IT WAS MORE A COMPANION.
SIGH... THOSE WERE SIMPLER TIMES. I DOUBT YOU'D SEE ANY OF THE PSYCHOPATHS WHO CALL THEMSELVES HEROES NOWADAYS CULTIVATING A RELATIONSHIP QUITE SO...QUAINT.
I DOUBT EVEN GREEN LANTERN WOULD RISK THE SCORN THAT WOULD UNDOUBTEDLY BE HEAPED UPON HIM BY HIS...AHEM...PEERS WERE HE TO BE SEEN IN THE COMPANY OF--
YOU CAME TO POSSESS IT...HOW?
IT WAS SOLD TO ME BY AN OLD FRIEND FALLEN ON HARD TIMES. NOT ALL OF US WERE LUCKY ENOUGH TO HIT THE LOTTERY, AS I'M SURE YOU UNDERSTAND.
"OLD FRIEND?"
I'D PREFER HIM KEPT OUT OF THIS.
CAN YOU TELL ME HOW HE CAME TO POSSESS IT?
IS THAT REALLY NECESSARY?
THEN PERHAPS YOU COULD TELL ME IF IT WAS ALIVE WHEN YOU RECEIVED IT?
ALIVE? I HONESTLY WOULDN'T KNOW I'M NOT A SCIENT FOR ALL I KNOW COULD STILL BE A BUT DORMANT. AL LIFE FORMS ARE MY AREA OF EXPERTISE.

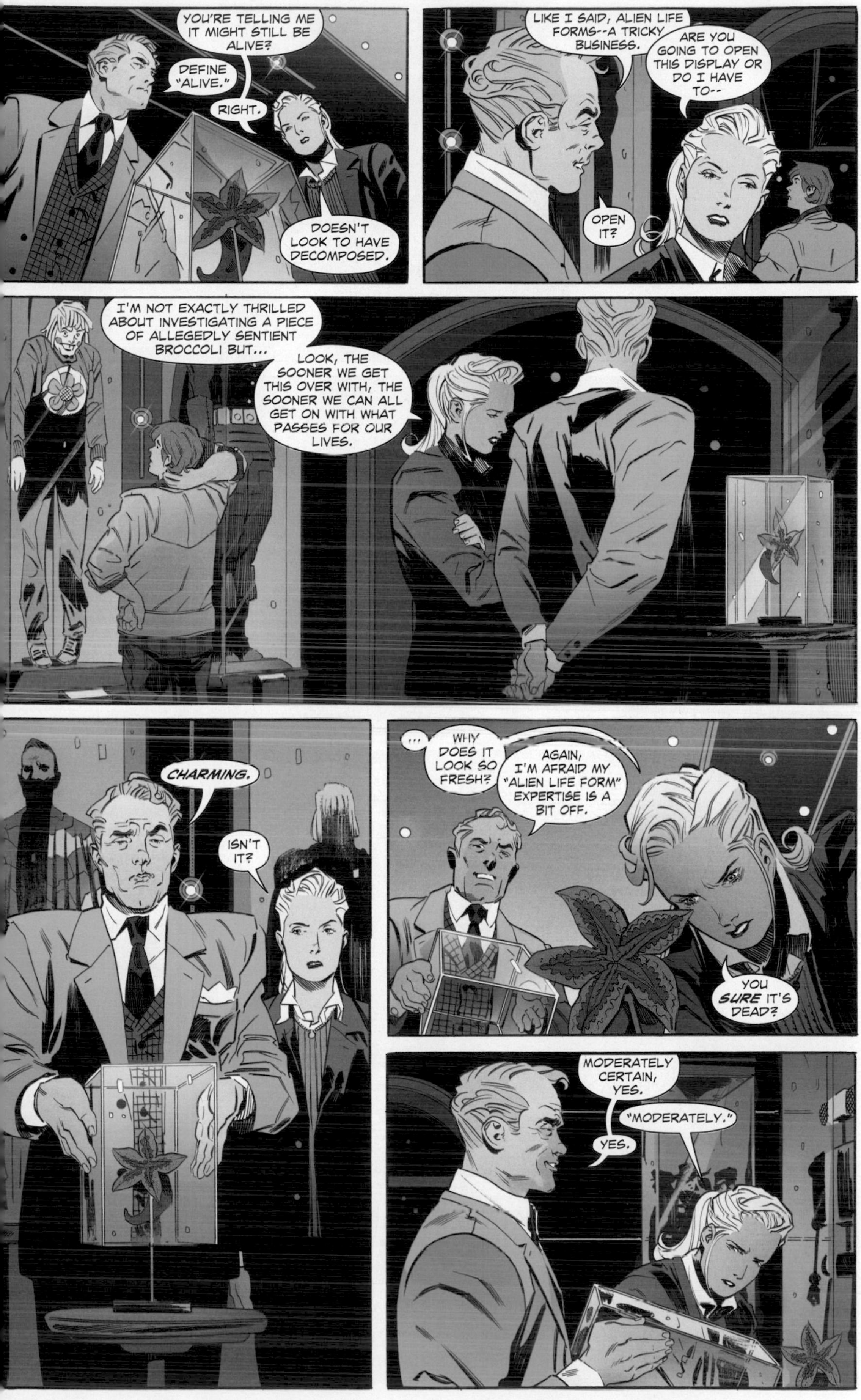
YOU'RE TELLING ME IT MIGHT STILL BE ALIVE?
DEFINE "ALIVE."
RIGHT.
DOESN'T LOOK TO HAVE DECOMPOSED.
LIKE I SAID, ALIEN LIFE FORMS--A TRICKY BUSINESS.
ARE YOU GOING TO OPEN THIS DISPLAY OR DO I HAVE TO--
OPEN IT?
I'M NOT EXACTLY THRILLED ABOUT INVESTIGATING A PIECE OF ALLEGEDLY SENTIENT BROCCOLI BUT...
LOOK, THE SOONER WE GET THIS OVER WITH, THE SOONER WE CAN ALL GET ON WITH WHAT PASSES FOR OUR LIVES.
CHARMING.
ISN'T IT?
...
WHY DOES IT LOOK SO FRESH?
AGAIN, I'M AFRAID MY "ALIEN LIFE FORM" EXPERTISE IS A BIT OFF.
YOU SURE IT'S DEAD?
MODERATELY CERTAIN, YES.
"MODERATELY."
YES.

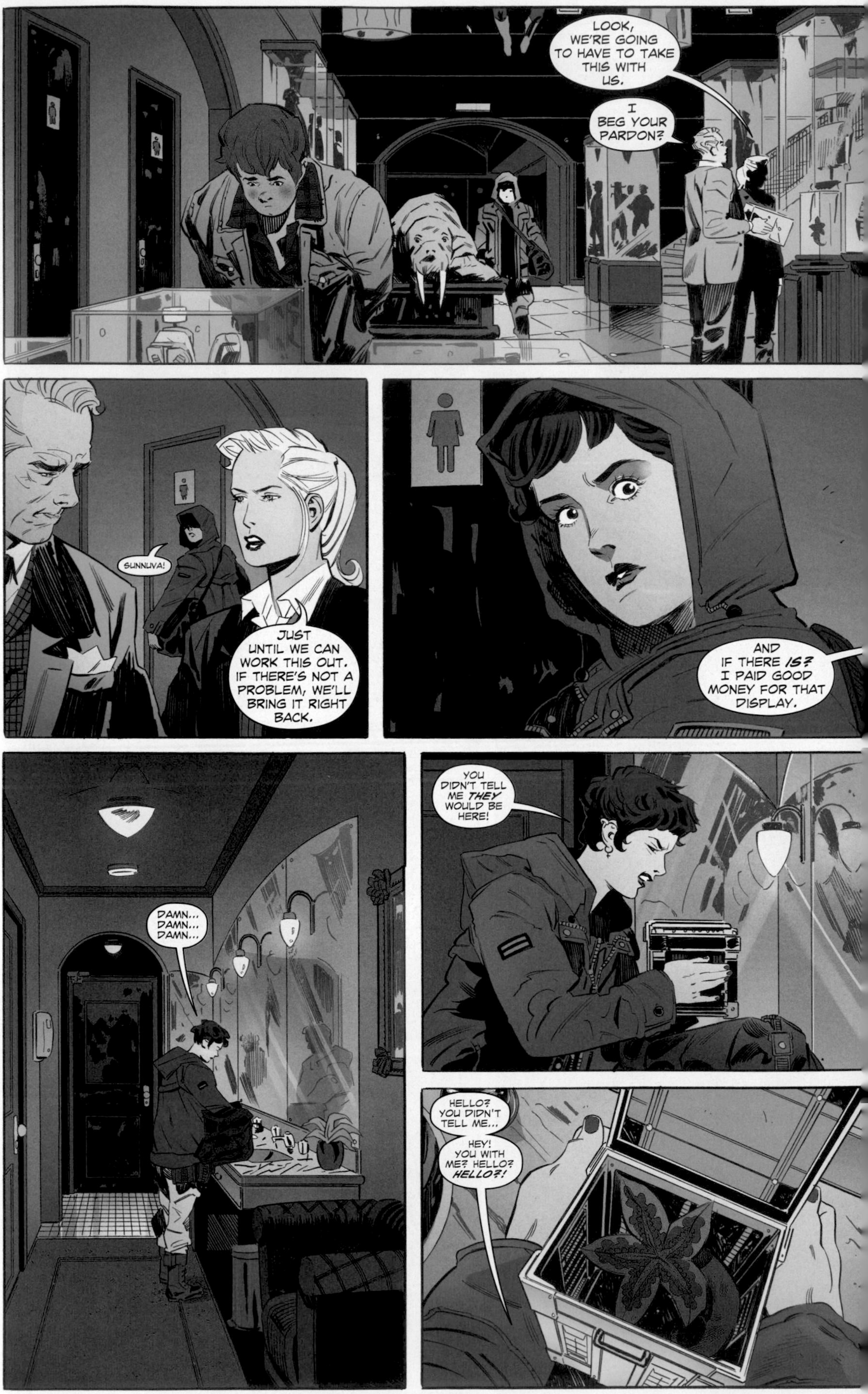
LOOK, WE'RE GOING TO HAVE TO TAKE THIS WITH US.
I BEG YOUR PARDON?
SUNNUVA!
JUST UNTIL WE CAN WORK THIS OUT. IF THERE'S NOT A PROBLEM, WE'LL BRING IT RIGHT BACK.
AND IF THERE IS? I PAID GOOD MONEY FOR THAT DISPLAY.
DAMN... DAMN... DAMN...
YOU DIDN'T TELL ME THEY WOULD BE HERE!
HELLO? YOU DIDN'T TELL ME...
HEY! YOU WITH ME? HELLO? HELLO?!

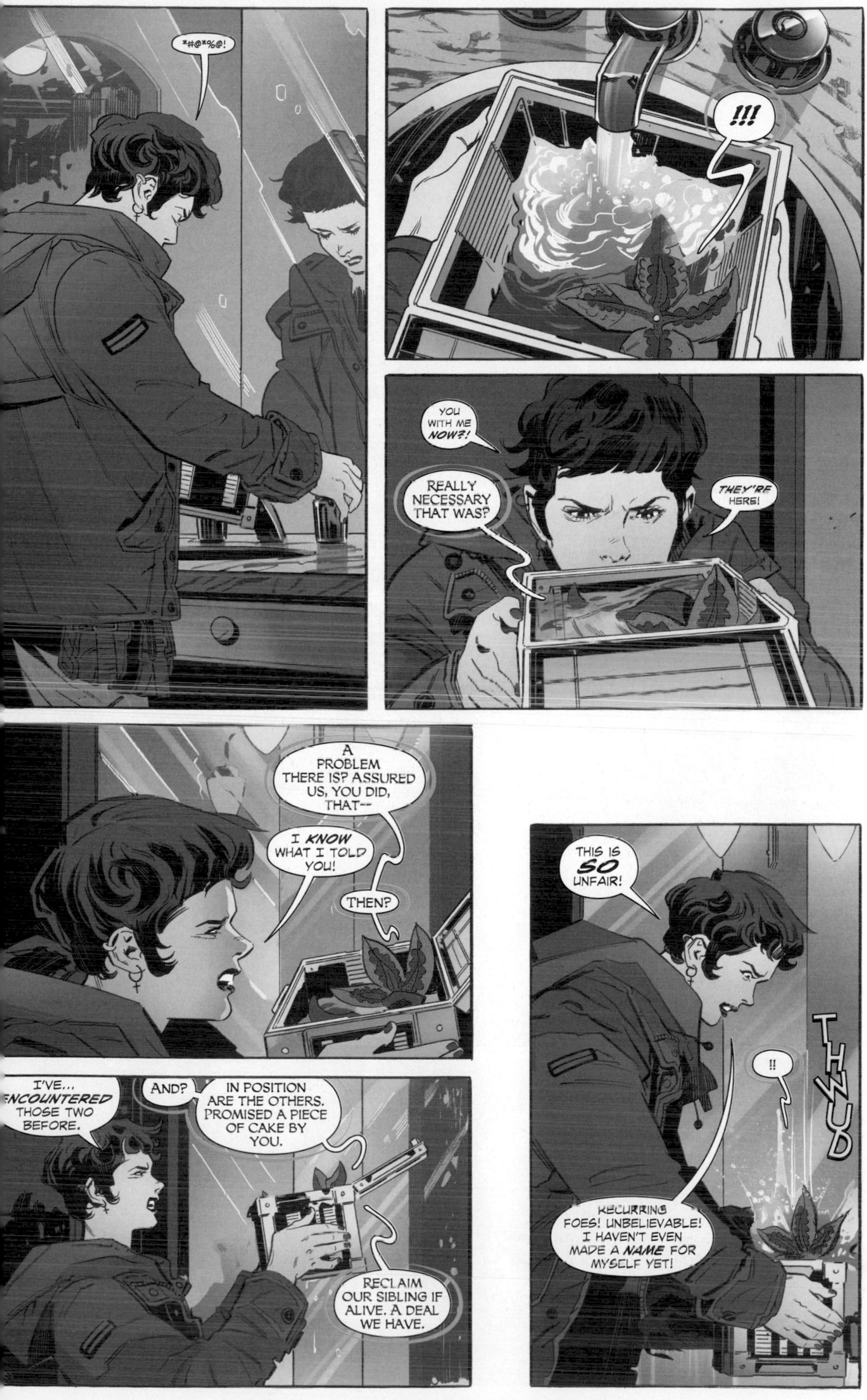
#@%@!
!!!
YOU WITH ME NOW?!
REALLY NECESSARY THAT WAS?
THEY'RE HERE!
A PROBLEM THERE IS? ASSURED US, YOU DID, THAT--
I KNOW WHAT I TOLD YOU!
THEN?
I'VE... ENCOUNTERED THOSE TWO BEFORE.
AND?
IN POSITION ARE THE OTHERS. PROMISED A PIECE OF CAKE BY YOU.
RECLAIM OUR SIBLING IF ALIVE. A DEAL WE HAVE.
THIS IS SO UNFAIR!
!!
THWUD
RECURRING FOES! UNBELIEVABLE! I HAVEN'T EVEN MADE A NAME FOR MYSELF YET!

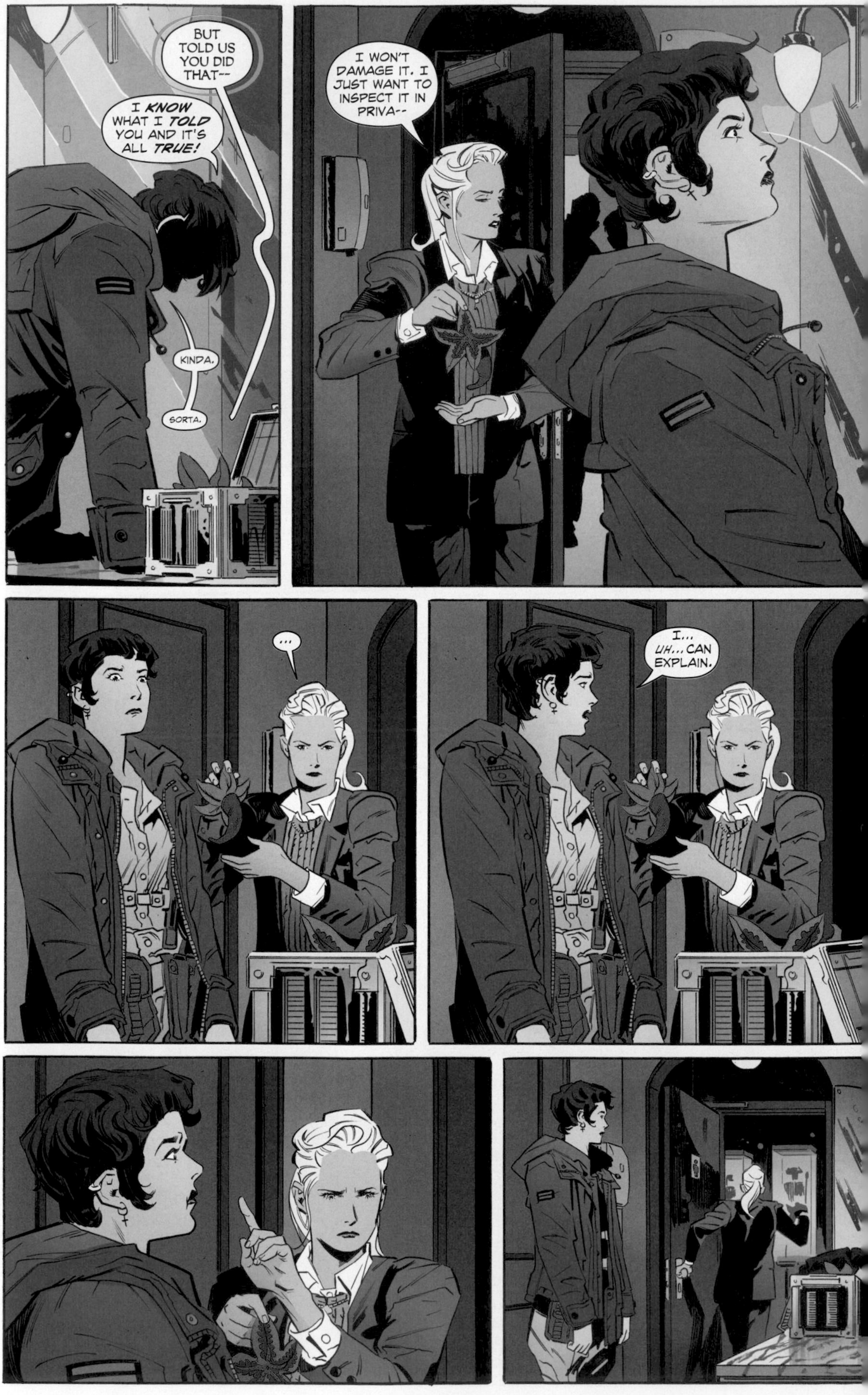
BUT TOLD US YOU DID THAT--
I KNOW WHAT I TOLD YOU AND IT'S ALL TRUE!
KINDA.
SORTA.
I WON'T DAMAGE IT. I JUST WANT TO INSPECT IT IN PRIVA--
...
I... UH... CAN EXPLAIN.

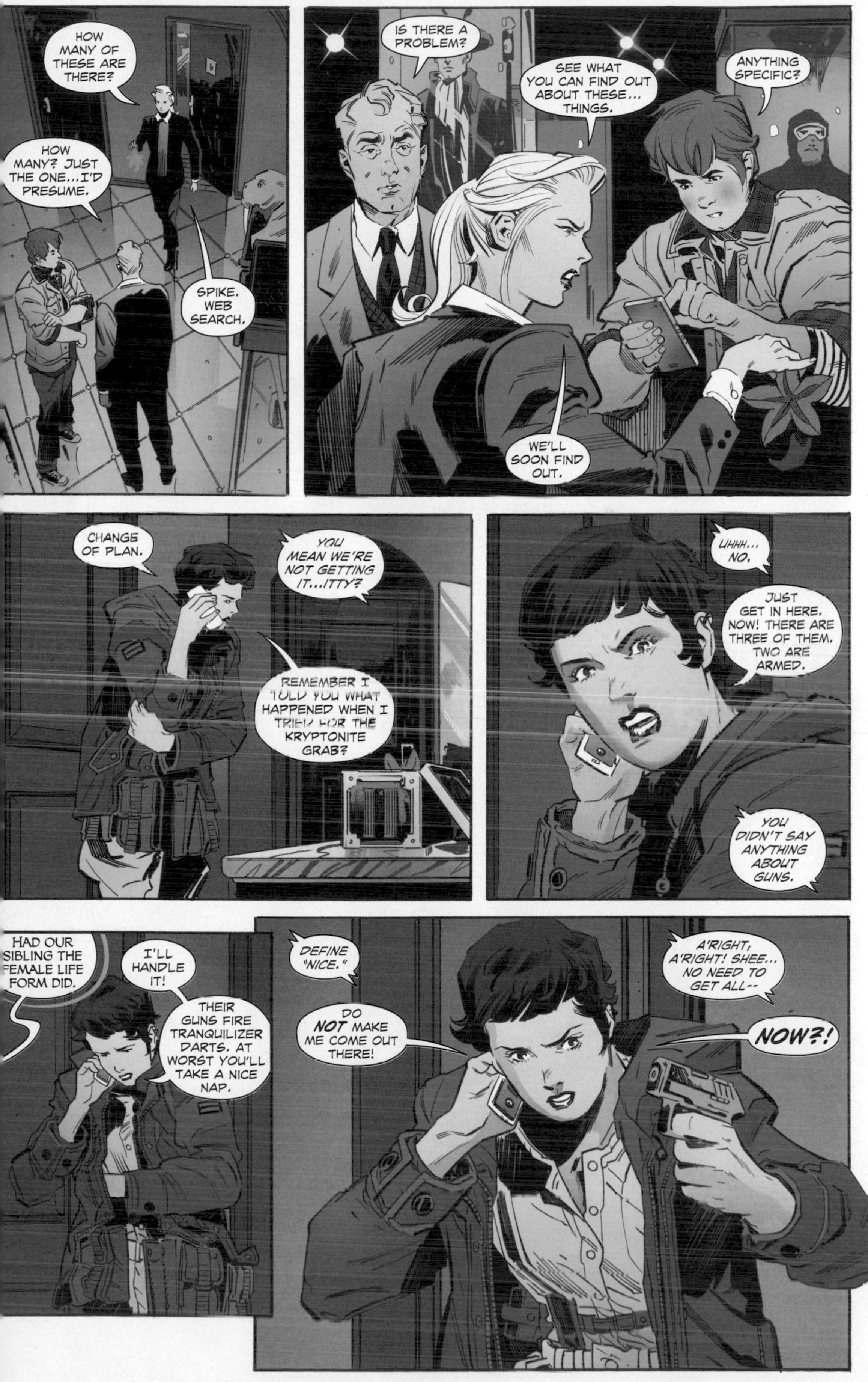
HOW MANY OF THESE ARE THERE?
HOW MANY? JUST THE ONE...I'D PRESUME.
SPIKE. WEB SEARCH.
IS THERE A PROBLEM?
SEE WHAT YOU CAN FIND OUT ABOUT THESE... THINGS.
ANYTHING SPECIFIC?
WE'LL SOON FIND OUT.
CHANGE OF PLAN.
YOU MEAN WE'RE NOT GETTING IT...ITTY?
REMEMBER I TOLD YOU WHAT HAPPENED WHEN I TRIED FOR THE KRYPTONITE GRAB?
UHHH... NO.
JUST GET IN HERE, NOW! THERE ARE THREE OF THEM. TWO ARE ARMED.
YOU DIDN'T SAY ANYTHING ABOUT GUNS.
HAD OUR SIBLING THE FEMALE LIFE FORM DID.
I'LL HANDLE IT!
THEIR GUNS FIRE TRANQUILIZER DARTS. AT WORST YOU'LL TAKE A NICE NAP.
DEFINE "NICE."
DO NOT MAKE ME COME OUT THERE!
A'RIGHT, A'RIGHT! SHEE... NO NEED TO GET ALL--
NOW?!

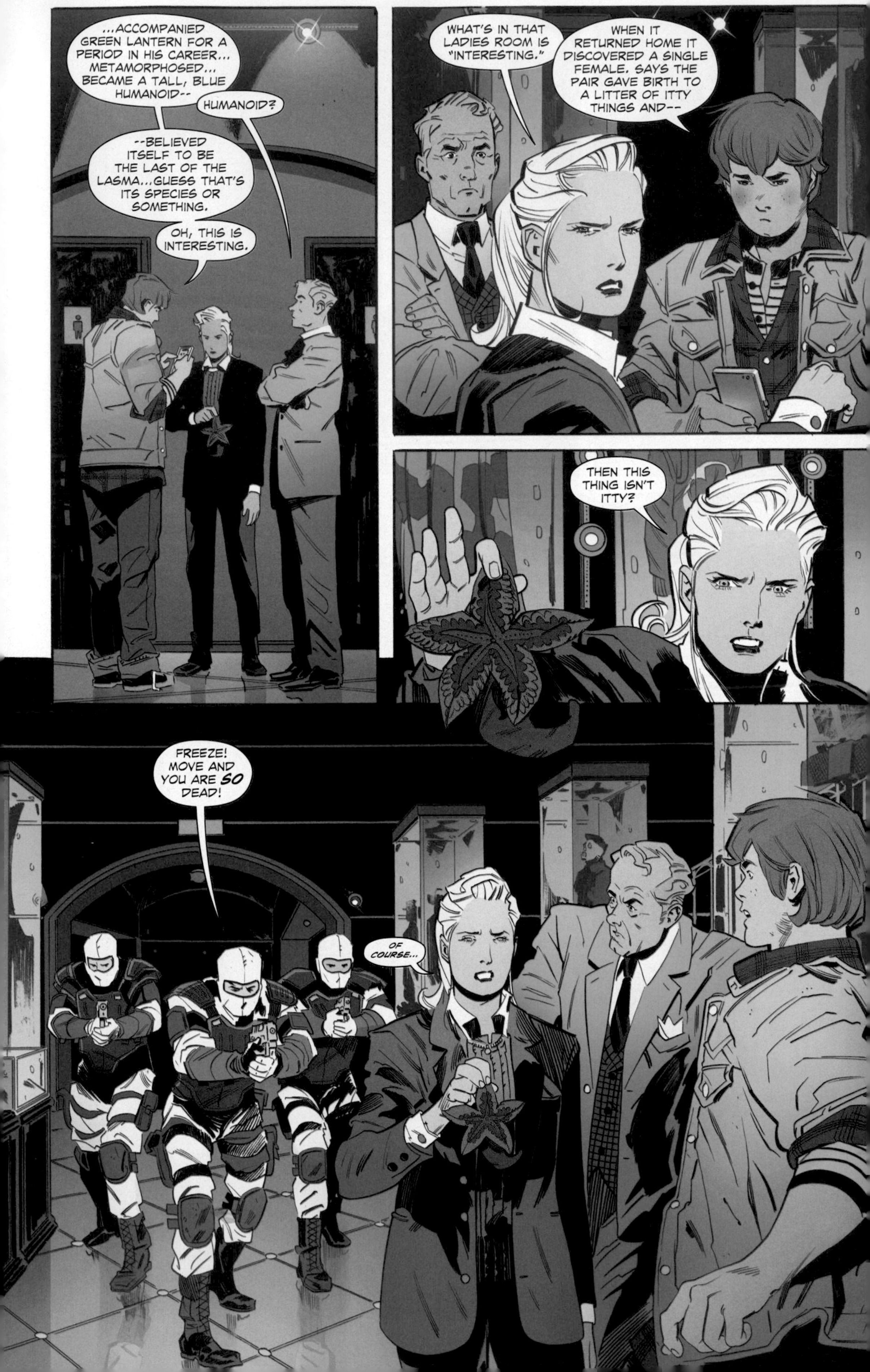
...ACCOMPANIED GREEN LANTERN FOR A PERIOD IN HIS CAREER... METAMORPHOSED... BECAME A TALL, BLUE HUMANOID--
HUMANOID?
--BELIEVED ITSELF TO BE THE LAST OF THE LASMA...GUESS THAT'S ITS SPECIES OR SOMETHING.
OH, THIS IS INTERESTING.
WHAT'S IN THAT LADIES ROOM IS "INTERESTING."
WHEN IT RETURNED HOME IT DISCOVERED A SINGLE FEMALE. SAYS THE PAIR GAVE BIRTH TO A LITTER OF ITTY THINGS AND--
THEN THIS THING ISN'T ITTY?
FREEZE! MOVE AND YOU ARE *SO* DEAD!
OF COURSE...

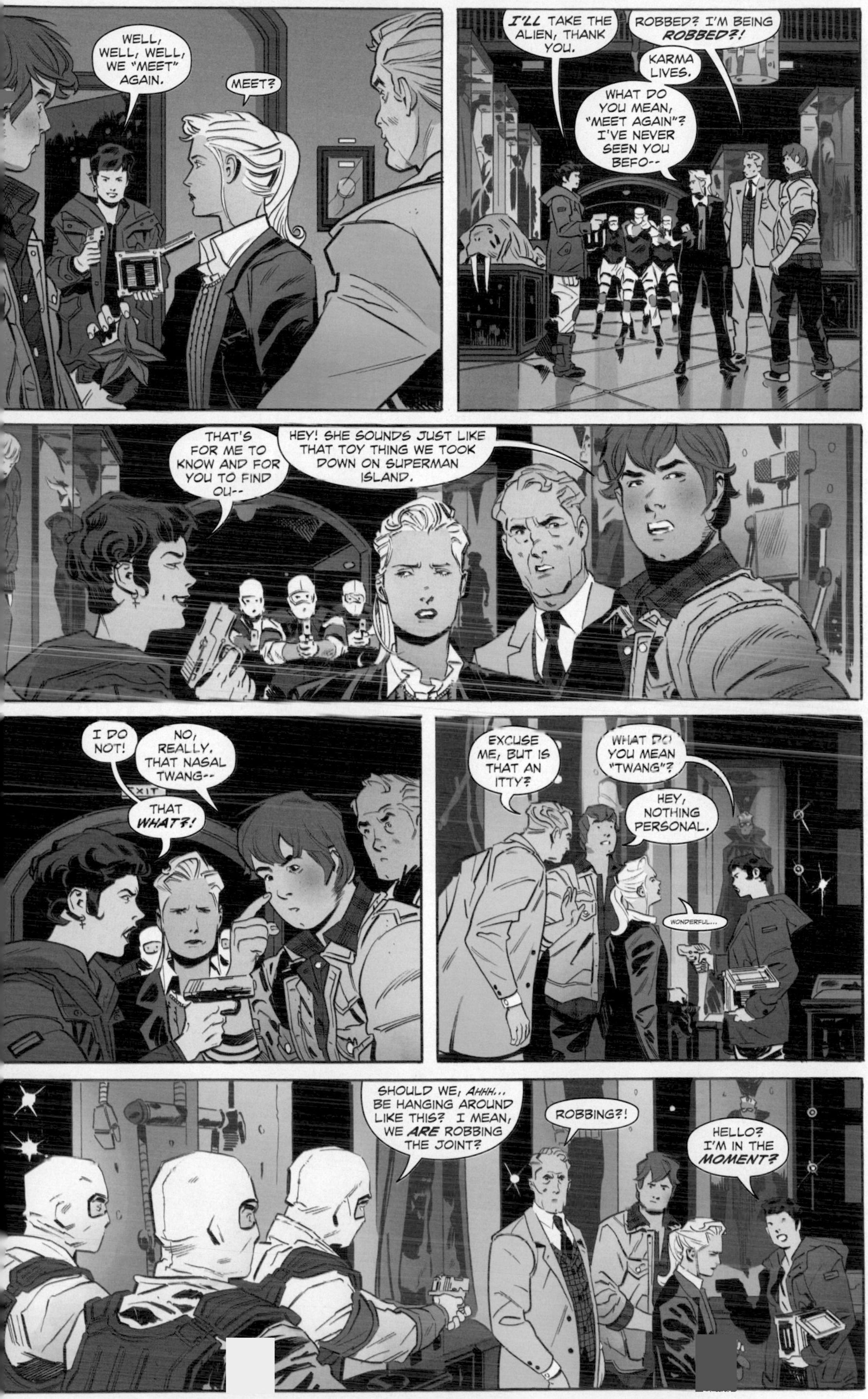
WELL, WELL, WELL, WE "MEET" AGAIN.
MEET?
I'LL TAKE THE ALIEN, THANK YOU.
ROBBED? I'M BEING ROBBED?!
KARMA LIVES.
WHAT DO YOU MEAN, "MEET AGAIN"? I'VE NEVER SEEN YOU BEFO--
THAT'S FOR ME TO KNOW AND FOR YOU TO FIND OU--
HEY! SHE SOUNDS JUST LIKE THAT TOY THING WE TOOK DOWN ON SUPERMAN ISLAND.
I DO NOT!
NO, REALLY. THAT NASAL TWANG--
EXIT
THAT WHAT?!
EXCUSE ME, BUT IS THAT AN ITTY?
WHAT DO YOU MEAN "TWANG"?
HEY, NOTHING PERSONAL.
WONDERFUL...
SHOULD WE, AHHH... BE HANGING AROUND LIKE THIS? I MEAN, WE ARE ROBBING THE JOINT?
ROBBING?!
HELLO? I'M IN THE MOMENT?

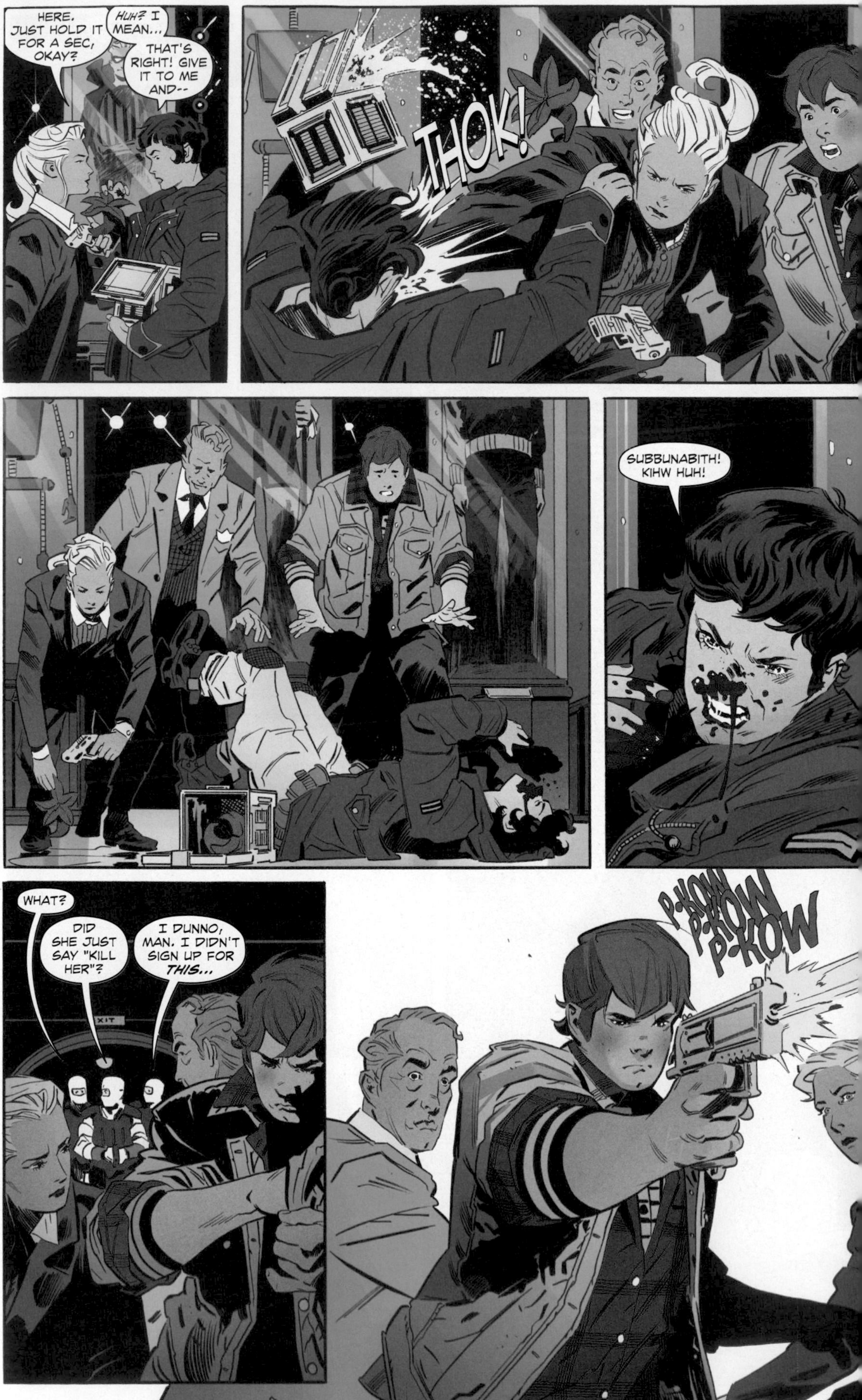
HERE. JUST HOLD IT FOR A SEC, OKAY?
HUH? I MEAN...
THAT'S RIGHT! GIVE IT TO ME AND--
THOK!
SUBBUNABITH! KIHW HUH!
WHAT?
DID SHE JUST SAY "KILL HER"?
I DUNNO, MAN. I DIDN'T SIGN UP FOR THIS...
P-KOW P-KOW P-KOW

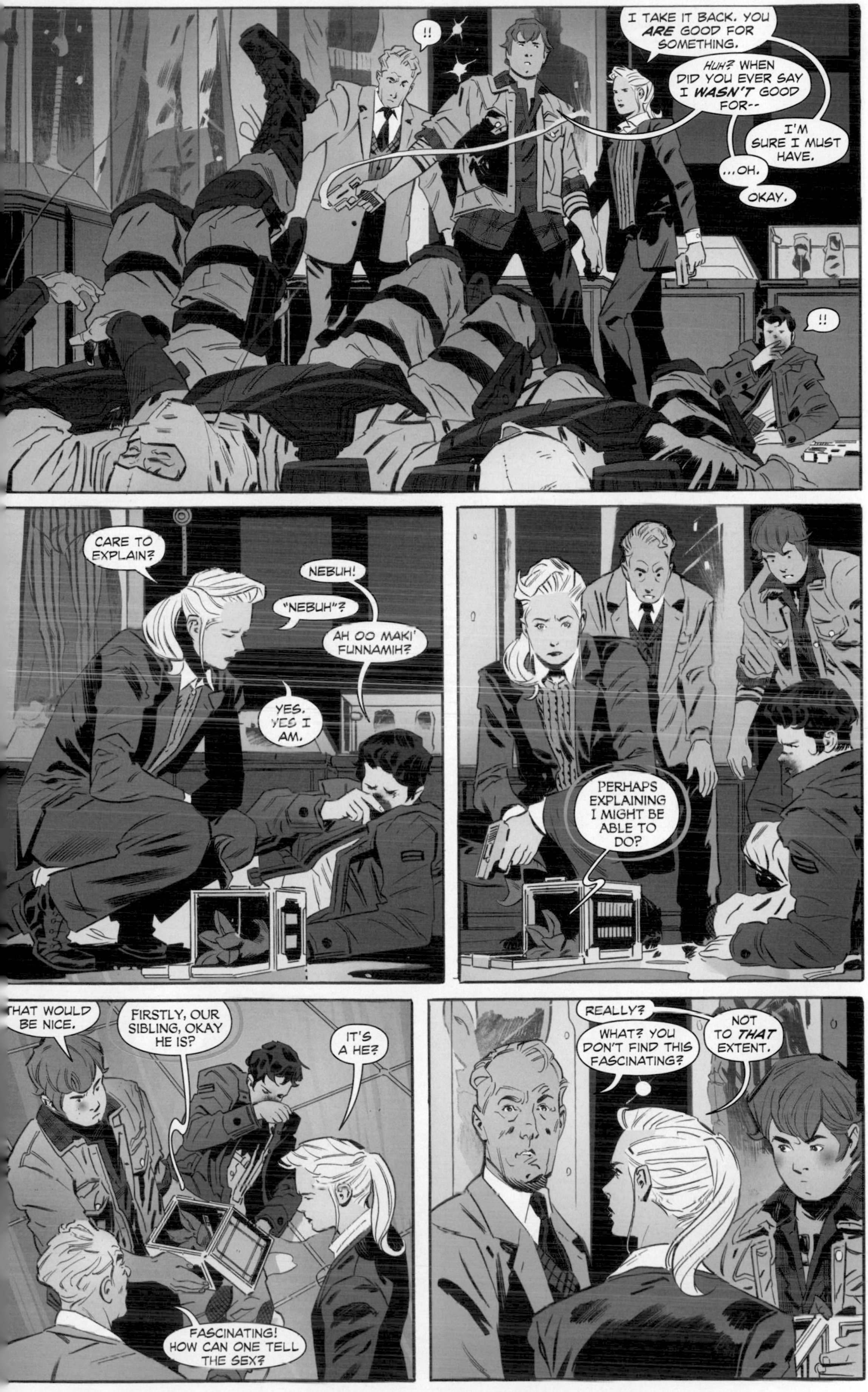
!!
I TAKE IT BACK. YOU ARE GOOD FOR SOMETHING.
HUH? WHEN DID YOU EVER SAY I WASN'T GOOD FOR--
I'M SURE I MUST HAVE.
...OH.
OKAY.
!!
CARE TO EXPLAIN?
NEBUH!
"NEBUH"?
AH OO MAKI' FUNNAMIH?
YES. YES, I AM.
PERHAPS EXPLAINING I MIGHT BE ABLE TO DO?
THAT WOULD BE NICE.
FIRSTLY, OUR SIBLING, OKAY HE IS?
IT'S A HE?
FASCINATING! HOW CAN ONE TELL THE SEX?
REALLY?
WHAT? YOU DON'T FIND THIS FASCINATING?
NOT TO THAT EXTENT.

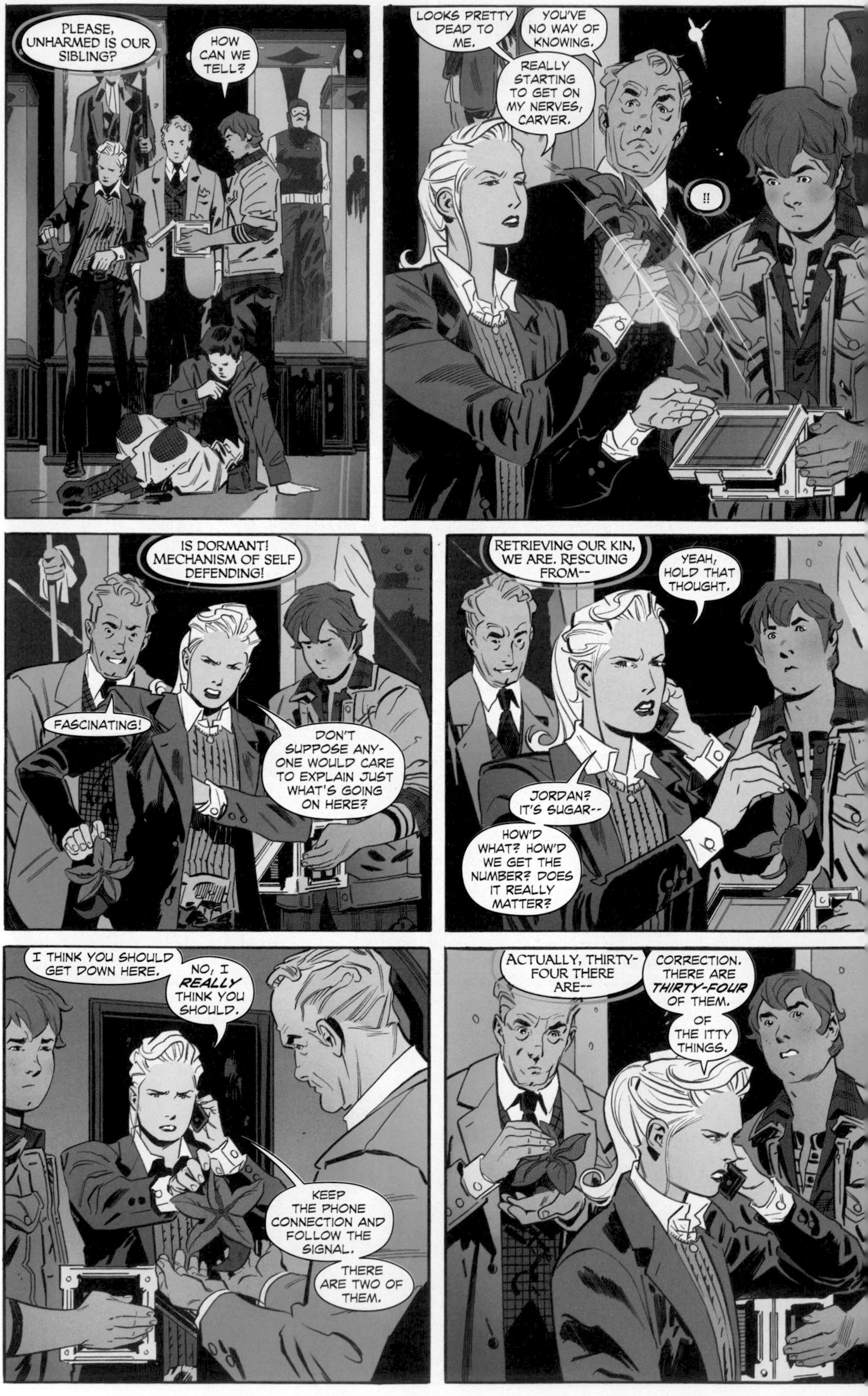
PLEASE, UNHARMED IS OUR SIBLING?
HOW CAN WE TELL?
LOOKS PRETTY DEAD TO ME.
YOU'VE NO WAY OF KNOWING.
REALLY STARTING TO GET ON MY NERVES, CARVER.
!!
IS DORMANT! MECHANISM OF SELF DEFENDING!
FASCINATING!
DON'T SUPPOSE ANY-ONE WOULD CARE TO EXPLAIN JUST WHAT'S GOING ON HERE?
RETRIEVING OUR KIN, WE ARE. RESCUING FROM--
YEAH, HOLD THAT THOUGHT.
JORDAN? IT'S SUGAR--
HOW'D WHAT? HOW'D WE GET THE NUMBER? DOES IT REALLY MATTER?
I THINK YOU SHOULD GET DOWN HERE.
NO, I *REALLY* THINK YOU SHOULD.
KEEP THE PHONE CONNECTION AND FOLLOW THE SIGNAL.
THERE ARE TWO OF THEM.
ACTUALLY, THIRTY-FOUR THERE ARE--
CORRECTION. THERE ARE *THIRTY-FOUR* OF THEM.
OF THE ITTY THINGS.

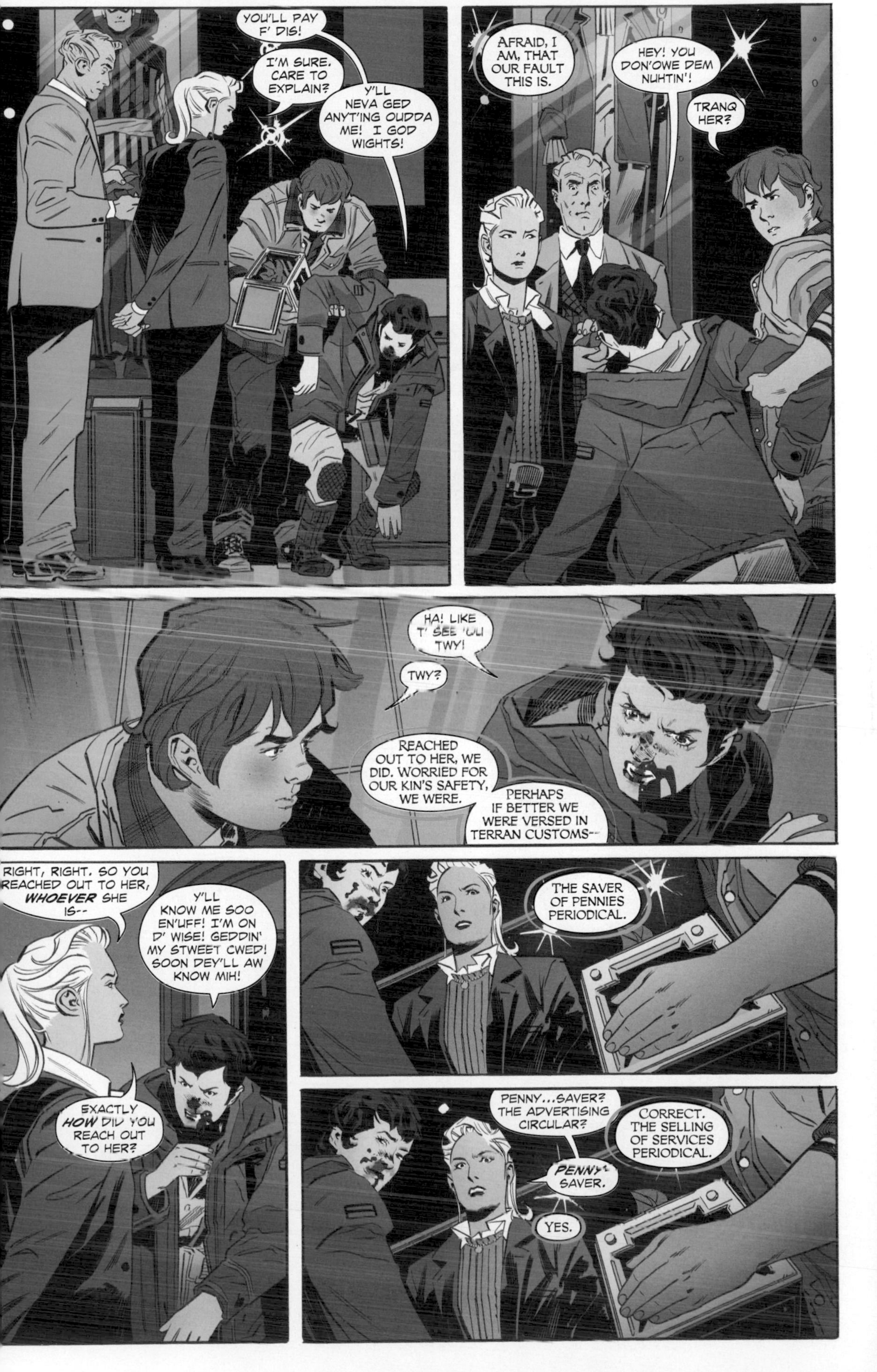

YOU'LL PAY F' DIS!
I'M SURE. CARE TO EXPLAIN?
Y'LL NEVA GED ANYT'ING OUDDA ME! I GOD WIGHTS!
AFRAID, I AM, THAT OUR FAULT THIS IS.
HEY! YOU DON'OWE DEM NUHTIN'!
TRANQ HER?
HA! LIKE T' SEE 'UU TWY!
TWY?
REACHED OUT TO HER, WE DID. WORRIED FOR OUR KIN'S SAFETY, WE WERE.
PERHAPS IF BETTER WE WERE VERSED IN TERRAN CUSTOMS--
RIGHT, RIGHT. SO YOU REACHED OUT TO HER, WHOEVER SHE IS--
Y'LL KNOW ME SOO EN'UFF! I'M ON D' WISE! GEDDIN' MY STWEET CWED! SOON DEY'LL AW KNOW MIH!
EXACTLY HOW DID YOU REACH OUT TO HER?
THE SAVER OF PENNIES PERIODICAL.
PENNY...SAVER? THE ADVERTISING CIRCULAR?
CORRECT. THE SELLING OF SERVICES PERIODICAL.
PENNY- SAVER.
YES.

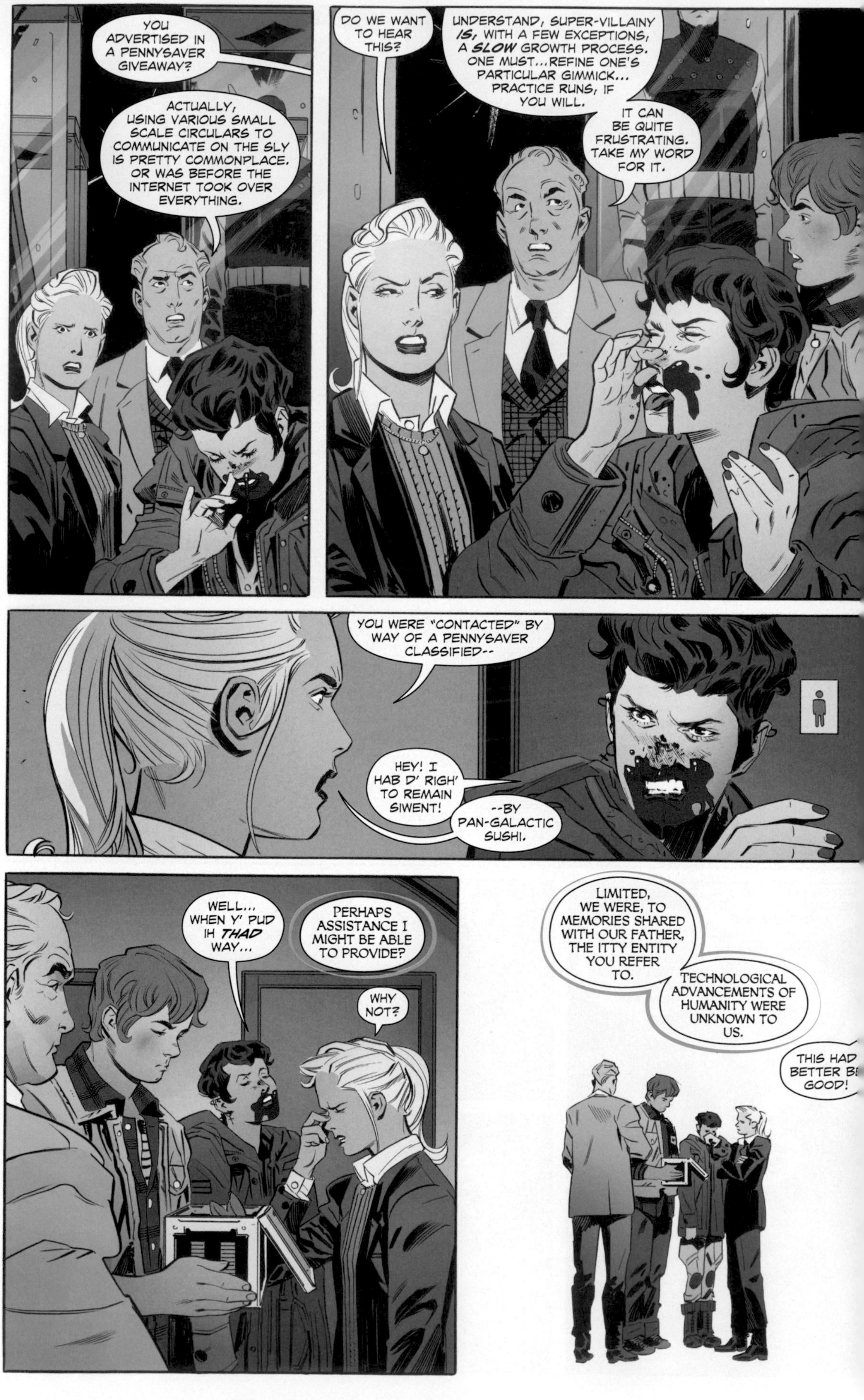

YOU ADVERTISED IN A PENNYSAVER GIVEAWAY?
ACTUALLY, USING VARIOUS SMALL SCALE CIRCULARS TO COMMUNICATE ON THE SLY IS PRETTY COMMONPLACE. OR WAS BEFORE THE INTERNET TOOK OVER EVERYTHING.
DO WE WANT TO HEAR THIS?
UNDERSTAND, SUPER-VILLAINY *IS,* WITH A FEW EXCEPTIONS, A *SLOW* GROWTH PROCESS. ONE MUST...REFINE ONE'S PARTICULAR GIMMICK... PRACTICE RUNS, IF YOU WILL.
IT CAN BE QUITE FRUSTRATING. TAKE MY WORD FOR IT.
YOU WERE "CONTACTED" BY WAY OF A PENNYSAVER CLASSIFIED--
HEY! I HAB D' RIGH' TO REMAIN SIWENT!
--BY PAN-GALACTIC SUSHI.
WELL... WHEN Y' PUD IH *THAD* WAY...
PERHAPS ASSISTANCE I MIGHT BE ABLE TO PROVIDE?
WHY NOT?
LIMITED, WE WERE, TO MEMORIES SHARED WITH OUR FATHER, THE ITTY ENTITY YOU REFER TO.
TECHNOLOGICAL ADVANCEMENTS OF HUMANITY WERE UNKNOWN TO US.

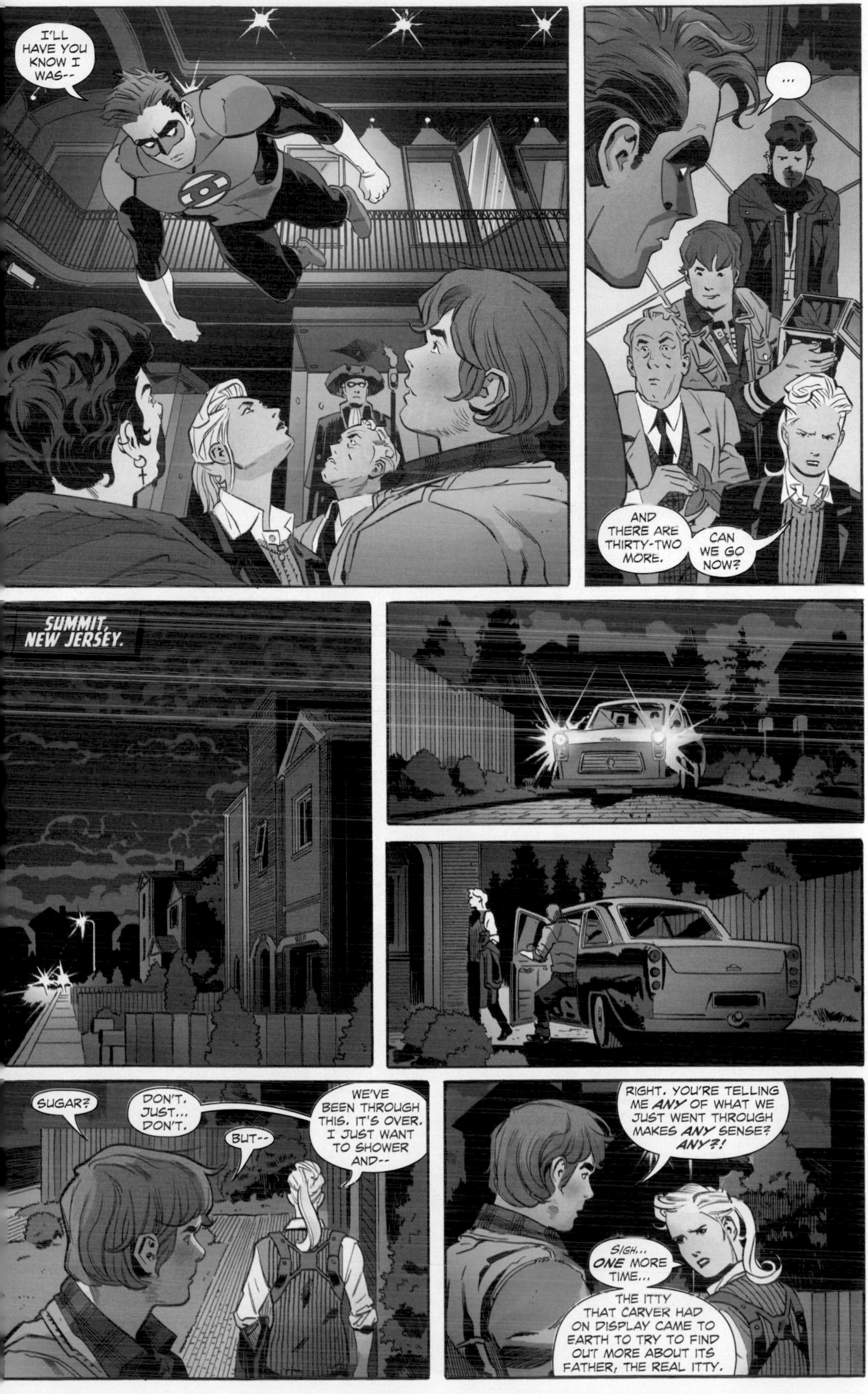
I'LL HAVE YOU KNOW I WAS--
...
AND THERE ARE THIRTY-TWO MORE.
CAN WE GO NOW?
SUMMIT, NEW JERSEY.
SUGAR?
DON'T. JUST... DON'T.
BUT--
WE'VE BEEN THROUGH THIS. IT'S OVER. I JUST WANT TO SHOWER AND--
RIGHT. YOU'RE TELLING ME *ANY* OF WHAT WE JUST WENT THROUGH MAKES *ANY* SENSE? *ANY?!*
SIGH... *ONE* MORE TIME...
THE ITTY THAT CARVER HAD ON DISPLAY CAME TO EARTH TO TRY TO FIND OUT MORE ABOUT ITS FATHER, THE REAL ITTY.

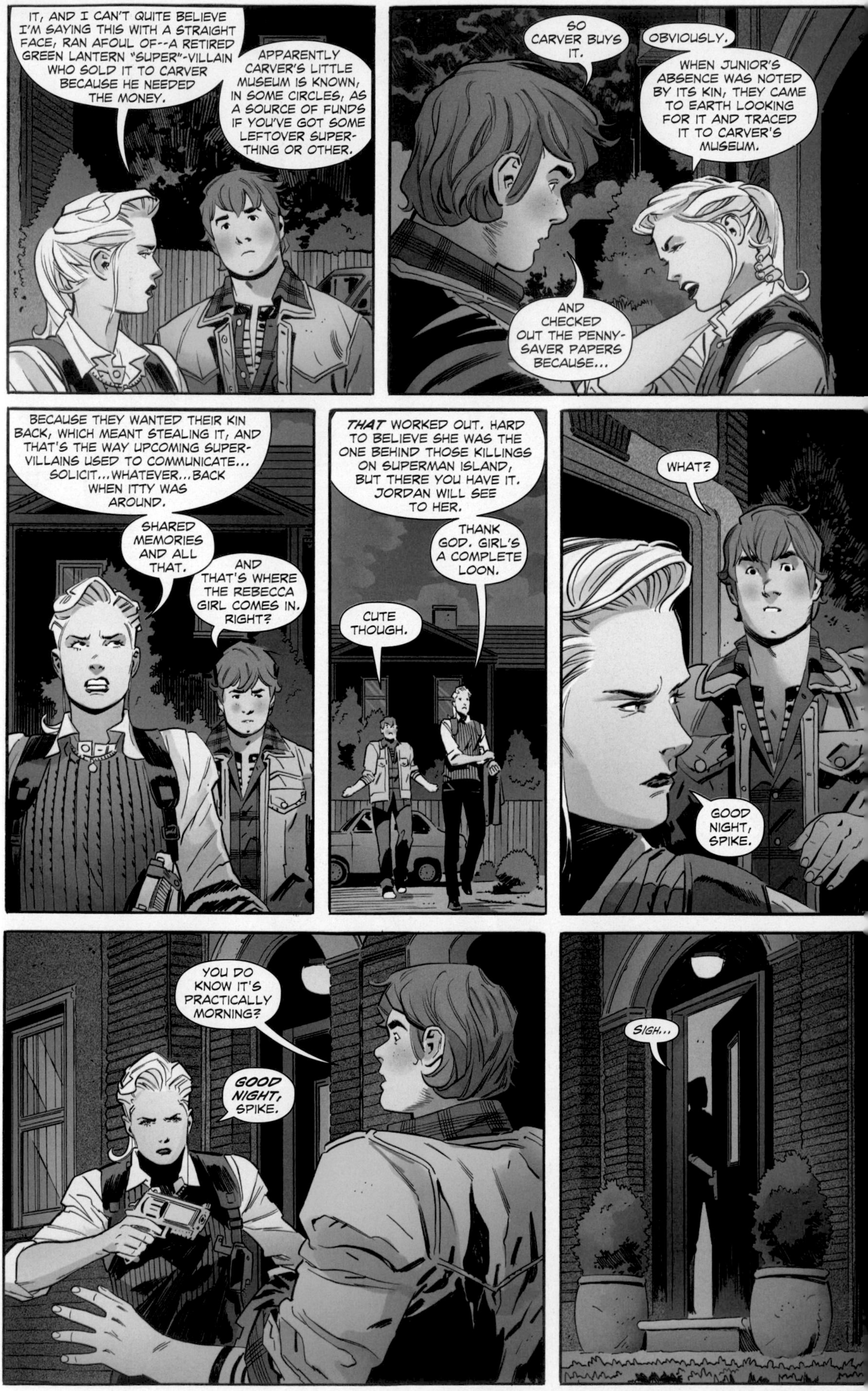
IT, AND I CAN'T QUITE BELIEVE I'M SAYING THIS WITH A STRAIGHT FACE, RAN AFOUL OF--A RETIRED GREEN LANTERN "SUPER"-VILLAIN WHO SOLD IT TO CARVER BECAUSE HE NEEDED THE MONEY.
APPARENTLY CARVER'S LITTLE MUSEUM IS KNOWN, IN SOME CIRCLES, AS A SOURCE OF FUNDS IF YOU'VE GOT SOME LEFTOVER SUPER-THING OR OTHER.
SO CARVER BUYS IT.
OBVIOUSLY.
WHEN JUNIOR'S ABSENCE WAS NOTED BY ITS KIN, THEY CAME TO EARTH LOOKING FOR IT AND TRACED IT TO CARVER'S MUSEUM.
AND CHECKED OUT THE PENNY-SAVER PAPERS BECAUSE...
BECAUSE THEY WANTED THEIR KIN BACK, WHICH MEANT STEALING IT, AND THAT'S THE WAY UPCOMING SUPER-VILLAINS USED TO COMMUNICATE... SOLICIT...WHATEVER...BACK WHEN ITTY WAS AROUND.
SHARED MEMORIES AND ALL THAT.
AND THAT'S WHERE THE REBECCA GIRL COMES IN. RIGHT?
THAT WORKED OUT. HARD TO BELIEVE SHE WAS THE ONE BEHIND THOSE KILLINGS ON SUPERMAN ISLAND, BUT THERE YOU HAVE IT. JORDAN WILL SEE TO HER.
THANK GOD. GIRL'S A COMPLETE LOON.
CUTE THOUGH.
WHAT?
GOOD NIGHT, SPIKE.
YOU DO KNOW IT'S PRACTICALLY MORNING?
GOOD NIGHT, SPIKE.
SIGH...

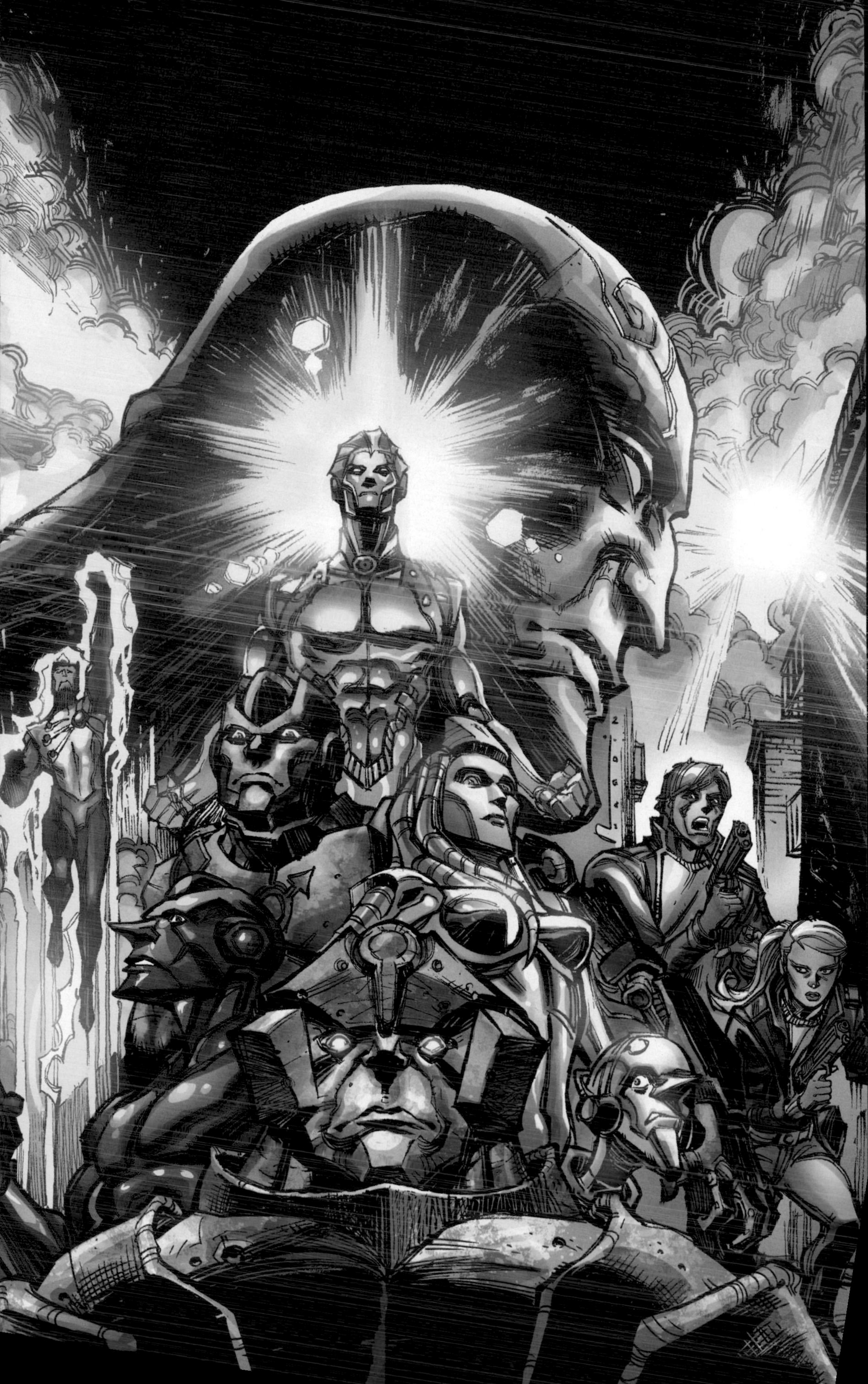

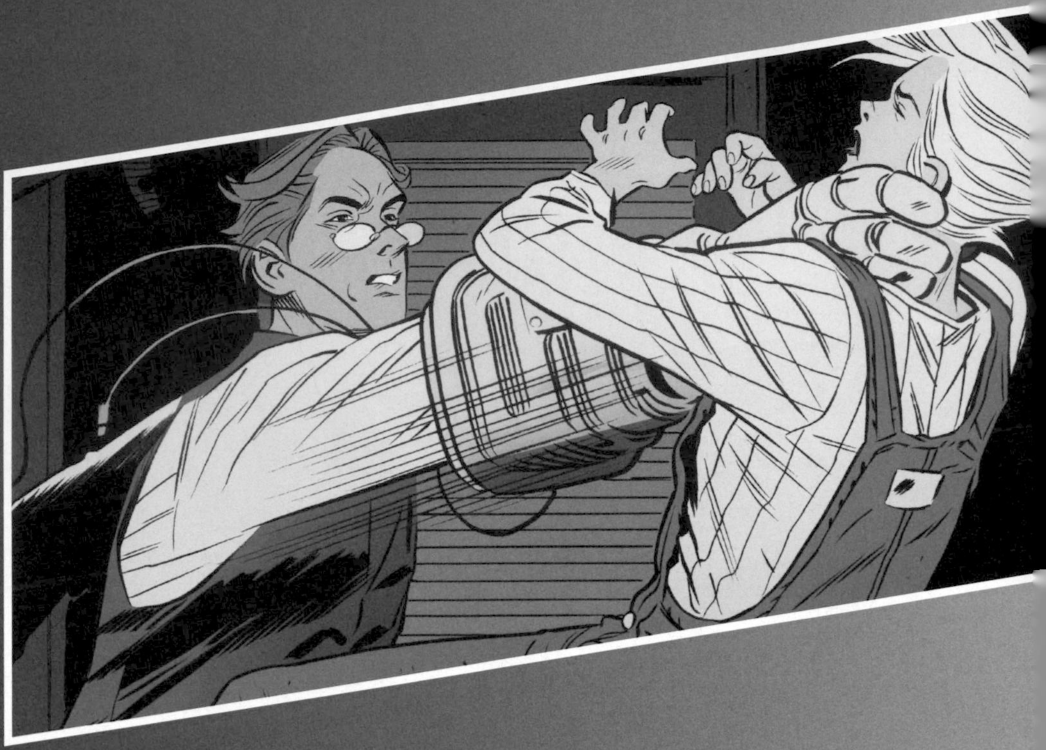

CHAD HARDIN
and **PAUL MOUNTS**
cover

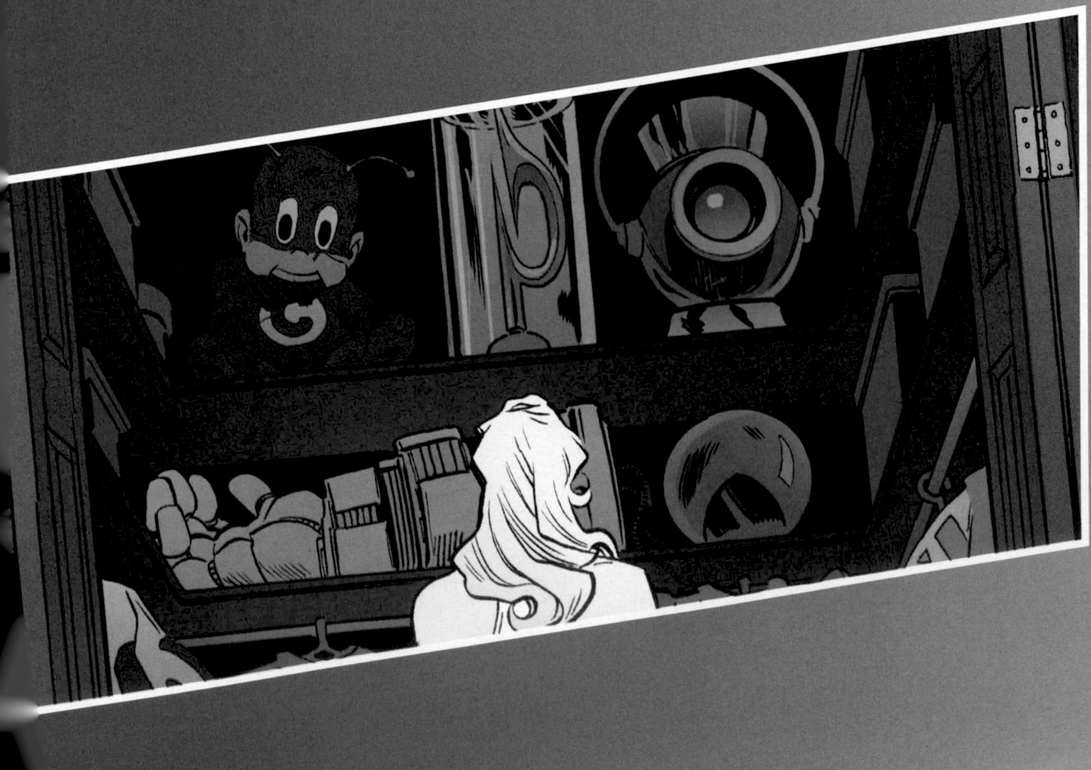

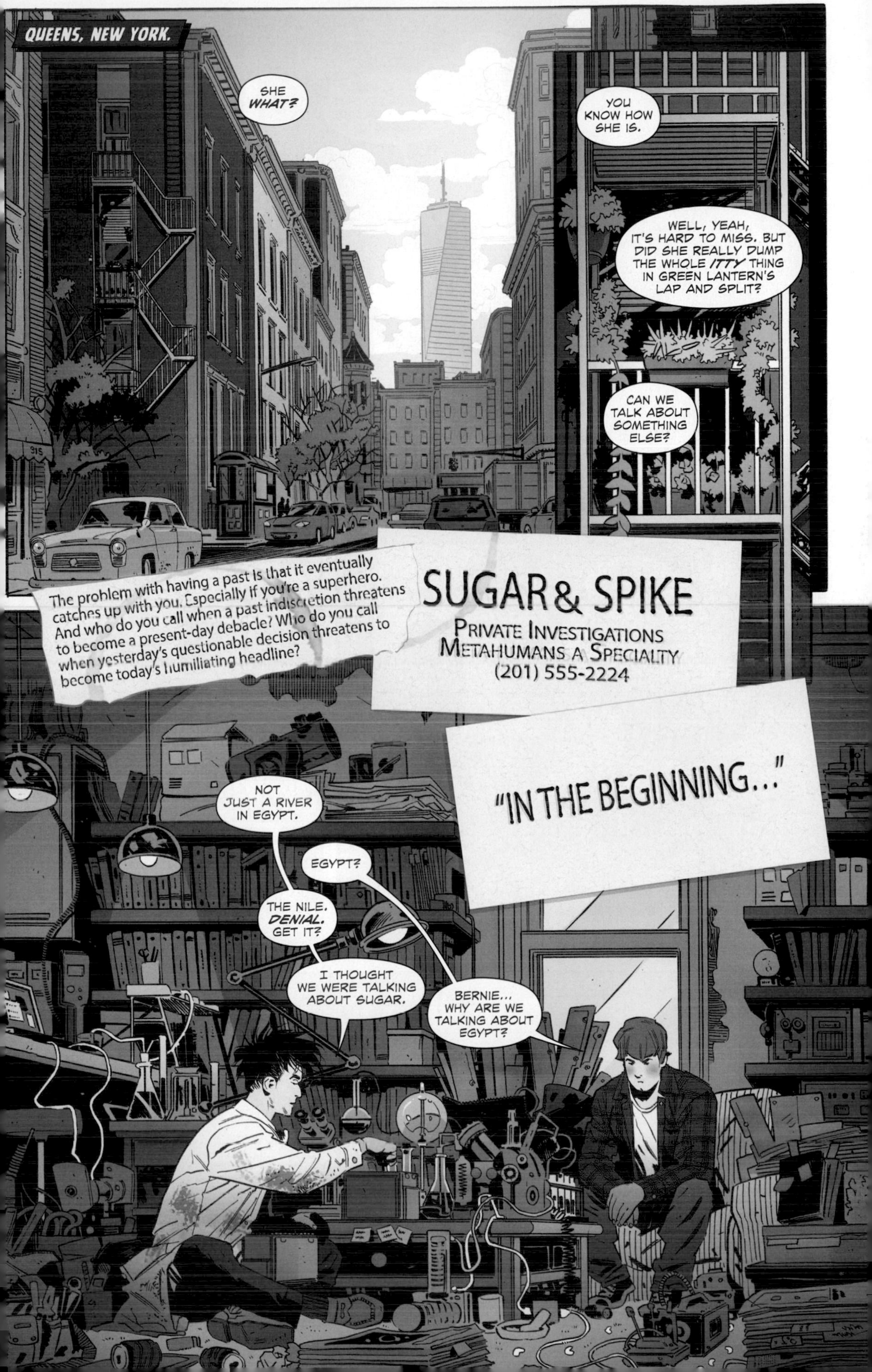

QUEENS, NEW YORK.
SHE *WHAT?*
YOU KNOW HOW SHE IS.
WELL, YEAH, IT'S HARD TO MISS. BUT DID SHE REALLY DUMP THE WHOLE *ITTY* THING IN GREEN LANTERN'S LAP AND SPLIT?
CAN WE TALK ABOUT SOMETHING ELSE?
The problem with having a past is that it eventually catches up with you. Especially if you're a superhero. And who do you call when a past indiscretion threatens to become a present-day debacle? Who do you call when yesterday's questionable decision threatens to become today's humiliating headline?
SUGAR & SPIKE
PRIVATE INVESTIGATIONS
METAHUMANS A SPECIALTY
(201) 555-2224
"IN THE BEGINNING..."
NOT JUST A RIVER IN EGYPT.
EGYPT?
THE NILE. *DENIAL.* GET IT?
I THOUGHT WE WERE TALKING ABOUT SUGAR.
BERNIE... WHY ARE WE TALKING ABOUT EGYPT?

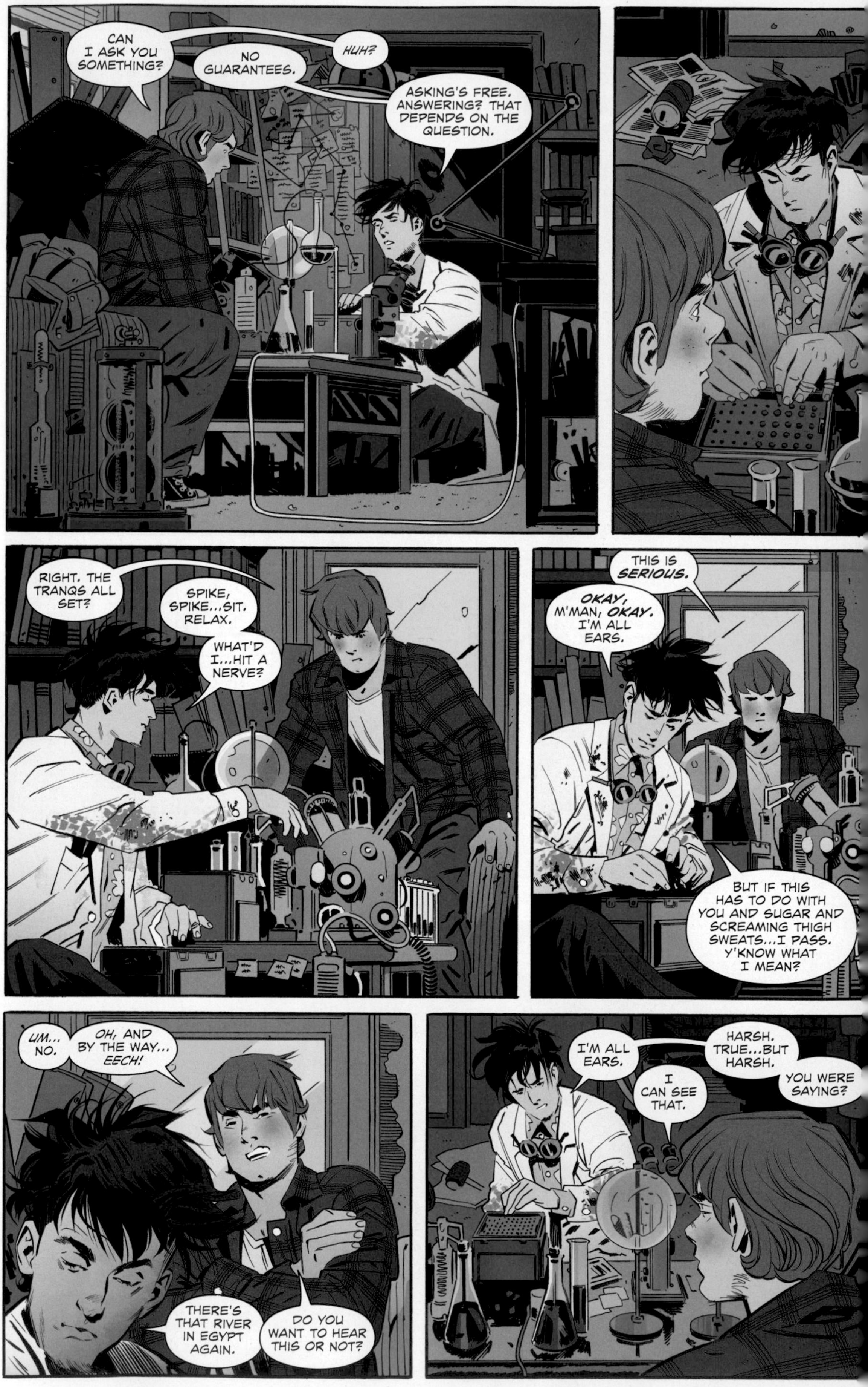
CAN I ASK YOU SOMETHING?
HUH?
NO GUARANTEES.
ASKING'S FREE. ANSWERING? THAT DEPENDS ON THE QUESTION.
RIGHT. THE TRANQS ALL SET?
SPIKE, SPIKE...SIT. RELAX.
WHAT'D I...HIT A NERVE?
THIS IS SERIOUS.
OKAY, M'MAN, OKAY. I'M ALL EARS.
BUT IF THIS HAS TO DO WITH YOU AND SUGAR AND SCREAMING THIGH SWEATS...I PASS. Y'KNOW WHAT I MEAN?
UM... NO.
OH, AND BY THE WAY... EECH!
THERE'S THAT RIVER IN EGYPT AGAIN.
DO YOU WANT TO HEAR THIS OR NOT?
I'M ALL EARS.
I CAN SEE THAT.
HARSH. TRUE...BUT HARSH.
YOU WERE SAYING?

...

THERE WERE... DEAD PEOPLE. MURDERED. ON THAT ISLAND CASE, THE KRYPTONITE STORAGE THING.

DEAD? YOU MEAN--

GOD, BERNIE, I MEAN *DEAD!* SHOT! IN COLD BLOOD!

BUT YOU GOT THE KILLER, RIGHT? THAT PSYCHO FROM THE MUSEUM?

THAT'S NOT WHAT I... I MEAN...

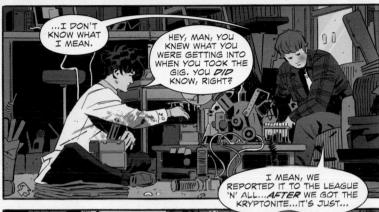

...I DON'T KNOW WHAT I MEAN.

HEY, MAN, YOU KNEW WHAT YOU WERE GETTING INTO WHEN YOU TOOK THE GIG. YOU *DID* KNOW, RIGHT?

I MEAN, WE REPORTED IT TO THE LEAGUE 'N' ALL...*AFTER* WE GOT THE KRYPTONITE...IT'S JUST...

NOT YOUR RESPONSIBILITY, MAN.

NOW YOU SOUND JUST LIKE SUGAR.

THAT WAS LOW.

I KNOW... SORRY.

LOOK, THE LEAGUE SAW TO IT, RIGHT?

I KNOW, BUT STILL--

I THOUGHT SUGAR WORKED THIS OUT WITH THE "COMMUNITY."

COMMUNITY?

THE SUPER GUYS. YOU TWO FOCUS ON YOUR MISSION--FOR LACK OF A BETTER TERM--AND THEY'LL HANDLE THE MESSY PARTS.

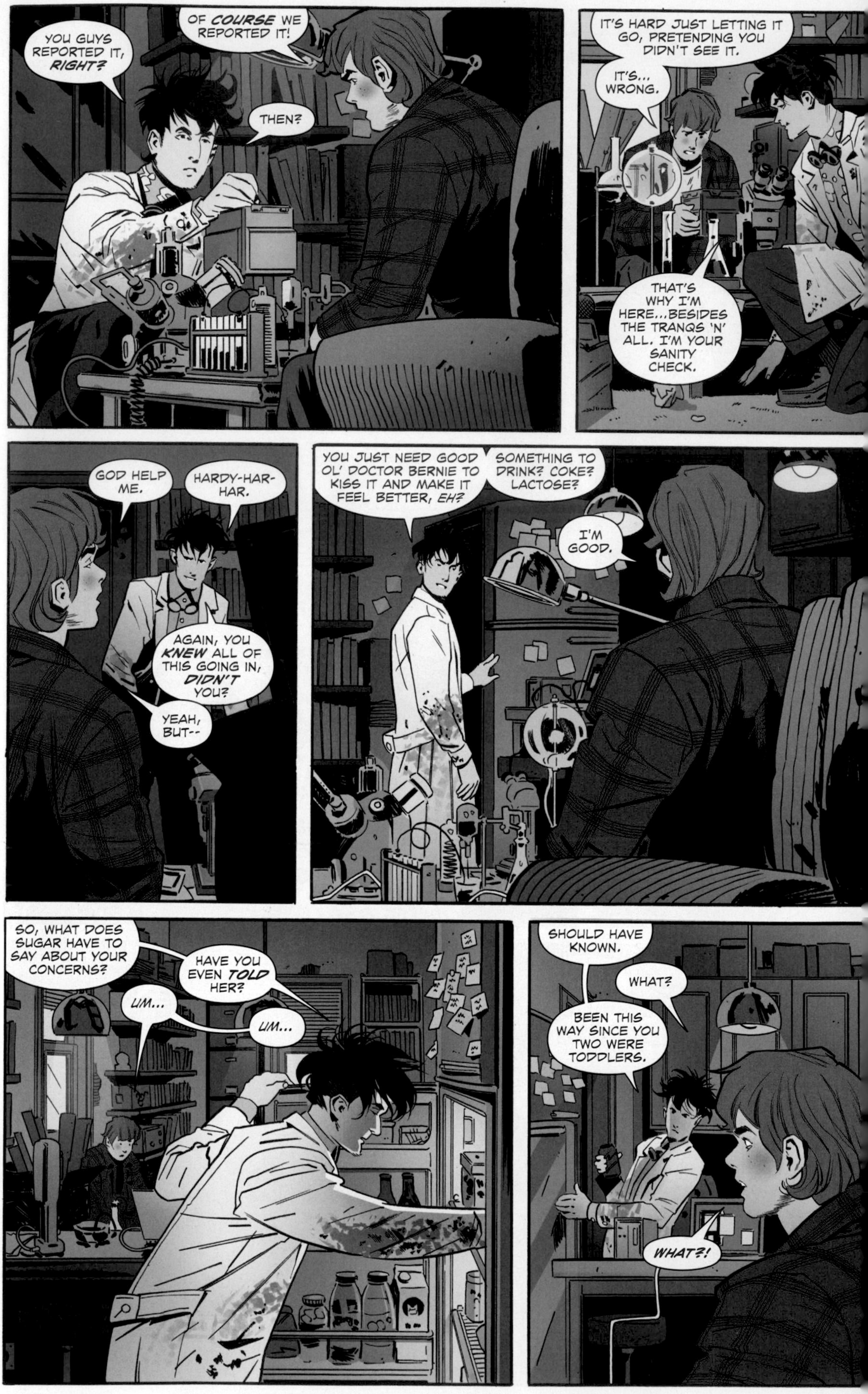
YOU GUYS REPORTED IT, RIGHT?
OF COURSE WE REPORTED IT!
THEN?
IT'S HARD JUST LETTING IT GO, PRETENDING YOU DIDN'T SEE IT.
IT'S... WRONG.
THAT'S WHY I'M HERE...BESIDES THE TRANQS 'N' ALL. I'M YOUR SANITY CHECK.
GOD HELP ME.
HARDY-HAR-HAR.
AGAIN, YOU KNEW ALL OF THIS GOING IN, DIDN'T YOU?
YEAH, BUT--
YOU JUST NEED GOOD OL' DOCTOR BERNIE TO KISS IT AND MAKE IT FEEL BETTER, EH?
SOMETHING TO DRINK? COKE? LACTOSE?
I'M GOOD.
SO, WHAT DOES SUGAR HAVE TO SAY ABOUT YOUR CONCERNS?
HAVE YOU EVEN TOLD HER?
UM...
UM...
SHOULD HAVE KNOWN.
WHAT?
BEEN THIS WAY SINCE YOU TWO WERE TODDLERS.
WHAT?!

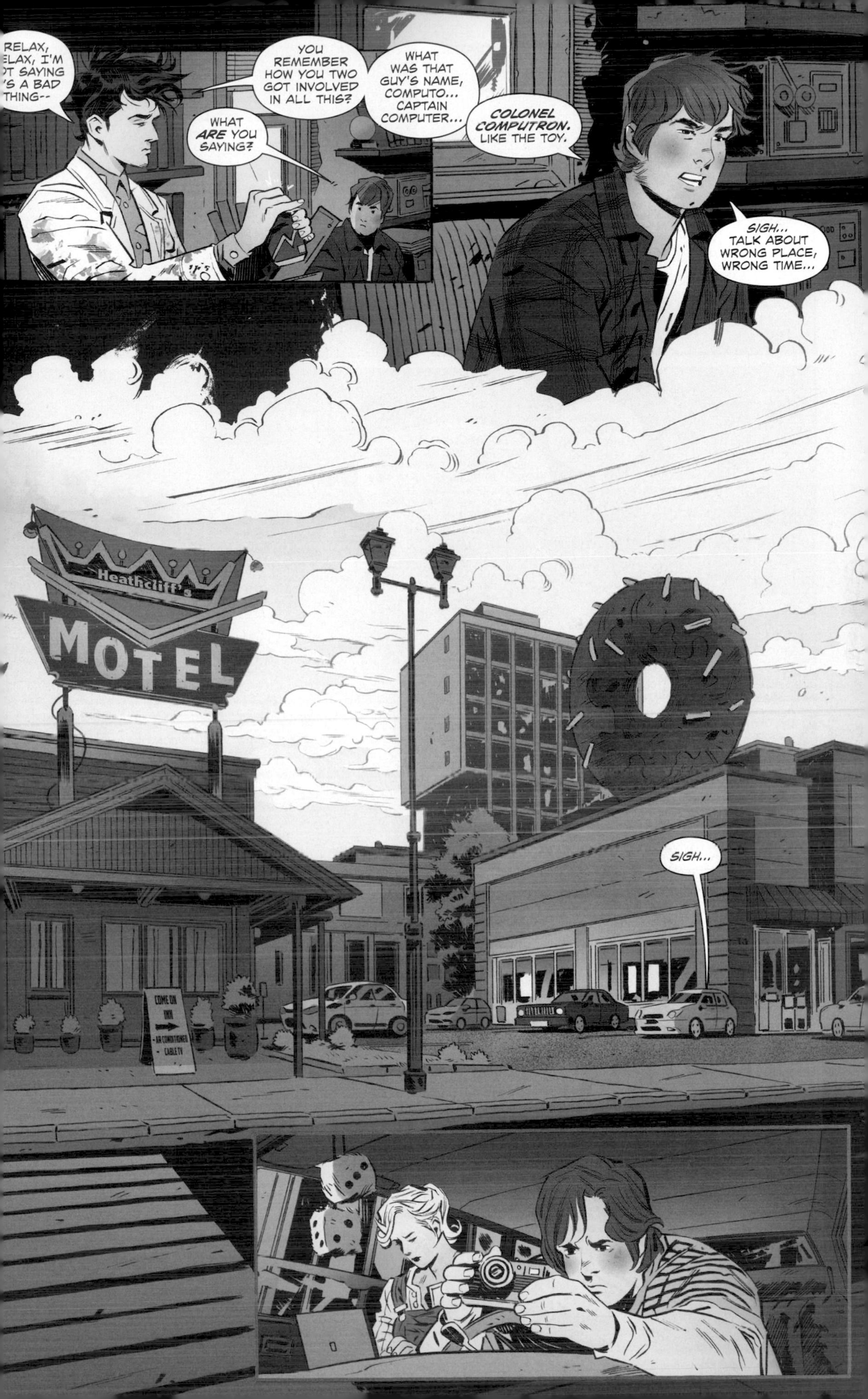

RELAX, ELAX, I'M OT SAYING 'S A BAD THING--
YOU REMEMBER HOW YOU TWO GOT INVOLVED IN ALL THIS?
WHAT ARE YOU SAYING?
WHAT WAS THAT GUY'S NAME, COMPUTO... CAPTAIN COMPUTER...
COLONEL COMPUTRON. LIKE THE TOY.
SIGH... TALK ABOUT WRONG PLACE, WRONG TIME...
Heathcliff's
MOTEL
COME ON INN
SIGH...

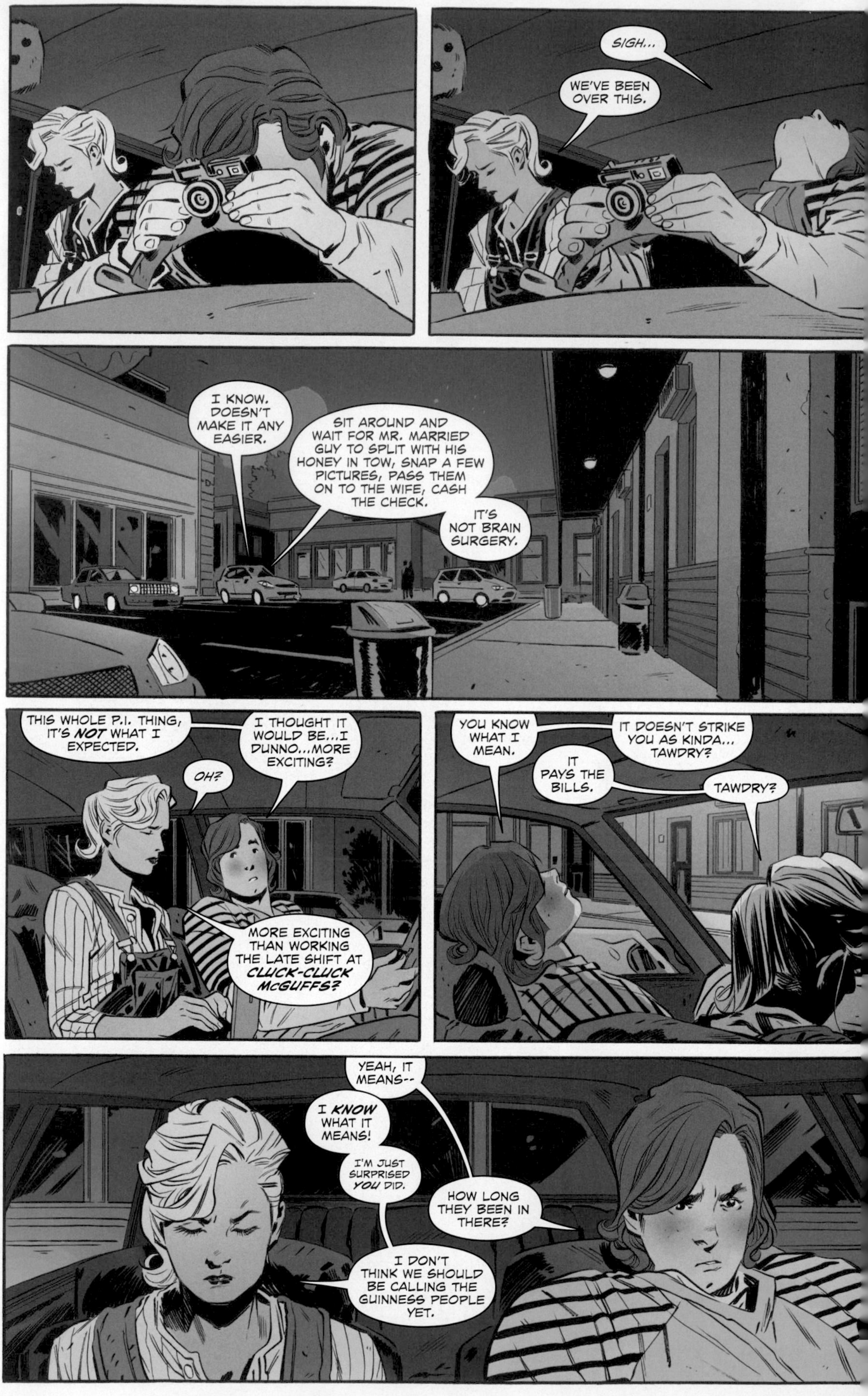
SIGH...
WE'VE BEEN OVER THIS.
I KNOW. DOESN'T MAKE IT ANY EASIER.
SIT AROUND AND WAIT FOR MR. MARRIED GUY TO SPLIT WITH HIS HONEY IN TOW, SNAP A FEW PICTURES, PASS THEM ON TO THE WIFE, CASH THE CHECK.
IT'S NOT BRAIN SURGERY.
THIS WHOLE P.I. THING, IT'S NOT WHAT I EXPECTED.
OH?
I THOUGHT IT WOULD BE...I DUNNO...MORE EXCITING?
MORE EXCITING THAN WORKING THE LATE SHIFT AT CLUCK-CLUCK McGUFFS?
YOU KNOW WHAT I MEAN.
IT DOESN'T STRIKE YOU AS KINDA... TAWDRY?
IT PAYS THE BILLS.
TAWDRY?
YEAH, IT MEANS--
I KNOW WHAT IT MEANS!
I'M JUST SURPRISED YOU DID.
HOW LONG THEY BEEN IN THERE?
I DON'T THINK WE SHOULD BE CALLING THE GUINNESS PEOPLE YET.

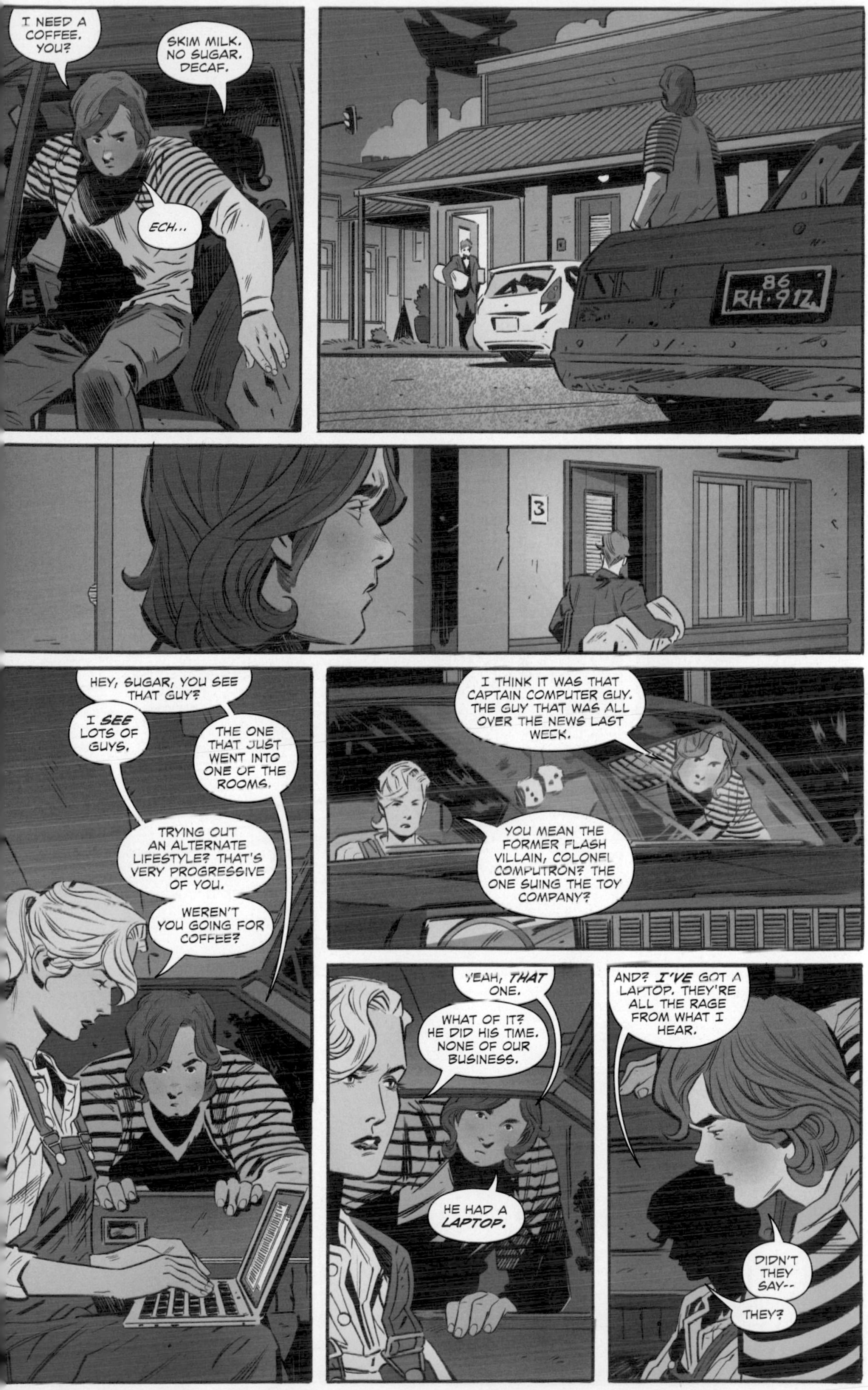
I NEED A COFFEE. YOU?
SKIM MILK. NO SUGAR. DECAF.
ECH...
86 RH·912
3
HEY, SUGAR, YOU SEE THAT GUY?
I SEE LOTS OF GUYS.
THE ONE THAT JUST WENT INTO ONE OF THE ROOMS.
TRYING OUT AN ALTERNATE LIFESTYLE? THAT'S VERY PROGRESSIVE OF YOU.
WEREN'T YOU GOING FOR COFFEE?
I THINK IT WAS THAT CAPTAIN COMPUTER GUY. THE GUY THAT WAS ALL OVER THE NEWS LAST WEEK.
YOU MEAN THE FORMER FLASH VILLAIN, COLONEL COMPUTRON? THE ONE SUING THE TOY COMPANY?
YEAH, THAT ONE.
WHAT OF IT? HE DID HIS TIME. NONE OF OUR BUSINESS.
HE HAD A LAPTOP.
AND? I'VE GOT A LAPTOP. THEY'RE ALL THE RAGE FROM WHAT I HEAR.
DIDN'T THEY SAY--
THEY?

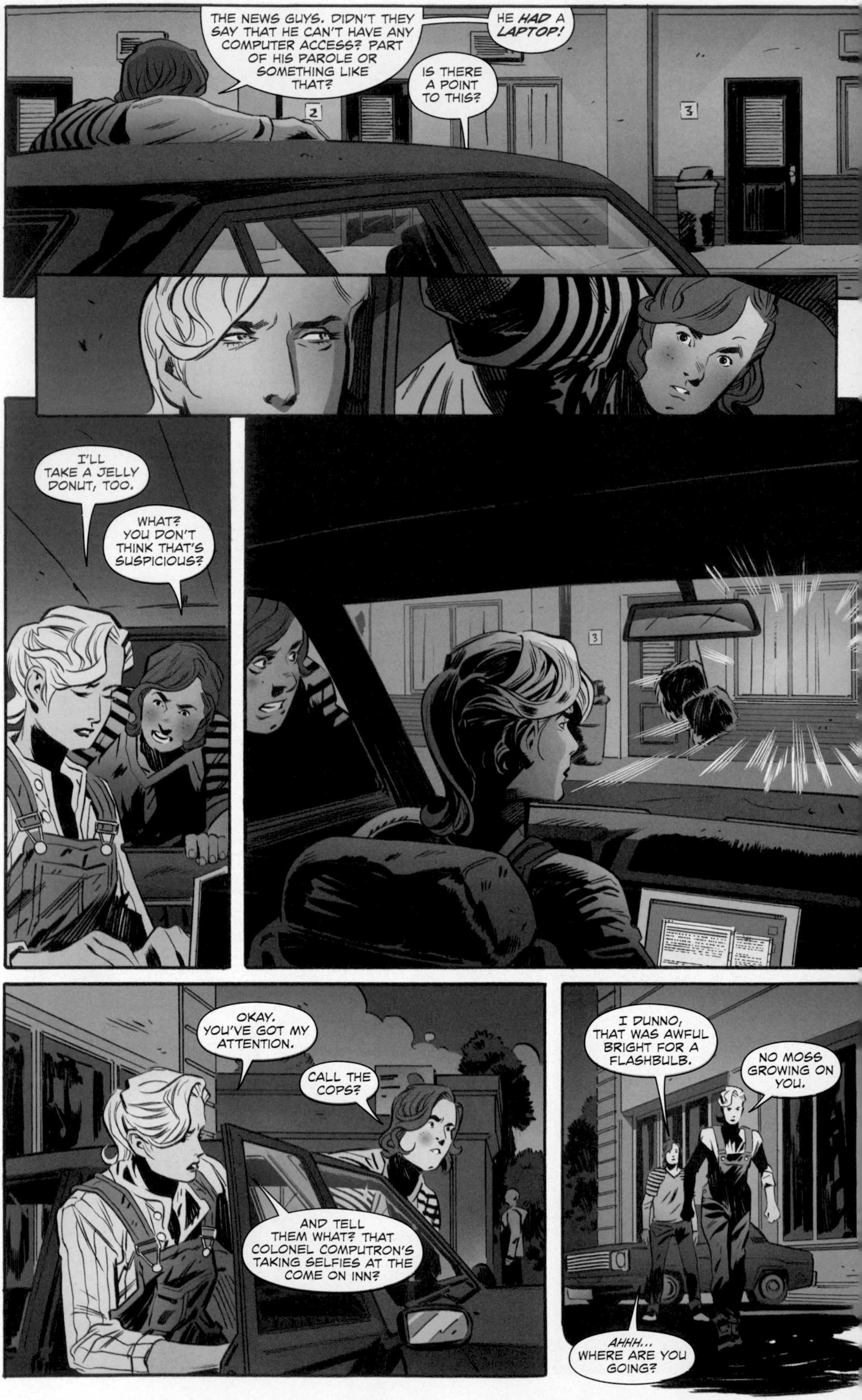
THE NEWS GUYS. DIDN'T THEY SAY THAT HE CAN'T HAVE ANY COMPUTER ACCESS? PART OF HIS PAROLE OR SOMETHING LIKE THAT?
HE *HAD* A *LAPTOP!*
IS THERE A POINT TO THIS?
2
3
I'LL TAKE A JELLY DONUT, TOO.
WHAT? YOU DON'T THINK THAT'S SUSPICIOUS?
3
OKAY. YOU'VE GOT MY ATTENTION.
CALL THE COPS?
AND TELL THEM WHAT? THAT COLONEL COMPUTRON'S TAKING SELFIES AT THE COME ON INN?
I DUNNO, THAT WAS AWFUL BRIGHT FOR A FLASHBULB.
NO MOSS GROWING ON YOU.
AHHH... WHERE ARE YOU GOING?

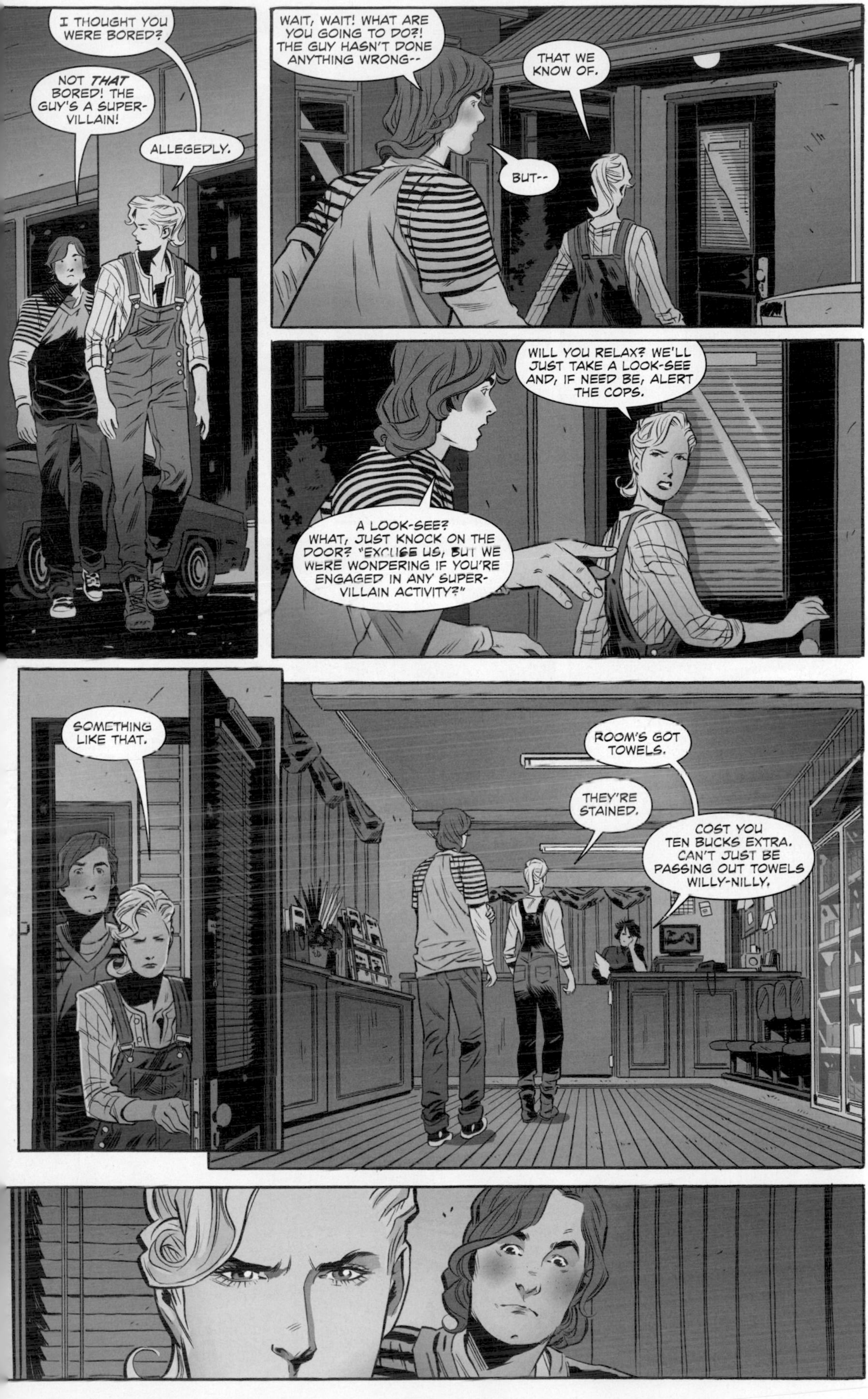
I THOUGHT YOU WERE BORED?
NOT *THAT* BORED! THE GUY'S A SUPER-VILLAIN!
ALLEGEDLY.
WAIT, WAIT! WHAT ARE YOU GOING TO DO?! THE GUY HASN'T DONE ANYTHING WRONG--
THAT WE KNOW OF.
BUT--
WILL YOU RELAX? WE'LL JUST TAKE A LOOK-SEE AND, IF NEED BE, ALERT THE COPS.
A LOOK-SEE? WHAT, JUST KNOCK ON THE DOOR? "EXCUSE US, BUT WE WERE WONDERING IF YOU'RE ENGAGED IN ANY SUPER-VILLAIN ACTIVITY?"
SOMETHING LIKE THAT.
ROOM'S GOT TOWELS.
THEY'RE STAINED.
COST YOU TEN BUCKS EXTRA. CAN'T JUST BE PASSING OUT TOWELS WILLY-NILLY.

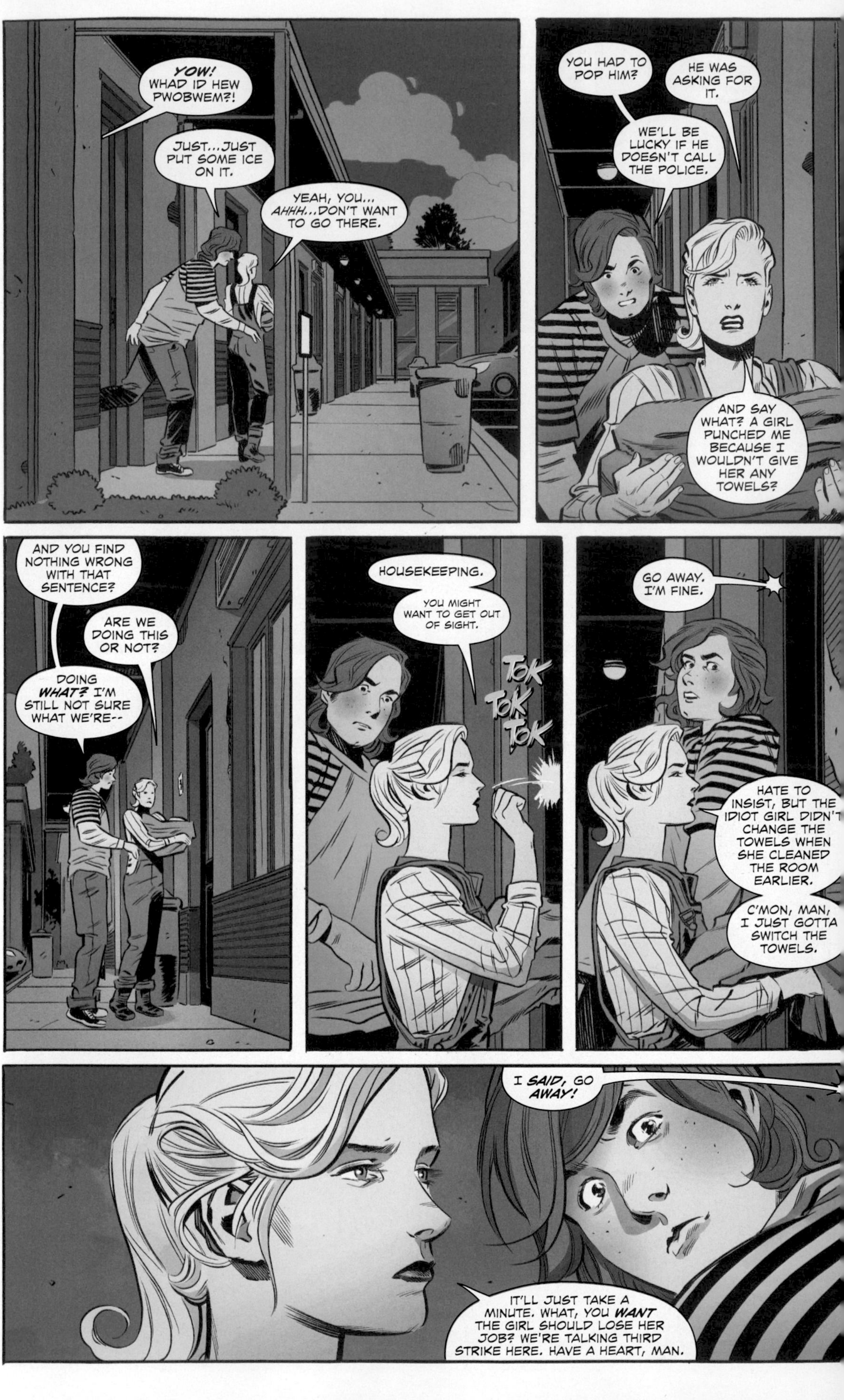
YOW! WHAD ID HEW PWOBWEM?!
JUST...JUST PUT SOME ICE ON IT.
YEAH, YOU... AHHH...DON'T WANT TO GO THERE.
YOU HAD TO POP HIM?
HE WAS ASKING FOR IT.
WE'LL BE LUCKY IF HE DOESN'T CALL THE POLICE.
AND SAY WHAT? A GIRL PUNCHED ME BECAUSE I WOULDN'T GIVE HER ANY TOWELS?
AND YOU FIND NOTHING WRONG WITH THAT SENTENCE?
ARE WE DOING THIS OR NOT?
DOING WHAT? I'M STILL NOT SURE WHAT WE'RE--
HOUSEKEEPING.
YOU MIGHT WANT TO GET OUT OF SIGHT.
TOK TOK TOK
GO AWAY. I'M FINE.
HATE TO INSIST, BUT THE IDIOT GIRL DIDN'T CHANGE THE TOWELS WHEN SHE CLEANED THE ROOM EARLIER.
C'MON, MAN, I JUST GOTTA SWITCH THE TOWELS.
I SAID, GO AWAY!
IT'LL JUST TAKE A MINUTE. WHAT, YOU WANT THE GIRL SHOULD LOSE HER JOB? WE'RE TALKING THIRD STRIKE HERE. HAVE A HEART, MAN.

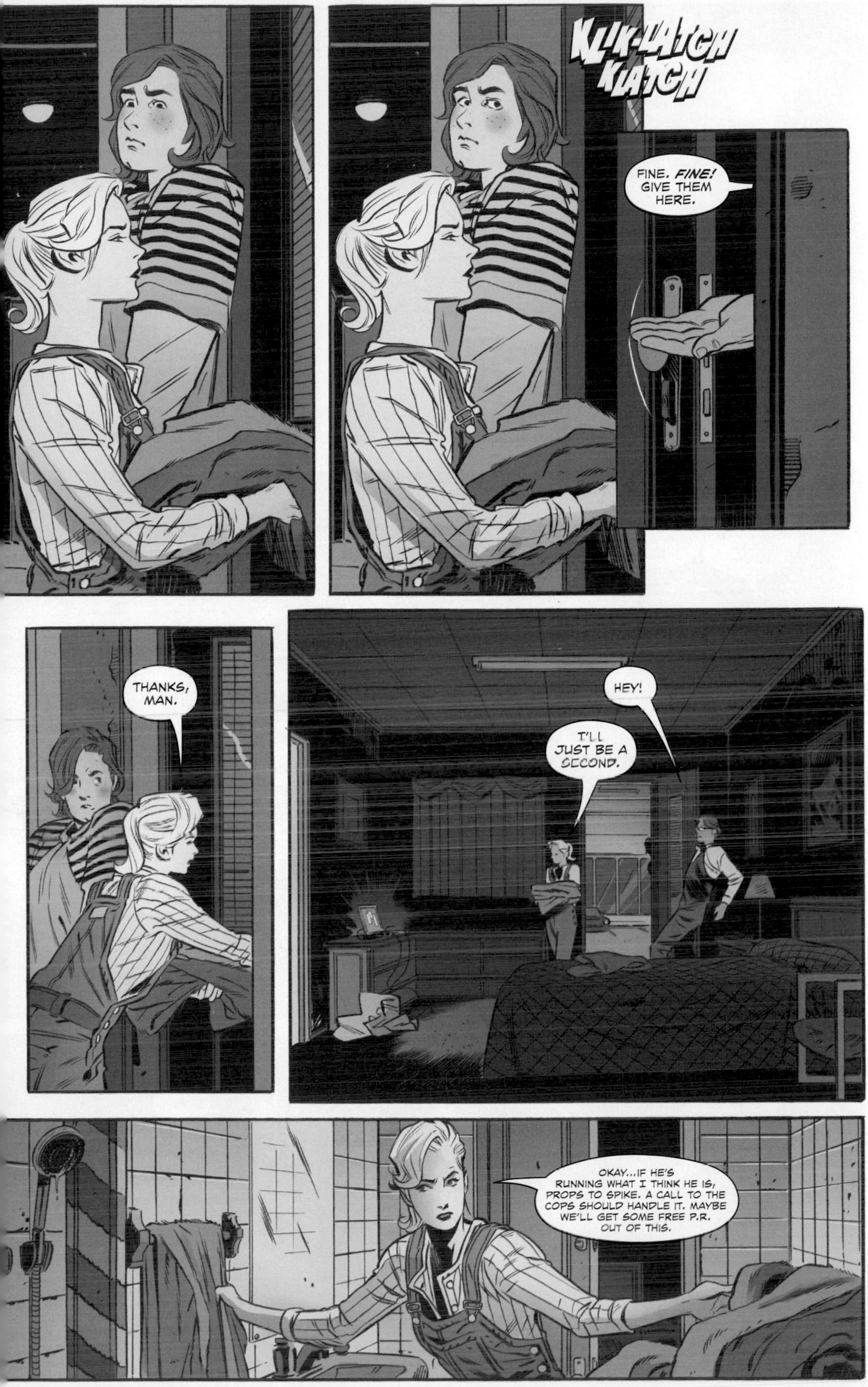
KLIK-LATCH
KLATCH
FINE. FINE! GIVE THEM HERE.
THANKS, MAN.
HEY!
I'LL JUST BE A SECOND.
OKAY...IF HE'S RUNNING WHAT I THINK HE IS, PROPS TO SPIKE. A CALL TO THE COPS SHOULD HANDLE IT. MAYBE WE'LL GET SOME FREE P.R. OUT OF THIS.

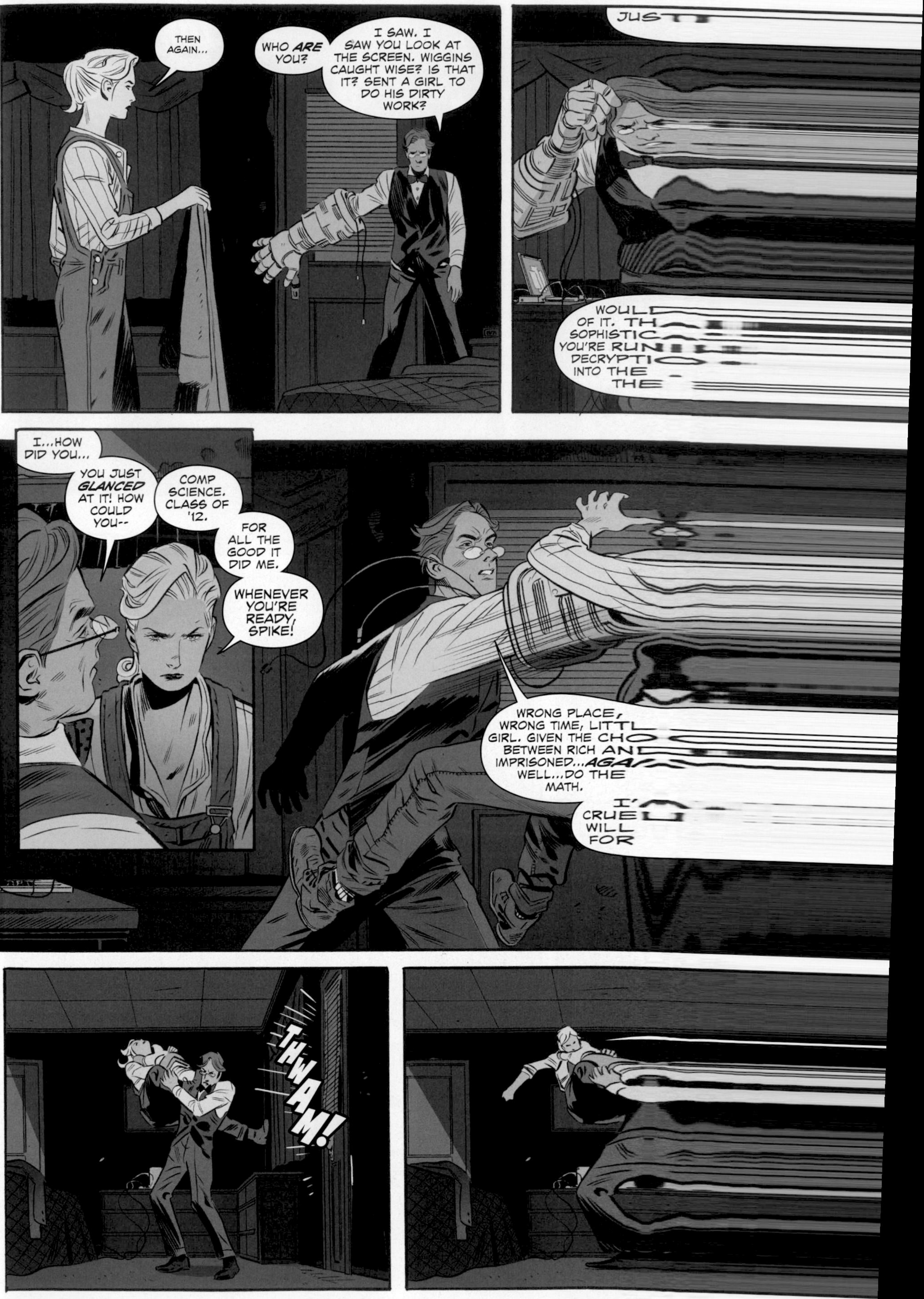
THEN AGAIN...
WHO ARE YOU?
I SAW. I SAW YOU LOOK AT THE SCREEN. WIGGINS CAUGHT WISE? IS THAT IT? SENT A GIRL TO DO HIS DIRTY WORK?
JUST
WOUL
OF IT. TH
SOPHISTICA
YOU'RE RUN
DECRYPTIO
INTO THE
THE
I...HOW DID YOU...
YOU JUST GLANCED AT IT! HOW COULD YOU--
COMP SCIENCE. CLASS OF '12.
FOR ALL THE GOOD IT DID ME.
WHENEVER YOU'RE READY, SPIKE!
WRONG PLACE, WRONG TIME, LITTL GIRL. GIVEN THE CH BETWEEN RICH AN IMPRISONED...AGA WELL...DO THE MATH.
I' CRUE WILL FOR
THWAM!

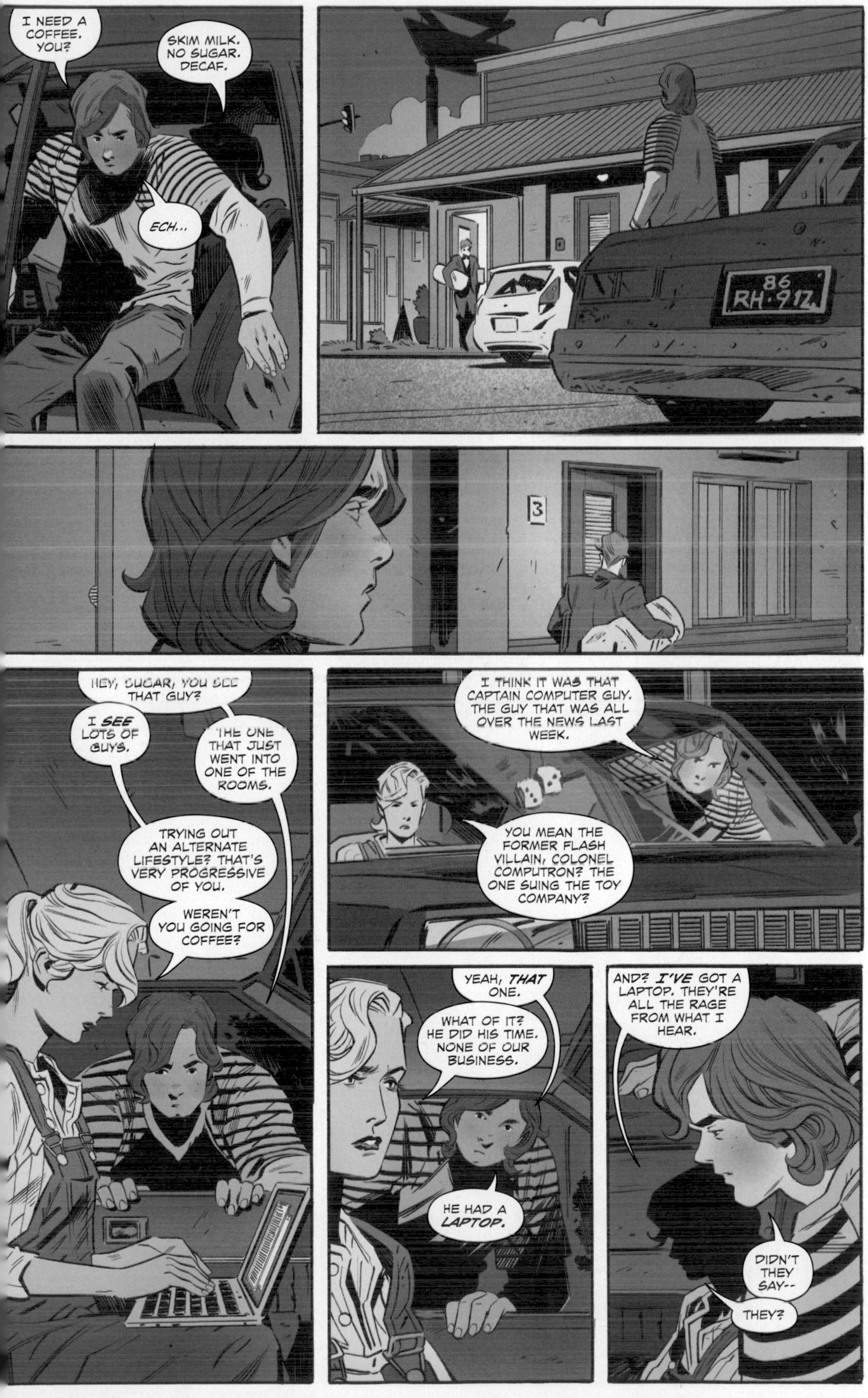
I NEED A COFFEE. YOU?
SKIM MILK. NO SUGAR. DECAF.
ECH...
86 RH·912
3
HEY, SUGAR, YOU SEE THAT GUY?
I SEE LOTS OF GUYS.
THE ONE THAT JUST WENT INTO ONE OF THE ROOMS.
TRYING OUT AN ALTERNATE LIFESTYLE? THAT'S VERY PROGRESSIVE OF YOU.
WEREN'T YOU GOING FOR COFFEE?
I THINK IT WAS THAT CAPTAIN COMPUTER GUY. THE GUY THAT WAS ALL OVER THE NEWS LAST WEEK.
YOU MEAN THE FORMER FLASH VILLAIN, COLONEL COMPUTRON? THE ONE SUING THE TOY COMPANY?
YEAH, THAT ONE.
WHAT OF IT? HE DID HIS TIME. NONE OF OUR BUSINESS.
HE HAD A LAPTOP.
AND? I'VE GOT A LAPTOP. THEY'RE ALL THE RAGE FROM WHAT I HEAR.
DIDN'T THEY SAY--
THEY?

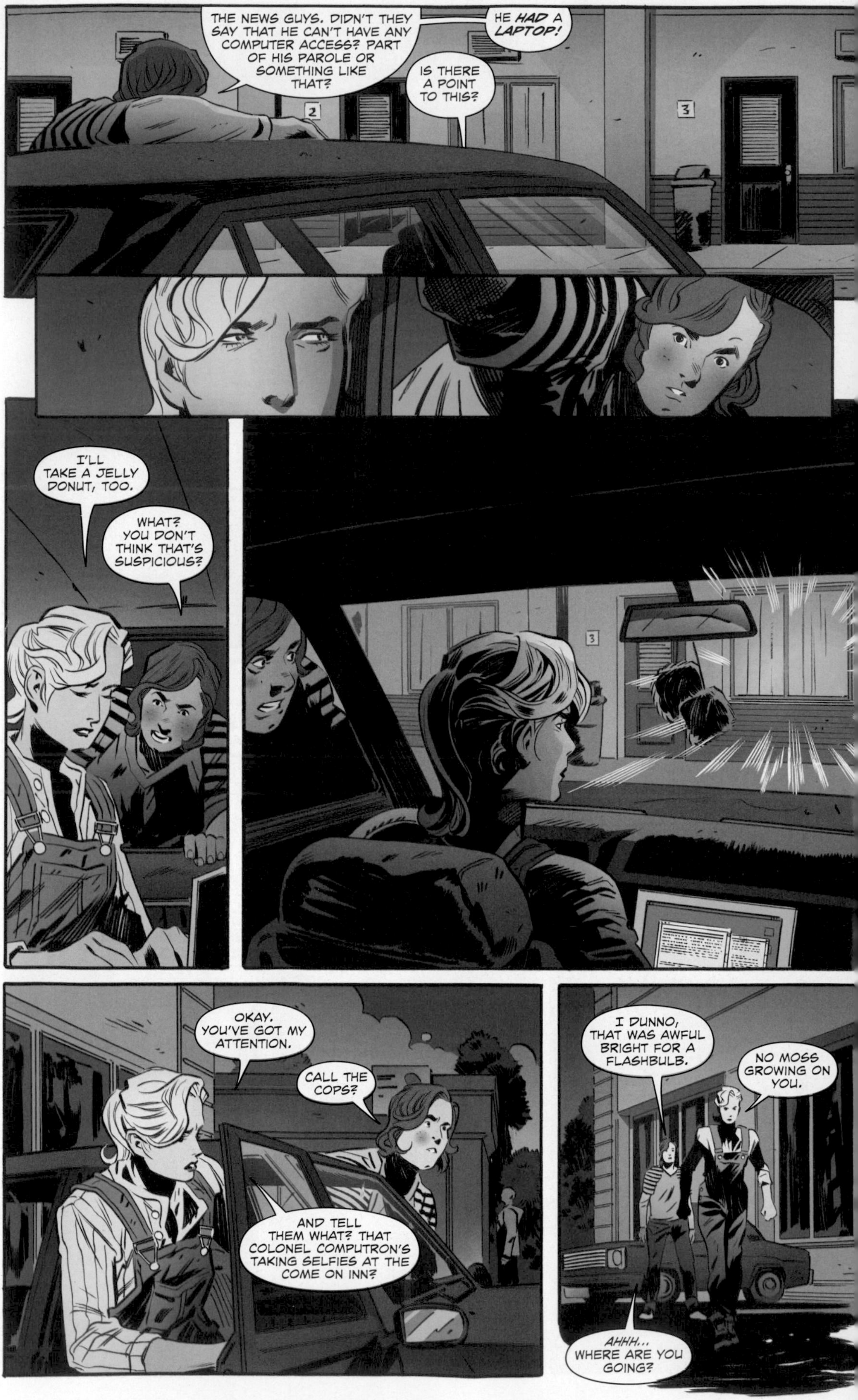
THE NEWS GUYS. DIDN'T THEY SAY THAT HE CAN'T HAVE ANY COMPUTER ACCESS? PART OF HIS PAROLE OR SOMETHING LIKE THAT?
HE *HAD* A *LAPTOP!*
IS THERE A POINT TO THIS?
2
3
I'LL TAKE A JELLY DONUT, TOO.
WHAT? YOU DON'T THINK THAT'S SUSPICIOUS?
3
OKAY. YOU'VE GOT MY ATTENTION.
CALL THE COPS?
AND TELL THEM WHAT? THAT COLONEL COMPUTRON'S TAKING SELFIES AT THE COME ON INN?
I DUNNO, THAT WAS AWFUL BRIGHT FOR A FLASHBULB.
NO MOSS GROWING ON YOU.
AHHH... WHERE ARE YOU GOING?

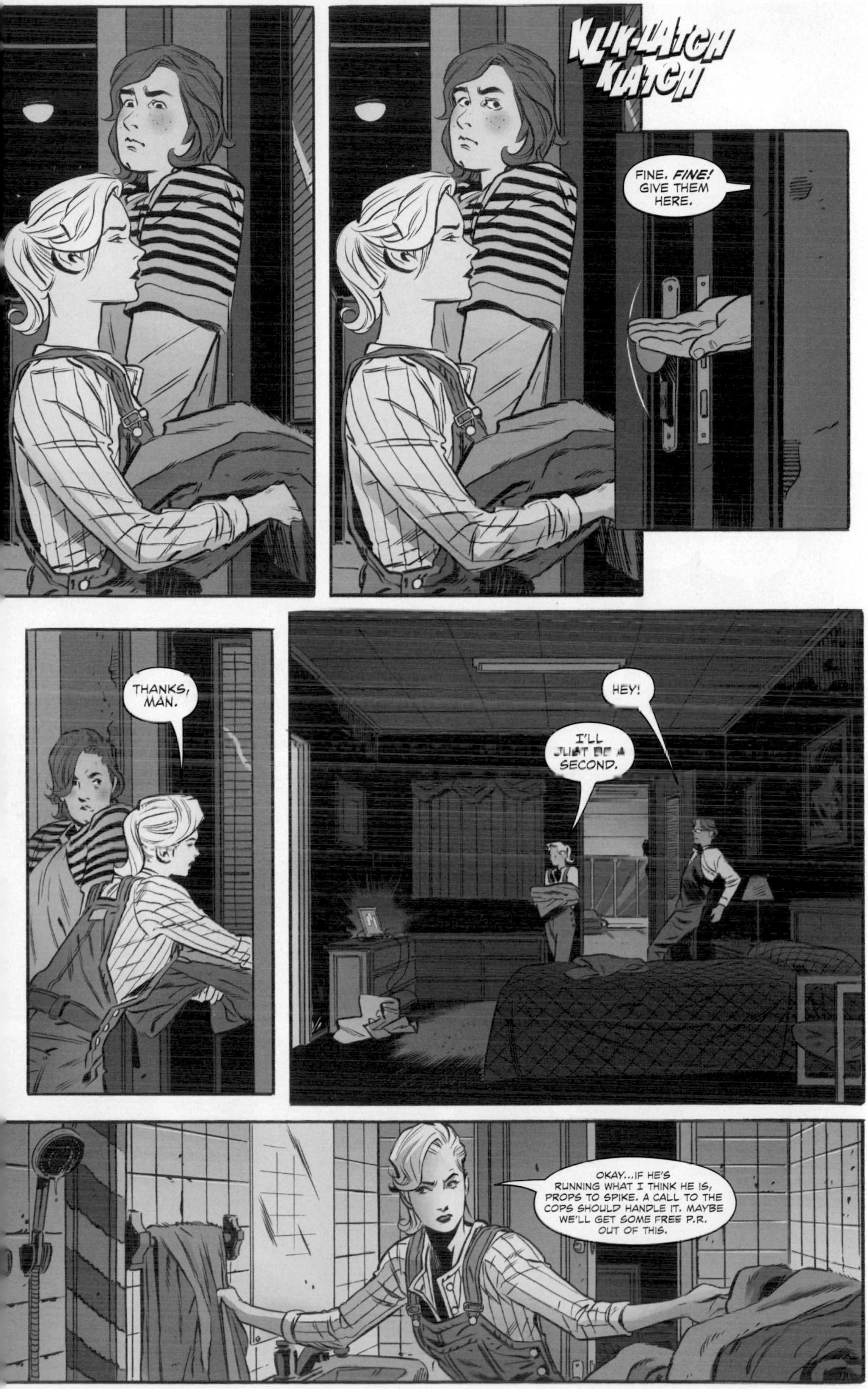
KLIK-LATCH KLATCH
FINE. *FINE!* GIVE THEM HERE.
THANKS, MAN.
HEY!
I'LL JUST BE A SECOND.
OKAY...IF HE'S RUNNING WHAT I THINK HE IS, PROPS TO SPIKE. A CALL TO THE COPS SHOULD HANDLE IT. MAYBE WE'LL GET SOME FREE P.R. OUT OF THIS.

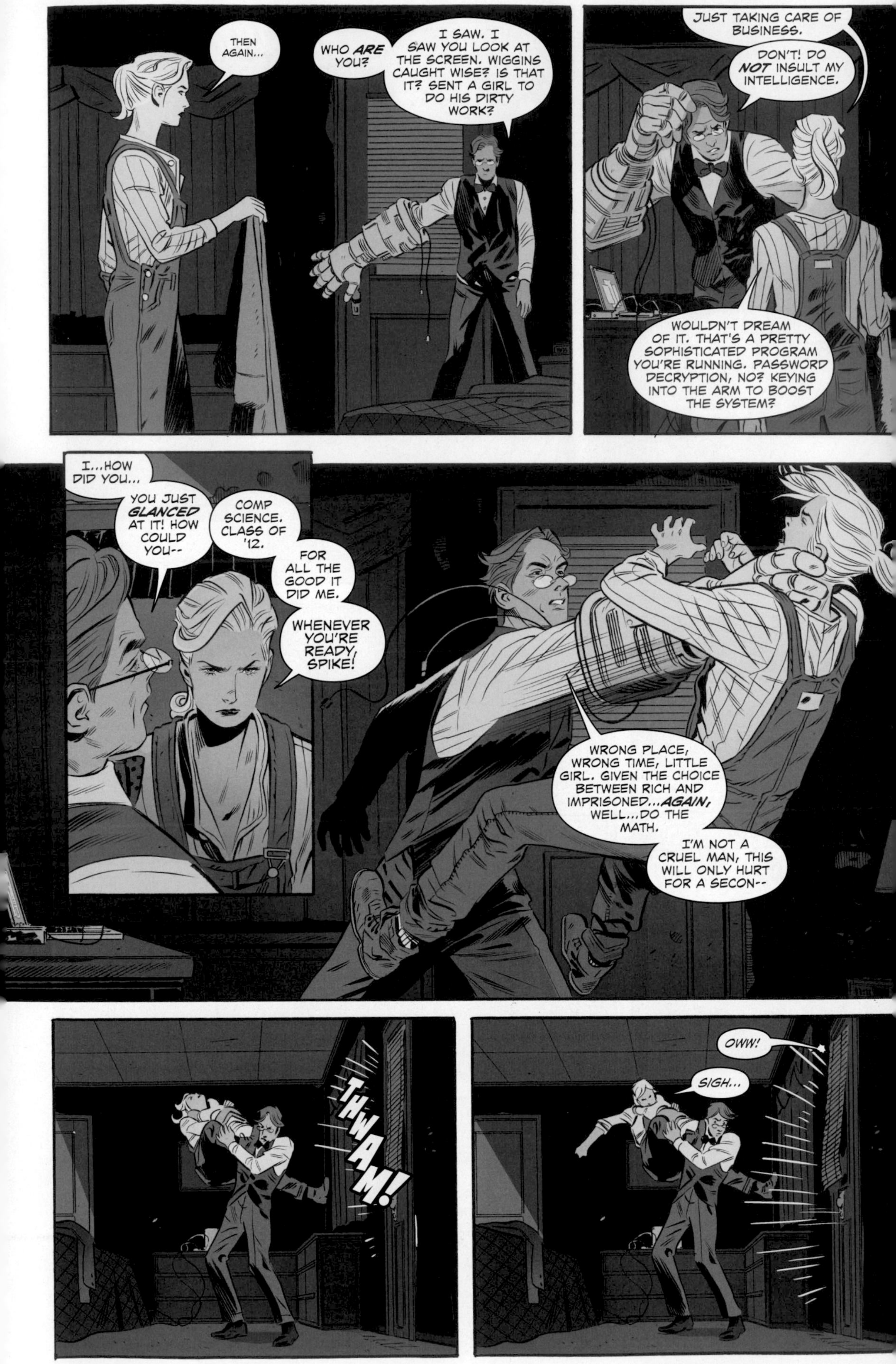
THEN AGAIN...
WHO *ARE* YOU?
I SAW. I SAW YOU LOOK AT THE SCREEN. WIGGINS CAUGHT WISE? IS THAT IT? SENT A GIRL TO DO HIS DIRTY WORK?
JUST TAKING CARE OF BUSINESS.
DON'T! DO *NOT* INSULT MY INTELLIGENCE.
WOULDN'T DREAM OF IT. THAT'S A PRETTY SOPHISTICATED PROGRAM YOU'RE RUNNING. PASSWORD DECRYPTION, NO? KEYING INTO THE ARM TO BOOST THE SYSTEM?
I...HOW DID YOU...
YOU JUST *GLANCED* AT IT! HOW COULD YOU--
COMP SCIENCE. CLASS OF '12.
FOR ALL THE GOOD IT DID ME.
WHENEVER YOU'RE READY, SPIKE!
WRONG PLACE, WRONG TIME, LITTLE GIRL. GIVEN THE CHOICE BETWEEN RICH AND IMPRISONED...*AGAIN,* WELL...DO THE MATH.
I'M NOT A CRUEL MAN, THIS WILL ONLY HURT FOR A SECON--
THWAM!
OWW!
SIGH...

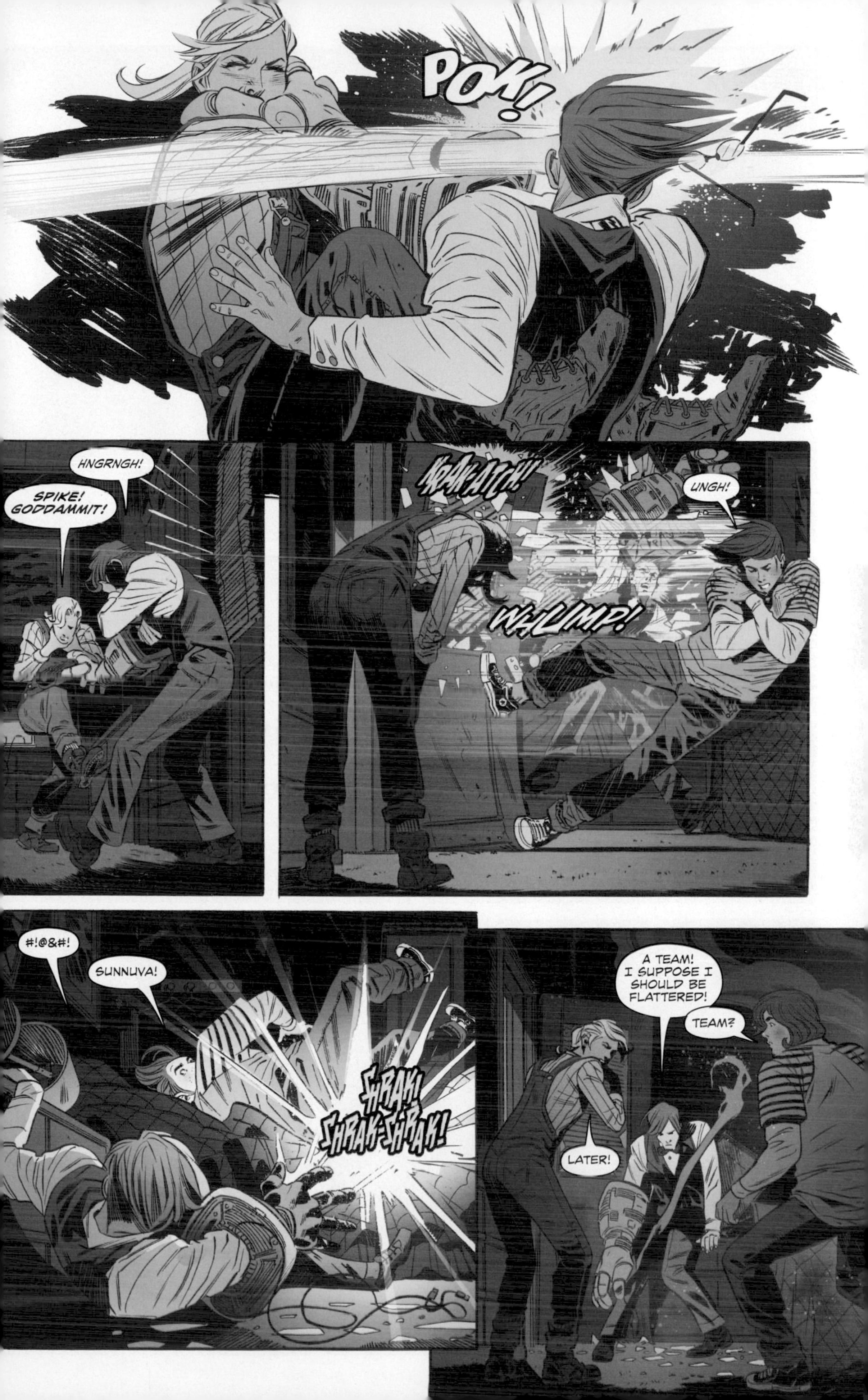
POK!!
HNGRNGH!
SPIKE! GODDAMMIT!
KRAKATCH!
UNGH!
WHUMP!
#!@&#!
SUNNUVA!
SHRAK! SHRAK-SHRAK!
A TEAM! I SUPPOSE I SHOULD BE FLATTERED!
TEAM?
LATER!

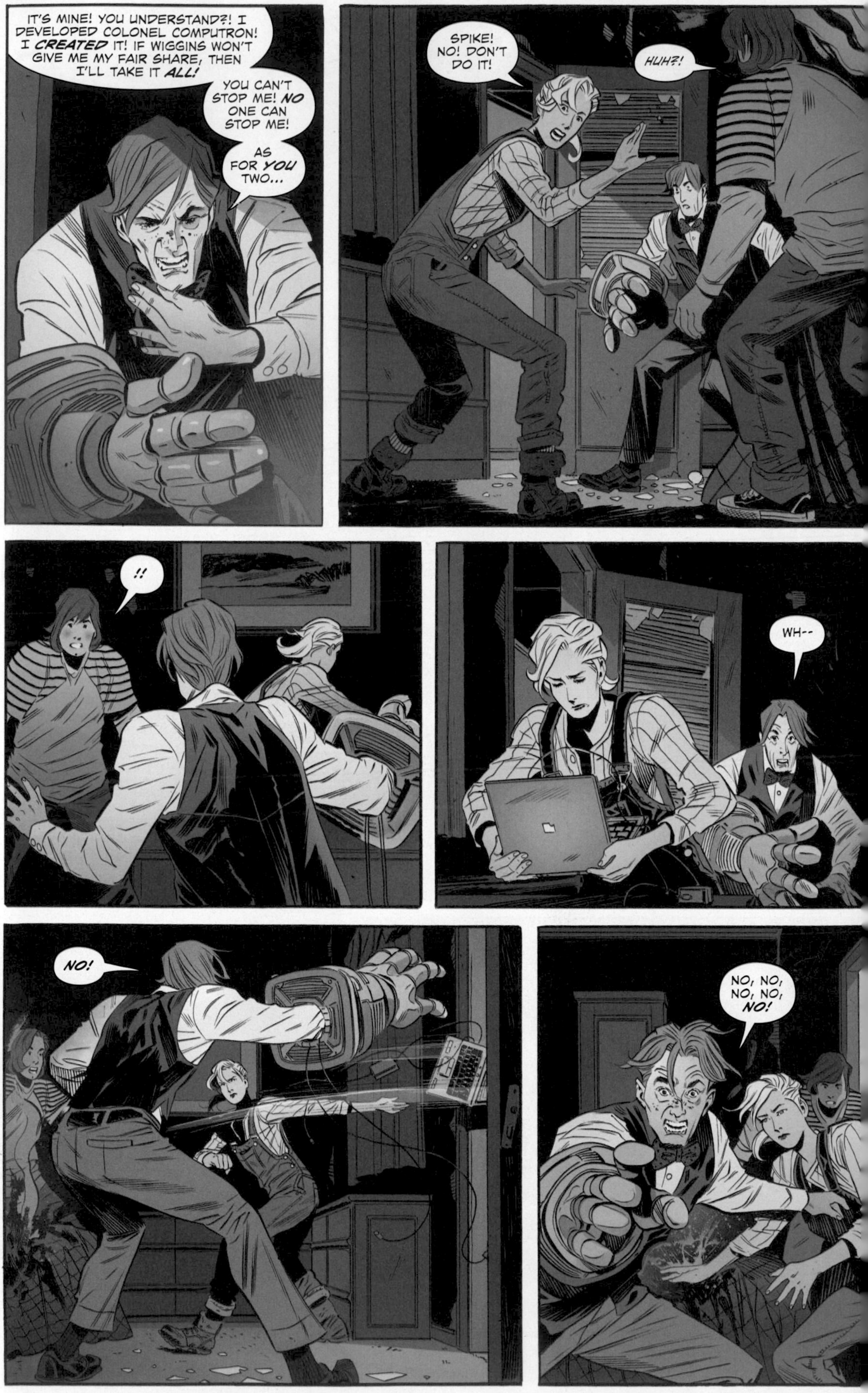
IT'S MINE! YOU UNDERSTAND?! I DEVELOPED COLONEL COMPUTRON! I CREATED IT! IF WIGGINS WON'T GIVE ME MY FAIR SHARE, THEN I'LL TAKE IT ALL!
YOU CAN'T STOP ME! NO ONE CAN STOP ME!
AS FOR YOU TWO...
SPIKE! NO! DON'T DO IT!
HUH?!
!!
WH--
NO!
NO, NO, NO, NO, NO!

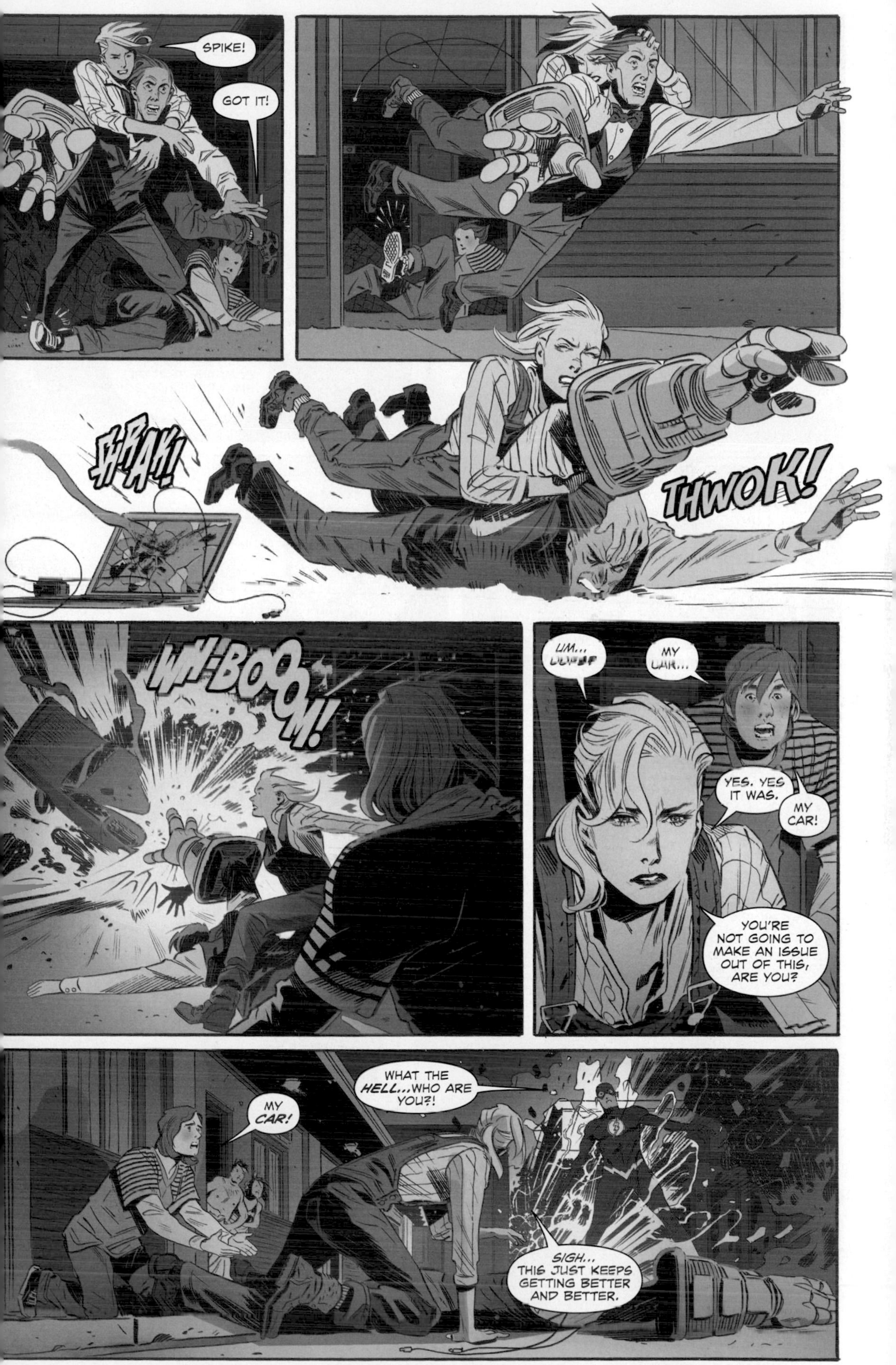
SPIKE!
GOT IT!
SKRAK!
THWOK!
WH-BOOOOM!
UM...
MY CAR...
YES. YES IT WAS.
MY CAR!
YOU'RE NOT GOING TO MAKE AN ISSUE OUT OF THIS, ARE YOU?
MY CAR!
WHAT THE HELL...WHO ARE YOU?!
SIGH... THIS JUST KEEPS GETTING BETTER AND BETTER.

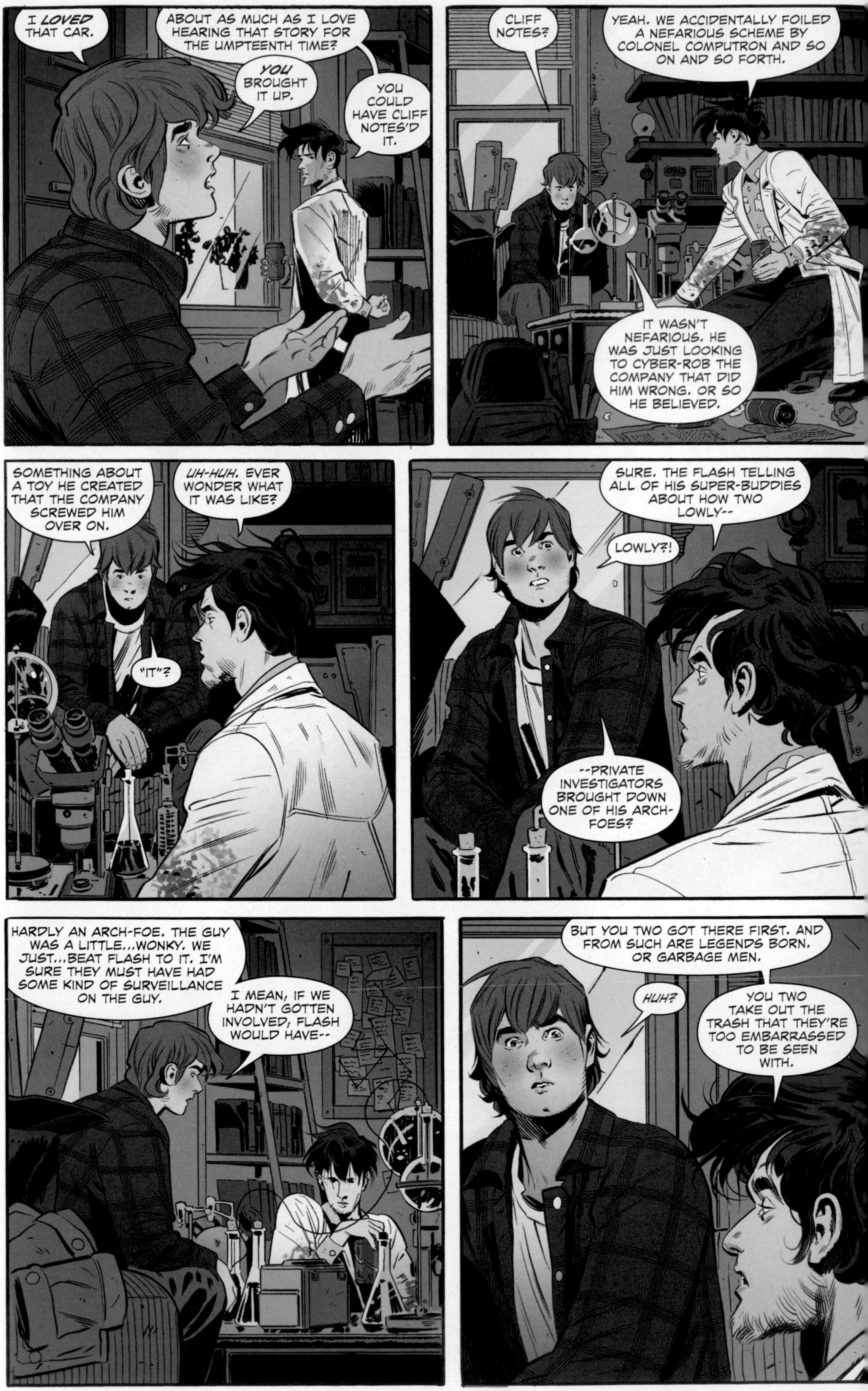
I *LOVED* THAT CAR.
ABOUT AS MUCH AS I LOVE HEARING THAT STORY FOR THE UMPTEENTH TIME?
YOU BROUGHT IT UP.
YOU COULD HAVE CLIFF NOTES'D IT.
CLIFF NOTES?
YEAH. WE ACCIDENTALLY FOILED A NEFARIOUS SCHEME BY COLONEL COMPUTRON AND SO ON AND SO FORTH.
IT WASN'T NEFARIOUS. HE WAS JUST LOOKING TO CYBER-ROB THE COMPANY THAT DID HIM WRONG. OR SO HE BELIEVED.
SOMETHING ABOUT A TOY HE CREATED THAT THE COMPANY SCREWED HIM OVER ON.
UH-HUH. EVER WONDER WHAT IT WAS LIKE?
"IT"?
SURE. THE FLASH TELLING ALL OF HIS SUPER-BUDDIES ABOUT HOW TWO LOWLY--
LOWLY?!
--PRIVATE INVESTIGATORS BROUGHT DOWN ONE OF HIS ARCH-FOES?
HARDLY AN ARCH-FOE. THE GUY WAS A LITTLE...WONKY. WE JUST...BEAT FLASH TO IT. I'M SURE THEY MUST HAVE HAD SOME KIND OF SURVEILLANCE ON THE GUY.
I MEAN, IF WE HADN'T GOTTEN INVOLVED, FLASH WOULD HAVE--
BUT YOU TWO GOT THERE FIRST. AND FROM SUCH ARE LEGENDS BORN. OR GARBAGE MEN.
HUH?
YOU TWO TAKE OUT THE TRASH THAT THEY'RE TOO EMBARRASSED TO BE SEEN WITH.

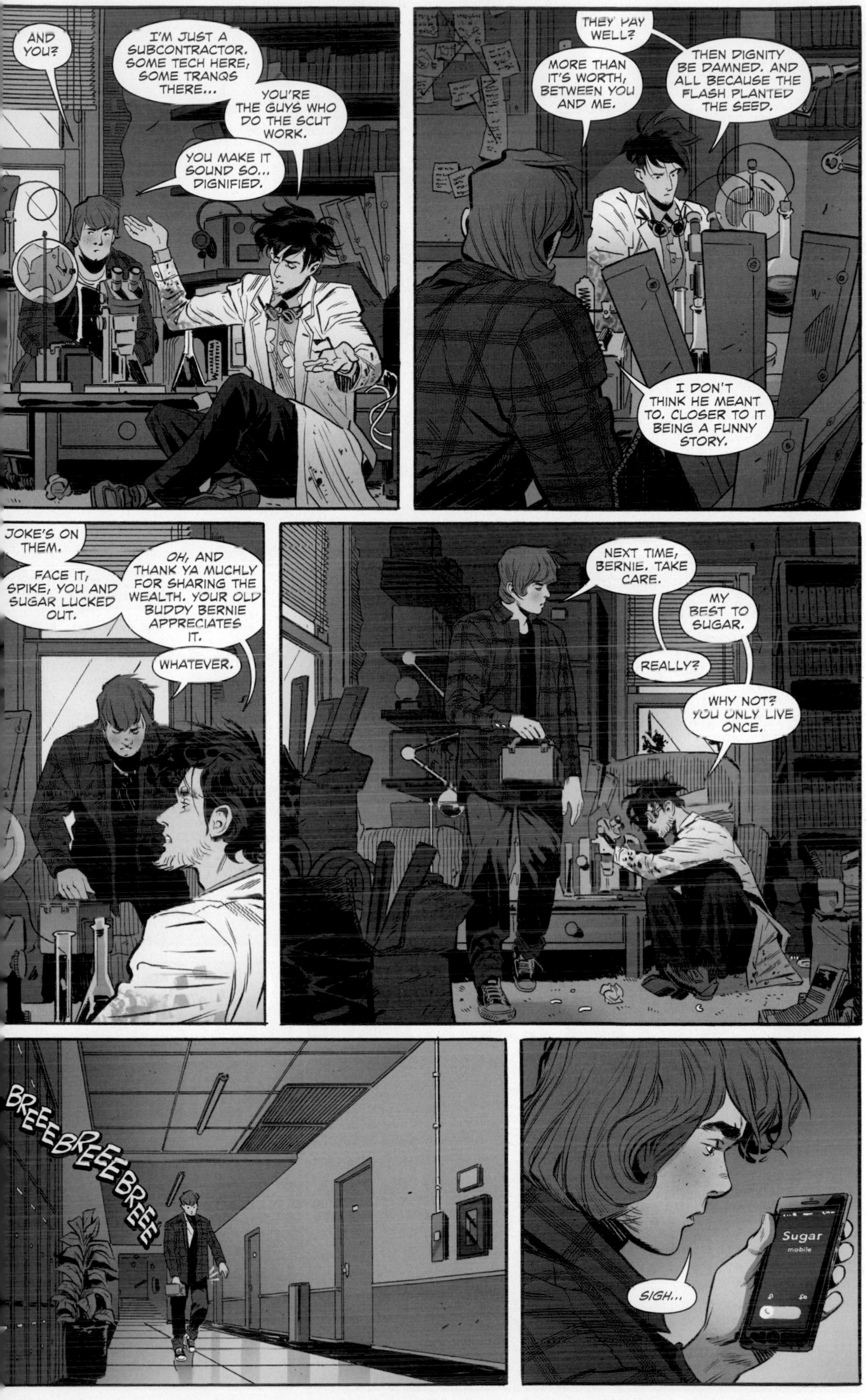
AND YOU?
I'M JUST A SUBCONTRACTOR. SOME TECH HERE, SOME TRANQS THERE...
YOU'RE THE GUYS WHO DO THE SCUT WORK.
YOU MAKE IT SOUND SO... DIGNIFIED.
THEY PAY WELL?
MORE THAN IT'S WORTH, BETWEEN YOU AND ME.
THEN DIGNITY BE DAMNED. AND ALL BECAUSE THE FLASH PLANTED THE SEED.
I DON'T THINK HE MEANT TO. CLOSER TO IT BEING A FUNNY STORY.
JOKE'S ON THEM.
FACE IT, SPIKE, YOU AND SUGAR LUCKED OUT.
OH, AND THANK YA MUCHLY FOR SHARING THE WEALTH. YOUR OLD BUDDY BERNIE APPRECIATES IT.
WHATEVER.
NEXT TIME, BERNIE. TAKE CARE.
MY BEST TO SUGAR.
REALLY?
WHY NOT? YOU ONLY LIVE ONCE.
BREEEBREEEBREE
Sugar
mobile
SIGH...

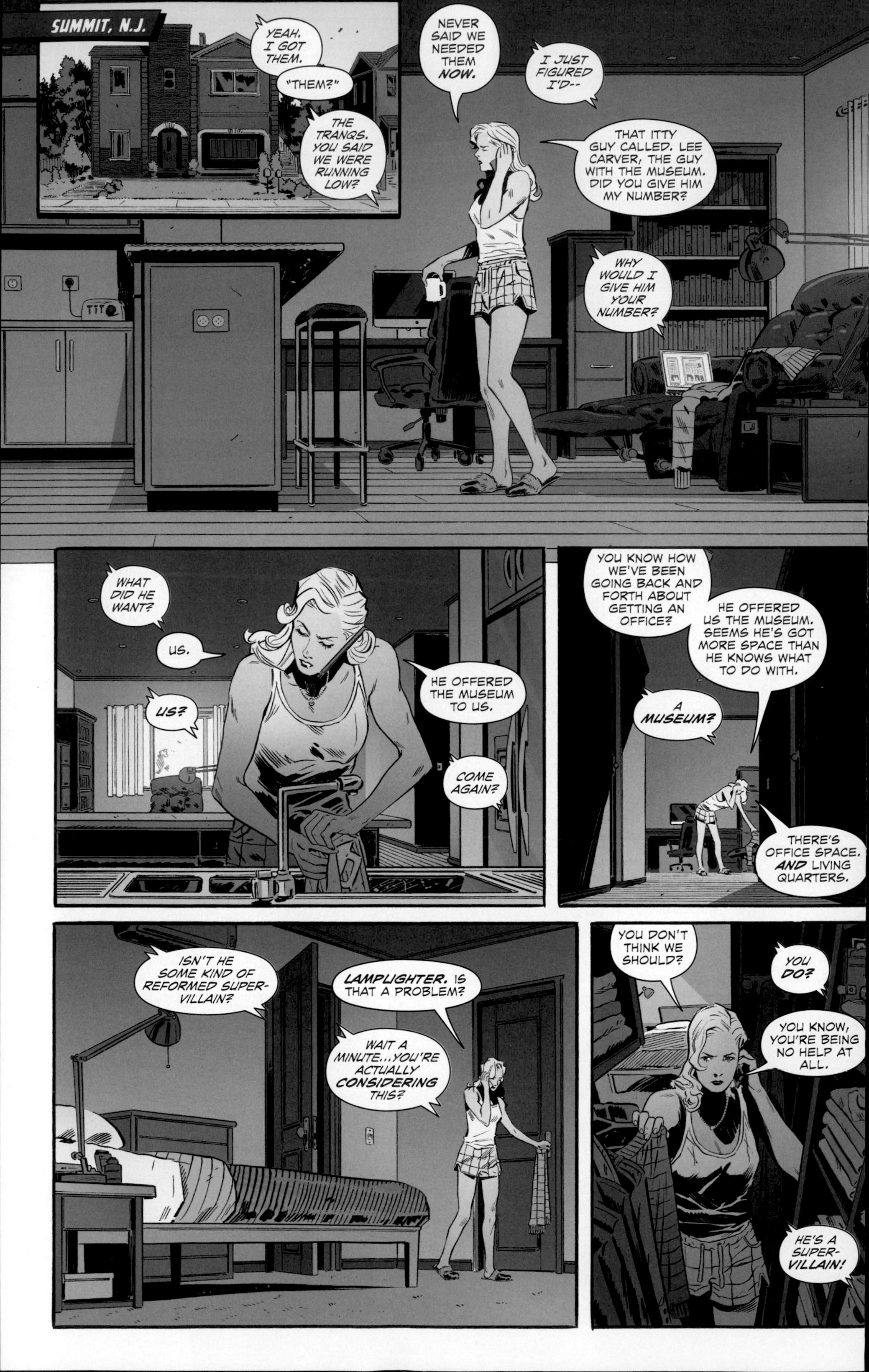
SUMMIT, N.J.
YEAH. I GOT THEM.
"THEM?"
THE TRANQS. YOU SAID WE WERE RUNNING LOW?
NEVER SAID WE NEEDED THEM NOW.
I JUST FIGURED I'D--
THAT ITTY GUY CALLED. LEE CARVER, THE GUY WITH THE MUSEUM. DID YOU GIVE HIM MY NUMBER?
WHY WOULD I GIVE HIM YOUR NUMBER?
WHAT DID HE WANT?
US.
US?
HE OFFERED THE MUSEUM TO US.
COME AGAIN?
YOU KNOW HOW WE'VE BEEN GOING BACK AND FORTH ABOUT GETTING AN OFFICE?
HE OFFERED US THE MUSEUM. SEEMS HE'S GOT MORE SPACE THAN HE KNOWS WHAT TO DO WITH.
A MUSEUM?
THERE'S OFFICE SPACE. AND LIVING QUARTERS.
ISN'T HE SOME KIND OF REFORMED SUPER-VILLAIN?
LAMPLIGHTER. IS THAT A PROBLEM?
WAIT A MINUTE...YOU'RE ACTUALLY CONSIDERING THIS?
YOU DON'T THINK WE SHOULD?
YOU DO?
YOU KNOW, YOU'RE BEING NO HELP AT ALL.
HE'S A SUPER-VILLAIN!

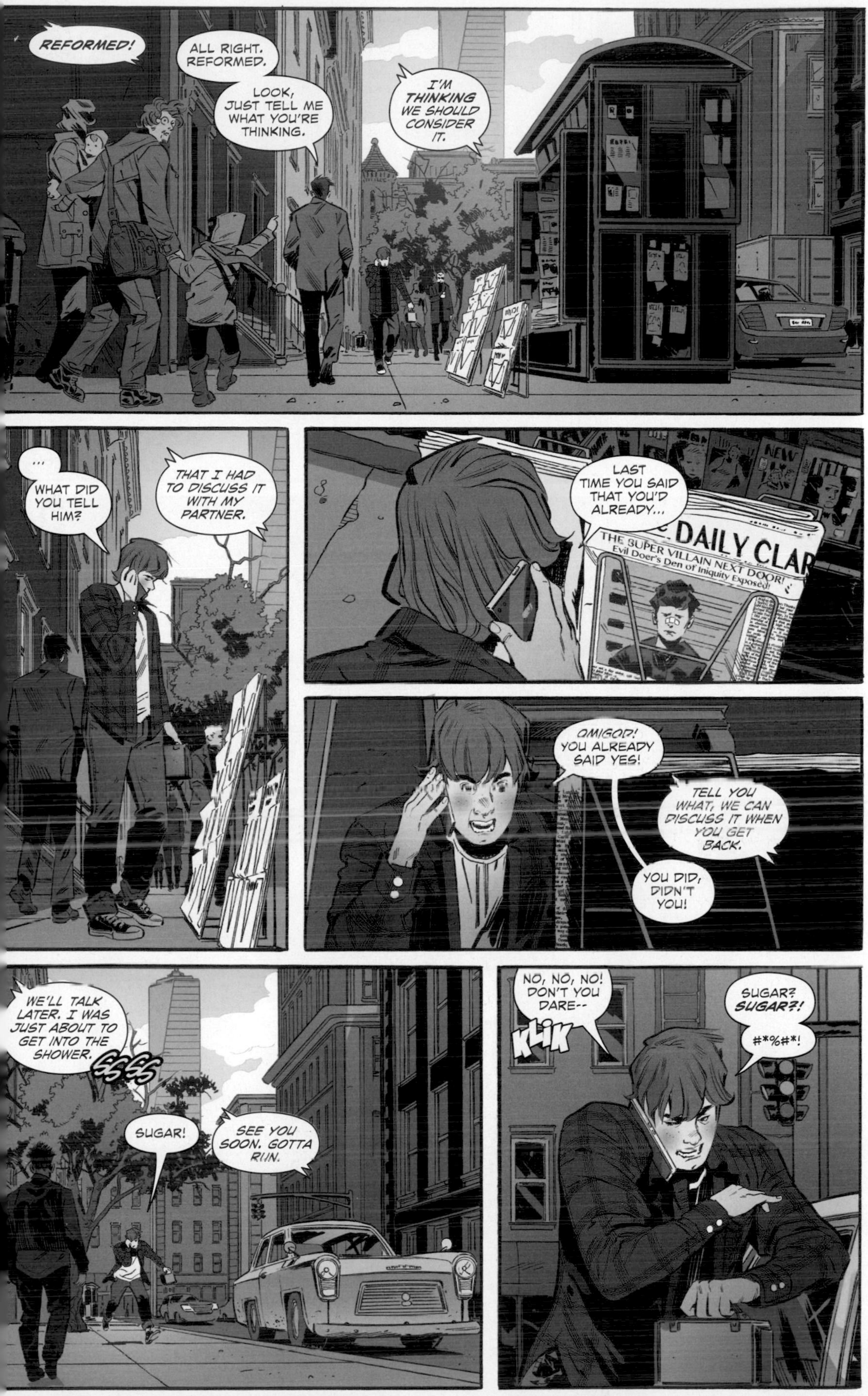
REFORMED!
ALL RIGHT. REFORMED.
LOOK, JUST TELL ME WHAT YOU'RE THINKING.
I'M THINKING WE SHOULD CONSIDER IT.
...
WHAT DID YOU TELL HIM?
THAT I HAD TO DISCUSS IT WITH MY PARTNER.
LAST TIME YOU SAID THAT YOU'D ALREADY...
DAILY CLAR
THE SUPER VILLAIN NEXT DOOR!
Evil Doer's Den of Iniquity Exposed!
OMIGOD! YOU ALREADY SAID YES!
TELL YOU WHAT, WE CAN DISCUSS IT WHEN YOU GET BACK.
YOU DID, DIDN'T YOU!
WE'LL TALK LATER. I WAS JUST ABOUT TO GET INTO THE SHOWER.
SSSS
SUGAR!
SEE YOU SOON. GOTTA RUN.
NO, NO, NO! DON'T YOU DARE--
KLIK
SUGAR? SUGAR?!
#*%#*!

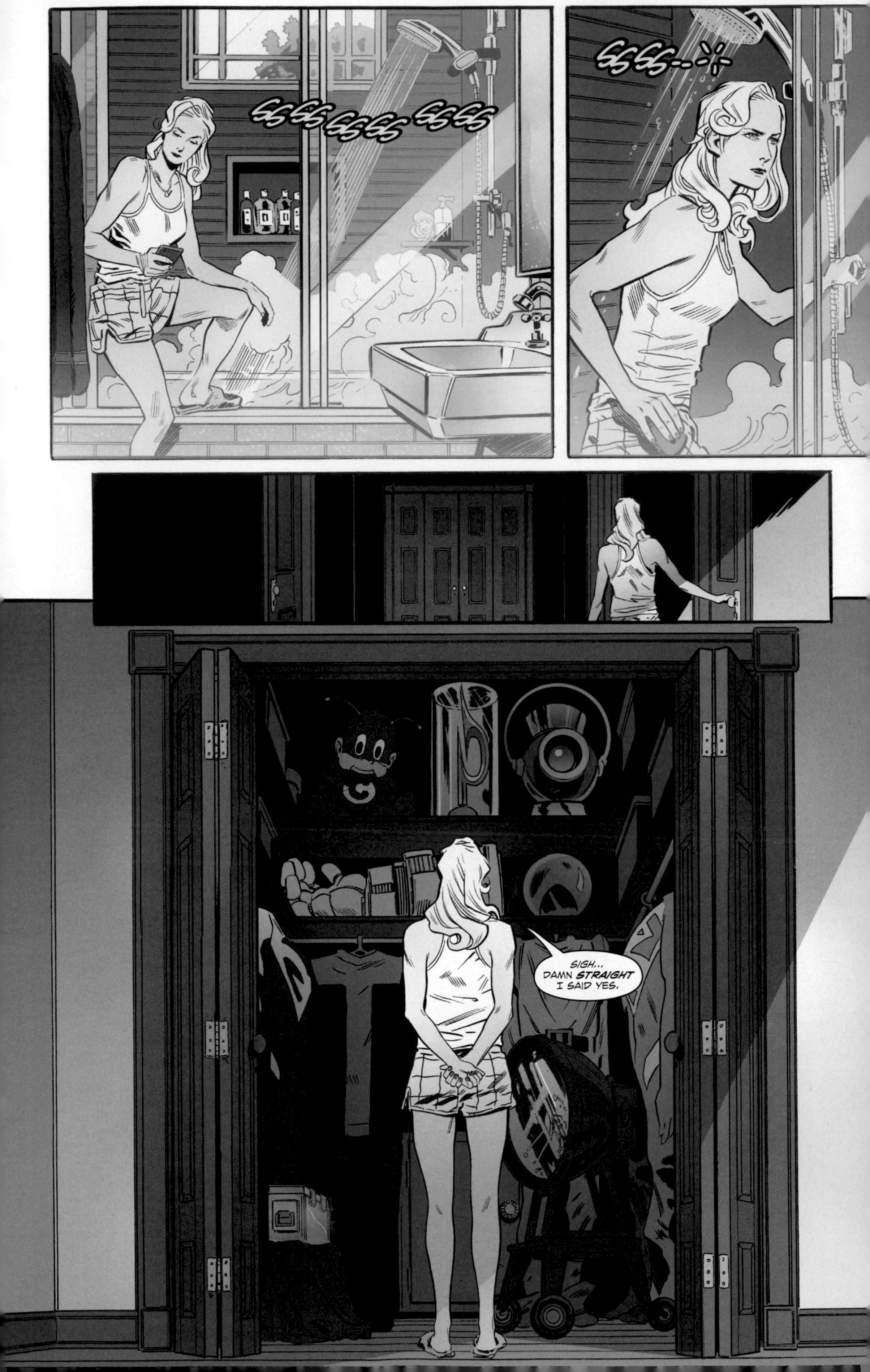
SSSS SSSS SSSS
SSSS--
SIGH... DAMN STRAIGHT I SAID YES.

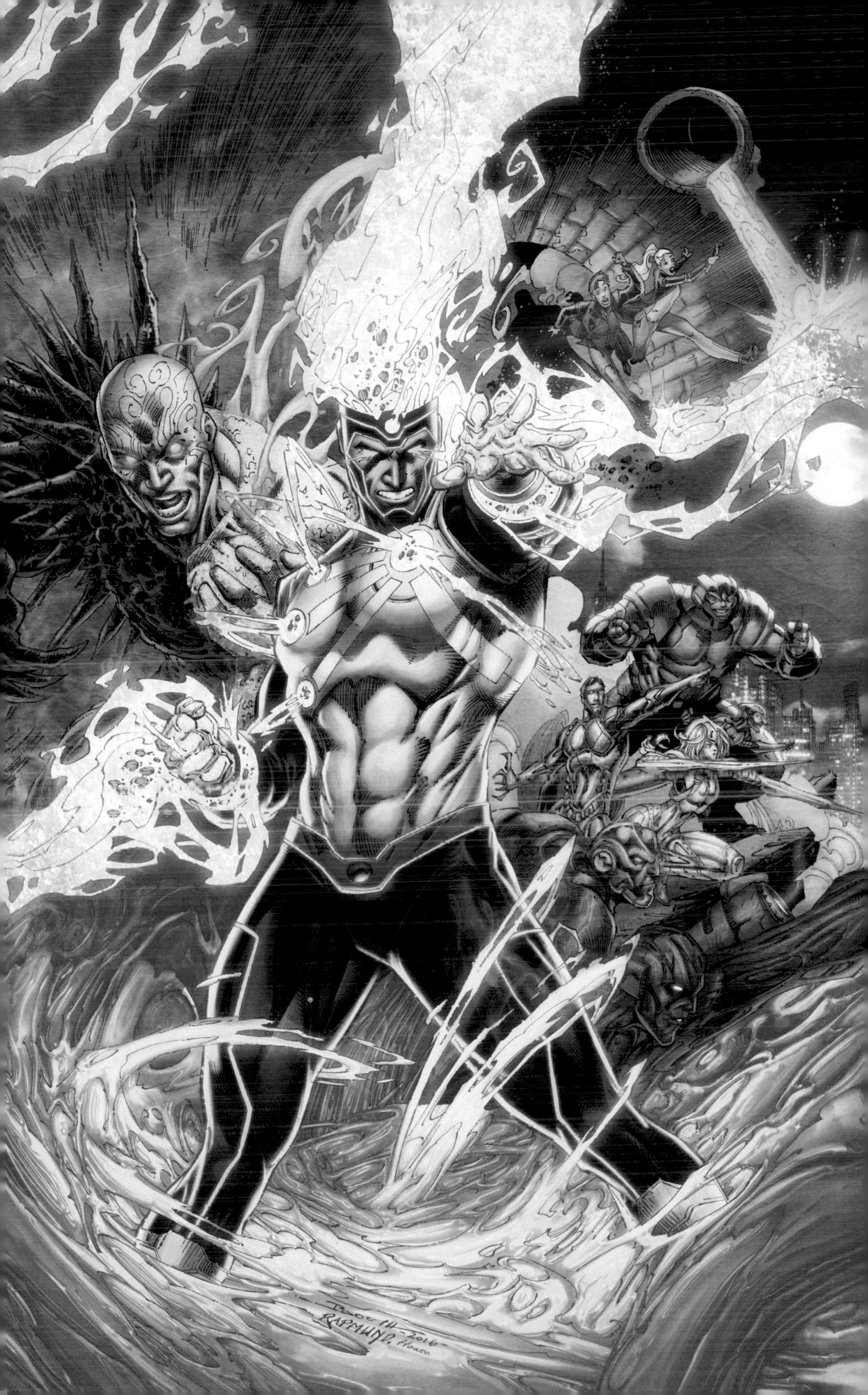

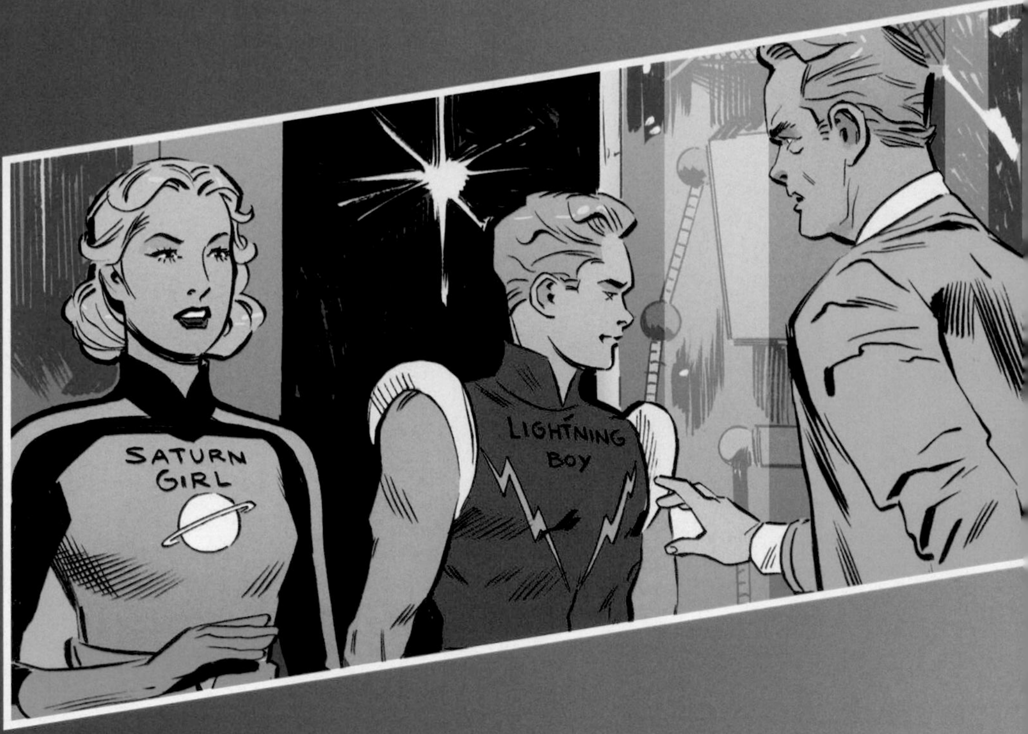
SATURN GIRL
LIGHTNING BOY

BRETT BOOTH
NORM RAPMUND
with **ANDREW DALHOUSE**
cover

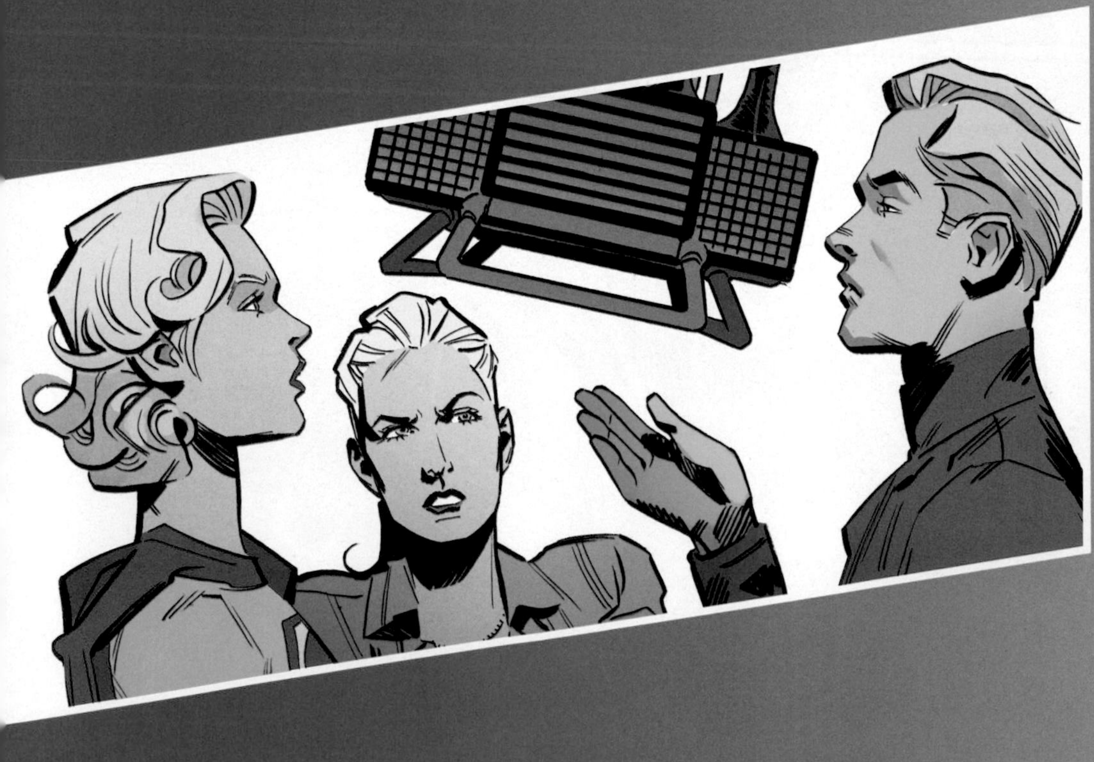

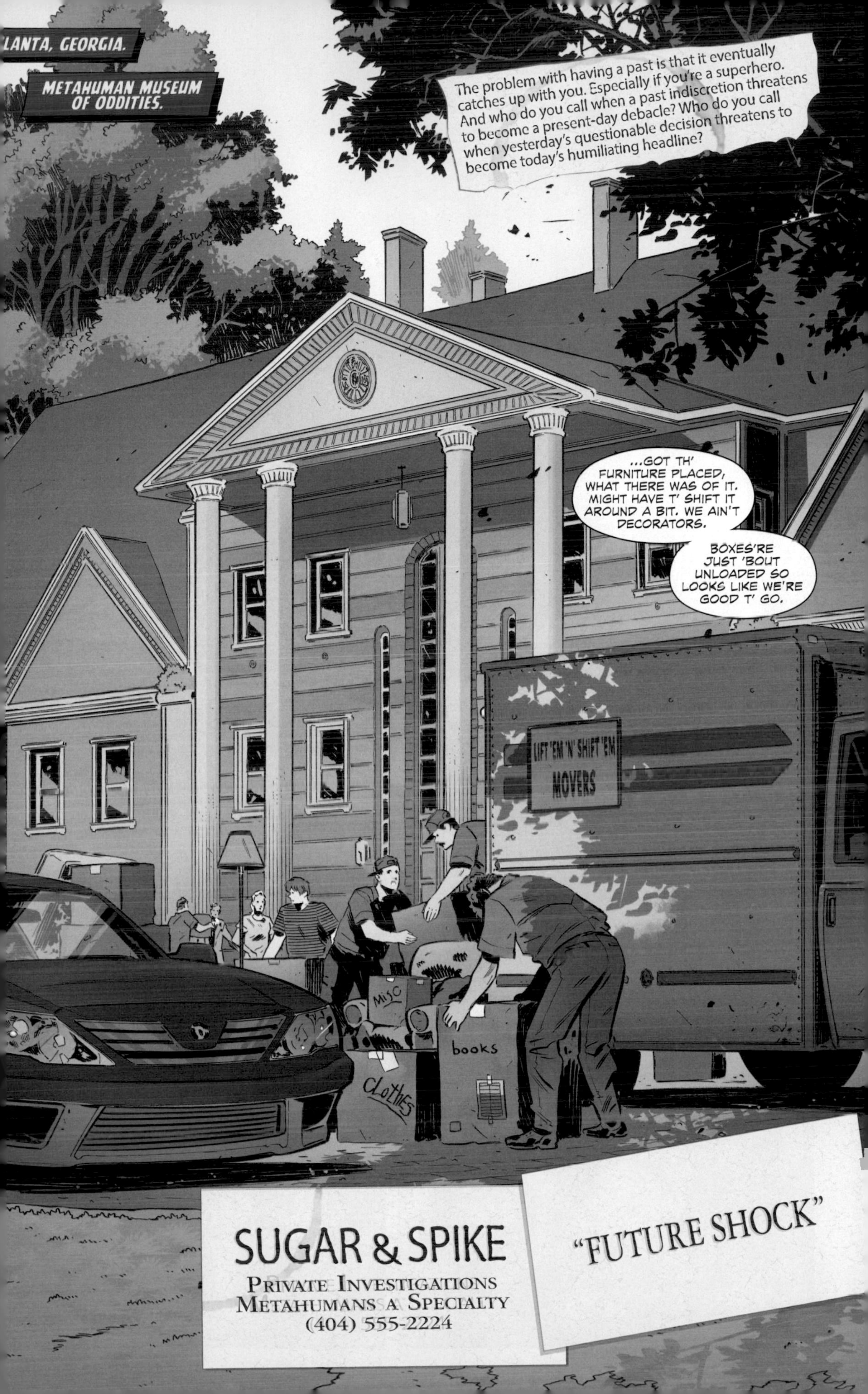
LANTA, GEORGIA.
METAHUMAN MUSEUM OF ODDITIES.
The problem with having a past is that it eventually catches up with you. Especially if you're a superhero. And who do you call when a past indiscretion threatens to become a present-day debacle? Who do you call when yesterday's questionable decision threatens to become today's humiliating headline?
...GOT TH' FURNITURE PLACED, WHAT THERE WAS OF IT. MIGHT HAVE T' SHIFT IT AROUND A BIT. WE AIN'T DECORATORS.
BOXES'RE JUST 'BOUT UNLOADED SO LOOKS LIKE WE'RE GOOD T' GO.
LIFT 'EM 'N' SHIFT 'EM MOVERS
MISC
books
CLOTHES
SUGAR & SPIKE
PRIVATE INVESTIGATIONS
METAHUMANS A SPECIALTY
(404) 555-2224
"FUTURE SHOCK"

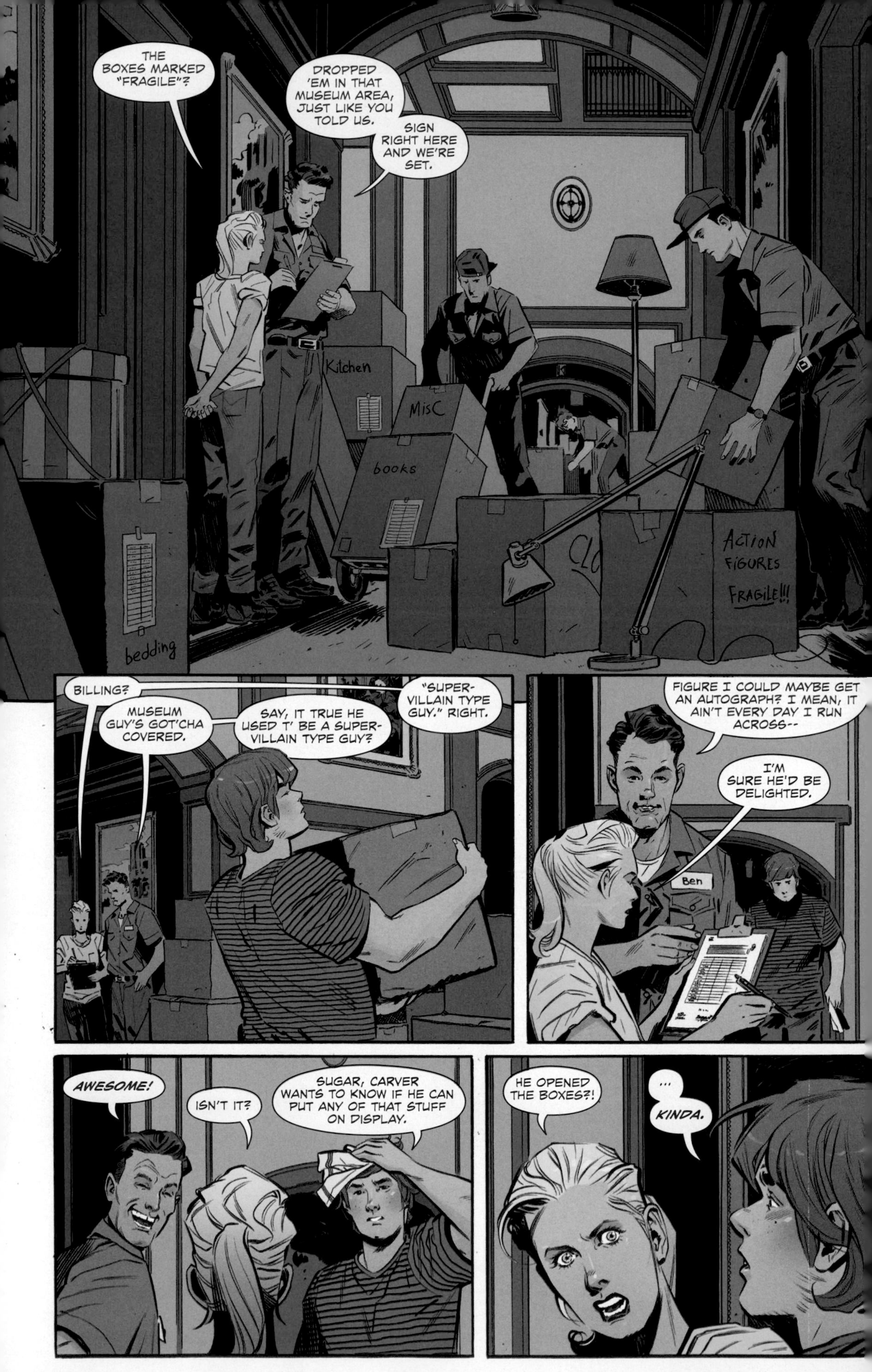
THE BOXES MARKED "FRAGILE"?
DROPPED 'EM IN THAT MUSEUM AREA, JUST LIKE YOU TOLD US.
SIGN RIGHT HERE AND WE'RE SET.
Kitchen
MisC
books
ACTION FIGURES FRAGILE!!!
bedding
BILLING?
MUSEUM GUY'S GOT'CHA COVERED.
SAY, IT TRUE HE USED T' BE A SUPER-VILLAIN TYPE GUY?
"SUPER-VILLAIN TYPE GUY." RIGHT.
FIGURE I COULD MAYBE GET AN AUTOGRAPH? I MEAN, IT AIN'T EVERY DAY I RUN ACROSS--
I'M SURE HE'D BE DELIGHTED.
Ben
AWESOME!
ISN'T IT?
SUGAR, CARVER WANTS TO KNOW IF HE CAN PUT ANY OF THAT STUFF ON DISPLAY.
HE OPENED THE BOXES?!
...
KINDA.

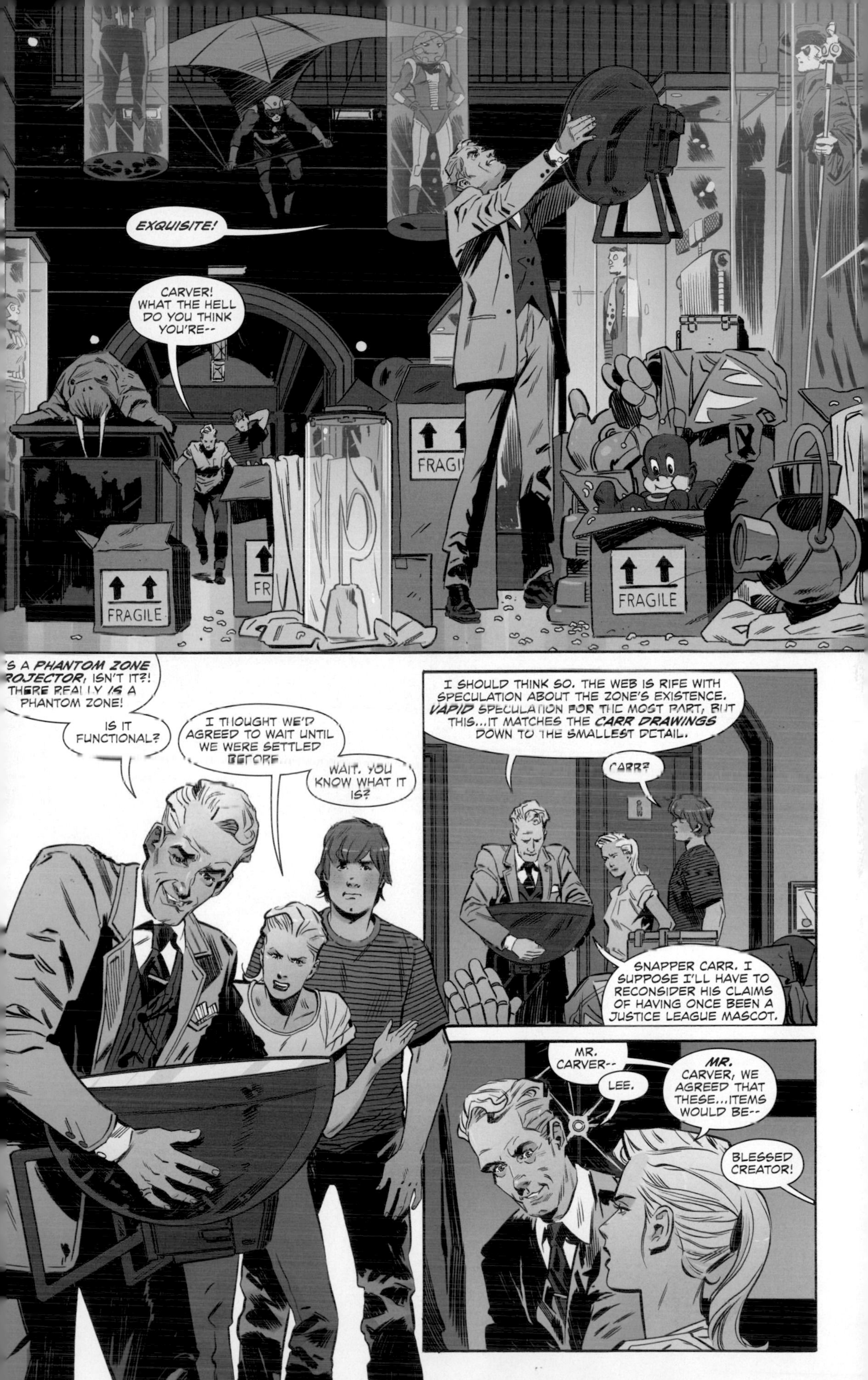
EXQUISITE!
CARVER! WHAT THE HELL DO YOU THINK YOU'RE--
FRAGILE
FRAGILE
FRAGILE
'S A PHANTOM ZONE ROJECTOR, ISN'T IT?! THERE REALLY IS A PHANTOM ZONE!
IS IT FUNCTIONAL?
I THOUGHT WE'D AGREED TO WAIT UNTIL WE WERE SETTLED BEFORE
WAIT. YOU KNOW WHAT IT IS?
I SHOULD THINK SO. THE WEB IS RIFE WITH SPECULATION ABOUT THE ZONE'S EXISTENCE. VAPID SPECULATION FOR THE MOST PART, BUT THIS...IT MATCHES THE CARR DRAWINGS DOWN TO THE SMALLEST DETAIL.
CARR?
SNAPPER CARR. I SUPPOSE I'LL HAVE TO RECONSIDER HIS CLAIMS OF HAVING ONCE BEEN A JUSTICE LEAGUE MASCOT.
MR. CARVER--
LEE.
MR. CARVER, WE AGREED THAT THESE...ITEMS WOULD BE--
BLESSED CREATOR!

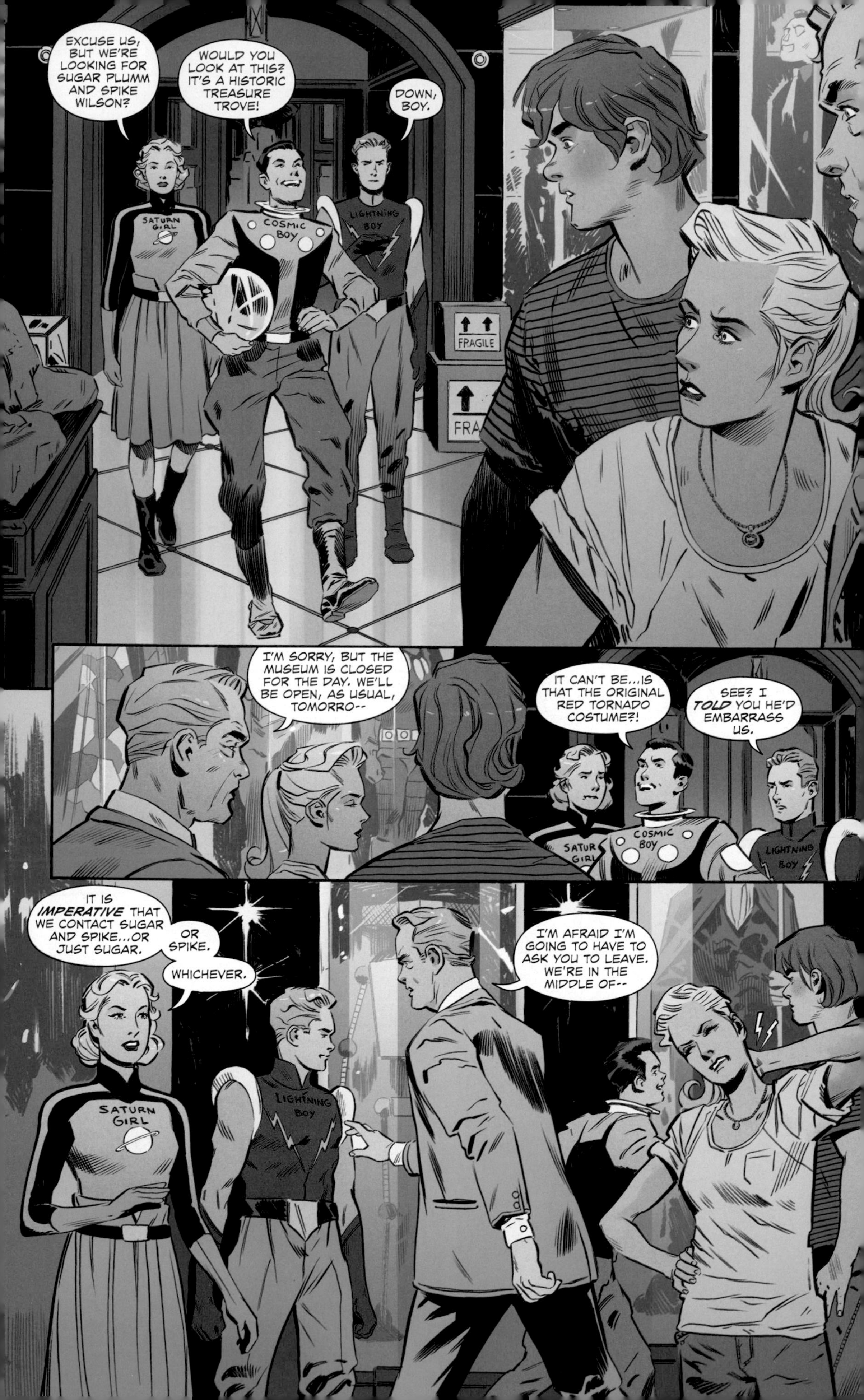

EXCUSE US, BUT WE'RE LOOKING FOR SUGAR PLUMM AND SPIKE WILSON?
WOULD YOU LOOK AT THIS? IT'S A HISTORIC TREASURE TROVE!
DOWN, BOY.
SATURN GIRL
COSMIC BOY
LIGHTNING BOY
FRAGILE
I'M SORRY, BUT THE MUSEUM IS CLOSED FOR THE DAY. WE'LL BE OPEN, AS USUAL, TOMORRO--
IT CAN'T BE...IS THAT THE ORIGINAL RED TORNADO COSTUME?!
SEE? I TOLD YOU HE'D EMBARRASS US.
IT IS IMPERATIVE THAT WE CONTACT SUGAR AND SPIKE...OR JUST SUGAR.
OR SPIKE.
WHICHEVER.
I'M AFRAID I'M GOING TO HAVE TO ASK YOU TO LEAVE. WE'RE IN THE MIDDLE OF--

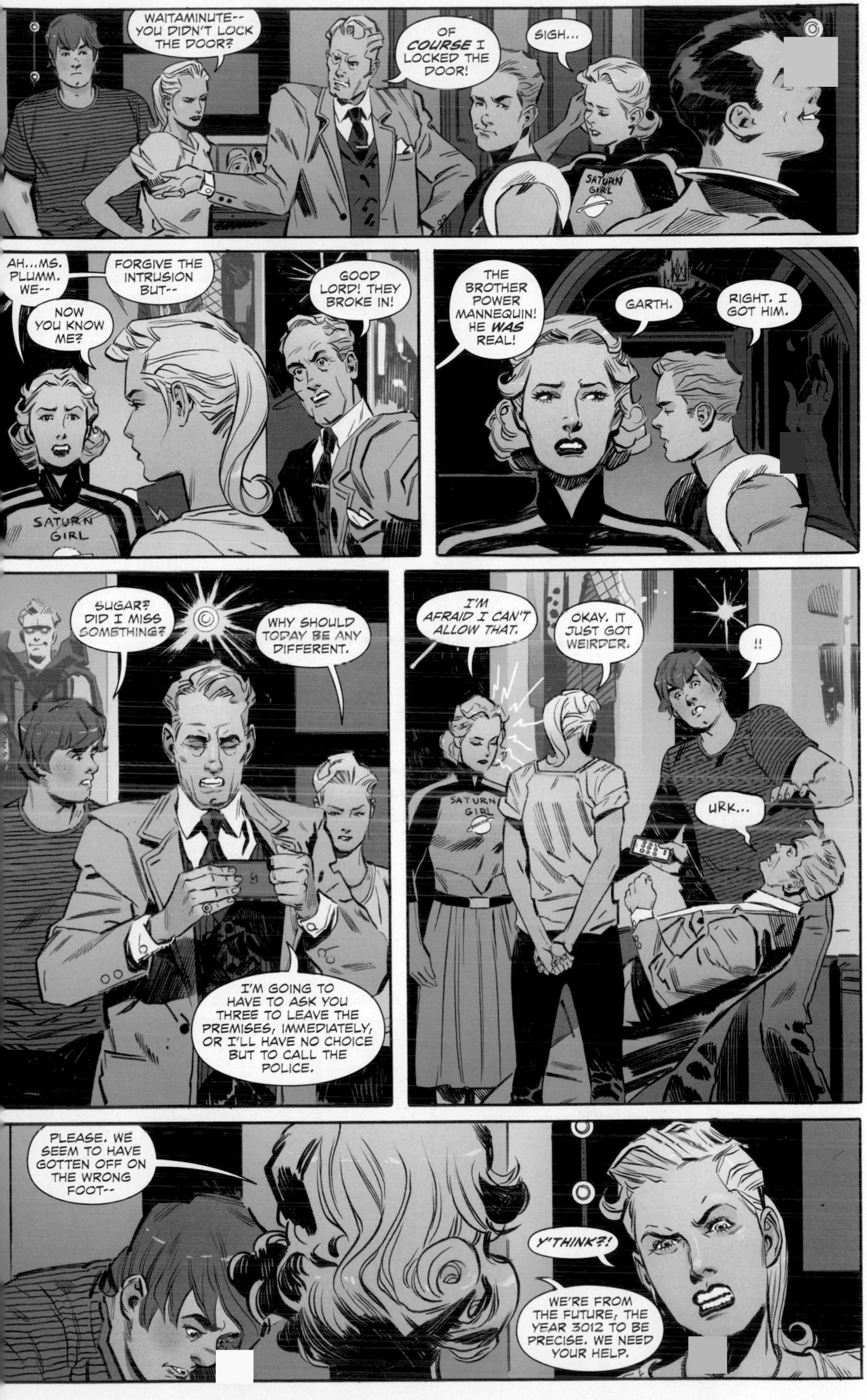
WAITAMINUTE-- YOU DIDN'T LOCK THE DOOR?
OF *COURSE* I LOCKED THE DOOR!
SIGH...
AH...MS. PLUMM. WE--
FORGIVE THE INTRUSION BUT--
NOW YOU KNOW ME?
GOOD LORD! THEY BROKE IN!
THE BROTHER POWER MANNEQUIN! HE *WAS* REAL!
GARTH.
RIGHT. I GOT HIM.
SUGAR? DID I MISS SOMETHING?
WHY SHOULD TODAY BE ANY DIFFERENT.
I'M GOING TO HAVE TO ASK YOU THREE TO LEAVE THE PREMISES, IMMEDIATELY, OR I'LL HAVE NO CHOICE BUT TO CALL THE POLICE.
I'M AFRAID I CAN'T ALLOW THAT.
OKAY. IT JUST GOT WEIRDER.
!!
URK...
PLEASE. WE SEEM TO HAVE GOTTEN OFF ON THE WRONG FOOT--
Y'THINK?!
WE'RE FROM THE FUTURE, THE YEAR 3012 TO BE PRECISE. WE NEED YOUR HELP.

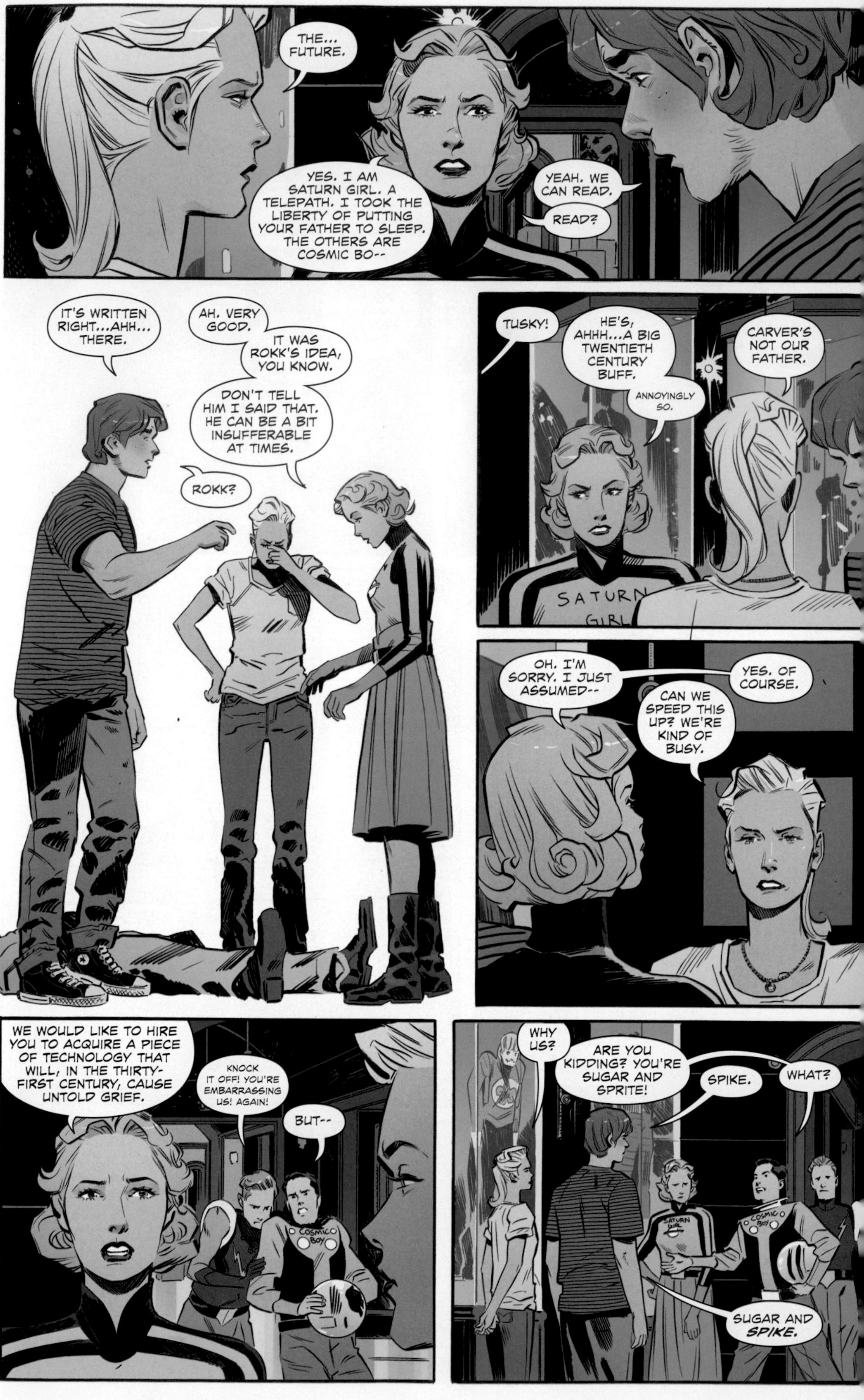
THE... FUTURE.
YES. I AM SATURN GIRL. A TELEPATH. I TOOK THE LIBERTY OF PUTTING YOUR FATHER TO SLEEP. THE OTHERS ARE COSMIC BO--
YEAH. WE CAN READ.
READ?
IT'S WRITTEN RIGHT...AHH... THERE.
AH. VERY GOOD.
IT WAS ROKK'S IDEA, YOU KNOW.
DON'T TELL HIM I SAID THAT. HE CAN BE A BIT INSUFFERABLE AT TIMES.
ROKK?
TUSKY!
HE'S, AHHH...A BIG TWENTIETH CENTURY BUFF.
ANNOYINGLY SO.
CARVER'S NOT OUR FATHER.
SATURN GIRL
OH. I'M SORRY. I JUST ASSUMED--
YES. OF COURSE.
CAN WE SPEED THIS UP? WE'RE KIND OF BUSY.
WE WOULD LIKE TO HIRE YOU TO ACQUIRE A PIECE OF TECHNOLOGY THAT WILL, IN THE THIRTY-FIRST CENTURY, CAUSE UNTOLD GRIEF.
KNOCK IT OFF! YOU'RE EMBARRASSING US! AGAIN!
BUT--
COSMIC BOY
WHY US?
ARE YOU KIDDING? YOU'RE SUGAR AND SPRITE!
SPIKE.
WHAT?
SUGAR AND *SPIKE.*

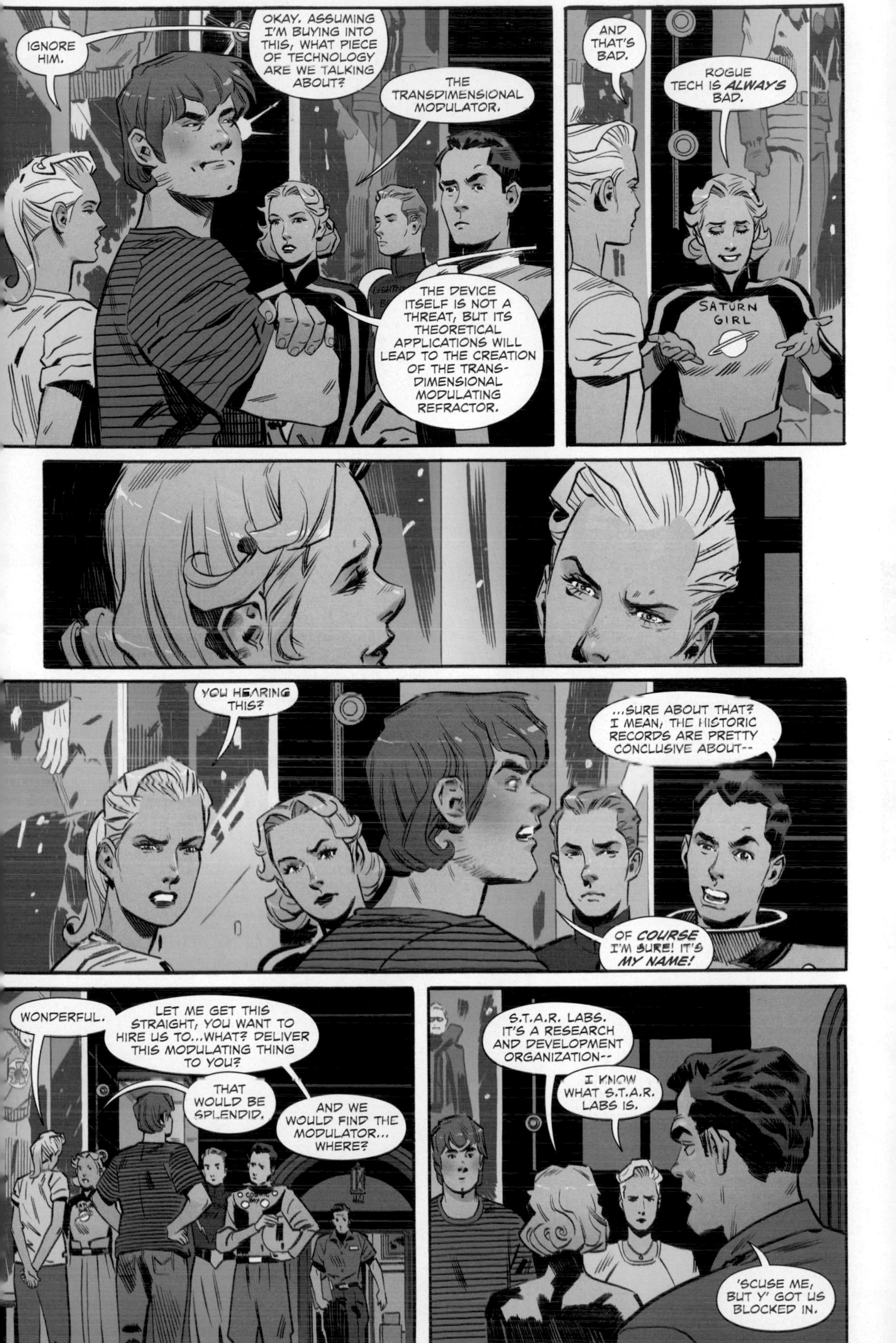
IGNORE HIM.
OKAY. ASSUMING I'M BUYING INTO THIS, WHAT PIECE OF TECHNOLOGY ARE WE TALKING ABOUT?
THE TRANSDIMENSIONAL MODULATOR.
THE DEVICE ITSELF IS NOT A THREAT, BUT ITS THEORETICAL APPLICATIONS WILL LEAD TO THE CREATION OF THE TRANS-DIMENSIONAL MODULATING REFRACTOR.
AND THAT'S BAD.
ROGUE TECH IS *ALWAYS* BAD.
SATURN GIRL
YOU HEARING THIS?
...SURE ABOUT THAT? I MEAN, THE HISTORIC RECORDS ARE PRETTY CONCLUSIVE ABOUT--
OF *COURSE* I'M SURE! IT'S *MY NAME!*
WONDERFUL.
LET ME GET THIS STRAIGHT, YOU WANT TO HIRE US TO...WHAT? DELIVER THIS MODULATING THING TO YOU?
THAT WOULD BE SPLENDID.
AND WE WOULD FIND THE MODULATOR... WHERE?
S.T.A.R. LABS. IT'S A RESEARCH AND DEVELOPMENT ORGANIZATION--
I KNOW WHAT S.T.A.R. LABS IS.
'SCUSE ME, BUT Y' GOT US BLOCKED IN.

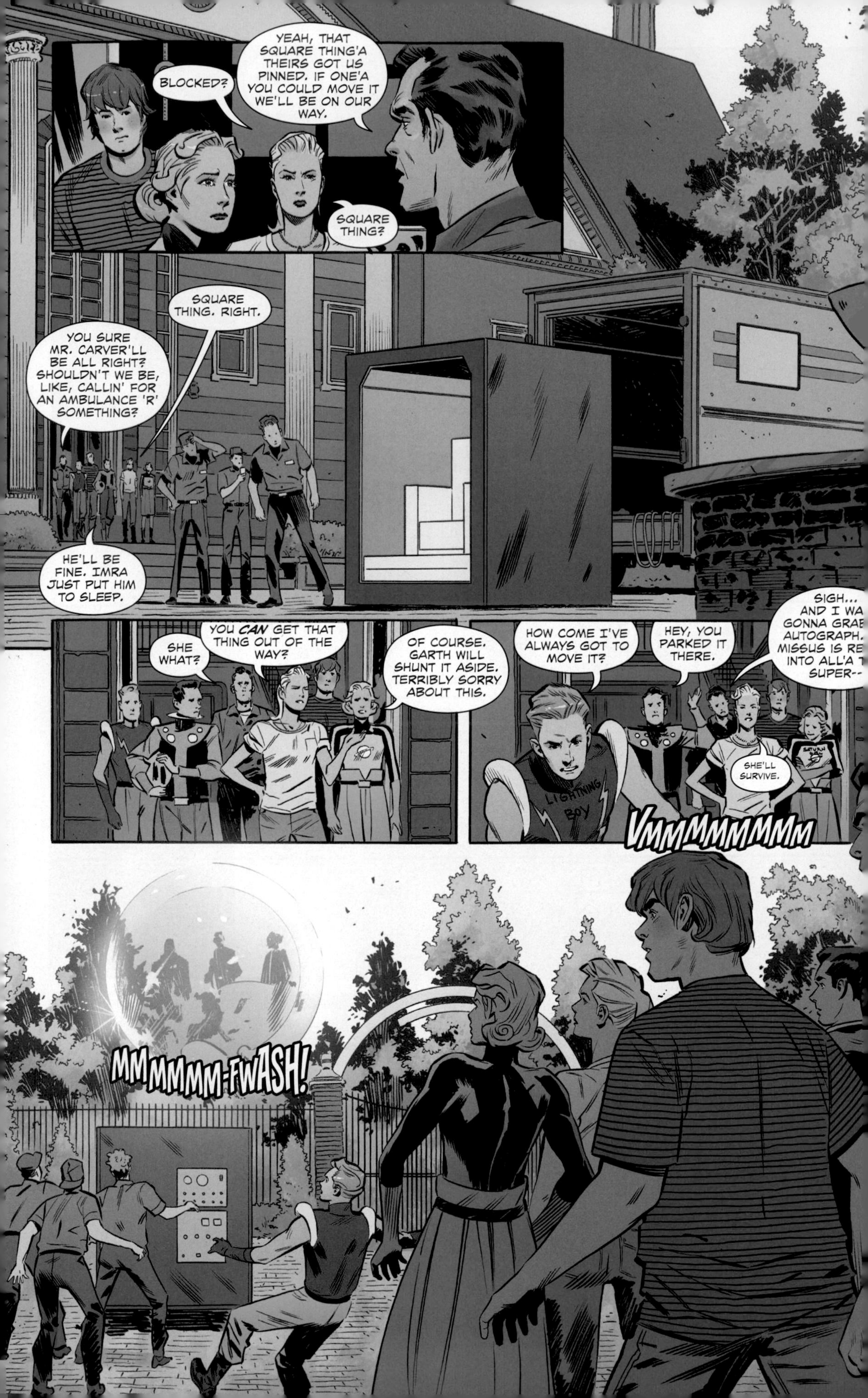
BLOCKED?
YEAH, THAT SQUARE THING'A THEIRS GOT US PINNED. IF ONE'A YOU COULD MOVE IT WE'LL BE ON OUR WAY.
SQUARE THING?
SQUARE THING. RIGHT.
YOU SURE MR. CARVER'LL BE ALL RIGHT? SHOULDN'T WE BE, LIKE, CALLIN' FOR AN AMBULANCE 'R' SOMETHING?
HE'LL BE FINE. IMRA JUST PUT HIM TO SLEEP.
SHE WHAT?
YOU CAN GET THAT THING OUT OF THE WAY?
OF COURSE. GARTH WILL SHUNT IT ASIDE. TERRIBLY SORRY ABOUT THIS.
HOW COME I'VE ALWAYS GOT TO MOVE IT?
HEY, YOU PARKED IT THERE.
SIGH... AND I WA GONNA GRAB AUTOGRAPH. MISSUS IS RE INTO ALL'A T SUPER--
SHE'LL SURVIVE.
LIGHTNING BOY
VMMMMMMMM
MMMMMM-FWASH!

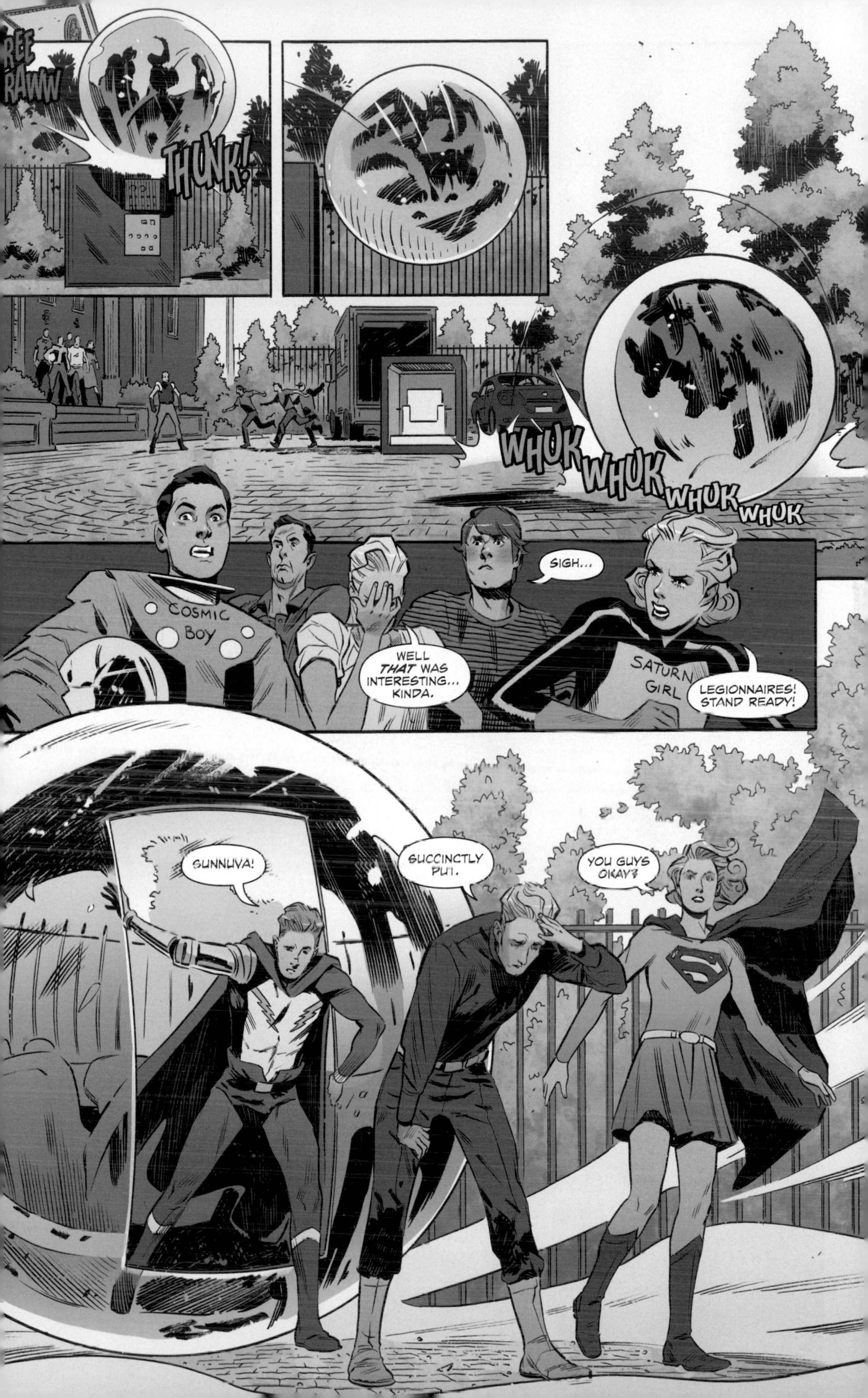
REE RAWW
THUNK!
WHUK WHUK WHUK WHUK
COSMIC BOY
SIGH...
SATURN GIRL
WELL *THAT* WAS INTERESTING... KINDA.
LEGIONNAIRES! STAND READY!
SUNNUVA!
SUCCINCTLY PUT.
YOU GUYS OKAY?

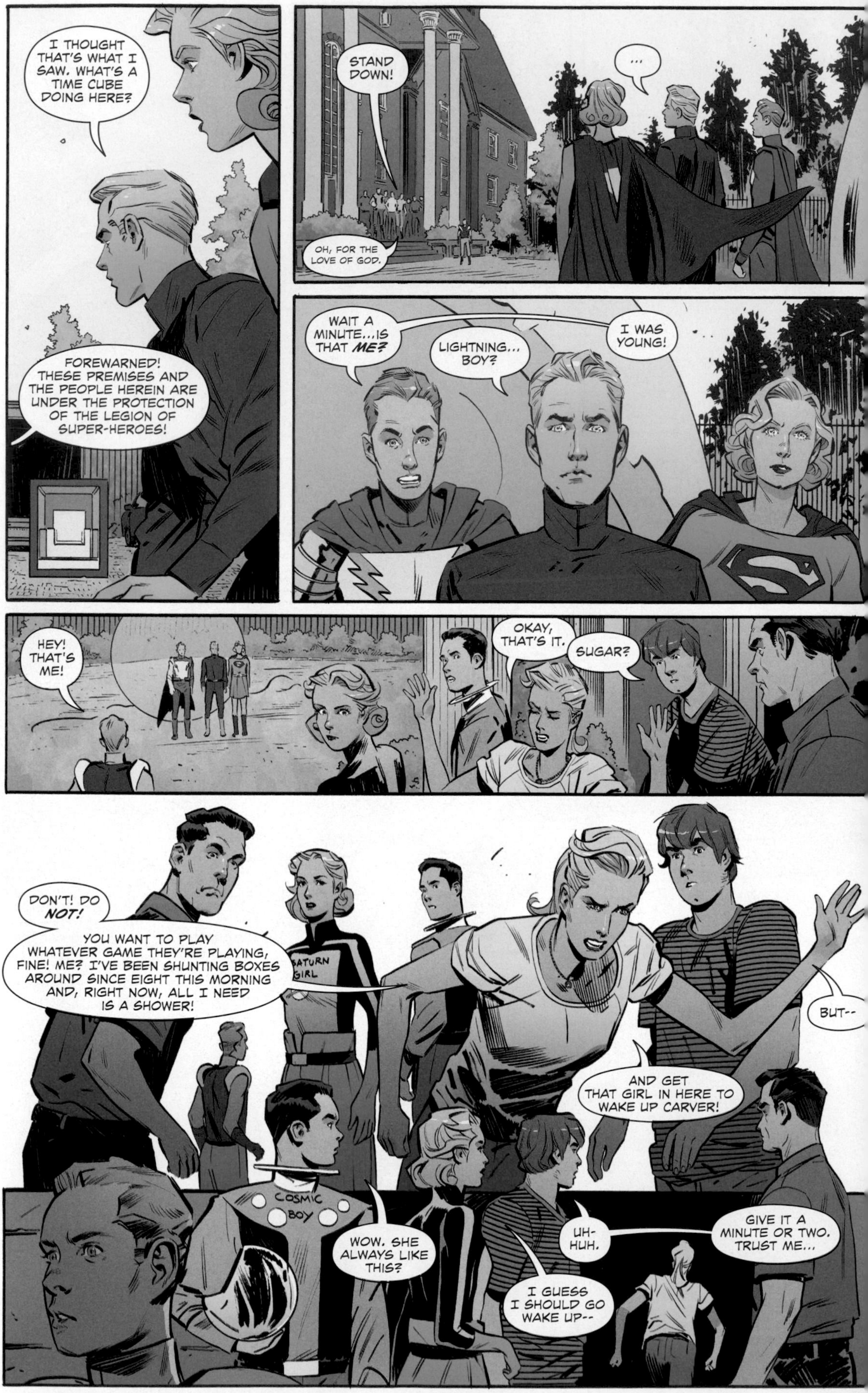
I THOUGHT THAT'S WHAT I SAW. WHAT'S A TIME CUBE DOING HERE?
FOREWARNED! THESE PREMISES AND THE PEOPLE HEREIN ARE UNDER THE PROTECTION OF THE LEGION OF SUPER-HEROES!
STAND DOWN!
OH, FOR THE LOVE OF GOD.
...
WAIT A MINUTE...IS THAT ME?
LIGHTNING... BOY?
I WAS YOUNG!
HEY! THAT'S ME!
OKAY, THAT'S IT.
SUGAR?
DON'T! DO NOT!
YOU WANT TO PLAY WHATEVER GAME THEY'RE PLAYING, FINE! ME? I'VE BEEN SHUNTING BOXES AROUND SINCE EIGHT THIS MORNING AND, RIGHT NOW, ALL I NEED IS A SHOWER!
SATURN GIRL
BUT--
AND GET THAT GIRL IN HERE TO WAKE UP CARVER!
COSMIC BOY
WOW. SHE ALWAYS LIKE THIS?
UH-HUH.
GIVE IT A MINUTE OR TWO. TRUST ME...
I GUESS I SHOULD GO WAKE UP--

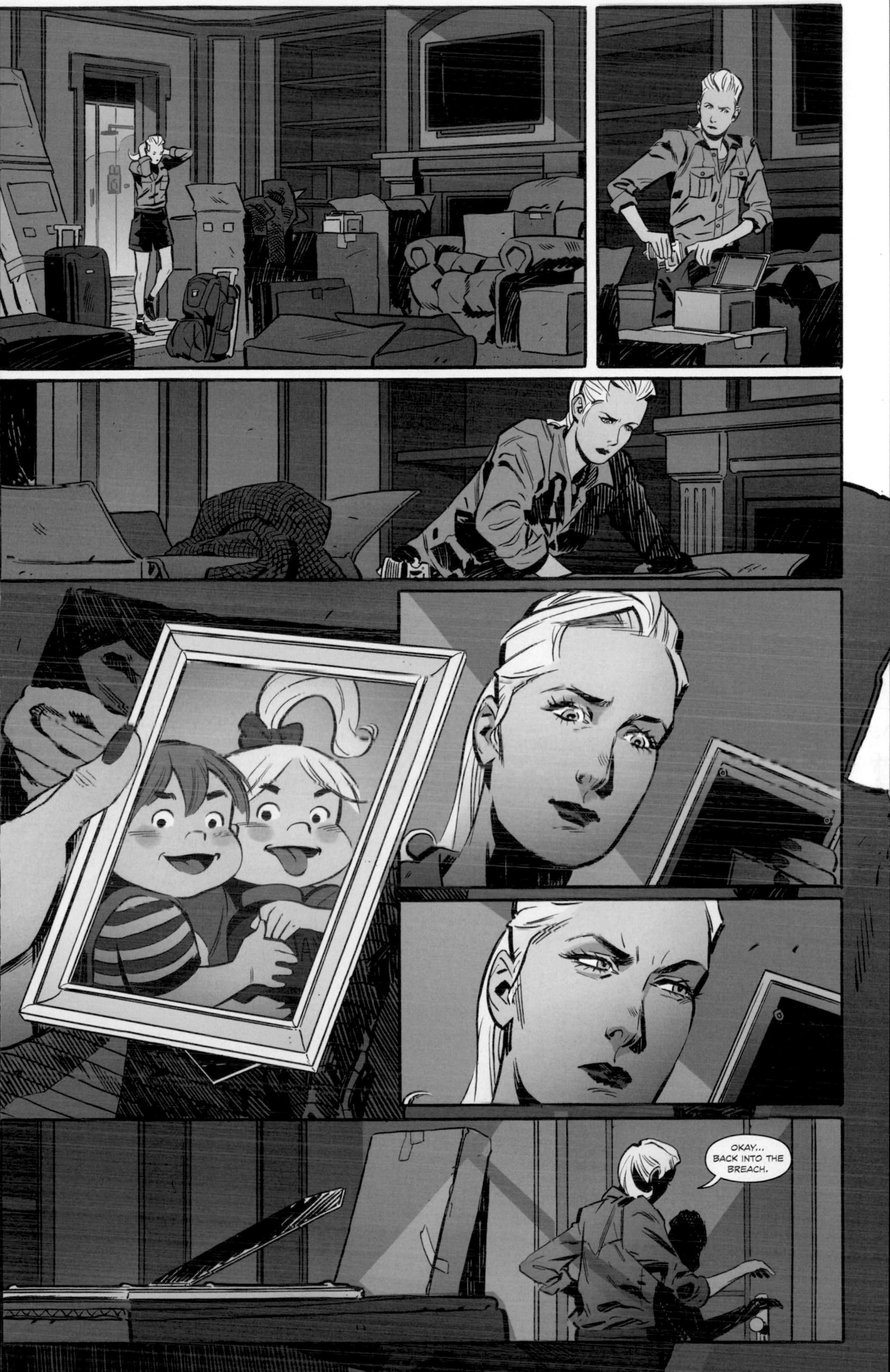
OKAY... BACK INTO THE BREACH.

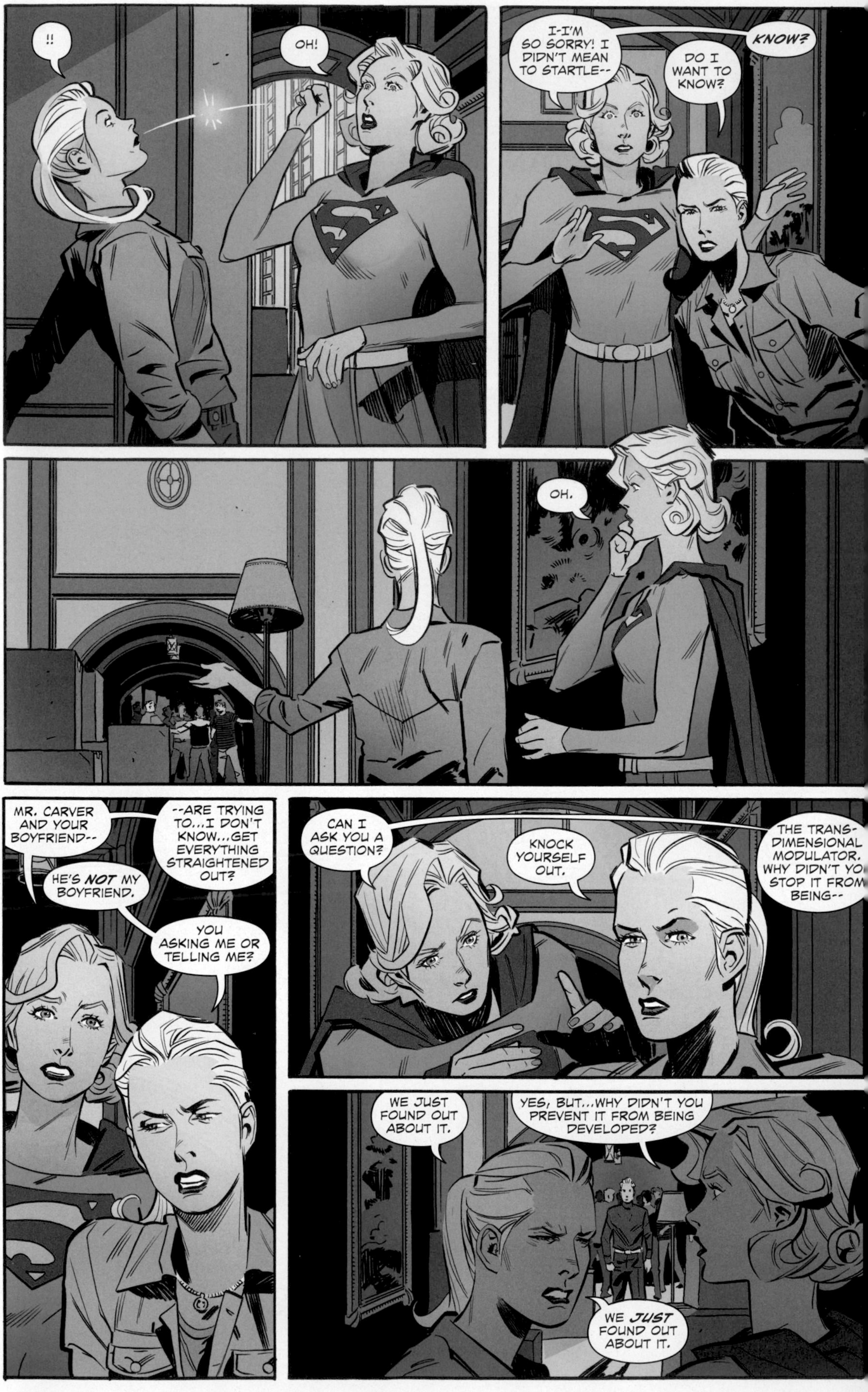
!!
OH!
I-I'M SO SORRY! I DIDN'T MEAN TO STARTLE--
KNOW?
DO I WANT TO KNOW?
OH.
MR. CARVER AND YOUR BOYFRIEND--
--ARE TRYING TO...I DON'T KNOW...GET EVERYTHING STRAIGHTENED OUT?
HE'S **NOT** MY BOYFRIEND.
YOU ASKING ME OR TELLING ME?
CAN I ASK YOU A QUESTION?
KNOCK YOURSELF OUT.
THE TRANS-DIMENSIONAL MODULATOR. WHY DIDN'T YO STOP IT FROM BEING--
WE JUST FOUND OUT ABOUT IT.
YES, BUT...WHY DIDN'T YOU PREVENT IT FROM BEING DEVELOPED?
WE **JUST** FOUND OUT ABOUT IT.

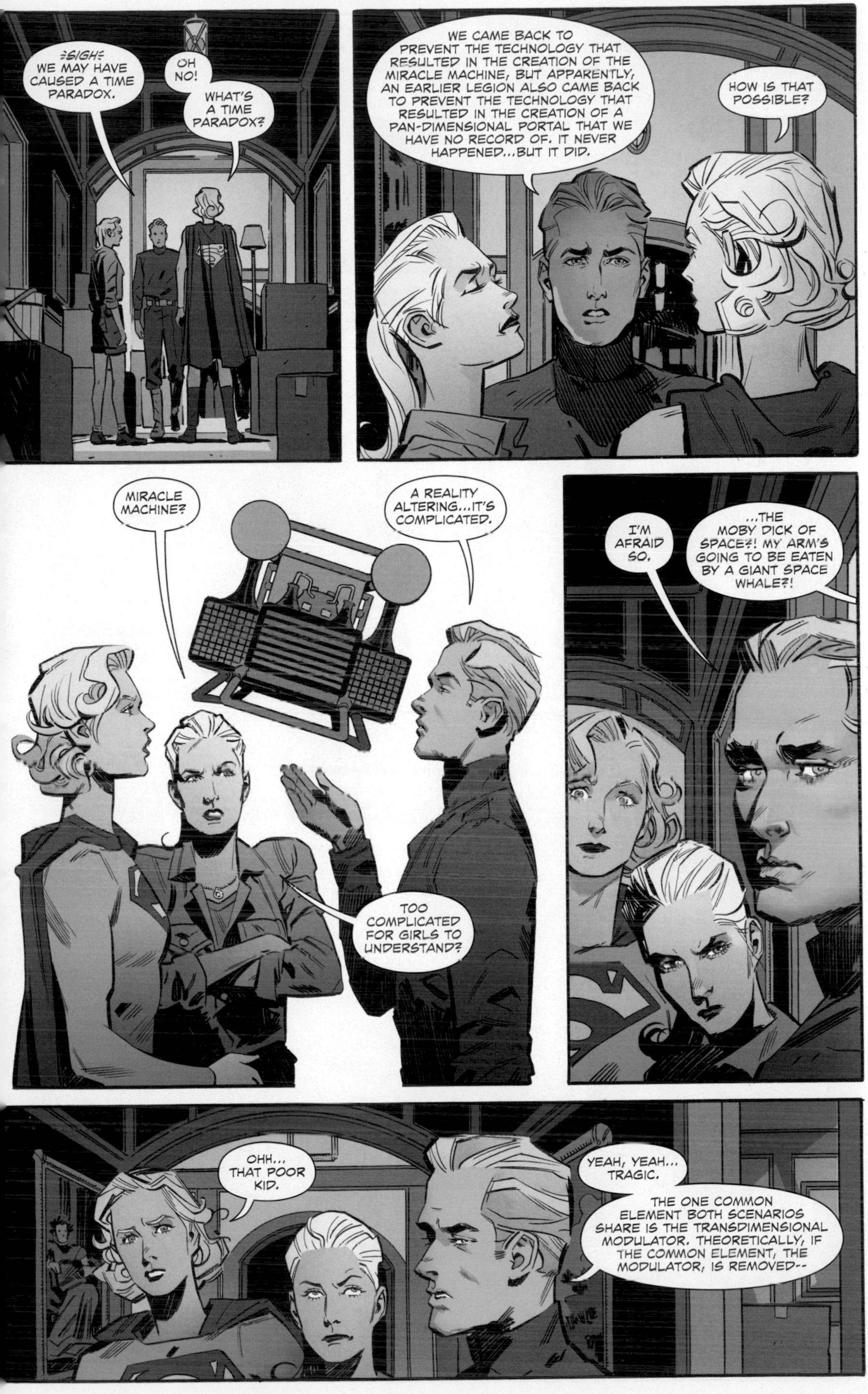
⁼SIGH⁼ WE MAY HAVE CAUSED A TIME PARADOX.
OH NO!
WHAT'S A TIME PARADOX?
WE CAME BACK TO PREVENT THE TECHNOLOGY THAT RESULTED IN THE CREATION OF THE MIRACLE MACHINE, BUT APPARENTLY, AN EARLIER LEGION ALSO CAME BACK TO PREVENT THE TECHNOLOGY THAT RESULTED IN THE CREATION OF A PAN-DIMENSIONAL PORTAL THAT WE HAVE NO RECORD OF. IT NEVER HAPPENED...BUT IT DID.
HOW IS THAT POSSIBLE?
MIRACLE MACHINE?
A REALITY ALTERING...IT'S COMPLICATED.
TOO COMPLICATED FOR GIRLS TO UNDERSTAND?
I'M AFRAID SO.
...THE MOBY DICK OF SPACE?! MY ARM'S GOING TO BE EATEN BY A GIANT SPACE WHALE?!
OHH... THAT POOR KID.
YEAH, YEAH... TRAGIC.
THE ONE COMMON ELEMENT BOTH SCENARIOS SHARE IS THE TRANSDIMENSIONAL MODULATOR. THEORETICALLY, IF THE COMMON ELEMENT, THE MODULATOR, IS REMOVED--

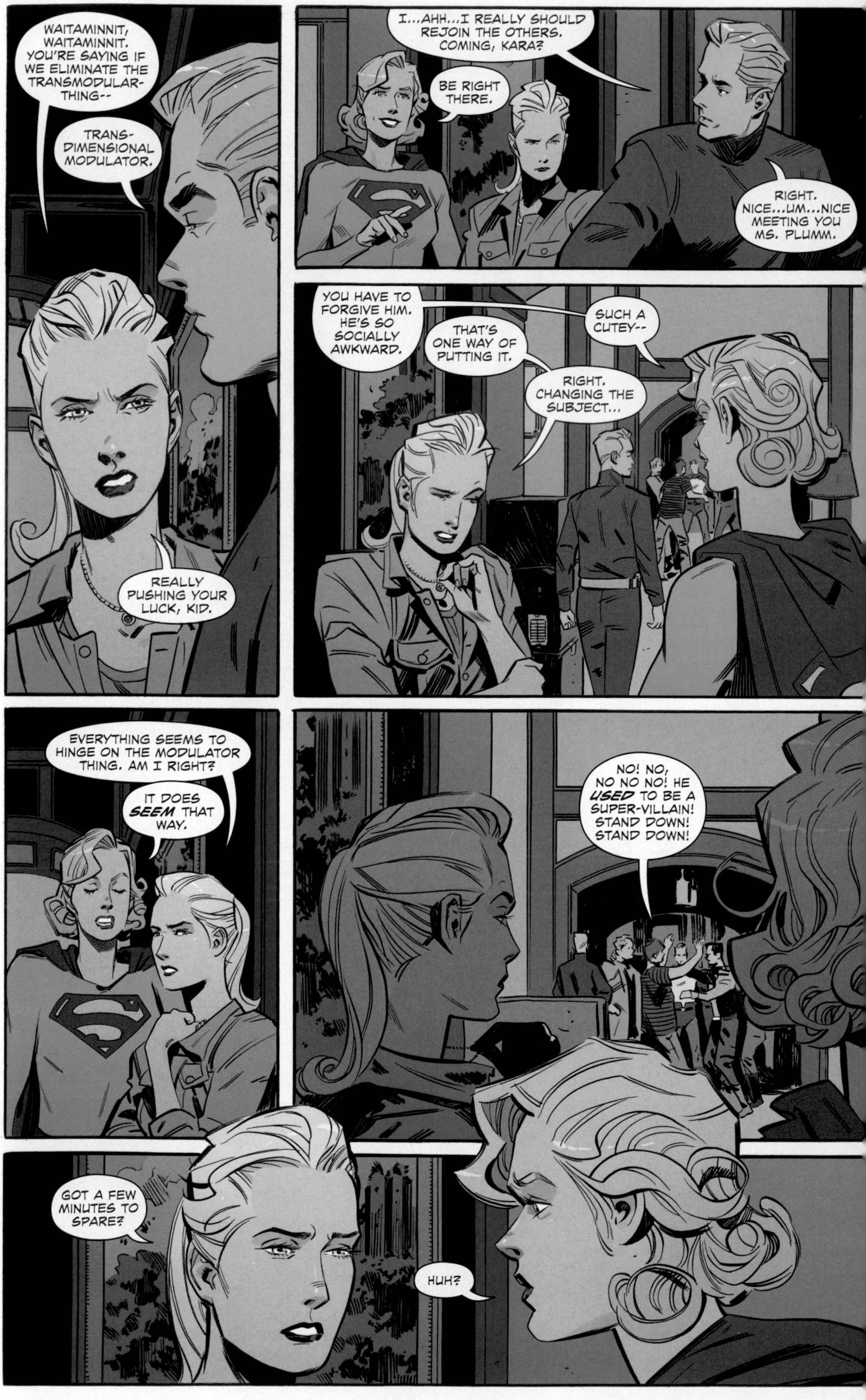
WAITAMINNIT, WAITAMINNIT. YOU'RE SAYING IF WE ELIMINATE THE TRANSMODULAR-THING--
TRANS-DIMENSIONAL MODULATOR.
REALLY PUSHING YOUR LUCK, KID.
I...AHH...I REALLY SHOULD REJOIN THE OTHERS. COMING, KARA?
BE RIGHT THERE.
RIGHT. NICE...UM...NICE MEETING YOU MS. PLUMM.
YOU HAVE TO FORGIVE HIM. HE'S SO SOCIALLY AWKWARD.
SUCH A CUTEY--
THAT'S ONE WAY OF PUTTING IT.
RIGHT. CHANGING THE SUBJECT...
EVERYTHING SEEMS TO HINGE ON THE MODULATOR THING. AM I RIGHT?
IT DOES SEEM THAT WAY.
NO! NO, NO NO NO! HE USED TO BE A SUPER-VILLAIN! STAND DOWN! STAND DOWN!
GOT A FEW MINUTES TO SPARE?
HUH?

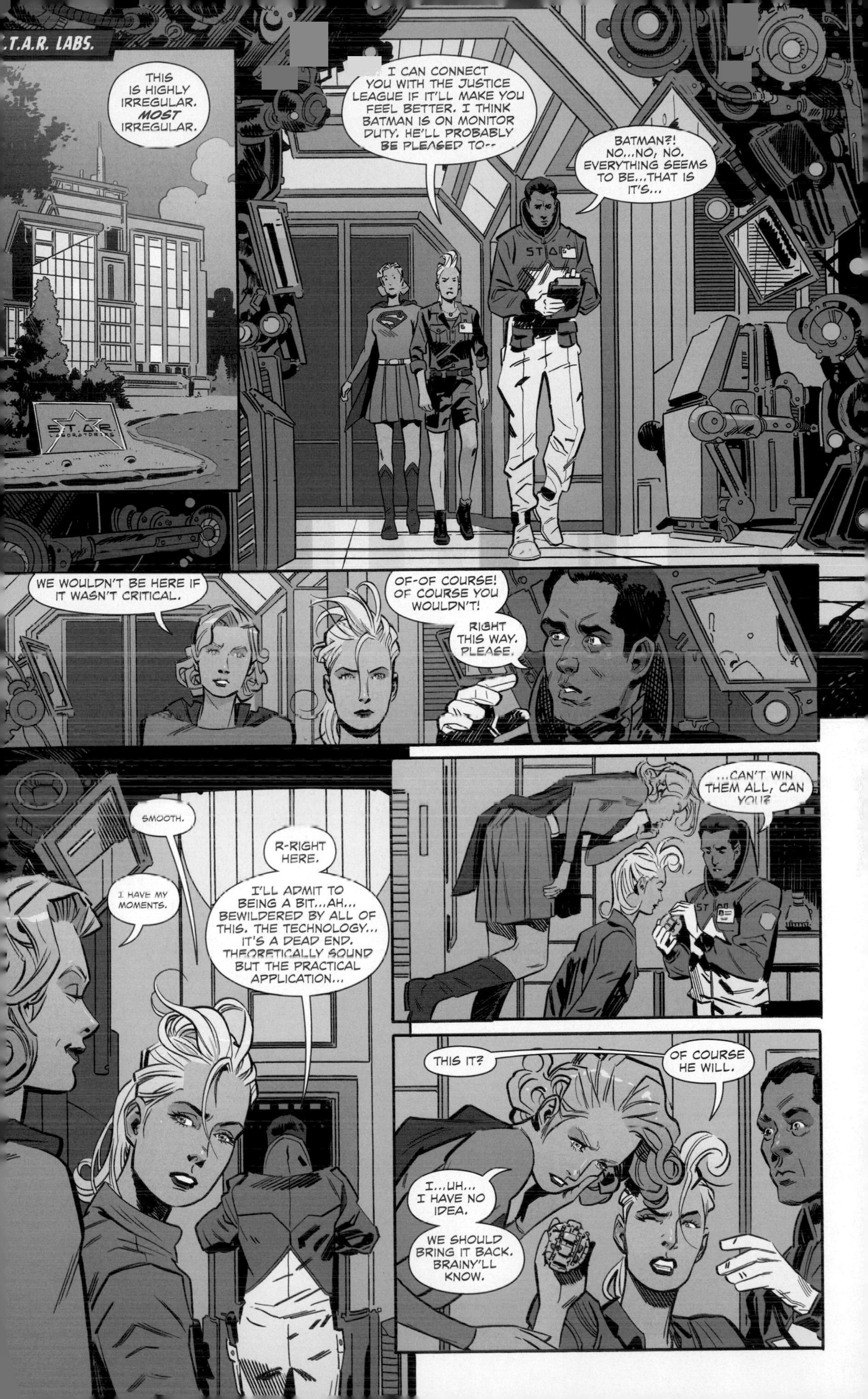
.T.A.R. LABS.
THIS IS HIGHLY IRREGULAR. MOST IRREGULAR.
I CAN CONNECT YOU WITH THE JUSTICE LEAGUE IF IT'LL MAKE YOU FEEL BETTER. I THINK BATMAN IS ON MONITOR DUTY. HE'LL PROBABLY BE PLEASED TO--
BATMAN?! NO...NO, NO. EVERYTHING SEEMS TO BE...THAT IS IT'S...
WE WOULDN'T BE HERE IF IT WASN'T CRITICAL.
OF-OF COURSE! OF COURSE YOU WOULDN'T!
RIGHT THIS WAY. PLEASE.
SMOOTH.
I HAVE MY MOMENTS.
R-RIGHT HERE.
I'LL ADMIT TO BEING A BIT...AH... BEWILDERED BY ALL OF THIS. THE TECHNOLOGY... IT'S A DEAD END. THEORETICALLY SOUND BUT THE PRACTICAL APPLICATION...
...CAN'T WIN THEM ALL, CAN YOU?
THIS IT?
OF COURSE HE WILL.
I...UH... I HAVE NO IDEA.
WE SHOULD BRING IT BACK. BRAINY'LL KNOW.

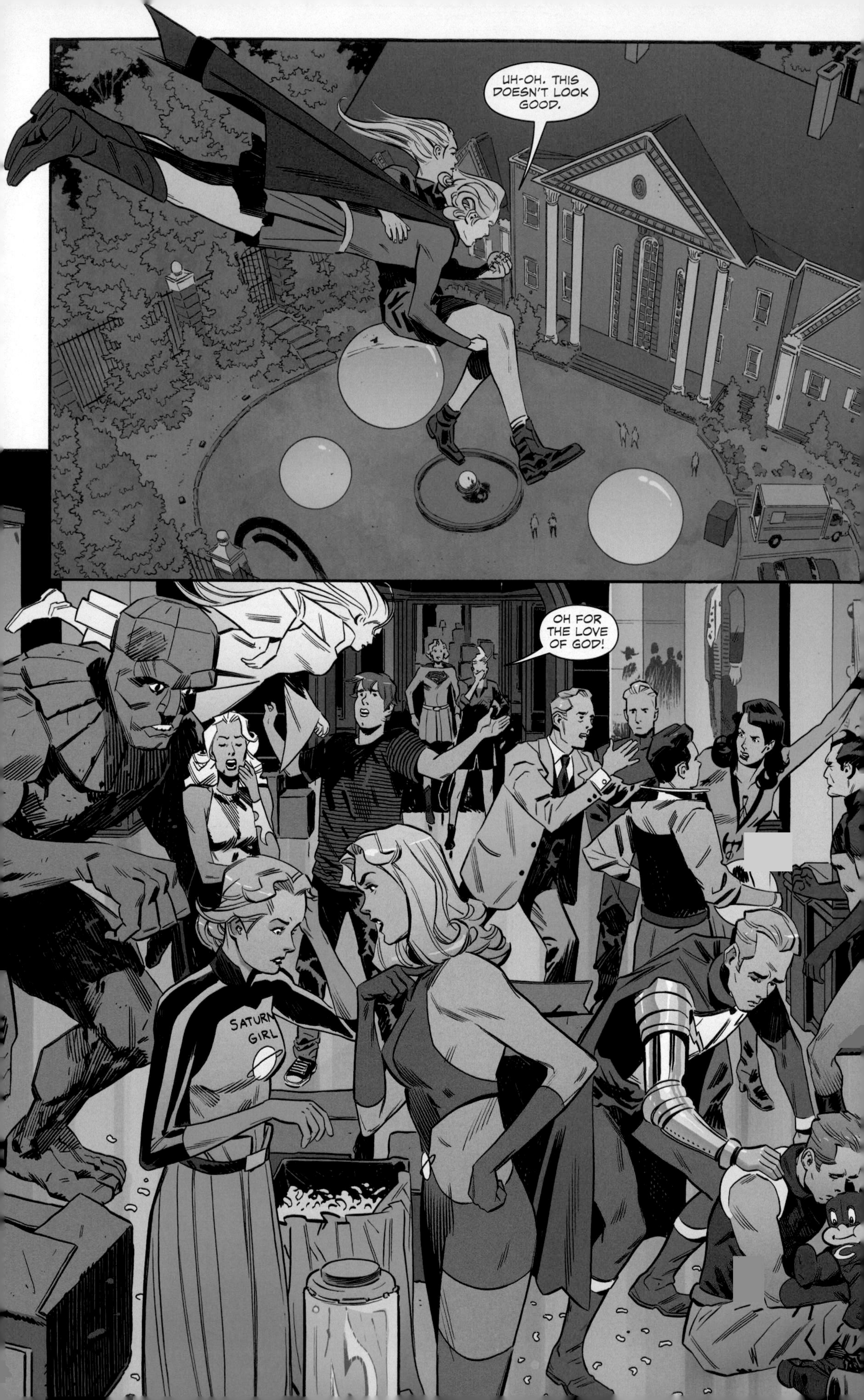
UH-OH. THIS DOESN'T LOOK GOOD.
OH FOR THE LOVE OF GOD!
SATURN GIRL

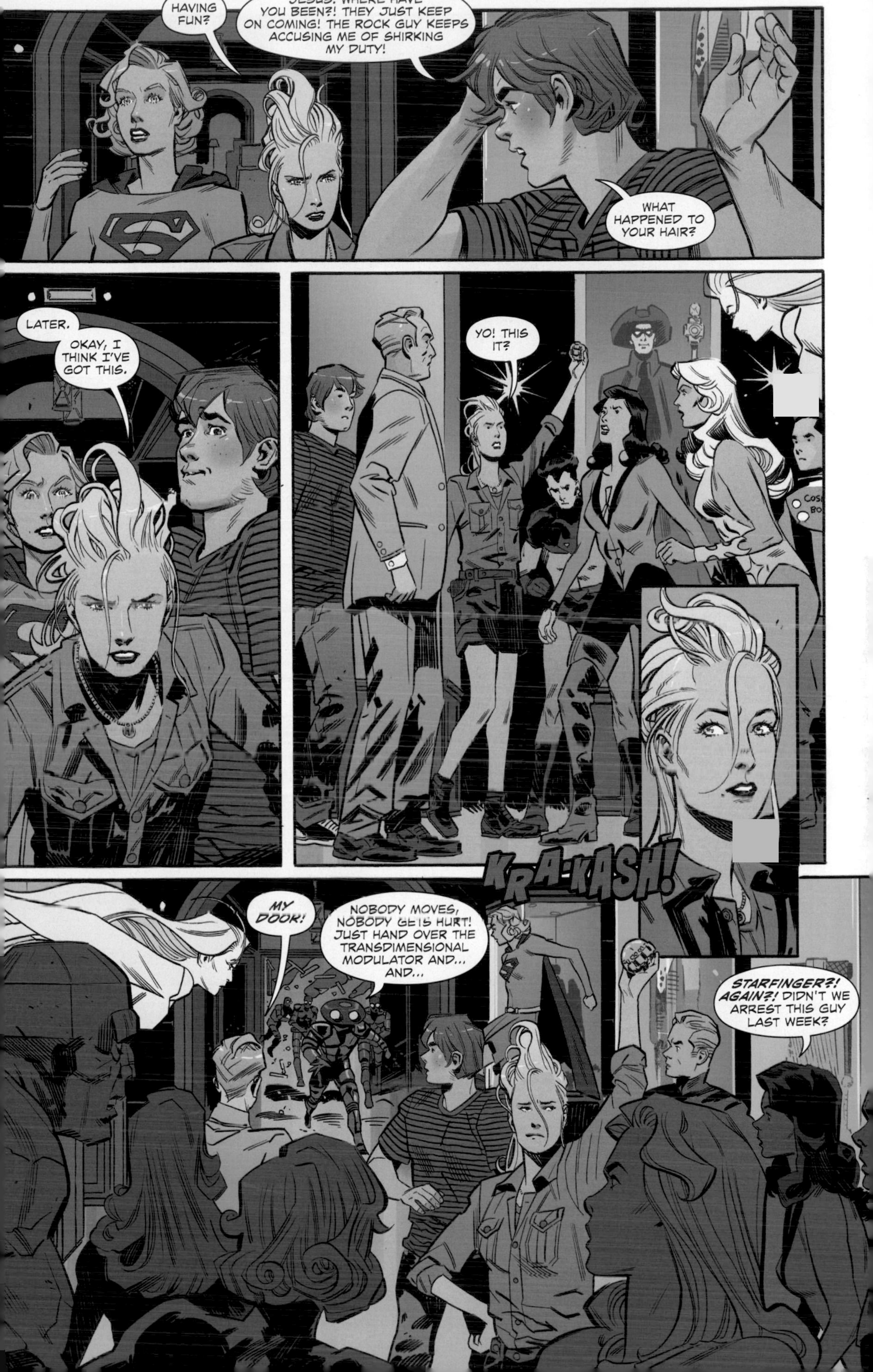
HAVING FUN?
JESUS! WHERE HAVE YOU BEEN?! THEY JUST KEEP ON COMING! THE ROCK GUY KEEPS ACCUSING ME OF SHIRKING MY DUTY!
WHAT HAPPENED TO YOUR HAIR?
LATER.
OKAY, I THINK I'VE GOT THIS.
YO! THIS IT?
KRA-KASH!
MY DOOR!
NOBODY MOVES, NOBODY GETS HURT! JUST HAND OVER THE TRANSDIMENSIONAL MODULATOR AND... AND...
STARFINGER?! AGAIN?! DIDN'T WE ARREST THIS GUY LAST WEEK?

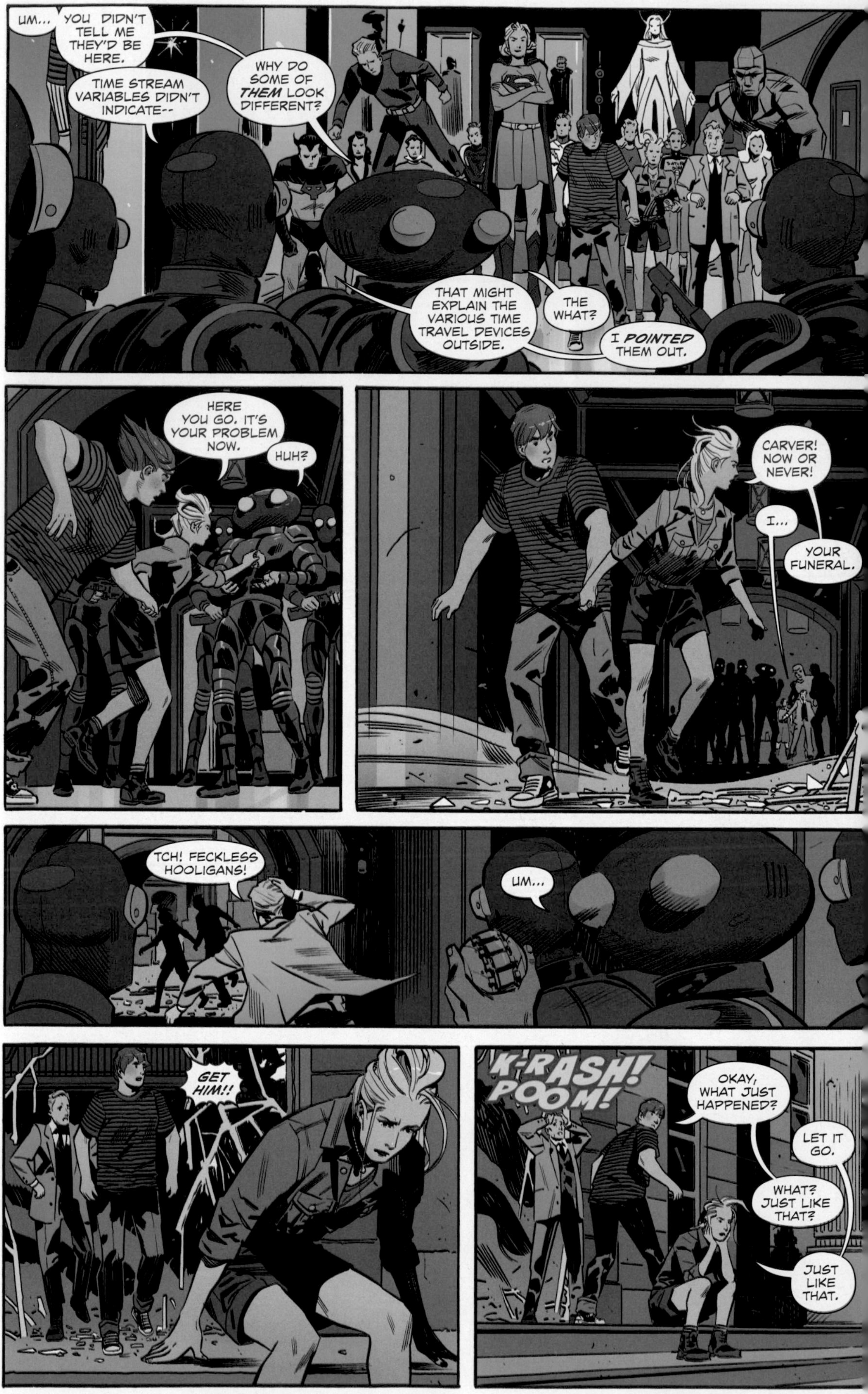
UM...
YOU DIDN'T TELL ME THEY'D BE HERE.
TIME STREAM VARIABLES DIDN'T INDICATE--
WHY DO SOME OF *THEM* LOOK DIFFERENT?
THAT MIGHT EXPLAIN THE VARIOUS TIME TRAVEL DEVICES OUTSIDE.
THE WHAT?
I *POINTED* THEM OUT.
HERE YOU GO. IT'S YOUR PROBLEM NOW.
HUH?
CARVER! NOW OR NEVER!
I...
YOUR FUNERAL.
TCH! FECKLESS HOOLIGANS!
UM...
GET HIM!!
K-RASH! POOM!
OKAY, WHAT JUST HAPPENED?
LET IT GO.
WHAT? JUST LIKE THAT?
JUST LIKE THAT.

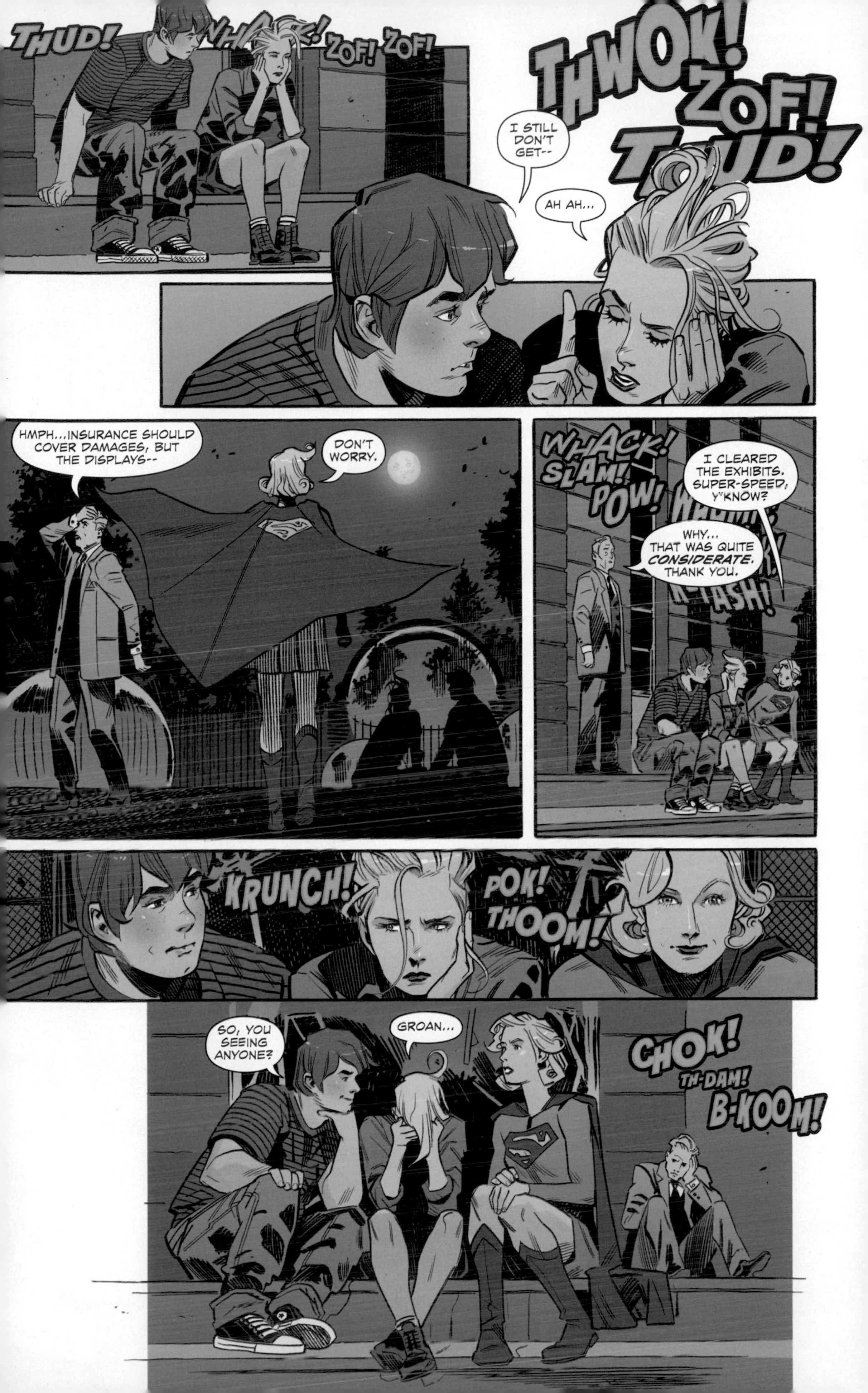
THUD!
ZOF! ZOF!
THWOK! ZOF! THUD!
I STILL DON'T GET--
AH AH...
HMPH...INSURANCE SHOULD COVER DAMAGES, BUT THE DISPLAYS--
DON'T WORRY.
WHACK! SLAM! POW!
I CLEARED THE EXHIBITS. SUPER-SPEED, Y'KNOW?
WHY... THAT WAS QUITE *CONSIDERATE*. THANK YOU.
KRUNCH!
POK! THOOM!
SO, YOU SEEING ANYONE?
GROAN...
CHOK! TH-DAM! B-KOOM!

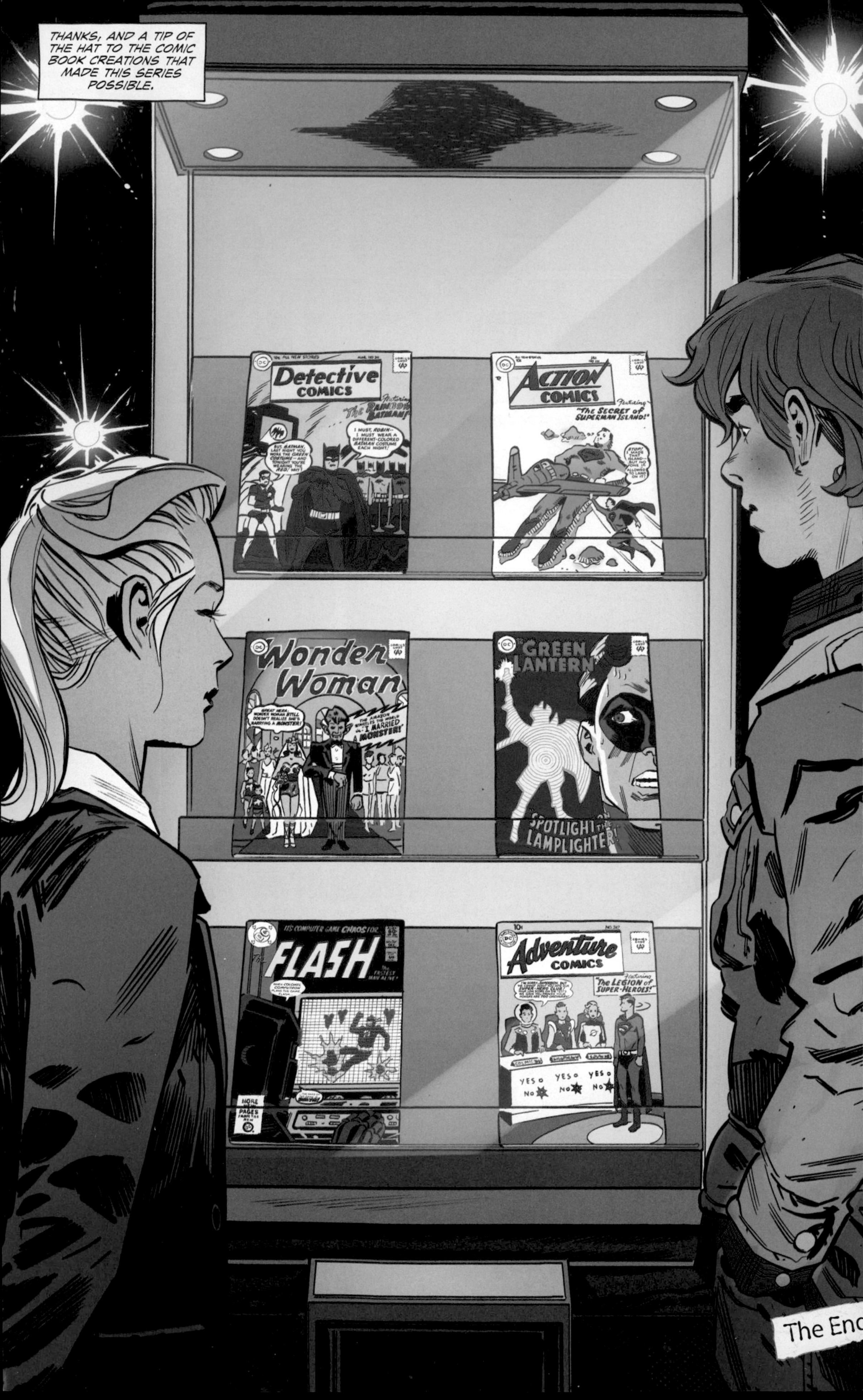
THANKS; AND A TIP OF THE HAT TO THE COMIC BOOK CREATIONS THAT MADE THIS SERIES POSSIBLE.
Detective COMICS
Featuring The RAINBOW BATMAN!
I MUST, ROBIN-- I MUST WEAR A DIFFERENT-COLORED BATMAN COSTUME EACH NIGHT!
ACTION COMICS
Featuring "THE SECRET OF SUPERMAN ISLAND!"
Wonder Woman
I MARRIED A MONSTER!
GREEN LANTERN
SPOTLIGHT ON THE LAMPLIGHTER!
IT'S COMPUTER GAME CHAOS FOR...
FLASH
THE FASTEST MAN ALIVE!
Adventure COMICS
Featuring "The LEGION of SUPER-HEROES!"
YES NO
The Enc

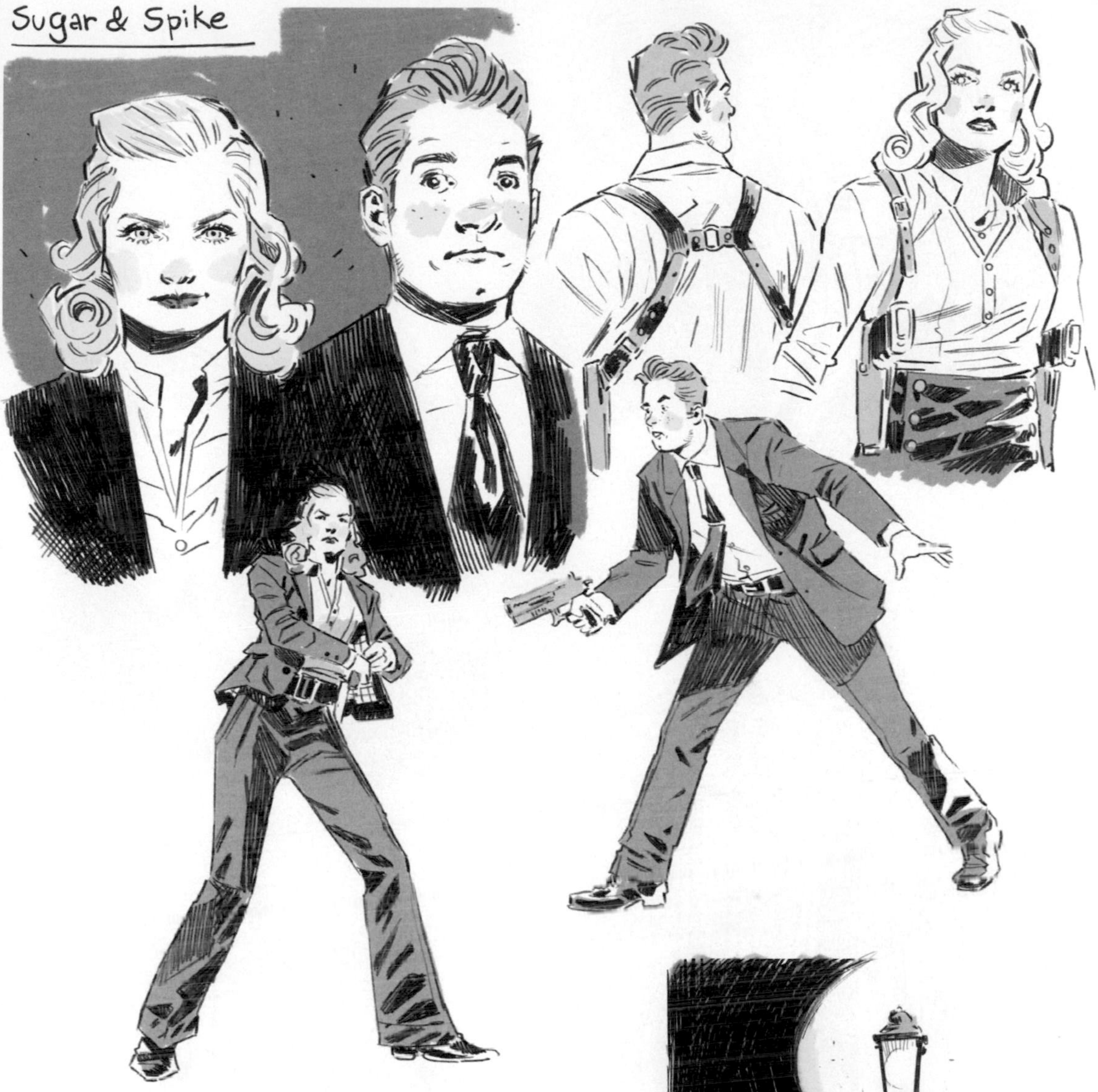
Sugar & Spike

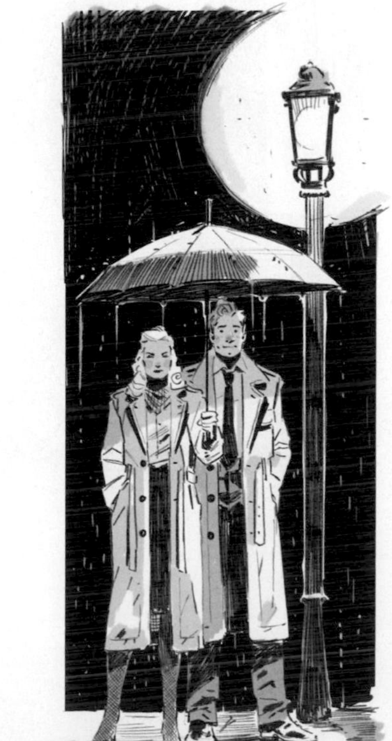

Character sketches by
BILQUIS EVELY

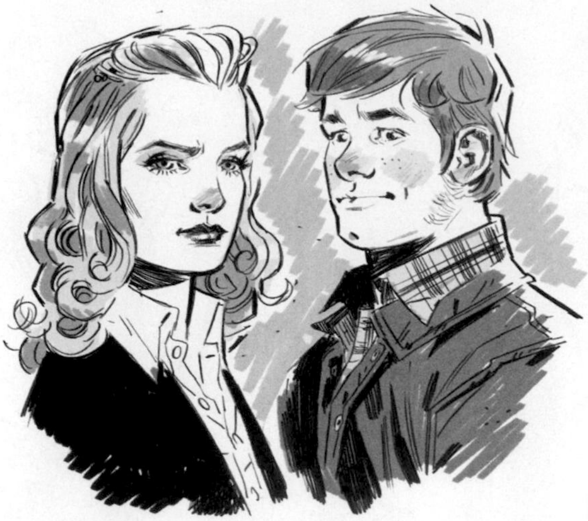

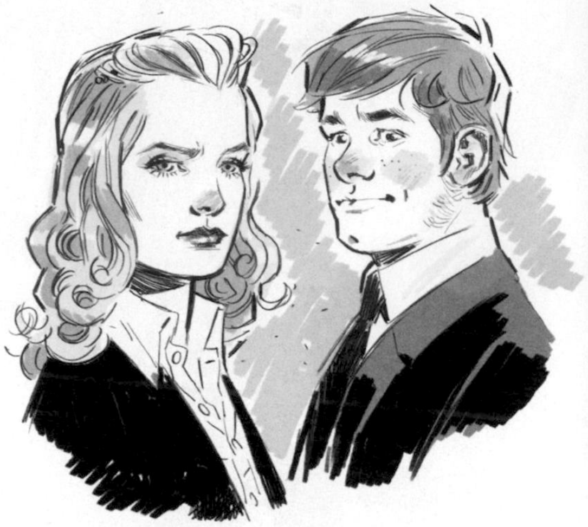

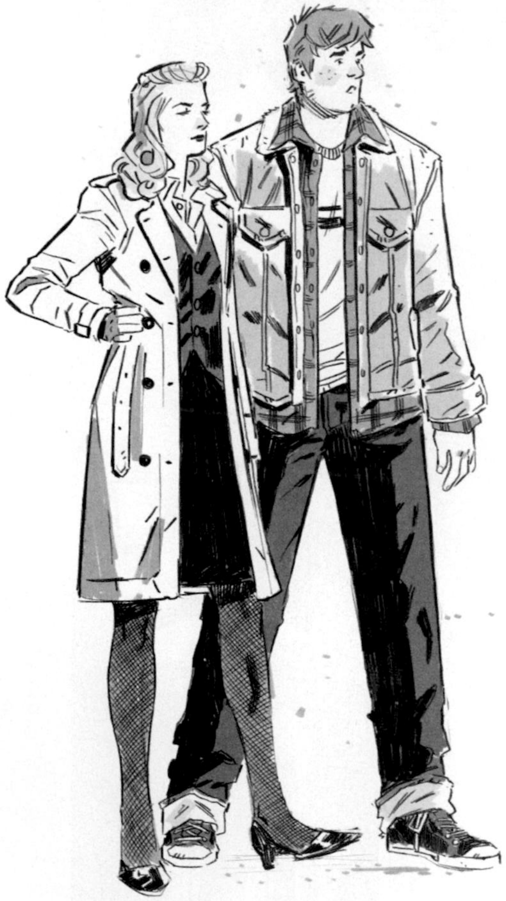

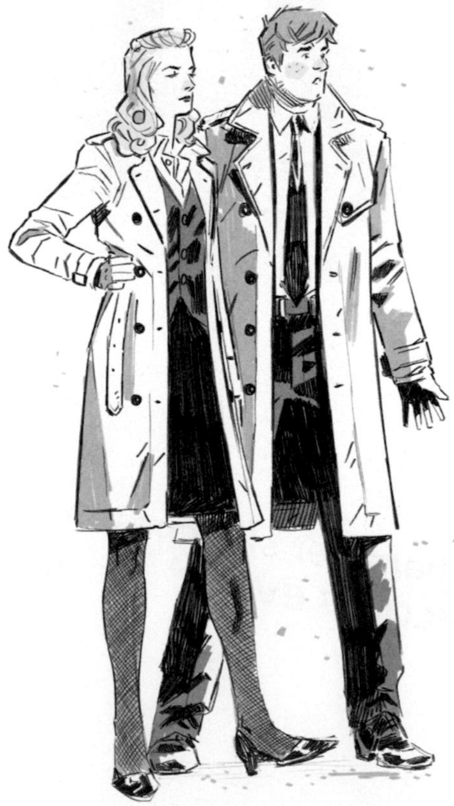

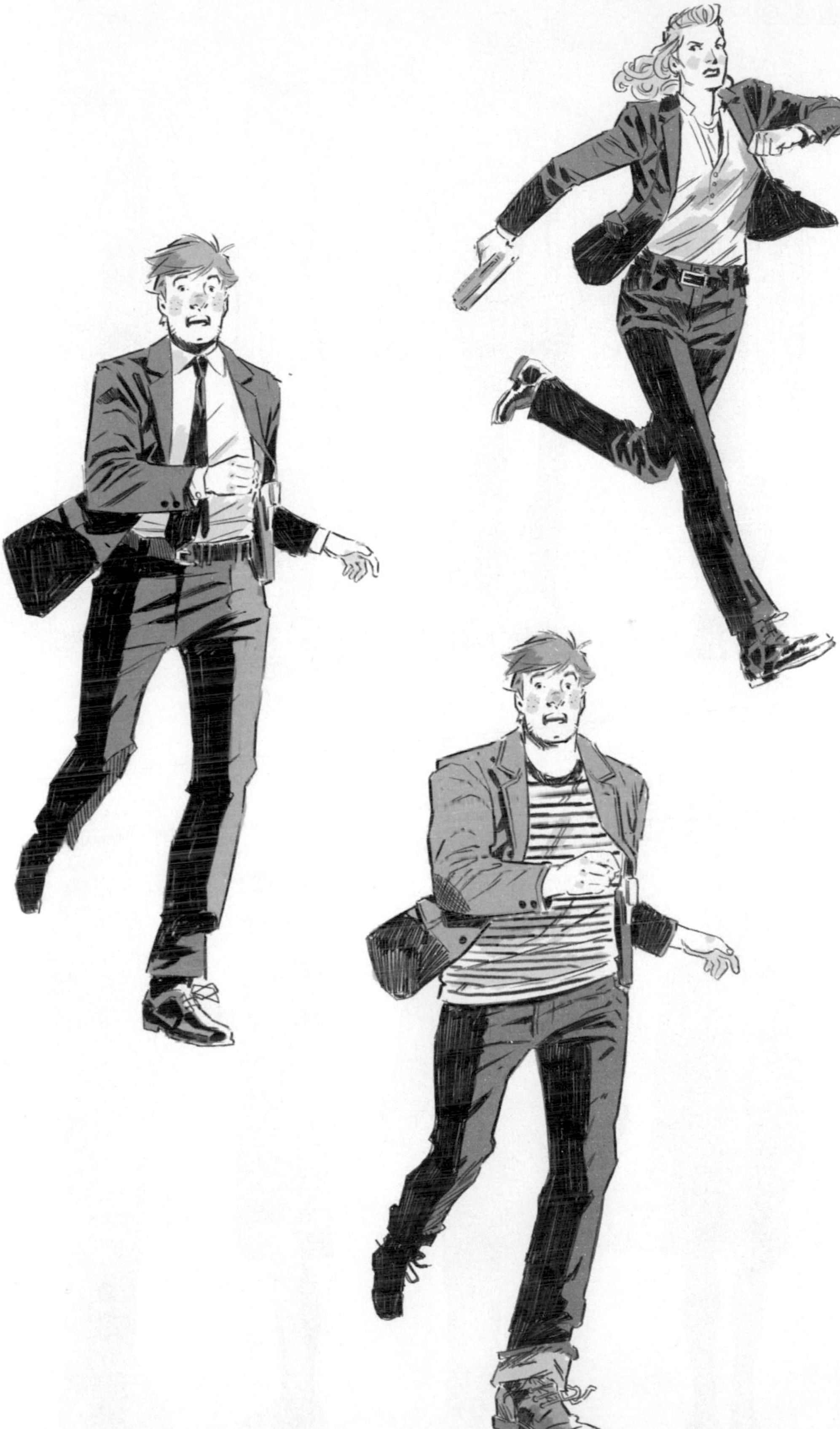

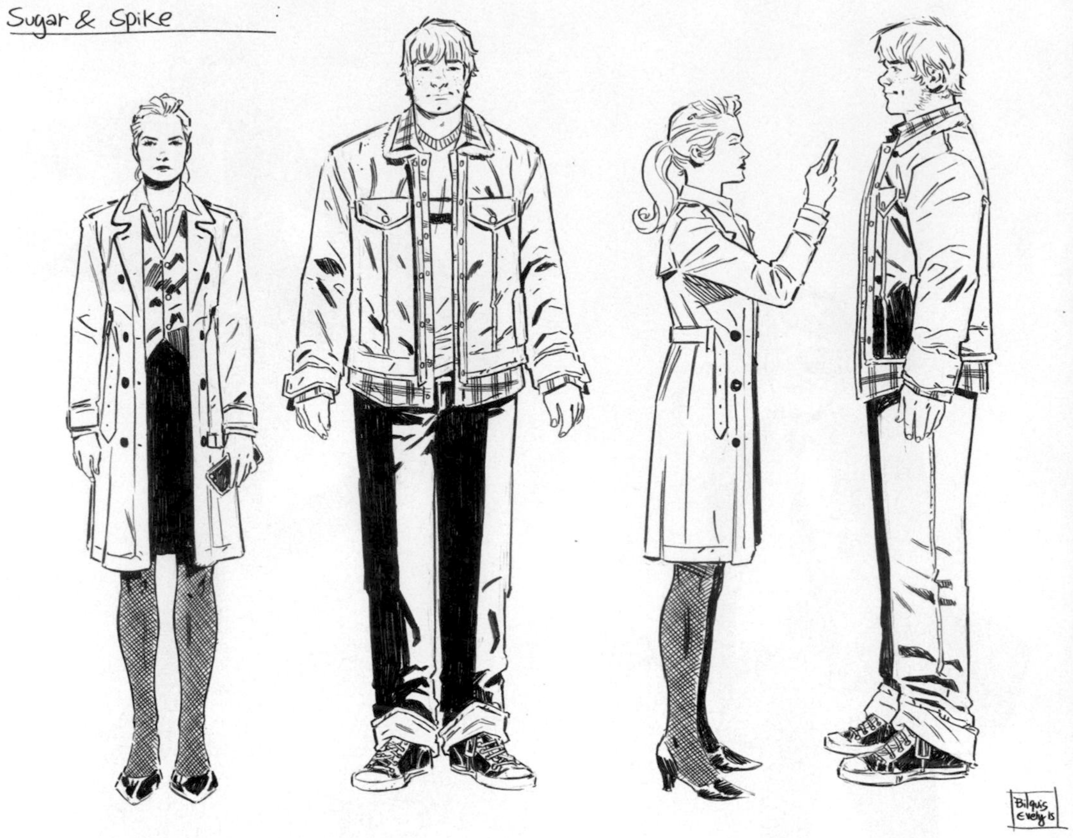
Sugar & Spike
Bilquis Evely 15

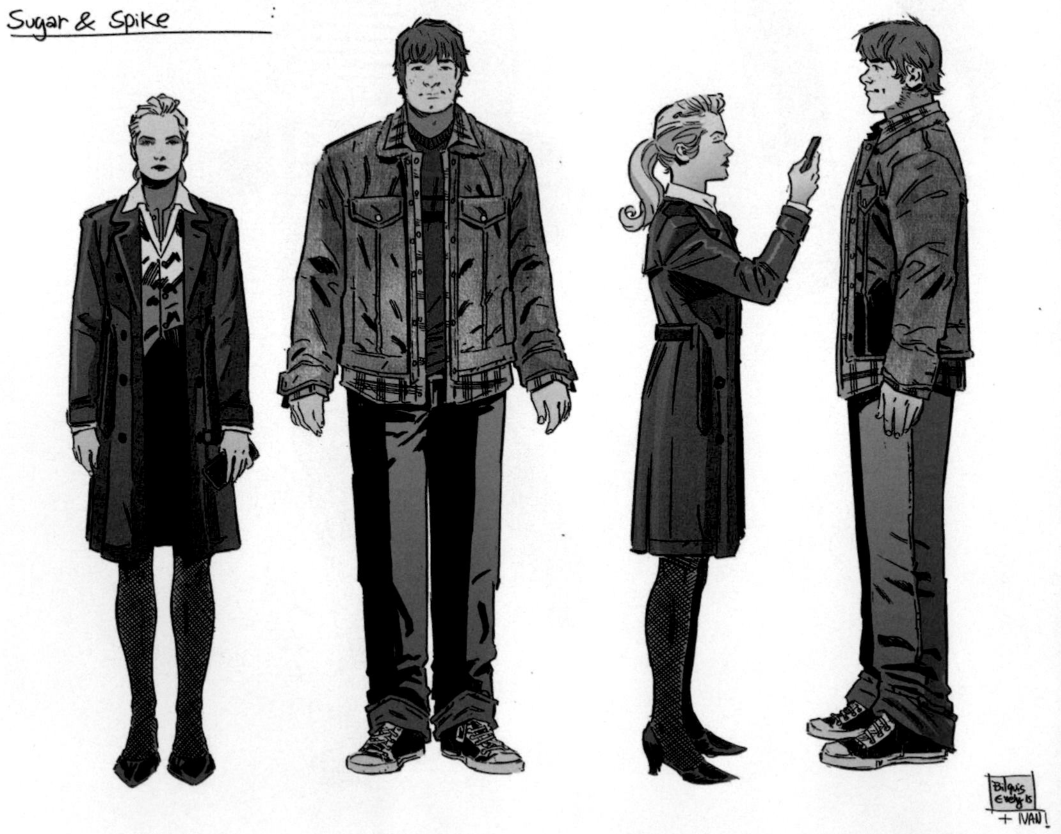
Sugar & Spike
Bilquis Evely 15
+ IVAN!

REBECCA - S&S

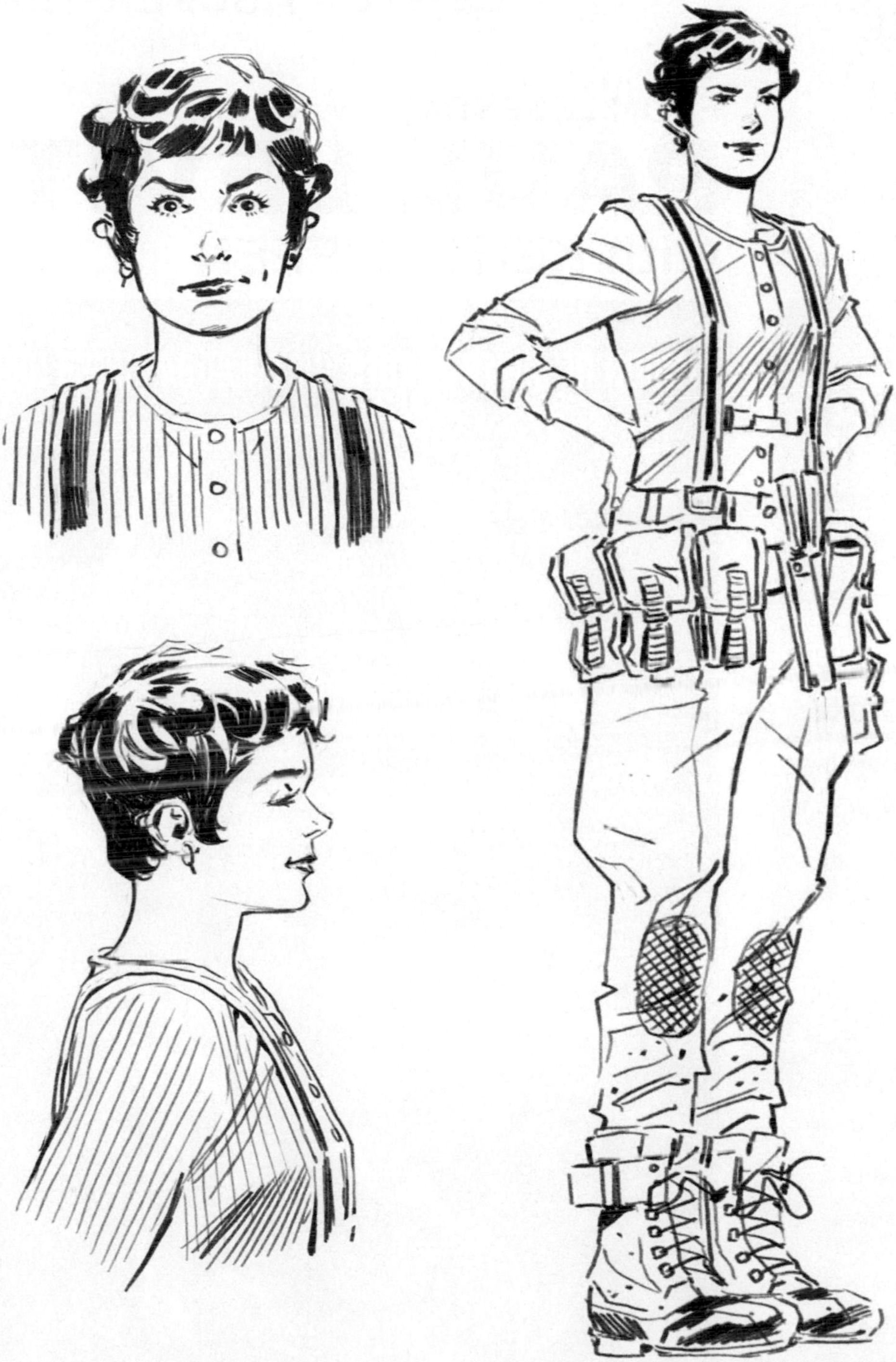

"One of the greatest comic book runs of all time."
—COMIC BOOK RESOURCES

TALES OF THE 31ST CENTURY SUPER-TEAM

FROM LEGENDARY WRITER
PAUL LEVITZ
with KEITH GIFFEN

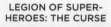

LEGION OF SUPER-HEROES: THE GREAT DARKNESS SAGA

PAUL LEVITZ
KEITH GIFFEN
LARRY MAHLSTEDT

DC COMICS

DC COMICS™

FROM THE WRITER OF *JUSTICE LEAGUE* & *GREEN LANTERN*

GEOFF JOHNS
with GARY FRANK

SUPERMAN: THE LAST SON OF KRYPTON

with RICHARD DONNER & ADAM KUBERT

SUPERMAN & THE LEGION OF SUPER-HEROES

with GARY FRANK

SUPERMAN: BRAINIAC

with GARY FRANK

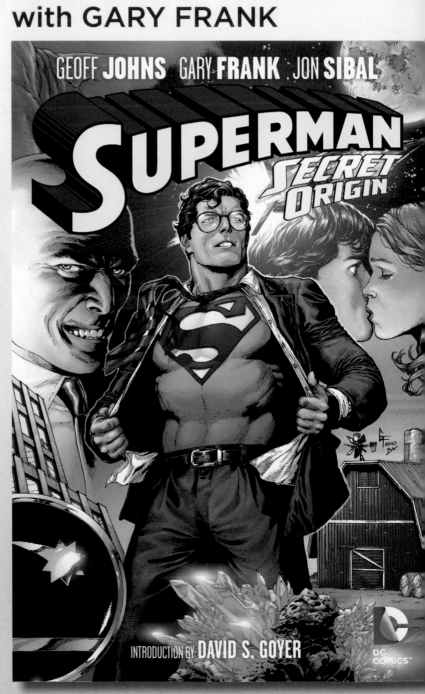